ALSO BY PICO IYER

*Cuba and the Night*

*Falling Off the Map*

*The Lady and the Monk*

*Video Night in Kathmandu*

These are Borzoi Books published in
New York by Alfred A. Knopf

*Tropical Classical*

# TROPICAL
# CLASSICAL

*Essays from Several Directions*

# PICO IYER

*Alfred A. Knopf   New York   1997*

THIS IS A BORZOI BOOK
PUBLISHED BY ALFRED A. KNOPF, INC.

http://www.randomhouse.com/

Owing to limitations of space, acknowledgments
for permission to reprint previously published material
may be found on page 317.

Library of Congress Cataloging-in-Publication Data

Iyer, Pico.
Tropical classical : essays from several directions / by Pico
Iyer.—1st ed.    p.   cm.
ISBN 0-679-45432-2
I. Title.
PS3559.Y47T76   1997
814'.54—dc20      96-38578     CIP

Manufactured in the United States of America
First Edition

*For the still points of my turning world—*
*my mother and Hiroko*

The sea canes by the cliff flash green and silver;
they were the seraph lances of my faith,
but out of what is lost grows something stronger

that has the rational radiance of stone,
enduring moonlight, further than despair,
strong as the wind, that through dividing canes

brings those we love before us, as they were,
with faults and all, not nobler, just there.

—DEREK WALCOTT

# CONTENTS

## THEMES

SQUIBS

Derek Walcott's poems hymn the constant, melodious effort to reconcile the pomme-arac and casuarinas of his unrecorded home with the cobblestones and pillared houses he learned to love on paper. For me, growing up in Oxford, the son of Indian parents, it often seemed that dialogue was playing itself out in reverse as I tried to matchmake the classical precepts of my upbringing with the tropical palms that came with my inheritance. Later, when we moved to California, I had to forge a different kind of peace, between my new home in the '60s, where anything seemed possible, and my fifteenth-century boarding school in England, where inmates were trained in all the imperial disciplines of stoicism and command; and as I shuttled back and forth, between one world that seemed to ask too much of life and another that seemed to ask too little, I began to feel that both our starriest hopes and our tiniest tics are only as strong as their acknowledgment of the other. Even our deepest convictions, it seemed to me, arise only out of a patient, step-by-step commitment to the details of the day, and only by paying the closest attention to the minutiae of this world could one begin to make out the lineaments of some other. You can see this in the churches of ancient Ethiopia, you can see it in the strand of hair escaping from behind a lover's ear.

The essays you may encounter here, therefore, are all aimed, one way or another, to romance possibility by looking at the everyday, and to undergird faith by taking in irony. I have three or four times as many pieces lying around in my drawer (and had hundreds more before a forest fire destroyed my home and all my files), but I chose these because they seemed to belong together; and though not always my favorites, and not always free of youthful brattiness or ungenerosity, they seemed to point in some of the same directions. They were, I hoped, thoughts or occasions that could profit from one another's company and even, now and then, throw light on one another and conspire; and I was interested in the way that some of them, though starting from radically different points, seemed to converge on some kind of common ground. The virtue of essays from several directions is, after all, that like other lines inscribed upon a page, they may, in unexpected ways, intersect around the outlines of a face.

.  .  .

I would like to thank some of the many colleagues who worked with me on pieces here, among them the late Ronald Kriss; Richard Duncan, James Kelly, Walter Isaacson, Christopher Porterfield, Anne Hopkins, and Ratu Kamlani; Klara Glowczewska, Gully Wells, and Thomas J. Wallace; Karsten Prager, José M. Ferrer III, and George Russell; William Phillips, Jane Uscilka, Alan Ross, Lindsay Duguid, Andrew Sullivan, and Robert B. Silvers; Marge Horvitz and Nelly Bly; and a host of others, whom it would be invidious to single out but who may recognize a few of these cadences and sentences. I would also like to thank some of the people who helped set me up in an enviable position whereby I could write for a living, among them Richard Marius at Harvard University, Timothy Foote at *Smithsonian*, Ray Cave and Henry Muller at *Time*, Charles Elliott, Harold Evans, Lynn Nesbit, and Sonny Mehta.

# PLACES

# Ethiopia: Prayers in the Wilderness

This is the New Jerusalem," said our guide, a former deacon. "These churches were built with the help of angels. Once upon a time, an angel came to King Lalibela and asked him to build a city in the heart of Ethiopia, in rock. This is heaven," he went on, pointing to the divide along which we were standing. "As soon as you step here, you have set foot in heaven."

We walked, in the silence, above the plain, across the Jordan, through Bethlehem and Nazareth, through all the places reconstituted here by the king so that the faithful would not have to journey to Jerusalem, and sitting outside one of the eleven seven-hundred-year-old churches carved entirely out of red rock—the only such places in the world—we let the centuries fall away, on this, Saint Mary's Day.

The next morning, at dawn, I went out to see the hillside beside the churches scattered with figures—hooded, robed figures all in white, with priests above, under rainbowed umbrellas, half obscured by the mists of their frankincense, reciting prayers and sermons from the tops of rock faces. Farther in, the complex of churches was alive: with the gaunt, ancestral faces of pilgrims called Bethlehem and Solomon and Abraham, who had walked two weeks—or two millennia—across the emptiness to be here; with withered nuns staring out from the darkness of their cells, small lightless spaces in round two-story huts, white crosses on their iron doors; with priests, burning-eyed and bearded, moving back and forth in purple robes to the ancient, hypnotic sound of drum and sistrum, golden crosses in their hands.

Motes of sunlight danced in the air, and boys flashed smiles, and, gradually, the silence descended, seeping out of the round huts, drifting through the network of underground passageways, floating into the chapels guarded by men with beards, swinging censers. Something in the air—the children playing in the light of ragged corridors, the aged pilgrims clambering toward the doors, the priests in raiment, stepping back into the Bible—made me think of Tibet. For I had never before seen such fervor and devotion except in the Himalayas. Sometimes, in the dark, I could see nothing but priests and their crosses; sometimes only the outline of figures, archetypal almost, bowing toward the altar.

I had heard for years that Lalibela was one of the secret, undiscovered wonders of the world, and now I was being told that it was paradise. But in fact this tiny village seemed something more valuable than that: a living, singing replica of paradise in our midst. And not just a collection of old buildings and stones for archaeologists, but a breathing, pounding, chanting place with a sense of worship so powerful that it made me shake.

Lalibela, like all the truly sacred places in the world, is distinguished, in fact, by all the things you cannot see: most of all, the silence, the sense of spun calm as luminous and clear as glass polished by forty generations and more of worship. You sit in the cool darkness of a church, light streaming through the cross-shaped windows, the sound of murmured prayers all around you, and you leave the world you know. And enter one you had forgotten you inhabited.


I hadn't come to Ethiopia to be spiritually awakened. Quite the opposite, in fact. I'd set off (for reasons that should remain obscure) with a box of plain Cheerios, some chocolate-covered espresso beans, and an English investment banker with a mosquito net. The I.B. (as I shall call him, for reasons of diplomacy) was a disciple of Waugh's, anxious to set back any Anglo-Ethiopian relations that might have healed since the great man's visit. The Ethiopian National Tourist Organization was, I had found, in the Ethiopian Airlines office in New York, but when I went there, they had no knowledge of it (or, indeed, of tourists) and fobbed me off instead with a months-old copy of the *Ethiopian Herald*. A large headline said: "Amateur Boxing Lacks Kock-out Appeal."

On the flight into Addis Ababa, one toilet was soon flooded to the point of being unusable, and the other needed to be reassembled by the time the feature movie—*Dennis the Menace*—began. Every five minutes, like clockwork, the armrest of the woman in front of me came down to concuss my knee. And, for some atavistic reason, wrenching country-and-western music accompanied us over the great plains of Africa, culminating in a stirring rendition of "America the Beautiful" as we touched down at Bole International Airport (which was dominated by a six-foot-high replica of a pack of Winstons and a sign that said: "Welcome to Ethiopia. Centre of Recreation and Relaxation").

Within an hour of arrival in the country, I found myself (unknowingly) in a house of ill repute, where a plump, denim-jacketed houri called Franca was shaking her hips and calling, "Rico, Rico," while a bearded man walked in and out, bearing a copy of *Franny and Zooey*. Another woman sat at a brazier in her shorts, cooking up coffee in some traditional fashion, while Kenny Rogers sang, "We don't need money," out of a super-woofer twin-drive radio. We were there because we had been picked up by an Eritrean named Haile ("Haile Unlikely," said the I.B.), who had promised that this was the only place where we could get a visa to his newly independent homeland.

A top dog in the Eritrean Embassy came here to "recreate himself," said Haile, red-eyed with drink and bad intentions. "If we make some trouble, maybe you can give us some favorable attentions."

"I got you," sang Kenny Rogers, "you got me, we got love."

A few hours later, still reeling from the twenty-four-hour flight, I found myself standing under a huge full moon outside the room of the Somali warlord Mohammed Farah Aidid. Aidid, the most wanted man in the world just a month before, was staying in the same hotel as we were, as it happened ("Oh, General Aidid—Room 211, over near the swimming pool," the receptionist had said), and now, surrounded by khaki-covered men with guns, his private secretary was pulling up his pants leg to show us the shrapnel he had received from "U.S. helicopter gunships."

The very next day, though, we drove out of Addis, away from Franca and Aidid, away from Kenny Rogers and Haile Unfortunate, and within minutes, we found ourselves in an utterly different world: a Stone Age world, almost, of antique figures and shawled old crones and donkeys who seemed to have walked in from the Book of Kings. "Abyssinia" has, of course, been veiled in mists and mysterious associations almost since the birth of Christ. It was the haunt of the Queen of Sheba and, by some accounts, the original site of the Garden of Eden. It is the oldest Christian country in the world and the only one in Africa to have defeated a European power (the Italians, in 1896). I had only to look at the ancient Phoenician script on my visa, with its air of old parchment and sacred Coptic texts, to realize that I was traveling into antiquity.

Compounding this remoteness in space—for Ethiopia is not really Africa, and yet not quite Arabia, either—is a remoteness in time, hardened by the watchfulness with which it has guarded its traditions. In medieval times, in Europe, Abyssinia was known primarily as the domain of Prester John, a Christian priest-king ruling a world of unicorns and pygmies; and for centuries, hidden away in the mountains, with the oldest written culture on the continent and its own distinctive community of Muslims, Christians, and Jews, it had kept up its own unlikely ways (whenever a crime was committed, the Eleventh Edition of the *Encyclopaedia Britannica* informed me, "a small boy is drugged, and 'whatever person he dreams of is fixed on as the criminal' "). Its sense of apartness from the world was only confirmed by the fact that Ethiopia still observed a pre-Julian calendar (so that there are thirteen months in a year there, noon is at 6 a.m., and the new year is celebrated in September,

four months before Christmas). "Encompassed on all sides by the enemies of their religion," as Gibbon wrote, "the Aethiopians slept near a
thousand years, forgetful of the world, by whom they were forgotten."

Even within my own memory, things were no less otherworldly. Just
twenty years ago, Addis was still the center of a feudal medieval court—
with pillow bearers and urine wipers and bodies suspended in front
of Saint George's Cathedral—ruled over by Haile Selassie (his heir
apparent, Prince Zere Yacob, walked the same high-school corridors as
the I.B. and myself). Then, in 1974, the King of Kings, Lord of Lords,
and Conquering Lion of the Tribe of Judah was taken off his throne and
driven away in a VW. There followed a more or less typical seventeen
years of guerrilla warfare, Marxist misrule, and desperate food shortages,
and when the country emerged again, in 1991, with a new "transitional
government," it had a per capita GDP of under $100 a year, and more
than four million people dependent on international food aid. Now,
under the thirty-nine-year-old Meles Zenawi, the 53 million Ethiopians
(up from just 42 million only ten years before) were experimenting with
a kind of democracy by trial and error—no easy task for a land that
had, not long before I arrived, held its first free elections in sixteen hundred years.

So as we journeyed out of Addis, along the well-organized "Historic
Route" that takes you through all the great historical sites of Ethiopia—
Lalibela, Gonder, Axum, and Lake Tana—we felt as if we were going
into prehistory, or into some dark and echoing otherworld. Rastafarians
famously consider Ethiopia to be the home of the Messiah; others believe
that the Ark of the Covenant, and part of the true cross of Christ, are
buried here. The high plateau is made for guerezas, geladas, guenons, and
dog-faced baboons, I read, as well as the greater and lesser kudu, duiker,
klipspringer, and dik-dik. The Ethiopian Orthodox Church is like
nothing else in the world, observing a practice of singing and dancing, as
in the time of King David, and a Monophysite creed. And even if (like
me) one doesn't go to see the Surma women with clay plates in their lips,
the tribes who still make fires with bows and sticks, or the "yellow
people" of the south, one is going into a world charged with something
spookily recessed.

As soon as we drove out of the capital, we were in a land of ancient
spareness: shepherds on horseback, driving their flocks along roads white
with dust; horses galloping across the openness; huge processions of petitioners, all in white, marching in long lines along the road to celebrate
Saint Gabriel's Day. The sky above the eucalyptus groves a burning blue,
the ridges of the mountains forbidding before us, and everywhere a landscape untouched by anything we knew. Sometimes we stopped and

joined little boys along the road at their games of *foosball;* sometimes we sipped sweet clove-and-cinnamon tea, while introducing our hosts to the Neville Brothers.

And as we drove, I realized that I had never, ever, seen a place so bare: there were no road signs here—no roads almost—and no amenities or shops or frills. Nothing, in fact. And nothing to take one away from the ageless, changeless rhythm of men with crooks and staffs, and women with blue crosses painted on their chins, and patriarchs staring out from unlit doorways. In late afternoon, as we drove through villages lit up by the sharp last light, and six-year-old shepherds drove their animals home, and the sun declined behind the purple mountains, surrounded by silence and vast emptiness, I could think only of the lilting cadences of Gray's "Elegy Written in a Country Churchyard." For this really did seem a world pre-fallen; an intimation of some pastorale that sang inside us like a long-lost melody.

"What would it take for news to reach here?" asked the I.B., hungry for a copy of the latest *Financial Times.* It never could, I realized. An atomic bomb in Hiroshima; a coup in Moscow; the whole of China swinging on its hinges: none of it, surely, could ever touch this world, or make sense even if it did get here. It belonged to a different age.

Driving in Ethiopia is not an easy experience—infrequent buses appearing on the wrong side of the road, children and donkeys swerving crazily in front of you, potholes sending you ricocheting from one side of the car to the other till you cannot move or talk or eat. And in our case, conditions were not enhanced by a Land Cruiser equipped with a tape deck that wouldn't work, seat belts that didn't engage, a front door that couldn't lock, and a driver who, when pressed, admitted that he'd been along this road only once before, twenty-eight years earlier, on a bus.

Yet still, there was redemption in the air itself, and in the unending vistas: camels, sometimes, running under a full moon; horses being ridden so fast, in impromptu races, that they raised up Mongol clouds of dust; village homes a blaze of apricot and sea blue and blinding green.

We drove past rolling hills and round straw huts, past monumental skies and conifers and hooded pietàs. "It's so cultivated," said the I.B., who had just come from Kenya, and though he was talking about the land, he could as easily have been talking about the sensibility: for there is nothing of the bush or the untended jungle here among these high mountain plateaus. And nothing without pride, and some degree of self-possession. At night, our first day on the road, hooded figures calling out directions in the dark, we stopped at a tiny rest house, and a man came out, cried, *"Buona sera!"* and served up, with a Milanese flourish, steak Bismarck and Axumite red wine, a napkin decorously wrapped around the bottle (which announced: "The peculiarity of this wine makes it appreciated by everybody").

In the morning again, at daybreak, it was like seeing the face of the world before it was born: like shapes and figures from one's deepest subconscious. In the early light, the mist still swaddled the mountains, and when I walked up the main street, little girls were skipping rope, women were sweeping the space before their huts, boys were carrying fuel home for their mothers. Cocks crowed. The mist began to lift. Horse-drawn carriages clattered over bumpy roads. It was not that there was so much poverty here; more that there was so little excess. No fat on the land, so to speak.

On a blazing blue day in Dese—the name means "My Joy"—we stopped to get our roof fixed. Across from us, men bathed naked in a stream, their wives sitting on the grass under parasols. Above them, on a hill, villagers were selling sheep and goats and donkeys on this market day, while below, in the central market, boys sold empty bottles of Johnnie Walker and presided over cans of European Economic Community rapeseed oil. The I.B. lost himself in Richard Price, and I walked into a local video store, which carried seven copies of *Return to Eden* (and one of *Romeo and Juliet*), under a huge mural of Bob Marley.

"The Sudan is primitive," the I.B. pronounced. "This is basic. There's a difference." And there was some truth to what he was saying, in this land where eight people out of every ten live a half day's walk from the nearest road, and 95 percent are still agricultural peasants. There was no sugar in the Ethiopian diet until recently, and there has always been a fierce wariness of the modern: even when Haile Selassie brought the first airplane from Europe, in the '20s, many of his people took him to be a necromancer, importing instruments of Satan.

We drove on, through enchanted light, over mountain passes where men in hoods were carrying whole beds of leaves, and when we got to Weldiya, we stopped to ask directions. If we went on, we were told, we would be attacked by bandits. "If they see us," the driver said, turning round, eyes wild, "they will take money, bags, everything. Even they will kill us. They do not care. They will kill us like the animals." Deciding not to put this prognosis to the test, we procured three rooms in a waterless shack, and beguiled the last of the light with games of Ping-Pong along the main street, fifty or so boys cheering and laughing all around us, and calling out "Bravo!" whenever one of my slams nicked the table.

The final five miles to Lalibela, over unpaved road, the car's wheels spinning in dry creekbeds, the fuel in the cans in back all but suffocating us, took almost three hours. It was, we noted sorrowfully, December 31. "The end of the year in the end of the world!" cried the I.B., with a gaiety brought on by hysteria.

And then, suddenly, we were there, in silence and in mystery. Inside the rock churches, the white figures were everywhere in the dim light, leaning against pillars, standing in front of windows, reading old, leathery, hand-size Bibles, or letting out unearthly mumbled chants that reverberated around the ancient spaces. Sometimes I could see only their eyes in the dark, and hear only their song.

Lean, gaunt-bearded priests with piercing eyes made strange movements with their crosses, and pilgrims slept in empty spaces, and somewhere in the rafters, pigeons whirred. Incense rose up from the shrine, and deacons sang, and figure after figure came into the darkness, kissing the cool stone before coming in. "I weary of writing about these buildings," said the first foreign visitor to describe them, a Portuguese priest in the early sixteenth century, "because it seems to me I shall not be believed."

From time to time in Lalibela, I simply sat on slopes and listened to the sounds around: the chatter of old men with crooks, gathered in the shade; a mother shouting to her child; the voices of other children, playing in the distance. Birds with gorgeous, iridescent turquoise wings—Abyssinian rollers, I later learned—lit up the branches. Often, there was nothing but the calling of the birds and the wind, whistling in my ears.

Occasionally, there were vultures in the trees and bells to summon priests to church. And everywhere, a sense of piety and fervor, a world inscribed by nothing but devotion. "This is Golgotha," said a deacon, pointing to an inner gate. "And this is Nazareth. And there, in the light of the church, are the graves of Abraham, Isaac, and Jacob."

"It isn't Africa," a Swiss medieval historian said over dinner that night, on New Year's Eve. "It's more like a cross between medieval Europe and Arabia. In this village, for example, there are seven thousand people. And one thousand of them are priests. That, too, is medieval: in Europe, in the Middle Ages, one-tenth of the population were priests."

The next day, the I.B. and I got on mules and rode through the dust-colored mountains, over a landscape as majestic and humbling as Monument Valley, the I.B. listening to Dead bootlegs on his Walkman, as we passed peasants, with long black beards, seated under trees, sharing food, and donkeys and cedar trees and olive trees and juniper. All around us, as so often in Ethiopia, it felt as if we were passing through an illuminated Bible from the thirteenth century, except that all the figures moved.

When we arrived in Nakutola'ab, where twenty-five anchorites live in

rock caves, we came upon a group of pilgrims—mud-grimed grandfathers and sunken-cheeked women and young girls in pockmarked
gowns—all of them clapping and singing their joy, ululating wildly and
pounding on drums, in a circle, to vent their pent-up pleasure after
arriving at the place that they had been dreaming of all their lives.

I asked one of the men (through a translator) how old he was—a strap-
ping man, tall and lean, his eyes alight with glee. He was seventy, he said,
and he had walked twelve days and nights to mark Christmas (celebrated
in Ethiopia on January 7) in this sacred site.

"And why do you come here?"

"Because this is heaven. We believe if we are here we go to heaven."

"Then I'll see you in heaven," said the I.B., clapping him on the
shoulder, and there were wild shouts of approval and laughs all round.


Lalibela was not just an extraordinary medieval mystery play in stone, I
thought, not just a place where the Emperor had come to pray when the
first of Mussolini's Blackshirts had arrived; not merely a marvel that had
taken twenty-three years to construct, with the help of angels, and
masons from Syria, from Greece, even from India. It was one of those
rare sites where the spirit vibrated not only through the buildings but
through all the spaces in between.

And then we took to the road again, and drove for hour after hour,
past deep canyons and bleak wasteland and lunar spaces, with nothing to
remind us of where we were, or when. It felt more than ever as if we were
driving through some ur-terrain, archaic, ancestral, through some lost
part of ourselves almost.

And everywhere the sheer grandeur of the mountains, and an immen-
sity of sky. A landscape before whose gravity and purity one feels very
small, and young. A bareness that takes you back to something essential
and elemental, almost to life before it was lived. In the Ethiopian language of Gallinya, I read, the word for "sky" is the same as the word for
"God."

I had seen empty spaces before I came to Ethiopia—in the Australian
outback, say, or Patagonia. But what made these so much more rending
and exalting was that there were people living amidst this nothingness,
walking across it, trying to eke out a living from it. Nomads pale with
grime, men wielding axes, women bearing staffs. And, in the midst of the
desolation, long lines of people, most of them rail thin, bedraggled, barefoot, long lines of people, walking, walking, walking, from nowhere to
nowhere. The sadness of Ethiopia is that even in the areas that are relatively prosperous, all the lean figures look as if they are walking out of the

photographs of famine that shocked the world a decade ago; next year, we were told, a million people would be without food, and there was nothing that could be done.

And the fervor and the desperation, the suffering and the piety, threw light on one another. Amidst this extreme deprivation, one could see how extreme devotion could arise; amidst this barrenness, the burning brightness of the religious rites and buildings made better sense. Prayers in the wilderness, I thought; water in the desert. It was easy, in Ethiopia, to understand how religions caught fire (easy, too, to see why people became monks, in a world that was already naked, unaccommodated, and bare); and it was possible in Ethiopia to see how people who have nothing will give everything to faith.

Every now and then, we stopped in cafés for the national staple of *injera*, or foam-rubber bread, the I.B. crying out, "This could be *injerious* to your health. Did you take out multiple *injera* insurance?" Sometimes, as we left, we heard the haunting, biblical cry of children in the distance, *"Abba, Abba!"* Every now and then, we saw figures in the distance, silhouetted against rocks or proceeding across the emptiness in search of shelter. The only signs of the world we knew were the occasional huts of relief agencies, or four-wheel-drive jeeps with "Love from Band-Aid" on their sides. Mostly, though, it was just emptiness stretching on and on toward the mountains.

After what seemed like days, or eons, of travel, we arrived in Gonder, and were reminded again of how sadness and fervor fuel one another here. There is a faintly threatening air to the old capital now, as its Amhara people chafe against the dictates of a non-Amhara government. A Martyrs' Memorial stands in the heart of town, with messages scrawled in blood red across it, and nearby is a large painting of a skeleton, with a fierce old woman holding the former governor of the province by the hair and crying, "You killed my child! Wherever you go, I will find vengeance!" Men in hoods watch you from dark corners in cafés, sipping their orange-colored mead, and boys in denim jackets tell you the difference between Kalashnikovs and M-14s, and how their fathers were killed by Communists, and their sisters raped by Sudanese soldiers. Strung between the pretty Italian buildings at the center of town, a banner proclaims: "Nov. 20 is the birth of the oppressed peoples!"

"All this the Italians built in five years," a local boy told us, motioning around the two main streets of town, and referring to the Italian occupation of 1936–41. "Some people are saying, if they stay ten years, Gonder becomes like Paris."

In Gonder, there was not a great deal to do. I bought some Yemenite sandwich biscuits, and visited the Falasha village where the last few remnants of Ethiopia's Jewish community, yet to be airlifted to Israel, stand by the side of the road and sell stone figurines of Solomon and the Queen of Sheba making whoopee. I parted with thirty-five cents to attend a wedding in Revolution Square, and saw groups of men in their best Bon Jovi T-shirts gathered around a video camera. And, dutifully, I went to the ruins of the castle of King Fasilades, with their Enigma Gate, and Gate of the Flute Players, and Castle of Songs. For all the lyrical names, however, they are much like ruins anywhere: dead clumps of stone, and broken towers, and piles of forgotten rubble.

Yet one Sunday morning, sitting in the corner of a tower and looking over the pieces of rock, suddenly I heard wild chanting and the steady, insistent pounding of drums and a trilling, thrilling ululation of women down below, and when I looked down, I saw them moving all as one, swaying back and forth, with the jacarandas behind them. When I went down, I found myself in a whole avenue of churches, crowded with worshipers, the streets all but palpitant with prayer, and, along the ancient mud walls, long lines of mendicants and beggars.

On every side, around the center, people were gathered under trees, and children were scampering around broken gravestones, and petitioners with white crosses chalked upon their foreheads were giving alms. There were golden robes and rows of multicolored umbrellas and bells tolling constantly and, lined up outside the round churches, a terrible, haggard row of people in rags: the leprous, the lame, the palsied, and the blind. The notion of a savior had never made more sense to me; I half expected to see Jesus and the Apostles walking down these muddy lanes.


The other site in Gonder that we inspected closely was the Ethiopian Airlines Office (which pins "Positive Attitude" posters from Fairfield, New Jersey, on its walls). E.T., as the experts call it, has a sterling reputation but is not without its extraterrestrial elements. Its schedules seem to follow the solar calendar, it insists on security checks at every stage of check-in, and in many places, the only terminals in sight are trees. "Ethiopia is a land where the great unknown yonder still exists in plenty," says the legend on every ticket.

Undeterred, we took our lives in our hands (and out of the hands of our driver, who had taken now to plaintive moans of "I am very suffering") and flew low over the high plateaus toward Bahar Dar. The town itself is a pleasant, palm-fringed settlement along the banks of Lake Tana. The Tisisat Falls are nearby, a rainbow punctually arcing across their rush of water every morning and marking the place where James Bruce excitedly hailed the waters of the Blue Nile. Boys cross the river on papyrus boats, and hoist stalks of sugarcane taller than themselves. On the quiet lake, there are tens of little islands, most of them given over to monasteries, some so strict that no female is allowed to set foot on them (even hens are not permitted). The round, dried-mud churches at their center, three hundred years old, swarm with naive, brightly colored murals bursting with angels and stories from the Bible and even—a typical Ethiopian anachronism—Jesus surrounded by gun-toting men.

That strain was beginning to hit me more and more forcibly. As soon as I went to change my money at a local bank, a security guard came up to frisk me, and to ask me to deposit my camera next to the rifles, laid neatly against the wall outside; an hour later, walking through quiet villages to see the falls, I was accompanied by a sharp-talking teenager and a barefoot peasant with a rifle (whether to ward off bandits or to perform banditry himself, I never knew). Pride is only a hairbreadth from machismo here, and when it does not take the form of guarding Jesus—or General Aidid—with guns, it involves overtaking around blind turns and driving the other man off the road.

The most obvious reason for this is that the country is only just emerging from decades of civil war. Ever since their region was annexed, in 1962, the Eritreans had been crossing the border to fight against central authority in Addis, and then their guerrillas had joined the local rebels to overthrow the Communists. Meanwhile, more than a hundred other ethnic groups were ardently pursuing their rivalries and interests in north and south and east. The result is that everywhere you go in Ethiopia, you see the scars and remnants of thirty years of war: airports are blasted, and their tarmac is littered with wrecked helicopters and junked Aeroflot planes. Rusted tanks line every road, and faded replicas of the hammer and sickle. Once, in Bahar Dar, coming upon a car crash (there are more crashes than cars in Ethiopia, it often seems), I ended up spending a long day in a local hospital, a place of terrible cries and whimpers, where boys with bandaged heads and sunken faces writhed under rough blankets. The doctors were courtly and efficient, but it was not a place where I would like to fall ill. "Are there many car accidents here?" I asked a pretty young nurse. "No," she said, nonchalant. "Usually it is bullet wounds. But that, too, not so often. Usually the people here shoot to kill, not wound. So we let them just go ahead with it." And, smiling, went off to another victim.

We explored Bahar Dar in an old car decorated with pictures of Rambo and Jesus on the windshield, driven by Solomon, with Mikael at his side, both of them breaking into smiles of good-natured perplexity as the I.B. recited a poem about a duck-billed platypus entering the diplomatic service. We visited the U.N. Shoe Shine store and the Marine

Bingo Club, and in the evening, we got the manager of the local cinema to screen *The Border* just for us, though the print was so washed out and mutilated that the picture was over in a matter of minutes, and somehow the classic last scene of Freddy Fender singing Ry Cooder's "Across the Borderline" was lost. Nonetheless, it was a cheerful experience, sitting on long wooden benches, like pews, in what looked like a school assembly hall, the boys in the balcony eating egg sandwiches and sipping *shai*, and scarcely missing Freddy Fender.


For the few foreigners who visit it, Ethiopia is a very small country, and when I arrived, I had no hesitation in calling up Richard Pankhurst, perhaps the West's leading authority on the country and a resident in Addis, on and off, since 1951. He was rather ill, he said, the first time I called, and the next time I tried, he was out of town. But one day, as I walked toward a monastery on an island in Lake Tana, suddenly I heard his inimitable Oxbridge tones, and when I looked round, there he was, in a green suit, explaining the iconography of the church to a group of birders from America: the usual Ethiopian gallimaufry of Saint George slaying the dragon, the "crucification" (as they always call it), the local saint Abbo, Moses, and the Virgin.

The Ethiopian Orthodox Church was unique, Professor Pankhurst explained, in that it still gives great honor to the Old Testament, believing not that the New supersedes the Old, but rather that the Old prophesies the New. The Ethiopian Bible contains all the books of the so-called Apocrypha, and in fact, the Book of Enoch comes down to us only in the ancient Ethiopian liturgical language of Ge'ez. Ethiopians also observe all the Old Testament rites of circumcision, fasting, and the like, to the point where many Ethiopians fast, one way or another, for roughly half the days of the year.

Ever since being brought here, in the fourth century, by Syrian missionaries, Christianity has taken a distinctive form in Ethiopia, not quite Coptic and certainly not Western. Nestled in the isolation of the highlands, unsettled by the constant threat of Muslim invasions, it has gone its own individual way—to the point where it is now almost a talisman of the nation (thus Muslims participate in Christian rites). It is wise to remember this when one flies out into the hot plains and scrubland of the east, for there one seems to have left the ancient land behind and entered Africa. Women in brilliantly colored robes, violet and green and pink, swirled like saris around their bodies, walk with a stately grace across the desolation of the desert. The air feels sultry, strutting, spiced with heat and menace.

Dire Dawa, my first stop in the east, had Stars of David on its doors, and signs for the Ethiopia-Somalia Democratic Movement among stores that were nearly always called "Moderen." Not far from the old *chemin de fer* station (there is a strong French influence here in this hot, dusty, squat, rectangular town, redolent of the Foreign Legion), I came upon a swirl of *calèches* and minivans and Peugeot taxis, tall boys with insolent stares, selling nuts and oranges. A man guffawed at my copy of *Le Rouge et le noir*, a boy with kohl-lined eyes ushered me into a van, women pulled up their saffron scarves, giving off a cloud of fragrances. A fight broke out nearby, and the combatants sprawled in the dust.

A couple of denim dudes collected our cash, and then we set off for Harar, passing proud dreadlocked girls and small, muddy African villages, tall cactus by the side of the road. Flirty teenagers jangled their bracelets, and stared back defiantly at passersby. The girl next to me had a ring on every finger.

Harar, at its heart, is all North Africa, all whitewashed passageways and Moorish curves, the cry of "baksheesh" from the boys, and, in the house where Haile Selassie once lived, a man called Sheikh Mohammed, offering traditional healing. ("The treatment is given by the help of God," his sign explains. "Although the Medicine is given without payment, the patient and all other peoples including organization help us if you can.")

I put myself in the tender care of a bleary-eyed gent called Astaw Warhu, and he gave me a highly colorful tour of a Muslim enclave that is like a rich and heady concoction: of tribal girls with yellow-chalked faces, and others with rolling white eyes; of Oromo women with red dots around their eyes, and men with lips of foaming green. As soon as I turned down the traditional healing, he whisked me along a tiny alleyway and then up some dusty stairs, to a place with panes of dirty stained glass, and a lightless room where two men were sprawled on cushions, phlegmatically chewing *qat* (the coca leaves of North Africa, of which Harar is the world's leading producer).

"You know Rimbaud?" asked Mr. Warhu, pointing to the two dazed men, who were splayed out like opium addicts. "This is where he lived. Sometimes he sells arms to Menelik II. Sometimes he is a postman." I thought, without joy, of the exiled author of *Une Saison en enfer*.

Then Mr. Warhu led me up some more stairs, to where there was some wallpaper covering the ceiling. "Rimbaud!" he declared. "All this he paints!"

We went down into the dust and confusion and red and yellow loudness of the market, surrounded by five gates and ninety-nine mosques, so they say, with *Les Jeunes Bonzes du temple de Shaolin* playing in the local cinema, and the children, without exception, crying out to me, *"Ferengi, ferengi!"* ("Foreigner, foreigner!") or, more often, "Cuba, Cuba, Cuba!"

"They think you are Cuban," said Mr. Warhu. "The Cubans are no good. They think every day, every night, about war. They are walking in town with guns, with pistols." This seemed an odd objection in a country where more people carried guns than handbags, but Mr. Warhu concluded, "Every people is come back to the gods."

Then, disconcertingly, he added, "You know Heinemann?"

Was he referring to the English publisher of V. S. Naipaul?

"Heinemann?"

"Yes. Heinie-man. Every night he feeds heinies. You can make photograph."

I decided to pass on the hyena man, while thinking that Harar had come a long way from its traditional status as a closed walled city, with its own chieftain, language, and coinage, a hidden metropolis that had never seen a European face till Sir Richard Burton stole into it in 1854. For centuries, ever since the Muslims had taken it over, it had flowered in secrecy behind its walls, closing its doors each night at dusk, and keeping all Christians out.

Harar today seemed to me stench, flies, dust: flashing-eyed girls in golden scarves; the cry of the muezzin above green-domed mosques; women with nose rings and dangling bangles, walking so straight they carried bundles of twigs on their heads. Along the main street was the Ogaden National Liberation Front and, next door to it, the Commission for the Rehabilitation of Members of the Former Disabled War Veterans East Haraghe Office (the CRMFDWVEHO?). I checked into the best— actually, the only—hotel in town, which promised "Both traditional comfort and modern hospitality." Did either of these include water? I asked the friendly receptionist. "No," she said. "There is no water in the town. For two months there has been no water."

Addis Ababa, through which almost every visitor must pass, while coming and going, is a sleepy, eerie, rather bedraggled town—less tranquil than torpid, and less a town, indeed, than a collection of grand monuments set against shacks and vacant lots and open ditches: a sad, rather abandoned place of relief agencies, and faded, sun-bleached ads for the United Colors of Benetton, and small, hand-painted signs along the road to the airport, directing you to embassies. It is, in fact, the most rural city I have ever seen, encircled by dun-colored hills and haunted by the recent discovery that the last Emperor was buried in a secret vault beneath the central palace. "Goats and cows grazed on the lawns along the main street, Churchill Road," wrote Ryszard Kapuscinski, "and cars had to stop when nomads drove their herds of frightened camels across the street." And that was during the Golden Age, when Haile Selassie ruled!

Indeed, what gives the city its forlorn, halfhearted air is that the half-finished relics of an imperial past are placed amidst the tin-roofed shanties. Addis—like much of Ethiopia—has the air of an exiled prince, long accustomed to grandeur and full of pride, but fallen now on very hard times. There are broad streets lined with jacaranda, and the Emperor's palace dominates the center of town ("At night the visitor can hear the lions roar from the grounds of the nearby palace," my 1969 guidebook said of the hotel where I was staying). There are boulevards named after Queen Elizabeth and King George VI, and ceremonial gates. There is even a Hilton Hotel. But incense clouds the lobby there, and the only papers on offer are ten days old.

Much of the capital feels remaindered now, and dispossessed (even the envelopes in my hotel proclaimed, not very ringingly, "Transitional Government of Ethiopia"). Along the streets where Haile Selassie used to cruise in his green Rolls-Royce, the signs say "Hope Enterprises Feeding Center" and "Life Saver Cafeteria." Across from the National Museum, there are stalls with names like "Neil A. Armstrong Typing Training School" (and typing in Amharic, with its 236-character alphabet, must be as difficult almost as walking on the moon) and hooded people clutching in-flight magazines as if they were glossy treasures. And the city of palimpsests still has a spooky, nerve-racked air, the air of a city with a bad case of the shakes, in the midst of a bad sleep troubled by dark dreams.

Yet on the day before Christmas—as flawless and blue as every other day I spent in Ethiopia—the streets were bright with cross-shaped wreaths of purple and gold, and as night began to fall, the bars put on their single tubes of neon lighting, and I could see bright candles in shacks, and twinkling trees in cafés. Children let off fireworks in small parks, and women in gorgeous silks, with painted feet, trooped into my hotel.

And on a misty Christmas Eve, the streets were filled again with white-robed worshipers. The bells of the Selassie (Trinity) Cathedral tolled and tolled and tolled, and soon all corners of the glowing church were crowded with gaunt white figures in hoods, and deacons in white with red crosses on their backs, and priests in black robes with small white hats, and women with gold sandals beneath their white: a whole swirl of half-mythic figures, ragged, barefoot, but upright, filling all the pews in the church's ornate interior, the green and red and yellow flag of Ethiopia fluttering above them.

Upstairs, in a gallery, a group of robed deacons was standing in a circle, chanting, slowly and solemnly, as if to some age-old rhythm. One of them, on the ground, banged a slow, slow drum, and all the men around him, clutching their T-shaped prayer sticks, slowly waving their sistrums, let out a slow, solemn, wailing chant that carried into the night and down into the nave below.

Outside, in the pitch blackness, worshipers were making deep prostrations, extending their whole bodies along the ground, and mumbling prayers, or standing in nooks and corners with their psalters. Candles had been placed in the hands of every saint, in all the twelve alcoves along the church, above the stained glass; believers circumambulated the darkened building bearing tapers, their figures making ghostly shadows on the walls.

From the trees, in the dark, I heard a banging drum. Cries and chants and ululations from somewhere among the gravestones. A haunting, unworldly, ancient chant that went through me to the core.

I followed the sound through the trees and the abject darkness, and came upon a wondrous sight: a whole avenue of people, on the ground, lit up by candles before them, outside the entrance to another church, old and small and round. Around it, on every side, barefoot, bedraggled, hooded bodies, all in white, more bodies than I could count, hardly visible by the light of the candles they were holding, and gathering in small groups under straw roofs, or standing against headstones, or assembled in a circle under a tree, just praying, or listening, in silence, to a sermon, or singing alleluias in the night.

Everywhere I turned there were figures, some of them asleep, for they had not eaten all day and many of them had been fasting for two months—no meat, no eggs. Others stood on either side of distant tombs, a candle on each side of them. Others were lined up in what looked to be a manger, their sweet high voices rising into the dark.

Within the church, there were so many people one could hardly move. Boys were playing oxskin drums, and lines of men in multicolored raiment, with gold and violet hats, were singing from their holy books, the altars in front of them shaking with their piety. Outside, one of the groups struck up a hymn and started clapping, and others picked up the rhythm, and then there was a wild ululation that signaled, thrillingly, glad tidings to the world, and the arrival of something bright.

All across the candlelit city it was like that on Christmas Eve, white-robed figures from another age, with laughing eyes and beads and crosses, chanting by the light of tapers. And sometimes, as I looked around me, at the round church, and the rough ground, and the ragged, hopeful figures sitting or standing and singing through the night, I felt that this must have been how it was in Bethlehem, two thousand years before. There was no sign of the modern world, no electricity or hype. Only ragged figures, with candles, singing their devotion.

"You really feel it," said the I.B., moved. "You really feel the joy that must have arisen when God was born." And he was right.

Before I went to Ethiopia, I had said, half facetiously, that I was going there to "get around Christmas," leaving, on December 25, to avoid the commercialism and loneliness and impossible expectations that constitute the holiday for us. I had not known that Ethiopia really was the way to get to the heart of Christmas, and of almost everything else. I am no Christian, but Christianity made sense to me in Ethiopia—and many things as basic as hope and dignity, necessity and faith—and as I looked at the stars through the branches and the flicker of candles, I really could imagine three wise men coming to a manger, following the skies. Everything revved up and complicated fell away, and I was left in Ethiopia with the small, forgotten soul of the whole thing: thanksgiving amidst hardship and songs of glorious praise.

(1994)

# Nepal: Movie Days
## in Kathmandu

There is a festive air in Bhaktapur today. Young wives are crowding through the tiny, dusty alleyways of the fairy-tale Nepali town, chattering excitedly, all in their Saturday finest, as they pose for cameras on brocaded swings or next to golden horses, while scores of others are standing in line to wander through a wonderland of silken canopies, next to a ceremonial pool, in front of ancient temples repainted in dazzling reds and golds. Little girls are huddled over bottles of hotel shampoo, and urchins are playing hide-and-seek around a silver van on which is written, simply, "Tao Film." Usually this is a grubby little square where men sell daggers, demon masks, and other kinds of spell, the poorest, most medieval part of a valley that is the heart of one of the poorest countries on earth. But today the "City of Devotees" is a blaze of colors, awash with gilded parasols, glittering with saris, like nothing so much as a toothless crone attending a wedding in her finest silks.

Amidst all the commotion on this dazzling winter's day (Nepal, as it is easy to forget, is more subtropical than California, and Kathmandu is on the same latitude as Miami), life goes on in its usual state of pell-mell calm. In one corner of the sunlit square, a man has laid out a carpet in the dust and is disappearing beneath a minivan that says "Ambulance" on its side; across the square, two Italians on cranes are poking into medieval windows and shouting down orders to a group of ragged laborers who are moving pieces of the town around. Nearby, a cow sits placidly against a plaster elephant. Preschool shopkeepers are luring shaven-headed nuns from Hong Kong into the Lovely Handicraft Thangka Centre. Somewhere in the sun, a flautist is playing—and playing and playing—the notes of "It's a small, small world."

The five-mile trip back to Kathmandu takes only forty-five minutes, traveling on a three-wheel motorized ricksha that bumps and lurches and stalls over roads well furnished with cows. "Speak the Truth," cries the sign across the road. "Perform your Dharma. Do Not Fall from Self-Studies." Most of the walls around it are scrawled with messages saying, "Vote for Sun" or "Vote for Tree," accompanied by pictures of these objects (since three Nepalis in every four cannot read, political parties here are designated by universal symbols, and ballot forms come with drawings as well as names).

Back in the city, in the Hotel Yak & Yeti—an opulent fantasy of a place that looks like the overheated daydream of some Victorian-educated Calcuttan who spent his youth around Saint Petersburg—a very different kind of show is taking place. Ponytailed Italians and Brits in leather jackets and a few bronzed trendies who look as if they've just stepped out of *L'Uomo* are sitting around chatting—as incongruous in this rugged town as a group of Nepali farmers would be along the Via Veneto. You can spot them from a hundred yards, with their expensive haircuts and silken scarves, talking, in accents redolent of Trastevere and Belgravia, of the Christian Dior wallet they've just lost or the BBC broadcast they caught by mistake on the hotel TV.

Today is a holiday, but call sheets are already posted in the lobby for tomorrow's predawn start. The two principals, Keanu Reeves and Rajeshwari, will have to be in Bhaktapur by sunup. This fairly typical day of shooting in Bernardo Bertolucci's latest epic will also require the services of "208 Members of the Court, 50 Court Guards, 36 Palanquin Porters, 12 Grooms, 11 Indian Girls and 8 Kapadi Players." "Special Requirements," the sign goes on, "10 Horses. Props: Palanquins (minimum of 3). Lunch: for 140 people (and for 350 extras)."

Right now, as the streets empty out (it is nearly 8:15 p.m.), the people, if not the extras, are gathered in the Yak & Yeti's tiny, nine-seat bar, half lit by the erratic flickerings of a black-and-white TV. The techies are propping up the bar, telling dirty stories; the rich women are sitting down, telling even dirtier stories. Their voices drift up above the Icebergs and Tuborgs they are drinking, above the chic assistants with their Tintin books, above the framed prints of maharajas and slain tigers. "This man over here with an Australian accent—he is Italian!" "A fire in Windsor Castle? You've got to be joking!" "See, he thinks he's D. W. Griffith. Matter of fact, I think so too."


It is the dilemma that every traveler faces—especially every traveler who wants to tell his friends about the Hidden Paradise he's discovered: the very fact of giving a name—or a face—to the place you love changes it till it becomes a place you hardly like. Talk about how unspoiled somewhere is, and you're almost inviting its despoliation. When someone gives you the address of the unknown Shangri-la he's found, you're forced to wonder whether he's serving its interests or his own.

And it is the dilemma that every developing country faces—especially a country as destitute and desirable as Nepal: when approached by the affluent modern West, do you take it in or take it on? Nepal has opted for the first solution, and smilingly accepted so much of the outside world that tourism is its largest source of foreign currency; Bhutan, nearby, has chosen the second option, and closed its doors so firmly that in all its history it has seen fewer tourists than visit Dodger Stadium on a single day.

It is also an issue that grows ever more urgent as filmmakers take themselves to ever more remote locations to shoot their zillion-dollar productions (Bertolucci's main rival for the Christmas market promises to be Oliver Stone's new Vietnam movie, *Heaven on Earth*, which is shooting, with almost exactly the same schedule, just a little farther down in Asia, in Phuket). As the developed countries recolonize their former properties on film—the French making three movies in a single year in Vietnam, the British sending television crews to every corner of the Empire—and as the dollar-for-dreams transactions multiply, so, too, do the questions. How does a poor country turn down the exposure and hard cash that a movie company promises? Yet how can it possibly acquiesce in a process that often ends up dismantling the place in life so as to reproduce it in art? Making a movie in Nepal can easily change the country so much that the "real Nepal" finally exists only in the moviemakers' cans.

In this instance, the plot is a relatively simple one. In recent years, Bernardo Bertolucci, the great maverick visionary of the modern cinema, has all but turned his back on the West in the hope of bringing something different—something wilder and maybe deeper—back to the rest of us. After shooting *The Last Emperor* in the Forbidden City and *The Sheltering Sky* in the Sahara, he decided to make his new film, based on his own story about a Tibetan lama and the life of Prince Siddhartha (later Lord Buddha), in the hidden kingdoms of the Himalayas. The movie itself has a kind of ascetic, renunciatory air to it: there are virtually no marquee names (save for Keanu Reeves, playing the Buddha, and Bridget Fonda, playing the mother of a contemporary American boy who's suspected of being a Tibetan incarnation), and the story will have a fairy-tale simplicity that leaves even its publicists a little speechless. The maker of *Last Tango in Paris* is shooting what he calls a "children's film." The laureate of revolutionary alienation is giving us a happy ending. Bertolucci is, in fact, hoping to bring Buddhism to a mass-market holiday audience.

But since Tibet is still more or less closed (and site now of some bloody oppression), the 120 moviemakers have descended on the fourteenth-century metropolis of Kathmandu. Having received the blessing of the Dalai Lama and having included in the cast a *rinpoche*, or reincarnated lama (who also happens to be the spiritual adviser to the king of Bhutan), they arrived last fall—for three months of shooting—in a country that is as dependent on foreigners for its livelihood as an actor on a director. His aim, said Bertolucci upon arrival, was to do for Nepal "what *The Last Emperor* did to China, and what the Department of Tourism has never done."

Done "to" or "for," though, is the question. And it is an especially immediate question when you consider that the budget of the $35 million movie could feed every person in the Kathmandu Valley for a year. When you know that *The Last Emperor* made more money than the whole of Nepal earned from exports in 1992. When you hear that a single night's stay in the Yak & Yeti would cost the man in the Bhaktapur street a year's salary. And when you bear in mind that the filmmakers will be shooting in—and largely remaking—Bhaktapur, a "living museum," in André Malraux's words, said to have been designed in the shape of the god Vishnu's conch; in Patan, the town once known to Tibetans as Yerang, or "Eternity," and thought to be the oldest Buddhist city in the world; and in Bhutan, a country so remote from the world that every citizen must still, by law, wear traditional medieval costume, and every building must be constructed in fourteenth-century style.

Four days later, Bhaktapur is transformed. There's an elephant over here, and over there a winged god. Whole buildings have disappeared entirely overnight, and twenty-foot walls have sprung up to enhance the square's symmetries. Local mask-sellers have been recast as courtiers, and school-girls—now princesses in priceless gowns—are clicking away at one another with Instamatics, hardly able to get over the fact that they are getting paid a whole year's wages just for lying down.

Around them, street kids in caps that say "Friend" (in America they'd say "X") are careening around boxes of Cinecittà lenses, or poring through containers piled high with orange filters. A few boys are crawling over temple roofs to set up banks of hypermodern lights, while old women are busy pushing electrical cords off temple platforms with their feet. Boys with "Assistant Crowd Master" buttons are doing everything possible to assist the crowd in making chaos, while, here and there, a few security guards are languidly peeling tangerines.

Occasionally, a duck walks into the square, or a raucous wedding procession, led by a marching band and a dervishing trumpeter (all in English military regalia). Occasionally, a red-dotted mendicant wanders in, or a howling madman. "The quality of the film is based on mystery," I remember Bertolucci telling a local newspaper, the *Independent* ("Beneath and Beyond the News"), when he arrived. "The serenity of the shooting wherever we go will be maintained."

Today is another blazing blue day, but the whole square is swathed in a mist so thick you cannot see three feet in front of you. Grannies are hobbling past with hankies to their mouths, and unshaven Italians are spluttering. Around them, the mist, billowing out of long cylindrical smoke machines, snakes in and out of all the passing bodies, compounding the reality games that everyone is playing. Is this art or is it Memorex? Which of these steeples have been here since Chaucer's time, and which arrived just yesterday? Which of these walls is five hundred years old, and which ones are only an eighth of an inch thick?

From the vantage point of my private perch (at an upstairs window of the tiny National Art Gallery, just above a collection of *Kamasutra* prints), I watch Bertolucci, in a white hat, and Keanu Reeves, with the long black ringlets and the ornate raiment of a privileged Indian prince (the unenlightened Buddha-to-be), steal over lines of sleeping figures. "Hey, give me two!" shouts a Bruno in the corner, with a pair of Nepali eyes on his baseball cap. "One boy and one girl!"

A little later, I venture into the Sahara Company Location Office in Bhaktapur. I find the Saharans on the second floor of the walk-up, rock-bottom Shiva Guest House (whose ninety-cent rooms are described as "small and spartan" even by the budget travelers' Lonely Planet guide). Across from the office is a sign: "Hot Shower (Only in Winter) from Morning to 10:30 a.m. Please Deposit your Precious Goods to the Manager for Safety (Otherwise no Responsibility). Cloth Washing is Strictly Prohibited."

Fighting back the impulse to cloth-wash, I wander farther in. One of the two Sahara Company Location Offices consists of nothing but a mat that says "Hallo." The other consists of three Nepali teenagers in blue jeans, who are taking their responsibilities very seriously. One of them presents himself as "Oasis" (he's certainly getting into the Sahara spirit!) and tells me, in bullet-trained, somewhat eccentric Japanese, of his struggles to get a visa for Japan. Behind him, on the wall, the shooting schedule calls for Lotus Tree, Ascetics, Snake, Mara's Army, a Mandala Cremation, Bamboo Screens, Fire Pit, and Stunt Horses. Of such small details are $35 million Oscar winners made.

Back in the Yak & Yeti that night, the main event is a reception hosted by the consul of the Maldives in honor of the finance minister of the Maldives. A few lamas in maroon-and-gold robes are clomping around, creating some strange reality games of their own. As soon as I enter, I am greeted by two somewhat plaintive boxes, seeking alms ("Help the Handicapped" and "Nepal Pediatric Society"), and a sign advising—as it does each day—that the Sunrise coffee shop is "Closed for Renovation.

Inconvenience Regretted." The nightly dinner show is going strong in the sumptuous palace theater in the old wing, where white-gloved waiters are serving up wild boar, but the electricity goes off promptly during the opening dance, leaving two twirling girls and two grinning boys to flail around madly in the dark.

The Yak & Yeti is a highly appropriate base camp for the visitors; it was, after all, the creation of Boris Lissarevitch, the "Father of Tourism in Nepal" and a White Russian who once danced with the Ballet Russe and was friend to Cocteau and Stravinsky. Today, however, it is home to a kind of traveling company, the entourage of Bertolucci that has been working together, in many cases, since 1970 and that reassembles every two or three years to make another epic in some beautifully impossible site. Their meetings have something of the air of a family reunion (the scripts are written by Bertolucci's brother-in-law Mark Peploe; the man who's responsible for the director's famously fluid tracking shots is now in his seventies; and, as one member of the cast says, "Everyone's someone's cousin here"). Thus most of the 106 names on the room list are Ruggeros, Fabrizios, Marcellos, and Vittorios. But in Room 314 you will find the *rinpoche*. In Room 447, one T. K. Lama. And in Room 515, the redoubtable Basil Pao.

Now, in the bar, a few of them are joining in the usual chorus—"You thought Morocco was bad, Antarctica was bad . . ." "Saw a couple of dead pigs. Live dogs, though. Three boxes of trekking shoes"—and around the room, hardened veterans of third-world campaigns are swapping hard-luck stories and hard-core horrors, one showing off a tattoo of his Mum, another a T-shirt that says, "Little Lama SFX Nepal 1992." There is even a rumor that there may be a disco in Nepal.


If Academy Awards were given for grace under pressure, for sheer bloody-minded persistence in the face of adversity (the Werner Herzog Award, it should be called), Bertolucci by now would merit a Lifetime Achievement Award. For *The Last Emperor*, he had to deal with thirty-two interpreters, three thousand extras, and a three-year-old star, filming in courtyards that had not been opened in fifty years. For *The Sheltering Sky*, he undertook a six-month shooting schedule, in annihilating heat, amidst beggars and nomads, which left him saying, admiringly, of Debra Winger, "I have never seen any actor capable of such suffering."

Nepal, though, promises to be the ultimate challenge. For it is still a wonky and somewhat off-kilter place, a country where women with babies stroll across the runway of the international airport as you land,

and men in solar topees spread out their newspapers along the landing strip. It is a country where, the minute it grew dark, two hours after I arrived, all the lights in town went off (as they did, more or less by law, every other day, from 5 p.m. to 7 p.m., and 6 a.m. to 8:30 a.m.). It is a country where, even in a five-star hotel, I needed an operator to place a call across the street (and usually failed in any case). The "Health" section of my guidebook was forty times longer than the "Tourist Information" section.

You know you're in a different world in Nepal—even before you learn that the country is exactly fifteen minutes ahead of India (and thirteen and three-quarters hours ahead of L.A.)—when you see the banners stretched across the road wishing you "All the Best Happiness of Happy New Year 1113." The local telephone directory (for the year 2049) devotes one entire page to a warning, "Beware of Fraud," and usefully advises you to "Use your fingers for dialing" (maybe that's why I could never get through); on the front page of the main newspaper, the *Rising Nepal*, the headlines shout: "HM Greets Albanian President" and "Cooperation Vital to Check Evils." In Nepal, restaurants still serve "roast buff" (in deference to the Hindu reverence for the cow, they slaughter water buffalo instead), and even in expensive hotels, the toilet paper comes on rolls that say: "This answer-book has 16 pages including the title-page. Make sure that it is so. Do not write your name or that of your College/ School/Examination Centre . . ."

"The Hotel Kathmandu," warns the sign that greets you at the airport (site of two major crashes in the weeks before the Bertolucci crew arrived). "Where Things Happen."

Things were certainly happening while I was there. One day, a generator gave out. The nine-year-old star of the movie, used to the polluted commotion of New York, got asthma as soon as he was set amidst the high, clear silences of Bhutan. Extras (who in *The Last Emperor* were People's Liberation Army soldiers, and nothing if not well drilled) did not infallibly turn up at the crack of dawn. Yet the gods, it seemed, had strange tricks up their sleeves. A little later, a cyclone swept through Nepal, up from Bangladesh: the next day, the snowcaps were sharper than they had been for twenty years.

The arrival of the Bertolucci traveling show to make a fairy-tale spectacular in Nepal ("Ten times more sumptuous than *The Last Emperor*," in the words of a New York publicist) has, of course, been the talk of the town—in fact, the country—for months. Everything seems to revolve around it. Shopkeepers reel off locations as if they were production assistants ("Now Bhaktapur, Durbar Square, then Patan, Swayambhu . . ."), and teenage entrepreneurs, between selling you Manjusri statues, will tell you of the businesses that received $1,200 a day for being redecorated. A whole kind of folklore has grown up around the production: there is the tale of how the Italians found the perfect tree (for the Buddha to find enlightenment under) just next to the perfect river—but not, alas, at the perfect distance from the perfect river, so they raised the tree onto a platform and gave it plastic roots. There is the tale of the chef who flew in from Rome to make pasta at the Yak & Yeti, and of the day Prince Andrew's former flame Koo Stark appeared on set—in Bhutan, no less—with photographic credentials and a zoom lens trained on Reeves.

A handful of local sophisticates profess to be unimpressed by all this. Nepal has seen a hundred productions come and go, they say; why, the place is now called "Kollywood." One day, indeed, I read in the *Weekend* newspaper how, ever since Dev Anand's *Hare Krishna, Hare Rama*, Nepal has hosted "an upteenth number of other directors from as far as Hong Kong, Japan and the USA, who have been coming out with films that have won critical acclaim and commercial success." The blockbusters it named were *The Himalayan, The Night Train to Kathmandu, Mahaan*, and *Story of Zen Master*. Another day, the local paper included a feature on the world premiere of *Pukar*, a Nepali production (with an $80,000 budget) that was being launched by a member of Parliament, at a party "attended by Nepali film luminaries." In truth, however, most of us know the place only from a few establishing shots with Eddie Murphy superimposed on them in *The Golden Child*. And Nepal is still too poor to be indifferent to money (is, in fact, distinguished by its merry mercantilism).

So local entrepreneurs around the valley will gladly tot up the numbers for you. "See, they have spent ten million [$220,000] just to redo Bhaktapur," says one man, twinkling over his tie. "They changed a whole row of fifty, sixty—no, a hundred—houses, and to every house they gave six thousand rupees. To some workers they are giving three hundred rupees a day [seven dollars], sometimes six hundred—to some it is even a thousand rupees. For us this is much money. Usually we make thirty, fifty rupees in a day." Stories are told of how a farmer was asked to stop burning wood for a day, since his smoke showed up in the background of a shot. Sure, he said, if you give me five thousand rupees. They did, and he received a whole year's wages for taking a whole day off.

It is easy—all too easy, perhaps—to cast the rich visitors as the villains here, and the poor country as their victim. On paper, at least, Nepal is one of the most helpless countries in the world. The statistics could hardly be more melancholy: five doctors for every 100,000 people; 4,700 hospital beds in the entire nation. One child in every five dies in the first few months of life; the average Nepali man is dead by fifty-five. Even when compared with twenty-five other countries of Asia, many of them among the most luckless in the world, Nepal is near the bottom. There is one telephone for every 680 people here (Taiwan, by comparison, has one for every three), and the infant mortality rate is four times worse even than China's. Though tourism has shot up in the last twenty-five years, population has increased even faster—from seven million to twenty million—so that as soon as money comes in, it trickles out.

Yet Nepal, it seems to me, is a paradoxical country, paradoxical enough to make things more complicated than they seem. More than most places, it leads a double life: the one in reality, which seems relatively tranquil and benign, and the one on paper, where it looks completely desperate. Yes, you could say, Bertolucci is making a movie in a Hindu kingdom ruled by a living incarnation of Vishnu; but you could also say that he's shooting in a country run by a graduate of Eton and Harvard (King Birendra wears all three caps). Yes, you could say, the whole country had only one restaurant as recently as 1955; but by now there are a hundred on every block, and nearly every one of them serves lasagna, moussaka, chop suey, tacos, and the continent's most celebrated apple pies.

Nepal is, in fact, something of an impossible phantasmagoria: at daybreak, its ancient streets teem with swamis carrying tridents, and dogs, and babies crawling through the mud. But around them, in the Rimini Pizzeria, teenage boys are briskly preparing a video triple bill: *Brain Donors, Frank and Joney*, and *Regarding Hennary*. At night, the old trade routes are all but deserted, and flickering candles turn faces into strange, medieval masks; but when you go into a candlelit stall, you find U2 throbbing across the system above the finest spinach-and-mushroom enchiladas you've ever tasted. Nepal is a little like a Hollywood conceit already: a halfway house between the conveniences of the regular world and the other world of Tibet. A modern world set against ancient props.

More than that, the country has long encouraged influences from abroad. In the 1950s, it was said to be *the* cosmopolitan capital of the Himalayas, thanks in part to King Tribhuvan (who plucked his eyebrows and sent porters across the mountains to bring back lounge chairs and gizmos chosen from mail order catalogues). By the late '60s, it was the Angel Food Capital of the East, a hippie-colonized Haight-Ashbury East, famous for Freak Street, Peace Corpsers, and the Eden Hash House.

Nepal cannot survive without foreigners, in fact: almost half its government revenue comes from foreign aid, and tourism is its bread and butter. In that context, Bertolucci is the biggest benefactor to touch down in years, and poised to make the lushest tourist brochure in the kingdom's history. "Peter Lucci is hiring twenty-five hundred Nepali people," one student tells me excitedly, leaning against a phallic Shiva temple. "Usually we are jobless. Nothing doing." Some of his profits the Italian is donating for the restoration of Bhaktapur, and already he has completed one fairy-tale ending by giving a major part to a ten-year-old shoeshine boy he encountered in the street.

"You see the beggars near Pashupathinath Temple?" one local travel agent asks me as we bump across squealing, squawking alleyways. "Begging for twenty-five paise, one rupee? If it were not for tourists, we would all be like that! And this film will be an advertisement for Nepal, an advertisement for Bhaktapur." He pauses. "But then the tourists will come, and it will not be like the movie. . . ."

Inevitably, the arrival of a group of Westerners to make a film about the founder of an Eastern philosophy has not been without controversy (imagine some Nepalis coming to the Middle East to shoot the life of Jesus!). The movie that is being called *Little Buddha* around the world will be known as *Little Lama* in India and Nepal, and in either case, the diminutive is not an ideal adjective (can one imagine a movie being called *Little Muhammad*?). Some Nepalis are complaining about a line in the script that has the Buddha being born in India, when it is well known that he was born in Lumbini, in Nepal (though he found enlightenment in India). Some Tibetans have grumbled about the lama's guru being played by a Chinese actor (while others have claimed that the Chinese are trying to discredit the inevitably pro-Tibetan script). Best of all, the tiny Communist Party of Nepal, which has its headquarters in Bhaktapur, has complained about the Sahara Company's wish to tear down advertising billboards. Sitting in their office, under a picture of Kim Il Sung, they are perhaps unaware that Bertolucci is the most famous leftist director of his generation, a card-carrying member of the Communist Party until 1978. As the upbeat Calcutta movie *City of Joy* discovered last year, the line between compassion and condescension, between exposing a country to the world and allegedly exploiting it, is as murky as in any love affair.

Yet it is hard really to find much substance to the charges, hard, for example, to see how Bertolucci will affect Nepalis' thinking any more than the usual groups that come here ("World Hindu Federation," says the welcoming banner strung across the main road; "International Symposium on Snow and Glacier Hydrology"), hard to see how he will do any more damage than Mira Nair, the Indian-born director of *Salaam Bombay!* and *Mississippi Masala*, who is planning her own $36 million movie of the life of Buddha across the border, in India. Nepalis can scarcely claim that the foreigner is taking liberties with something that should remain invisible when the first thing that greets arrivals at Tribhuvan International Airport is a somewhat cartoonish mural showing highlights of the Buddha's life. And a country that specializes in pizzas and spaghetti can hardly complain too loudly about an Italian making a movie on the East.

Nor is his scenario implausible. As I was passing the Restaurant at the End of the Universe one day, high in the shadow of the Himalayas—and only an hour from Bhaktapur—I ran across a German television cameraman who'd just returned from seven weeks in Tibet shooting the Karmapa, a young lama discovered only last year, and the subject already of considerable debate (some Tibetans feel he's authentic, some say he's a Chinese puppet). The cameraman, no starry-eyed believer, told spellbinding tales of how music was heard through a valley three days after the child's birth, of a map that led to his home that corresponded to a dream the Dalai Lama had had five years ago, of the boy's preternatural wisdom in dealing with the Chinese authorities, and of faxes sent from India to Rio to confirm the child's position. Bertolucci's script—about a boy in the Pacific Northwest who is taken to be a Tibetan lama, and comes to Tibet to undergo tests and to learn about the Buddha—is commonplace by comparison.

Most of all, it can hardly be said that Bertolucci is bringing corruption to an otherwise unspoiled country. For Nepal has developed at the speed of light (and flight) in the last twenty years, and it seems to know how to take the world in without being undone by it. Inevitably, elegies are as much a growth industry as Buddhist scrolls in a country that has gone from roadlessness to smog in just two decades. One thirty-two-year resident—now an honorary consul, among a variety of other roles—recalled for me the time when there was no main drag here, when there were no buildings designed to be hotels, when the first air conditioner arrived, the first private car, the first escalator. Only two years ago, it was still illegal to change religion in Nepal, and two hundred people were sitting in jail because of their Christianity, while other parts of the country, like Mustang (where the CIA once trained Tibetan freedom fighters), opened up—just a crack—only last year. Television arrived in Nepal only during the Reagan administration, and Bertolucci was already planning his first film by the time electricity came to Nepal. Even now, democracy is all but unknown in the private kingdom.

Nepal, though, is hardly a passive victim. A country that establishes places called the Hotel Iceland and the Tibet Holiday Inn—there is even a Yak and Yuppie Hotel here—is hardly unaware of the ironies of tourism. And those anxious about how the film will affect Tibet need only listen to the Tibetan *rinpoche* who has declared that "The making of this movie is more important than the building of a hundred monasteries." Five years ago, the National People's Congress in China was busy debating Bertolucci's presence at the very moment when the Academy of Motion Picture Arts and Sciences was conferring on him nine Oscars. Suddenly, next morning, the debate was over.

One winter day, in Dattatraya Square, three elephants are acting up in front of the *faux* wall, and Bertolucci is shouting, "I like it!" and occasionally a mad bull storms through the cordon to engage the elephants, and the whole gawking crowd sags in the middle and a few peasants try to restrain the crazy beast. Nearby, the signs say: "Vote for Cow" and "Vote for Moon and Star" and "We Love Tree." "See, but with Love," advises the fender on a bus.

The production is running a little behind schedule, and the Saharans are working hard to wrap before the ominous month of Poush, a time so ill starred that weddings and religious ceremonies and new projects are all canceled then. In the Yak & Yeti, a sign is up that the company will have to vacate fifty-five rooms next week, and crew members are asked to double up because of "a limited number of rooms available in Kathmandu of an acceptable standard."

Meanwhile, the crew prepares to shoot a glorious procession out of a temple, past a hundred redone houses, with a cast—quite literally—of thousands, dropping petals from the windows. Over there, Oasis is running around, in a "Tartaruglino Jnr." cap, asserting his newfound authority and flashing his Sahara Company badge. Over here, every other ambassador in town has found a way to take a holiday and to bring himself—and his local girlfriend—onto the set. This is the biggest thing to hit Nepal since Thai Airways first landed in 1968.

It's impossible not to wonder what will happen to the "crowd masters" when the movie strikes its tents, and goes off to its next locations—in Pinewood and Seattle—and the boys who worked for a thousand rupees a day are back to a thousand rupees a month, and the people who saw their hometown garlanded in silks are back to seeing it bare and are waiting for the next multimillion-dollar epic to come to town. The schoolgirls will be left with their bottles of hotel shampoo, and Oasis will be back with his visa application for Japan. That is the tease of every foreign visit: a sudden windfall, followed by a just as sudden withdrawal. Love you and leave you.

Yet it's impossible, too, not to wonder what "Peter Lucci" and his thirteen-Oscar crew will bring back from this hidden treasure of everyday magic, and what kind of beauty they will bring to our local cinemas. At the beginning of *The Sheltering Sky*, John Malkovich's character referred to the now familiar distinction between the "traveler" and the "tourist," and Bertolucci is one of the few modern directors to bring that distinction to the screen, to dig beneath exotic surfaces to find something even truer and more troubling, to go beyond postcard vistas and tourist shots to a sense of how places can not only surround you, but transform you. He is one of the few men of the cinema to produce the equivalent of travel literature on the screen—not a David Lean epic, that is, but something more individual and strange, full of irreverent majesty and eerie with a sense of the inextricability of terror and seduction, the way in which fear can be romantic as much as romance can be fearful. Bertolucci is one of those rare artists who take us to places inside ourselves, and so domesticate the alien (as suggested by the French title of *The Sheltering Sky*, "A Tea in the Sahara"). And in film after film, as he makes grandeur intimate and brilliance lucrative, one recalls that he was first and foremost a poet, the son of a poet, and the winner of a prestigious poetry prize at Rome University before he ever turned to film. His is the cinema not of sight but of vision, and the story of a prince surrounded by decadence and turning his back on it to pursue self-study is one that he has been exploring—and perhaps experiencing—for half a lifetime.


There is in Nepal a kind of transaction you encounter every day. You go into a store and are greeted by a nine-year-old businessman. He shows you a piece of "authentic Nepal culture" that is, in all likelihood, made by, and for, a group of Germans. You know it's not quite genuine, but it's beautiful nonetheless. You mention a price. He mentions another. You come up, he comes down, and the deal is finally done. Both of you know that the price agreed upon is a little high, and ridiculously low. Both of you know that his annual income is less than your weekly one—and that this does not entitle him to cheat you. Both of you also know that by the time you leave, the kid's got your cash, you've got a lovely object that you can show off to your friends as the *echt* Nepal, and both parties have a warm sense of profit.

That, I hope, is how it will turn out when the Buddha comes to the cineplex. Bertolucci will probably give Nepal a more alluring and uplifting face than it has ever had before. Nepal will probably end up $4 million richer and better able than ever to sell itself as a place of unspoiled wonders. And we? We can get a taste of Himalayan magic, and of the transformative powers of an ancient kingdom, all for a mere $7.50. Not a fairy-tale ending, perhaps; but surely a Nepali one.

(1992)

# Tibet: The Life and Times
# of the Potala Palace

Everywhere you go in Lhasa, you see the majestic structure, towering hundreds of feet above the streets and temples, stretching for a thousand feet or more along the ridge that separates the city from the distant snow-caps, gazing serenely across the

*The Potala is the Paradise of Buddhas,*
*Palace of Chenrezi.*
*To east, west, south, and north*
*There is a Potala on this Earth.*
*From the Land of Snows to the Lho Potala,*
*Potala of the Southern Seas.*

—TIBETAN SAYING

windswept plains. And from every part of the Tibetan capital—from the roof of the Jokang Temple, from the scattered buildings of Sera and Drepung monasteries, from houses and muddy alleyways—the thousand-chambered phenomenon reveals a different face: sometimes a gold-turreted castle that seems to float above the ground, sometimes a huge white stone fortress, scribbled over with 125 zigzagging steps, sometimes a solid maroon temple seemingly carved out of sheer rock. Even at night, as you walk the pitch-black streets, the thousand eyes of the Potala seem to watch you, and follow you.

And everywhere you go in contemporary Lhasa, even (or especially) in the parts guarded by Chinese soldiers, you see images of the Potala, the classic, almost defiant emblem of a free Tibet. In the showpiece Everest Room of the newly built Holiday Inn, there are only four decorations along the walls, and all four represent the Potala. In every shop, office, even billiards hall, in the Tibetan quarter rests an image of the sovereign symbol of Tibet, and of its former resident, the fourteenth Dalai Lama, draped reverently in traditional white silk scarves. As firmly as the Taj Mahal means India to the world, and the Eiffel Tower Paris, the Potala Palace, rising thirteen stories above the "Forbidden City" and hidden from modernity, two miles above the sea, denotes the "Land of Snows."

Unlike the other great residences of the world, however, the Potala is not just a golden edifice, nor even just a crowning symbol of its country; it is, in a very real sense, the center of an entire culture, and a faith. The Potala is not just a palace, but a temple, a storehouse, a meeting place for the National Assembly, and a home for a living godhead, as if West-minster Abbey, Buckingham Palace, and the Houses of Parliament were all combined in one. Largely built in the mid-seventeenth century by the fifth Dalai Lama, the first ruler of a unified Tibet, it was designed to serve, quite literally, as the place where temporal and spiritual worlds converged, the heart of a new theocracy. In that sense, it occupies a place in its country for which there is no equivalent. For fourteen million Tibetan Buddhists, not only in Tibet but in Mongolia, Nepal, Sikkim, India, and, increasingly, the West, it is the focus of their devotion—their Vatican, Mecca, and Jerusalem. For all the rest of us, it is the one great symbol of the most secret country in the world, a mysterious land that inspired notions of Shangri-la. And for more than six million Tibetans, who have chafed under occupying Chinese rule since 1959, when the Dalai Lama fled to India, it is the one immovable emblem of their own distinctive culture, and of a beloved leader they have not seen in half a lifetime.

For centuries our only image of the Rooftop of the World came from a handful of foreign visitors who fought their way, over some of the highest mountains on earth, into the "Forbidden City," and nearly every one of them described the first, heart-stopping sight of the Potala's golden roofs, rising like tongues of fire, visible from twelve miles away and betokening the imminence of the Holy City. Even Han Suyin, an apologist for Beijing, could not help marveling at the building's 10,000 chapels and 200,000 statues, and wrote, palpitatingly, of seeing "on a high hill, looking as if it floated in air, majestic and awesome in its perfection, the Potala, with glittering golden roofs above its massive white walls, a castle upon a fortress upon a mountain."

"Buildings in other countries may challenge comparison with the Potala," wrote Freddie Spencer Chapman, a tough-minded member of a British mission to Lhasa in 1936, "but to my mind no edifice, so perfect in itself, is placed in such incomparable surroundings." Peter Fleming, after traveling the globe, simply called it "the most extraordinary building in the world." And for devout Tibetans, it has always been something more: the central feature of the "Abode of the Gods," which many of the faithful will travel a thousand miles or more, prostrating themselves every step of the way, to see before they die. Even Heinrich Harrer, the Austrian mountaineer who escaped from a British prisoner-of-war camp in India in 1942 and walked for two years through the Himalayas with his friend Peter Aufschnaiter before arriving in Lhasa, found himself humbled when he first set eyes on the building. "We felt inclined," he wrote, "to go down on our knees like the pilgrims and touch the ground with our foreheads."

Yet for all its monumental remoteness, the Potala remains an entirely human place. In his recent autobiography, the fourteenth Dalai Lama, Tenzin Gyatso, gives a movingly full account of a building that was home to him from the age of four and a half. For him, as doubtless for most of the child kings who occupied it, the formidable "Palace of the Gods" was also a playpen. He remembers skating on its polished floors and devising jumping games with the palace sweepers, tinkering with his Meccano set in its hallowed hallways and peeping through windows and skylights to see the country's justices at work. From his schoolroom, adjacent to his bedroom, he could watch the red-beaked blackbirds who built their nests in the rafters of the ancient building, and hear the Master of the Ritual, sometimes chanting his sutras next door and sometimes trailing off. On occasion, he recalls, he could hear, while at his prayers, the songs of cowherds going home, and on occasion, he admits, he half wished he could be among them.

His youngest brother, Tenzin Chogyal, himself an incarnate lama, once recalled for me how he used to visit his godly sibling in the Potala, and how the two of them would go out on the roof and make flying saucers out of *tsampa*, or Tibetan dough, and send them winging across the roofs of the town. When I said that the Potala seemed a rather bleak and forbidding place, he looked surprised. "Bleak? No, I wouldn't call it that. For I never, ever, saw a speck of dust there. It was dark, yes, but it was *alive*. The thing to remember about the Potala is that it was always a *loved* place. And that care brought life and light to it. It was like an old car that you wash every day so it shines!"

Deeply loved, yet above the world, omnipresent yet detached, pre-siding over the city—and the country—with the watchful care of a father, the Potala was, in a very specific way, a symbol of the Dalai Lama at its center: at once divine and down-to-earth; in part an incarnation of Chenrezi, the Tibetan god of compassion, and in part, as the fourteenth Dalai Lama habitually calls himself, "just a simple monk."


Fittingly enough, the Potala was essentially built, nine centuries apart, by the first great king and the first great Dalai Lama of Tibet. A small building—some say a chapel, some a fortress—was initially erected by the beloved Tibetan ruler Songtsen Gampo, on the top of Marpori, or Red Hill, in the seventh century. In the tumultuous years that followed, attackers from China and Mongolia reduced nearly all of the building to ruins. But in 1645, three years after the Mongol khan invaded Tibet and killed the ruler of the day, the "Great Fifth" Dalai Lama, supported by his Mongol patrons, set about building a great symbol of a new Tibet, where church and state could meet.

Constructed with primitive tools in a land that had never even seen the wheel, each stone carried by donkeys or men from many miles away, the Potala "gives the impression," as Spencer Chapman points out, "not of having been built by men, but of having grown there, so perfectly does it fit in with its surroundings." Some Tibetans to this day believe that the monument cannot be touched because it is the handiwork of angels and protector deities who secretly worked on its construction every night.

In 1682, with the project still unfinished, the Great Fifth, having virtually created the modern nation of Tibet, died. His chief minister (and some believe his son), Sanggye Gyatso, realizing that the building had to be completed, kept the death a secret for an entire decade, telling the world that the Great Fifth had gone off to meditate alone. In a stone in the third story, however, lies a secret inscription recording the date when the Great Fifth departed to the "Heavenly Field" and memorializing the history of a project that is, like the Taj Mahal's in its way, the story of a love.

From the beginning too, the Potala was a home for both sacred and secular sides of Tibet, with one foot in the heavens and one foot solidly on earth. For though it was built by the great reforming spirit of Tibetan Buddhism, the fifth Dalai Lama, its first real occupant was the sixth Dalai Lama, a famous god-about-town who celebrated his love of taverns and local girls in lyric poetry. Every night, it is said, Tshangyang Gyatso (the name means "Ocean of Pure Melody") would steal out of his enormous palace, long hair flowing above his nobleman's silks, and go down into the drinking places below. The "man of many loves" even had a three-hundred-yard-long lake constructed behind the northern face of the Potala, with a Serpent House pavilion at its center, in which he could entertain his lady friends. "I dwell apart in Potala, / A god on earth am I," read one of his most revealing poems, "But in the town the chief of rogues / And boisterous revelry."

To this day, many questions surround the sixth Dalai Lama, who died, abruptly, on his way to exile, at the age of twenty-five. Yet his songs of life and love are among the most cherished poems in Tibet, and the majority of Tibetans still revere him, some believing that he was, in fact, conducting Henry V–like tests on the subjects with whom he mingled, others admiring his divinity all the more for its obviously human aspects. Certainly, he was, by all accounts, an engagingly unpretentious man, who kept no servants, made tea for anyone who visited, and walked around the town alone. Even today, the yellow-washed houses in the village of Shöl, at the foot of the palace, are the ones the "Merry One" blessed with his presence.

. . .

The setup of the Potala (named after the celestial home of Chenrezi) was carefully planned to accommodate its many roles. Its central, maroon section is the place of sanctity, a dark maze of temples, shrines, and the tombs of eight departed Dalai Lamas, their golden canopies jutting through the roof. On either side of the sacred heart are irregular, asymmetrical whitewashed wings: an eastern wing containing government offices, a school for monastic officials, and meeting halls of the National Assembly; and a western wing, added later, that was home to the 175 monks of the Namgyal (or "Victorious") Monastery. On the roof are golden turrets that will, according to Tibetan belief, lift the building above the waters when a great flood sweeps the land. And since all the windows in the Potala are narrower at the bottom than the top, it often seems as if the whole monument is leaning back, and pushing into the clear blue heavens.

Yet the image of massiveness and gravitas is always offset by the festive awnings above each window and, most of all, by the fact of a thousand windows. "Yes, in some places it gets dark," the Dalai Lama's younger brother told me, "underground and in parts of the treasury. But still, you must always remember that the Potala is a place of windows, thousands of windows." Through those windows comes the high Himalayan light, and a sense of easy commerce between the temple and the town.

The visitor making a trip to the Potala—on New Year's Day, for example—would have approached it through the shacks and shops (and, nowadays, the grimy buses at the central bus station) of Shöl. Here too—to the west—was the printing press on which were published government documents, and, nearby, the infamous dungeon in which highborn malefactors were incarcerated (as recently as 1947, when the presiding regent led an aborted coup, he found himself in the dark place at the foot of the Potala). With a child king generally enthroned at the age of five, in a building full of politicians and overseen by a regent, it was hardly surprising that the Potala saw as much chicanery and bloodshed as any royal residence, and the current Dalai Lama has likened the prison to the Tower of London. At the same time, however, he records the sense of kinship he felt with the prisoners as he watched them from his golden cage, they and he taking their walks at once, all of them savoring a rare sense of freedom.

The bottom floors of the Potala are largely underground caverns and storerooms, and in the lower rooms there are also believed to be shrines to the dark deities of the ancient Tibetan animist religion of Bön. A little farther up are the rooms of state, throne rooms, and assembly halls.

Highest of all are the Dalai Lama's private apartments, still fresh and airy openings through which the sunlight floods. Nonetheless, the god-king's bedroom is hardly sumptuous. "Pitifully cold and ill-lit," writes the current Dalai Lama, "everything in it was ancient and decrepit and behind the drapes that hung across each of the four walls lay deposits of centuries-old dust." Toilets in the palace were merely holes in the ground, and at night, as he slept in his boxlike wooden bed, in his twenty-five-square-foot cell, the god-king could feel mice scrambling over his body.

Above these living quarters was the famous rooftop, from which the Dalai Lama could watch the lives of Lhasa spread out before him—pilgrims and caravans, colorful paper dragons flapping from the rooftops, crowds prostrating before the Jokang Temple, wisps of smoke emerging from a hundred altars. From here he could see the two great monasteries of the "Holy City," and the silver curve of the Kyi-chu ("Happy") River. He could also get tantalizing glimpses of a world he could never enter: sometimes, he recalls, he used to watch through his telescope all the other little boys of Lhasa, playing in the streets. And each time his only young companion in the palace, his elder brother Lobsang Samten, returned home, he remembers "standing at the window, watching, my heart full of sorrow, as he disappeared into the distance."

The visitor to the Potala would generally ascend it along the steep steps that crisscross the great southern face. Clambering up in an awkward state of anticipation, spinning prayer wheels as he walked, and out of breath, he would arrive at last at the Pilgrims' Main Entrance, where he would turn a huge prayer wheel, twenty feet high, from which would issue the sound of a deep-toned bell. Towering above him now was the steep wall of the Red Palace. It was in this magical courtyard that I once followed a cluster of dusty Tibetan votaries toward a dark opening in the wall, and there, for a few pennies, was given a stack of beautiful *thangkas*.

The setting of the great building was also highly propitious: it sits in the very center of the Tibetan capital, commanding everything around it. On either side are the two great monasteries established in the fifteenth century, Sera and Drepung, and across from it is Iron Hill, long the site of a college of medicine. The Potala mediates between the green valley and the mountains rising to eighteen thousand feet behind; and as with the *dzongs*, the huge, whitewashed temple-fortresses scattered across Tibet and Bhutan, its place on high, on a lofty promontory, serves a strategic purpose too, allowing it to keep an eye out for intruders. No other building in Lhasa may rise above two stories or challenge its high eminence.

There are three great pilgrims' circuits that trace large circles around Lhasa, and the greatest of them all, the Lingkhor, or Park Circle, circumambulates the Potala. Every day, hundreds of devout Tibetans walk around the building, moving clockwise, the temple always on their right; muttering prayers, they tell their rosaries as they watch it disclose its different faces. The Potala is not the holiest site in Lhasa: that distinction belongs to the Jokang, built at the center of town. But it is, in its way, the most significant.

Inside the thick white walls were incalculable riches, all that might be imagined of a head of state—and living god—dwelling in one of the largest buildings in the world. There were huge statues stuffed with jewels and scriptures, storerooms crammed with gifts from khans and emperors, chapel after chapel decorated with astrological murals, *thangkas*, silk banners, and antiques. There was a silver Chenrezi with a thousand arms and eyes, a chapel in which everything was made of gold, jewel-encrusted thrones, and perhaps the world's finest collection of Chinese porcelain and cloisonné.

In one library alone, the fourteenth Dalai Lama recalls, was the whole history of Tibet: seven thousand enormous volumes, some of them weighing more than a pair of book-filled suitcases. Another two thousand illuminated volumes were written in inks made of powdered gold, silver, iron, copper, conch shell, turquoise, and coral, each line in a different ink. And everywhere there were frescoes and murals, depicting the lives of the Dalai Lamas, the construction of the Jokang Temple, even the erection of the Potala itself.

Particularly prized among the treasures left him by his luminous predecessor were some of the modern curiosities: an air rifle, a telescope, and two old hand-cranked movie projectors with several rolls of film (on one of which he was able to watch the coronation of George V). Somewhere in the building was a motorbike brought back by one of four Tibetan boys educated at Rugby. And the fourteenth especially delighted in pottering around within the armory, where he found old suits of armor and flintlock guns; he also acquired an elephant, which lived in a special stable in the Potala and, taken to be an "Enlightened One," appeared at certain processions, dressed in precious finery.

Thus the Potala was, among other things, a living history of Tibet, a cultural autobiography in a thousand rooms, and a register of all who had lived in it: two rooms are believed to have been left over from the building originally created by Songtsen Gampo, in the eighth century, and in them you can find life-size effigies of Tibet's great king, flanked by his wives, and a chapel believed to be the holiest in the building. There are hair clippings from the head of the Great Fifth, and handprints of the thirteenth. There are also, now, in defiance of the Chinese, so many snapshots, paintings, and even newspaper clippings of the exiled Dalai

Lama, filling almost every inch of every shrine, that he seems to breathe here, and every room is irradiated with the presence of his smiling face.

Perhaps the greatest of all the Potala's wonders, though, are the eight mausoleums that contain the bodies of departed Dalai Lamas, stuffed, inside, with jewels and gold vases, and studded, on the outside, with turquoises, amethysts, sapphires, rubies, and diamonds. The greatest of them entomb the two greatest Dalai Lamas: the forty-nine-foot mausoleum of the Great Fifth, decorated all in gold leaf, with a bell at its cone, on which are engraved the rising sun and the moon; and the seventy-foot-high resting place of the thirteenth, wrapped in gold leaf weighing half a ton, with four-foot-high butter lamps of solid silver burning at its base. All day, monks would pray and beat gongs before these two great stupas, which rise three stories above the ground and burst onto the roof in golden towers. The Potala actually had to be revised to accommodate the tomb of the thirteenth, yet the addition is of a piece with all the rest. Everywhere, the building marks the selflessness of its makers: each hand that worked on it has chosen to efface its identity in the creation of a building that seems almost to have built itself.

Beyond all this, of course, there are treasures beyond counting. Heinrich Harrer, who ended up becoming a friend and informal tutor to the current Dalai Lama, was once given permission to enter any room in the palace to make for the god-king a movie of his home. He writes of seeing chamber after chamber, some pitch black, their windows blocked by piles of lumber, some alight with Buddhas. Yet the Austrian could see that for his Tibetan friend, the Potala must have been "a golden prison," and Harrer writes movingly of how, whenever the people of Lhasa, at their parties, saw the young ruler watching them from his roof, they would hide themselves, so as not to cause him more sadness. When Harrer was finally compelled to leave Lhasa, in 1951, after the arrival of Chinese forces, he remembers getting into a yakskin boat to sail away down the Kyi-chu River, and looking back at the Potala, knowing that the Dalai Lama would be watching him from the roof.

In its heyday, therefore, the Potala was less a palace than a whole city on a hill, a huge network of worlds buzzing with activity. Peter Fleming describes monks and officials busying themselves along its terraces and parapets, and up its enormous staircase would come a constant, gaily colored procession of porters, pilgrims, petitioners, and nomads. Every official who left Lhasa had to report at the Potala before he departed and after he returned; and every foreign newcomer to Lhasa was expected to have an audience there. Lowell Thomas, Jr., remembers, when he visited, the chanting of hundreds of monks, "the roll of drums, the clash of cymbals, the whir of prayer wheels, and the throb of deep bass horns," and Colonel Younghusband, the head of a British expedition to Lhasa in 1906, insisted that his treaty with the Tibetans be signed in the great Audience Hall, his hosts giggling helplessly as his men scrambled up and down the hall's steep ramps, slippery with the butter of centuries. Many, too, have described visiting the Dalai Lama, seated on his six-foot-high Lion Throne, the regent on a lower throne beside him, and others seated on silk cushions in an audience hall hung with *thangkas*. One official would taste his food, and another would prostrate himself on behalf of visitors (such as Christians) who did not feel able to do so; at other times, monks and officials would walk in a long line past him, each receiving a divine hand on their heads, or blessings from a tassel suspended from a rod. Bells tolled every hour, and conch shells sounded at noon; at night, watchmen would trudge through all the darkened corridors, ensuring that every bolt was fastened.

Nearly all the great holidays of the Lhasa calendar centered on the Potala, and each one would turn it into a festival of color. The most celebrated of them welcomed in the Tibetan New Year. On the twenty-ninth day of the last month of the year, a troupe of monks, wearing the masks of animals and grinning skeleton heads, a Black Hat magician amidst them, would fling arms out to their sides in a wild dance of exorcism, watched in a Potala courtyard by all government officials (and behind yellow curtains, from an upstairs window, by the Dalai Lama himself). Then, on New Year's Day—Losar—the whole place was thrown open to the public, and 100,000 pilgrims or more would clamber up the steep stairs and race through the ill-lit passageways to receive the god-king's blessing. Alexandra David-Neel, the extraordinary Frenchwoman who, at the age of fifty-four, traveled for four months through the Tibetan winter, disguised as a local pilgrim (together with her adopted son, the Sikkimese lama Yongden), describes arriving in Lhasa at the time of this gleeful pandemonium. Reluctant to enter alone, they persuaded two rustics to accompany them—a kind of moving four-legged camouflage—and proceeded toward the sloping steps. At the top, however, the unlikely group was stopped by a temple doorman (a fat novice of about ten years old), who ordered David-Neel to remove her fur-lined hat. Knowing that the Chinese ink with which she had dyed her hair had worn off, and that her disguise would be shot, she refused at first but at last did as she was told and spent several hours walking around the palace unhindered, none of the Tibetans noticing anything amiss about what they took to be an eccentric Ladakhi.

After the formal greeting of the New Year, on the rooftop of the

Potala, there would be a ceremony in the great Throne Room, with tea served from golden, dragon-patterned teapots, and spirited monastic debates. As Mönlam, the "Great Prayer Festival," spread across Lhasa, the whole city would light up with parties and games (including one, in later years canceled, during which men would shoot down a yak-hair rope from the roof of the Potala to the foot). Twelve days after the three-week festival ended, a more solemn "Small Prayer Festival" would welcome in the spring, and at its conclusion, a long line of people carrying masks and flags would march to the foot of the Potala; there, after ceremonial dances, for a few hours an enormous silk banner ("certainly the largest in the world," writes Harrer), carried by fifty monks or more, and representing the thousand Buddhas who guard the world, would be slowly unfurled across the building's great white face.

Every September, the royal building, like all the homes in Lhasa, received an autumn cleaning; the black yak-hair curtains were taken down from the windows, and a team of specially trained workers, on yak-hair ropes, poured color on its walls from buckets, or droppers, every day for two weeks, till it shone.

The most colorful pageant of all, however, took place twice a year, on the days when the Dalai Lama moved. Toward the end of the eighteenth century, a summer palace had been constructed two miles to the west, the Norbulingka, or "Jewel Park," a lovely hundred-acre walled garden lyrical with peach trees and pear blossoms, and later adorned with an artificial lake, cool pavilions, even a private zoo. The cheerful orange buildings in the park, most of them built in this century, by the two most recent Dalai Lamas, exude a holiday spirit, and even today Tibetans enjoy picnics and make merry in the grounds. In one two-story house, a visitor can see the Philips gramophone that the Dalai Lama used to enjoy in his bedroom, and, nearby, the room in which his mother slept (in the Norbulingka, unlike the Potala, he was allowed to stay with his family).

At the official coming of the spring each year, on the eighth day of the third month, members of the court would change into summer dress, and the Dalai Lama would move out of the Potala. This was not, of course, a casual procession. Trumpets would sound, and then there would come an exotic line of monks carrying banners, musicians on horseback, porters bearing the god-king's favorite songbirds and his choice possessions, wrapped in yellow silk. Then, through a cloud of incense, you could see the Dalai Lama himself, seated behind curtains on a golden palanquin carried by thirty pigtailed men in green silk cloaks and red caps, with fierce and enormous *sing gha*, or monk policemen, beating back the eager crowds with whips. Behind him would follow more lay officials, a giant doorkeeper, even the faint strains of a band playing "God Save the King." Inevitably, the young ruler could not help but rejoice as he moved from a sepulchral palace to a light-filled park full of peacocks and flowers. "The day that I quit my gloomy room in the Potala," the fourteenth Dalai Lama writes, "was undoubtedly one of my favorite days during the whole year."

On the twenty-fifth day of the tenth month, winter would officially begin, and the whole procession would accompany him back to his winter palace. The thirteenth Dalai Lama, however, found a way more or less to play hooky, and having had two Austins and a Dodge brought to him (in pieces) over the Himalayas, he would use them to slip out of his "winter prison" and back into the Norbulingka. Indeed, save for three or four weeks around the New Year's festivities, the thirteenth managed, at the end of his days, to live almost entirely outside the Potala.

For the first two centuries of its life, the Potala, as the centerpiece of one of the most hidden countries on earth, was free from the intrusions of the world. But by the late nineteenth century, as more and more of the Great Game players (Britain, Russia, and even China) began to conceive designs upon the strategically vital region, and as more and more adventurers made it their ambition to breach the "Forbidden Land," Tibet, inevitably, was drawn into the world. In 1910, when Chinese troops reached Lhasa, the Dalai Lama was forced, for the first time in history, to leave Tibet; and though he returned two years later, more and more foreign envoys could now be seen in Lhasa (one of them, Sir Charles Bell, the British political officer who translated the poem of the sixth Dalai Lama quoted earlier, became a close friend of the thirteenth Dalai Lama and, in the process, the first foreigner to live inside the Potala). Meanwhile, bad omens continued to mount. Two lama magicians traditionally employed to prevent hail from falling on the palace failed in their duties. And just a few months before his death, in 1933, the thirteenth Dalai Lama, one of the strongest and most reform-minded in the entire line, delivered a chilling prediction of how misery and bloodshed would come to the land.

In 1940, the present Dalai Lama, not yet five and only recently brought in from the countryside, was lifted onto the Lion Throne, in the Hall of All Good Deeds of the Spiritual and Temporal World, and in the years that followed, he had to learn quickly how to deal with the world. By 1942, a group of emissaries was visiting him from Franklin Roosevelt, and by 1948, just before the Chinese Communist revolution, all Tibet was beginning to be haunted by terrible auguries. In the words of Hugh Richardson, the British envoy to Lhasa at the time: "A great comet blazed nightly in the sky for several weeks; monstrous births were reported; and the canopy of an ancient stone pillar at the foot of the

Potala fell one night, inexplicably, to the ground." To many devout Tibetans, it seemed that the palace itself, the image of their homeland, was shaking on its foundations.

Two years later, Chinese troops stormed into Lhasa, and the Dalai Lama, at the age of fifteen, was hastily given the Golden Wheel, symbolizing his assumption of temporal power. In 1956, as the pressure continued, the young ruler fled to India, sending fifty or sixty strongboxes of treasures from the Potala before him. Though he was able to return again after only a few months, by 1959 the Tibetan uprising was so intense that he fled for good. During the bitter fighting that ensued, Chinese guns destroyed part of the Dalai Lama's own rooms in the Potala, and the government school, and some of the houses of Shöl. One shell fell at the foot of the glittering stupa of the Great Thirteenth. Soon, huge pictures of Mao were hanging from the face of the great palace, and mass rallies were being held at its foot. Yet, almost miraculously, while all but thirteen of Tibet's 6,254 monasteries were destroyed in the years that followed, the Potala was spared—some say at the behest of Zhou Enlai, who sent his private bodyguards to protect it.

For the last thirty-five years, then, the Potala has been the symbol of a divided Tibet: on one side, to the north, Tibetans still set up tents, drink beer, and enjoy picnics on Sunday afternoons around the lake created by the sixth Dalai Lama; on the other side, the Chinese have erected what they call a "Cultural Palace" and a beautiful reflecting pool in which the Potala shines with the glassy perfection of a postcard: a symbol of how it has been turned by its new rulers in Beijing from a sacred site into a photogenic image for tourists. For a few years, at its base, the Chinese also set up a museum to chronicle the "atrocities" of the ancient "feudal" Tibet.

Thus today, in a sense, the Potala is the site of a clash of symbols. For the atheistic Marxists of Beijing, the great temple-fortress is a mere spectacle, a fairy-tale house of treasures and, they believe, a paradigm of priestly wealth and oligarchic cruelty: what Han Suyin typically calls "an evil, parasitic monster." For Tibetans, however, as the eldest brother of the Dalai Lama, Thubten Jigme Norbu, writes with characteristic firmness, "the Potala is a symbol of the spiritual rather than the temporal greatness of the Fifth [Dalai Lama]." For the Chinese, its position above the town suggests hierarchical oppression; for observers like Heinrich Harrer, its charm lay precisely in its place above, but within sight of, the filthy streets, like the classic Buddhist image of a lotus floating in mud. It often seems as if the very soul of the building is being subjected to a tug-of-war: the last time I visited, my young Tibetan guide (adamantly pro-Tibetan, but trained in history by her employers in Beijing) told me that the Potala was not a temple but a palace; it took two young Buddhist tourists from Lancashire to remind her that, in the true Tibetan tradition, the two were one and the same.

The first time I ever set foot in the Potala, in 1985, just a few months after Tibet was opened to the world, it was a revelation. I had never seen an image of such majesty and calm, never felt so removed from everything I knew. Yes, there were still bullet holes in the walls, and sundry treasures had apparently been looted. According to many Tibetans, most of the statues still remaining were papier-mâché replicas of originals long since whisked off to China: one former servant of the Dalai Lama's family recalls being compelled to work from eight in the morning till midnight every day for six months, transporting crates of treasures from the Potala to waiting Chinese trucks. And as if the building had not endured enough, a fire the year before had destroyed scores of priceless *thangkas*.

Yet still the Potala was alive. Everywhere I looked, there were Tibetans: wild mountain men in filthy sheepskin rags; gold-toothed ladies spinning prayer wheels; fierce Khampa bandits with red tassels in their hair; strange nomads with faces old as parchment. And everywhere there was a sense of intensity and devotion like nothing I had ever seen before. Old men in their eighties were clambering up the steep wooden ladders, grandchildren behind them, to place banknotes on the altars, and tiny, shaven-headed monks were sitting in every other room, rocking back and forth above their sutras. More fashionably dressed Tibetans from India were looking around in wonder at the place they had been dreaming of for almost thirty years. Once, when a tourist gave a monk a picture of the Dalai Lama, I saw the Tibetan's eyes fill with tears.

Sometimes, in the dark, weathered faces lit by flickering candles, the rumble of monastic chants thickening the shadows, everywhere the artichoky smell of butter lamps, and strange statues in the gloom, I felt taken back to an almost mystical Tibet. Strange cowboy hats sat against the walls, and huge stacks of scriptures, under which the faithful would crawl in the hope that the wisdom might enter their heads. Much of the palace was dark, a place of hidden doors and secret passageways lit only by a few naked lightbulbs. Much of it, too, was radiant, sunlight streaming through its windows, flashes of a cobalt sky outside. I felt as if I had been lifted out of the world of time.

When I returned to Lhasa five years later, the place seemed the symbol of a new Tibet, a culture closed and occupied, a country under siege. The Potala was under scaffolding now and was open only two mornings a week; many of its rooms were padlocked, and others were heaped with piles of rubble. Tibetans were not allowed admission to the place that means so much to them, and were left to walk around the circuit at its base, gazing wistfully at the tourists who were whisked up to the back entrance in tour buses to see treasures that, in many cases, meant nothing at all to them. ("Just a load of paintings," somebody said behind me.) The Potala really did feel like a prison, chilly, dark, and melancholy, with locked doors on every side, and soldiers in every corner, and army jeeps circling around it. Tourists had to pay fifteen dollars for taking photographs. And it seemed almost apt that the sightseers were led through the temple backward, from the death of the Buddha to his birth, and were not allowed to ascend the steps that traditionally gave every approach something of the air of a pilgrimage.

The Potala really had become a kind of haunted house, almost literally a shadow of its former self, a museum piece ruled by the ghosts of all who had loved it and left. And yet there was still a subversive magic to it. At one point, suddenly, just as I was beginning to lose heart, the lights went out, and suddenly the whole thousand-chambered palace was returned to mystery, and itself. One of the seventy or so Tibetans who lived in the building stole over to me, and told me what it was like to stay there, and slipped me a note before disappearing into the dark. He was not a special person, he said with characteristic Tibetan humility; but he was privileged to live in a special place. Then the lights came on again, and the tour resumed. Yet those few moments in the dark, among statues and stupas lit only by the flicker of the butter lamps, with the shadows given room to speak, brought home to me how the Potala grows ever more precious as Tibet grows more precarious, and how today, more than ever, it is the last stubborn and indestructible symbol of a culture that has almost been effaced, the one common link between a whole generation of Tibetans who have never seen their exiled leader and a whole generation of Tibetans in exile who have never seen their homeland. When the no-nonsense Spencer Chapman first saw the Potala, in 1936, he admired its "untamed dignity," the "inspired simplicity of its lines," and "the exquisite workmanship of many of the smallest details." But what made it live for him, and what distinguished it from any other building that he had seen, was an "indefinable quality of magic," some "transcendent quality" and sense of "divine excellence" that made it seem more lasting than mere stone, and more precious than a world's worth of gold.

(1990)

## The East India Company:
## Oxbridge-on-the-Hooghly

Images of the Raj are everywhere we look these days. On television we can watch the divided rulers of Paul Scott's *Jewel in the Crown* sipping their tea in flowery hill stations and swapping local gossip in the marbled palace of a prince. At movie houses, we can savor all the hot intensities that blast an arriving visitor the minute she steps ashore after a passage to India, to be swallowed up in a whirlwind of mendicants, elephants, snake charmers, and crowds. In best-selling books like *Freedom at Midnight*, we can relive the struggle of two great cultures, powerful opposites with a twinned destiny, as they set about trying to disentangle both themselves and their feelings. And at our leading museums, we can marvel at all the silks and sapphires of the Festival of India and, even more, at the opulent world they evoke: of bejeweled miniatures in the Mughal courts; of constant drama in the streets; and of all the imperial dilemmas confronting the British as they sought to bring order to one of the wildest and most complex lands on earth.

Behind all the glamour and the fanfare, though, lies one of history's more mischievous ironies. For the Raj, in fact, was nothing but the final act in a long and crooked drama, and the Empire, in a sense, was nothing but an accident. The British had not originally wished to impose their authority on India; it had imposed itself on them. When the London merchants of the East India Company first sent ships to the east, in 1601, they were bound not for India but for the Spice Islands of Java and the Moluccas. When English traders first set foot on the subcontinent a little later, they were determined to avoid conquest at all costs. And even after the Company had set up a chain of factories around the country, its directors constantly reiterated that expansionism could only cut into profits. "All war is so contrary to our interest," they reminded their employees in 1681, "that we cannot too often inculcate to you our strictest aversion thereunto."

Yet as "John Company" sought to protect its interests in a land riddled with factional rivalries, it was forced to defend its trading posts with companies of soldiers. Before long, the trading posts became cities, and the companies, small armies. As its responsibilities mounted, the Company came more and more under the control of the Crown. And gradually, almost against their will, the traders who had come out as supplicants became soldiers, and the soldiers became rulers.

By the time the Company was at last disbanded, in 1858, hardly a thousand British officers were in virtual command of all of India, an area the size of Europe in which two hundred million people spoke more than a thousand different dialects. By then, the East Indiamen had already carried home such Indian terms—and niceties—as "bungalow," "veranda," "punch," and "pyjamas." They had also imported back to Britain such "pukka" habits as smoking cigars, playing polo, and taking showers. And they had laid the foundations for what would later become the most ambitious empire, and perhaps the most anguished, in modern history.

The East India Company was originally conceived in September 1599, when a group of London merchants resolved to raise £30,000 for sending ships to the East to collect silks, spices, and jewels "upon a purely mercantile bottom." Such hopes had no doubt been buoyed by Sir Francis Drake's recent circumnavigation of the globe, and by reports of the riches being harvested by the Dutch from the islands that are now Indonesia. On the last day of the sixteenth century, Queen Elizabeth I gave her blessing to the merchants' dream.

By 1601, five British vessels were setting sail for the East Indies. Upon their arrival in Sumatra, however, they found that the Dutch were far from eager to share their profits. Deciding to turn their attentions elsewhere, the British therefore dropped anchor in India in 1608, and Sir William Hawkins proceeded to the imperial court in Agra to seek permission to set up a trading post. His was not, however, an encouraging welcome. The Portuguese, who had staked a claim on India when Vasco da Gama landed in 1498, proved quite as reluctant as the Dutch to part with their monopoly. And the Mughal court, which had enjoyed a remarkably sophisticated and tolerant administration during the forty-nine-year rule of Akbar, had recently passed into the hands of his undisciplined son, Jahangir.

As the court dithered and the Portuguese connived, the British took to backing up their requests with force. Finally, after capturing some Indian ships and destroying some Portuguese, they were granted permission in 1612 to establish a trading post around the western town of Surat. By 1639, English traders were on the eastern coast, too, and leased, for £600 a year, a harborless sandbar, just five miles long and one mile wide, which they christened Fort Saint George (later Madras). In 1668, they picked up a third site, when Charles II handed over, for a paltry £10, a barren

western island, called Bombay, that had been part of his dowry from
Catherine of Braganza. A generation later, after a series of small skir-
mishes, the Company completed its set by winning permission to set up
shop in a stinking mudflat in the east, which it quickly developed into
Fort William (later Calcutta).

The India that the British came to occupy was a thoroughly bewil-
dering place—a vast country of Hindu peasants ruled by a small number
of Muslims from a court whose brilliance could put any in Europe to
shame. The Mughals, a band of intruders of mostly Turkish and Mongolian origins, had formally established their empire in India in 1526; by the
time the British arrived, they ruled most of northern India save for a
few individual fiefdoms still controlled by tribute-paying Hindu rajas.
Though ruthless in advancing their interests, the Mughals were also
remarkably cultivated in their tastes, especially for Persian-flavored gardens, poems, and miniatures: the young emperor Jahangir, for example,
boasted of slaughtering seventeen thousand animals and nearly fourteen
thousand birds, yet the same man was also a great patron of the arts; his
successor, Shah Jahan, climbed to the throne on the backs of his rivals,
yet he was also the romantic who built an exquisite white palace, the Taj
Mahal, as a shrine to his beloved.

Under Akbar, the greatest of the Mughals, the empire had developed
into a system as enlightened as it was well organized: the prudent Muslim
emperor married Hindu princesses, observed Hindu festivals, and even
placed Hindus in high office. Thus even those he displaced were inclined
to see him not as the head of a Muslim state but simply as the Muslim
head of a nonpartisan India. As soon as Akbar died, however, the court
degenerated into a series of vicious successional struggles animated by the
principle of *takht ya takhta* ("throne or coffin"). During the forty-nine-
year rule of Aurangzeb, starting in 1658, the Mughals began demolishing
Hindu temples, applying special taxes to Hindus, and, in effect, sowing
the seeds of the furious Hindu-Muslim animosities that would shadow
British India till the end.

Against this turbulent background, the British were free to ply their
trade as they wished, selling silver and gadgets and firearms in return for
not only spices but also silk, cotton, indigo, opium, and jewels. Before
long, indeed, the East India Company was one of the largest employers in
all London, with its own dockyards, warehouses, and sawmills. In India,
meanwhile, each of its four settlements quickly developed into a self-
sufficient little community, appointed with its own forts, warehouses,
and dormitories, even its own courts and civic corporations. To defend
its "civil servants" from local marauders, each of the trading posts also
kept a company of "military servants."

The highest authority in every Company settlement was a governor (the governor of Madras from 1687 to 1692 was one Elihu Yale, who ended up leaving his post to help found a college in New Haven), and many of these senior officials soon developed a taste for the regal extravagance they had seen in the courts of local potentates. By 1700, the governor of Bombay would emerge from his private quarters only in palanquined splendor, attended by forty servants and preceded by underlings waving silver wands. At dinner, each of his courses was announced by a fanfare of trumpets. Nor were these meals simple meat-and-potatoes affairs: when the local nawab came to supper in 1701, the governor of Madras offered him six hundred different dishes.

For junior employees, of course, life was altogether more modest—most "griffins" arrived in India in their early teens, expecting to earn just £10 a year as "writers," or clerks. As soon as they became factors or merchants, however, they could bask in a lazy affluence inconceivable at home. Work was generally confined to the hours between nine o'clock and noon; the rest of the day was given over to brawling, gambling, drinking, and more drinking. At night, there were fifteen-course dinners, followed by such exotic diversions as hookahs, sometimes loaded with opium, and titillating *nautch* dances. In India, even the most ill-born of Company servants could enjoy the luxury and luxuriousness of the most privileged undergraduates.

If the rewards of an Indian posting were high, however, so, too, were the risks. "Two Monsoons are the age of a Man," ran the gloomy local saying, and many an East Indiaman never survived his first six months amidst the punishing heat and dust. If he was not laid low by malaria, cholera, or smallpox, he was likely to be felled by such exotic threats as snakebite, heatstroke, or jungle fever. Just as often, the British in India were simply undone by their own intemperance, as they blithely went about consuming huge meals in the midday heat, picking up diseases from local dancing girls, or drinking themselves into the ground. None of this was helped, of course, by amateur doctors who thought the best cure for cholera was a red-hot iron on the heel. Small wonder that Bombay soon became known as "the burying ground of the English," and Calcutta as "Golgotha," or the place of skulls.

By 1750, moreover, a passage to India resembled more than ever a great lottery offering all the riches of El Dorado. As the Mughal Empire began to collapse, a host of contenders swarmed into the vacuum. In 1739, the Persian Nadir Shah marched on Delhi, slaughtered its people, and carried its treasures, including the Peacock Throne, back to Tehran. Meanwhile, the predatory Marathas from the west were carving out a sizable chunk of the empire for themselves. The Afghans, too, made intermittent raids.

And for all the Company's attempts to discourage "interloping," more and more freelance adventurers kept flocking in from Europe, equipped with forged trading passes and a hunger for quick killings.

The threat that most unsettled the English, however, came from the French, who had arrived in India only in 1668 but were fast gaining ground in the south. As soon as the Austrian War of Succession broke out in Europe, the French went on the offensive in India. In 1746, they seized Madras, and in 1750, its governor, Joseph François Dupleix, set about installing a puppet ruler in nearby Trichinopoly. The British cause seemed doomed—until a daring suggestion arose from a moody young soldier who had come over as a clerk just seven years before: why not trump the French by seizing the provincial capital of Arcot? Commanding a force of five hundred inexperienced men and three small field guns, Robert Clive somehow managed to make good on his plan: first he seized Arcot back from an army many times bigger than his own; then he held on to it through a fifty-day siege. The French challenge had effectively been silenced. Hardly had the British begun to collect their breath, however, than another threat emerged, up the coast, where the new nawab of Bengal, Siraj-ud-Daula, had spotted an opening in Calcutta. Leading thirty thousand foot soldiers, twenty thousand horsemen, and four hundred trained elephants on a crumbling and ill-fortified garrison defended by scarcely two hundred soldiers, he took it without much difficulty. That night, he had his European captives locked up in a brig known as the "Black Hole," an eighteen-by-fourteen-foot chamber, with a door on one side and, on the other, a small iron-barred window leading onto a veranda. The stifling claustrophobia inside the room was compounded both by the swelter of a midsummer day and by the heat from the blazing buildings outside. By the time morning broke the following day, the cell was littered with corpses.

Many scholars today believe that early claims made for the "Black Hole of Calcutta"—describing 123 dead out of 146—were inflated by a factor of three. Even so, the British could hardly fail to be chilled, and outraged, by an episode that dramatized all their worst fears of dark suffocation. Two British captives were said to have survived the internment only by sucking the sweat off their shirts. Sixteen-year-old Mary Carey was rumored to have stayed alive, while her husband, her mother, and her ten-year-old sister died, by drinking her own tears.

Determined to avenge the tragedy, Robert Clive sailed up the coast from Madras and, one year after the "Black Hole," led eight hundred troops and roughly two thousand native sepoys against a force of more than fifty thousand at Plassey. There, Clive defied the odds once again by routing Siraj-ud-Daula. He then defied the Company by playing politician and installing as the new nawab an elderly Mughal general named Mir Jafar. By now, the crumbling Mughal Empire was in no position to resist; indeed, in 1765, the emperor actually made Clive his *dewan*, or revenue collector, for the whole state of Bengal. Thus the Company now found itself controlling the richest province in the land, source of almost two-thirds of all Britain's Asian imports. The Empire had begun.

With the takeover of Bengal, relations between the two cultures were suddenly turned on their heads. No longer were British tradesmen confined to their collegiate settlement in Calcutta; now they were free to roam around the province, helping themselves to the fruits of the land by extorting bribes and exploiting peasants. Where once they had given "presents" to the all-powerful nawabs, now they were in a position to receive them instead. Suddenly they could not only live with local kings; they could live like them too.

The result was a riot of helter-skelter development. With their "honourable masters" nine months passage and seven thousand miles away, the East Indiamen began "shaking the pagoda tree" to their hearts' content, unsupervised and uncircumscribed. Clive was given £211,500 by the nawab he had installed and, eighteen months later, another grant assuring him of £27,000 a year for life. That much perhaps was his due. But one Mr. Watts was rewarded for his bravery at Plassey with £117,000. Another British merchant established his own work force of fully thirteen thousand men. Still another set up his own mint.

As news of the profligate profiteering reached London, the city was scandalized. Before long, every young man wanted a position in India, and local panjandrums, no strangers to corruption themselves, were accepting £2,000 or more to secure them such positions. "Animated with all the avarice of age and all the impetuosity of youth," Edmund Burke told Parliament, the traders "roll in one after another; wave after wave; and there is nothing before the eyes of the native but an endless hopeless prospect of new birds of prey and passage, with appetites continually renewing for a food that is continually wasting."

Most outrageous of all to many in the British squirearchy was the fact that the self-appointed English nawabs—"nabobs," as the corrupted term had it—were beginning to overturn the country's age-old social structure. Clive, for example, had gone to India the unpromising son of a penurious country gentleman. By the time he returned, in 1760, he was a peer, a millionaire, and a local hero rich enough to repair his family home, buy another one nearby, purchase an estate in Ireland, and snap up a house in Mayfair. Just for good measure, he also helped himself to a seat in Parliament, in one of the notorious rotten boroughs of the time. Even as its employees were growing fatter, however, the Company itself was being pushed toward bankruptcy. In 1773, the directors had to appeal to the Bank of England for a £1.4 million loan.

Though the government complied, it made in return its first great claim on the Company's military and administrative authority. Under the Regulating Act of 1773, all British business in India was to be overseen by a governor-general in Calcutta, who would put an end to both "private trade" and "presents." Eleven years later, the Crown brought the company even further under its sway with the India Act, which established a six-man Board of Council, including two members of Parliament, to sit above the Company directors. As British control over India increased, it also passed steadily from private hands to public.

The first man chosen to restore some order was Warren Hastings. The new governor-general could not have been further removed from the idle and indulgent nabobs: even as de facto ruler of British India, he rode eight miles each day before breakfast, drank nothing stronger than tea, took cold baths, and turned in each night at ten. Under his principled eye, extracurricular profits were quickly cut down and salaries somewhat increased.

The Company's first governor-general brought to the country more than just a new sense of discipline, however. He brought a fresh sense of civility. Unlike most of his predecessors, Hastings was an educated man, schooled in Persian and Bengali and firmly convinced that the British should treat local customs with respect, deepening their mutual agreements with a sense of mutual sympathy. Toward that end, he began importing a new kind of British official, much more refined than the clubbable hearties of old—bright and well-born young men who had studied local languages and traditions, and were more devoted to cause and progress than to self. In time, such industrious and idealistic types would form the backbone of the body that became perhaps the brightest creation of the Raj: the Indian Civil Service.

As the British began to assume a more commanding and upstanding role in India, more and more men—and women—streamed into the subcontinent: not just *boxwallah* traders now but soldiers, scholars, and sophisticated young administrators. And as they tried to make themselves at home in the alien land, the newcomers laid the foundations of that closed society of splendor and heartache that would later so fascinate Forster and Scott. Where the rough-and-ready traders of old had lived like local princelings—hunting, feasting, and puffing on hubble-bubbles with local maharajas, or setting up house with Indian dulcineas—the new arrivals preferred to live like well-heeled Britons. Tom-toms were gradually replaced by drum-and-fife corps, curries by English dishes, and local clothes by the latest (or almost the latest) London fashions. Country houses began to spring up along the Hooghly River in Calcutta, complete with tidy Kent or Sussex gardens. Places like the "Bread and Cheese Bungalow," the Jockey Club, and the Eden Gardens (named after the two Misses Eden) cropped up around the "City of Palaces." Calcutta came to resemble a sweet-and-sour Bath.

In this imported version of Britain, intensified and exaggerated by its distance from home, the British diligently pursued their own rites and rituals. Every morning, before the heat of midday, the entire *beau monde* would travel en masse to the local racecourse, and every day at dusk, it would take the air along the Embankment in carriages. Days would pass in one long rondelay of social calls and siestas, evenings in one heady round of card games, recitals, dinner parties, and balls. Fireworks were let off to celebrate the recovery of the distant monarch from an illness, masked balls were held to mark some success in war. Musical entertainments like *The Poor Soldier* began to be staged at a theater behind the Writers' Building, and even in small country stations, where only a handful of Englishmen were posted, farces were bravely attempted, with ladies' parts being taken by "awkward giants with splay feet, gruff voices and black beards." Before very long, even that last deficiency was being taken care of: each October, shiploads of eligible young ladies arrived with the cooler weather, in what came to be known as the "Fishing Fleet"; each spring, a few "Returned Empties" sadly took the long journey home.

And though the pell-mell hedonism of the nabobs was now a thing of the past, the British society still shone with an air of gilded gentility. Silken canopies graced the private boxes at Calcutta theaters, while carriages with golden bells and embroidered curtains rolled down Saint Thomas Road. A typical bachelor in Calcutta in the 1780s kept sixty-three servants. Even a man at war did not consider relinquishing his sense of privilege: a captain going to the southern front in 1780 was generally accompanied by a steward, a cook, a "boy," a housekeeper, a grass-cutter, a barber, a washerman, and, of course, a mistress. He also had to bring along at least fifteen coolies to transport his double bed, his camp stools, his folding table, maybe six trunks of tableware, dozens of bottles of wine, a hamper of live poultry, a goat, and an extra tent for supplies.

Such extravagance and eccentricity were hardly confined to the British side, of course. Against them were arrayed such colorful adversaries as Hyder Ali and his son Tipu Sultan, who seized control of the predominantly Hindu state of Mysore and proceeded to run it as their own private empire-within-an-empire. For decades, the father and son were a

constant menace to the British presence in the south, setting fire to the
fine houses of Madras and leading their mercenary *lootywallahs* on one
pillaging expedition after another.

Not far away, the British faced exactly the opposite kind of resistance
from the infinitely courtly Muhammad Ali, whom they had installed as
nawab of Arcot. Though constantly entwined in shady deals and entangled in a ceaseless series of financial wrangles with the Company's
council, the tall and dignified gentleman somehow contrived to live like a
king for fifty years. Each day outside his Chepauk Palace, palanquins
would line up, filled with Europeans determined to collect their debts;
each night, the same men could be seen retreating, still unpaid but thoroughly won over by his dignified apologies and charming ways. At his
death, the nawab left behind outstanding debts of more than £30 million—and, paradoxically, a blur of warm memories among his creditors,
who still recalled with fondness the sumptuous public breakfasts he threw
and the grand hunts he attended on the back of an elephant. A place in
the nawab's service was, moreover, the making of many a nabob: Paul
Benfield, for example, a renegade who was dismissed by the Company on
four separate occasions, returned at last to England with a fortune of
£500,000, thanks in large part to the free-spending nawab.

As the eighteenth century drew to a close, however, the British presence in India became increasingly self-enclosed, a smaller and smaller
world governed by its own distinctive caste system. The raffish young
sports of the Governor's Ball would hardly dream of fraternizing with the
"Low Europeans"—the retired sailors, the Eurasians, and the Catholic
tavern keepers—who lived outside the cantonment in the hugger-mugger
chaos of the "Black Town." Nor were well-bred young officers eager to
consort with soldiers. Even within the army, all kinds of regimental divisions obtained. It seems only fitting that the first British magazine to
appear in India was a gossip rag, *Hickey's Journal,* run by a solicitor whose
name is even now synonymous in Britain with scurrilous social reporting.

The first great victim of all these feuds and factions was, ironically
enough, Hastings. In spite—or maybe because—of his success in bringing some order to India, the governor-general was challenged by junior
rivals, and in 1787, after returning to London, faced impeachment
charges blaming him in effect for almost everything that had gone wrong
in India (of which he was later acquitted). The new ruler, who arrived in
the following year, was an entirely different kind of man: Lord Cornwallis, the patrician soldier who had surrendered to George Washington
at Yorktown just five years earlier. To some extent, Cornwallis extended
Hastings's program of moral reform, establishing auditors to oversee
expenses, enforcing an absolute distinction between those who governed

and those who traded, even refusing a Company posting to the prince regent. Yet the new ruler had few of Hastings's wide sympathies: summarily removing from high office every Indian but one, he sought to stamp out the threat of corruption by attacking the spirit of cooperation.

Typical, perhaps, of the Cornwallis method was his renovation of the zamindar system. For decades the zamindar had been an all-powerful intermediary between ruler and peasant, an amphibious creature, half tax collector and half judge, whose operations lubricated a system in which ruler cheated peasant, peasant cheated ruler, and zamindar cheated everyone. To cut through these ambiguities, Cornwallis passed the Permanent Settlement: from 1793 on, British officials were to collect, directly from peasants, a fixed revenue based on annual averages. Though workable enough in Britain, perhaps, such an organized scheme was singularly ill suited to a wildly heterogeneous rural society in which harvests varied and customs differed. In India, the abolition of one kind of intermediary could only mean the emergence of another.

In 1798, another military aristocrat, Lord Wellesley, took over as governor-general. Self-confident and self-governing, Wellesley was a man of action who was not about to ignore the territorial openings he saw on every side. Realizing that his overseers at home were preoccupied with the threat from Napoleon, the "glorious little man" rationalized his assertiveness by pointing to the French march into Egypt and briskly set about extending British authority with a Napoleonic vigor of his own. Leading his troops south, he defeated Tipu Sultan, trounced the long-troublesome Marathas, and annexed Indian territory wherever he saw the chance. By the time he was recalled in 1805, British influence could be felt across two-thirds of the subcontinent.

Yet if Wellesley had some of Cornwallis's no-nonsense toughness, he also had some of Hastings's tolerant liberalism. In 1805, without the knowledge of his directors, he collected a levy from all his civil servants and set up in Calcutta a kind of Oxbridge-on-the Hooghly named Fort William College. Here young Englishmen were to learn from Brahminical scholars such languages as Arabic, Persian, and Hindi, while cultivating a deeper understanding of local traditions.

Thus Wellesley came to embody both of the main strains that would compete for preeminence throughout the rest of the Raj: imperialism and a higher Orientalism. Suddenly, and a little reluctantly, the Company had found itself in control of much of India; now it had to decide whether to treat the place as treasure chest, military base, branch office, or independent nation. As the British set about improving India, for better and for worse, some were driven by an arrogant sense of rightness, others by an earnest sense of duty. Out of those mixed motives arose all the mixed blessings and mixed feelings that would ultimately give the Raj so bittersweet a tang.

Through it all, John Company continued to be steadily subsumed by Parliament. In 1813, the Company's charter was renewed, but it was stripped of its Indian monopoly. Twenty years later, it was again allowed to survive, but its assets were liquidated, its ships dispersed, and its directors left with no power except dismissal of the governor-general. At the same time, Indians, though still unable to become covenanted employees, were for the first time allowed to hold administrative posts.

Yet for all its diminishing power, the last fifty years of John Company's presence in India marked in many respects a kind of Golden Age. This was due in large part to the arrival of a group of thoughtful and high-minded young Englishmen who regarded themselves as nothing more than guardians of a fledgling state, committed to giving it the faculties and facilities it would need to govern itself. Gentlemen scholars and gifted amateurs who preferred to deal with the locals directly, and in their own language, these educated Orientalists believed that their highest duty, in the words of Mountstuart Elphinstone, was to "prevent people making laws for [India] until they see whether it wants them."

Typical of the best of them was Charles Metcalfe, of Eton and Fort William College, a solitary and introspective soul who first proved his mettle at twenty-three, when he was sent to deal with Ranjit Singh. Famous for his harem, his opium addiction, and his possession of the Kohinoor diamond, the one-eyed Singh had established a powerful kingdom among the warlike Sikhs, guarded by a well-trained army led by European mercenaries. Yet somehow, in an unexpected development that was to become one of the most moving and oft-repeated features of the Raj, the British scholar and the flamboyant Indian chieftain struck up a mutual affection, which they sealed with a treaty of mutual respect.

In recognition of this diplomatic coup, Metcalfe was made Resident at Delhi at the tender age of twenty-seven. There, he presided over an area that was half the size of Britain—and in many respects more enlightened. By encouraging agriculture, Metcalfe virtually quadrupled revenues in only six years; more important, perhaps, he abolished the slave trade and outlawed capital punishment—at a time when the former was still going strong in the United States and the latter was often the lot of a forty-shilling thief in Britain. "Our dominion in India is by conquest," wrote Metcalfe in a typically clear-sighted moment. "It is naturally disgusting to the inhabitants and can only be maintained by military force. It is our positive duty to render them justice, to respect and protect their rights, and to study their happiness."

While such men sought to nurture Indian culture, another group steadfastly believed that Britain had a very different kind of moral mission to perform in India—to rescue the locals from the darkness of heathen superstition. During its trading days, the Company had never been notably pious: indeed, because of a ruling that forced ships with more than five hundred men to carry a chaplain, the directors had for sixty years sent out vessels with exactly 499 men. Now, however, a new kind of evangelical revival was abroad in England, and the spirit of doctrinal zeal found a perfect outlet in India. No longer were Hinduism and Islam regarded as strange, or even distasteful; now they were often seen as positively immoral. Even William Wilberforce, England's leading crusader against slavery, told Parliament in 1813 that he hoped to see the subcontinent "exchange its dark and bloody superstition for the genial influence of Christian light and truth."

Both conflicting impulses came together in the last of the Company's great governors-general, William Bentinck. A Burkean aristocrat and a moderate Evangelical, Bentinck was determined to promote British glory—but only by increasing Indian happiness. Thus he set about building railways to link the cities scattered across the enormous land, and established a canal system that would later become the most extensive in the world. He also weeded out the last remnants of corruption and, after canvassing the opinions of Hindus, prohibited the custom of suttee (whereby Hindu widows would fling themselves onto their husbands' funeral pyres).

Perhaps the most urgent challenge before him was the rising threat of thuggee, the practice of ritual murder that had begun to claim some twenty thousand victims each year. Working in small groups, the Thugs—our word originated here—would fall in with travelers crossing the vast distances of India and journey by their side for days or even weeks at a time, often under the pretext of protecting them from murderers. Then one night, when the moment was right, the Thugs would fall upon their companions and strangle them with consecrated bandanas knotted in one corner, before flinging them into graves as offerings to Kali, goddess of destruction. More than forty such cells were at large in India—one man alone boasted 719 murders—until Bentinck, through a young captain called Sleeman and a system of informers, brought them all to justice.

As the British came to govern more and more of India, however, they also seemed more and more removed from it. While the British presence had grown less dissipated, it had also, ironically, grown somewhat less sympathetic—more imperious as well as imperial—and in place of the

hurly-burly fraternalism that had linked the British to their Indian colleagues a century earlier, there was now a stronger spirit of paternalism,
with all the kindness and condescension such an attitude implies.

This new separation of the races had been intensified by the increasing
presence of English women on the subcontinent. Not only did the memsahibs inevitably cut down on the number of interracial relationships;
they also led more insulated lives than their husbands and, rarely seeing
the locals, were more apt to fear or disdain them. By now, therefore,
Indians were no longer sharing dinners, or *nautch*es, with their English
neighbors, and the British were no longer paying courtesy calls to local
maharajas. The view of many memsahibs was sadly reflected in the dis-
missive judgment of one Mrs. Graham, in her *Journal of a Residence in
India:* "These [Indian] people, if they have the virtues of slaves, have their
vices also. They are cunning and incapable of truth; they disregard the
imputation of lying and perjury and would consider it folly not to prac-
tise them for their own interest."

For their part, many Indians were growing increasingly alarmed to see
their landscape transformed and their customs changed. Their unease was
hardly soothed when Britain responded to a humiliating defeat in
Afghanistan—ten days after a company of 16,500 retreated from Kabul,
only one of them was still alive—with a flourish of saber rattling. In 1842,
the British seized the province of Sind, in 1848 they annexed Punjab, and
in 1856 they took over the large and corrupt province of Oudh. The
*talukdars*, or robber barons, of Oudh were incensed. Many peasants still
chafed at the continuing power of moneylenders, while many landowners
worried that they were being ignored in favor of peasants. High-caste
sepoys feared that they would soon be defiled by the secular spirit of
the age.

In 1857, all these separate grievances flared up into a blaze. The final
eruption was sparked by a relatively small charge: the introduction of a
new kind of Enfield rifle, whose cartridges, it was rumored, had to be
greased not with wax and vegetable oil, as before, but with animal fat.
The British were sensitive to the fact that no Hindu would touch cow fat,
and no Muslim pig fat; somehow, however, their orders got either confused or distorted. When eighty-five sepoys in Meerut were thrown into
jail for refusing to accept new cartridges, their enraged comrades stormed
the prison and threw open the gates, and the whole blood-crazed mob set
to murdering every foreign man, woman, or child it could find.

While a few pockets of the country got caught up in the bedlam of the
"Mutiny," most parts remained fairly calm. Nobody, however, could
ignore the tales of atrocities on both sides. At Cawnpore, hundreds of
British men, women, and children surrendered on guarantee of safe pas-

sage, and all were promptly slaughtered. In response, the British staged mass hangings and bayoneted sepoys on sight. Near Amritsar, the incident of the Black Hole was horribly repeated, and reversed, as one Major Cooper executed 237 captives, only to find that another 45 had died of suffocation in the tiny police station to which he had committed them. Amidst the cacophony, however, there were also stories of devoted old retainers risking their necks to protect British women and children, or of loyal sepoy regiments giving their lives to ensure that their country would remain in British hands.

When at last the Mutiny was put down, after five months of bloodshed, British rule had entered upon a new phase. Commerce had now formally given way to Empire. And despite the protestations of its chief executive, James Stuart Mill, the company that had been signed into being by one queen was now signed into extinction by another. Its army was reorganized into the Indian Army; its governor-general, Lord Canning, became the first viceroy of India. Thus began the last act of a drama that would culminate, ninety years later, in Gandhi's campaign of nonviolent resistance and the heart-torn figures of Paul Scott stranded in an imperial twilight. By the time India gained independence in 1947, it was hard for anyone to recall that the whole adventure had begun by accident almost 350 years earlier, with a group of merchants in search of nothing more than a "quiet trade."

(1987)

## Bombay: Hobson-Jobson
## on the Streets

All cities are best seen in the dawn, but in Bombay this is especially the case, for only when the day is fresh and young, and the city still uncrowded, can you see what this swampy spit of land is, what it was, what it will be. Go to Sassoon Dock at break of day, and there before you are the two unchanging forces of Bombay—commerce and the sea—in jostling, clangorous, Technicolor profusion. As the sun rises behind rows of multicolored fishing boats, blue and orange and aqua, and as birds begin circling the pinkening sky, the small, slippery, partly covered area becomes almost unimaginably crowded with women carrying baskets on their heads, baskets piled high with the night's silver catch, and people slipping coins from palm to palm.

Shacks on all sides advertise "Fish Industries" and "Batteries for Launching Boats," and the area stinks of fish, and as you make your way through a courtyard full of trucks, with people clinging to their sides, you can see nuns urging themselves forward, tiny, pinch-cheeked women pushing them aside, flirty-eyed girls barking numbers back and forth, and determined matrons flinging themselves into the crush like battering rams, hands on the shoulders of the person in front of them. The fishermen stand in their holds, watching the yelling chaos on shore, and the noisy fishwives in their tropicolored saris bustle around with their tattoos and jangling bracelets and tiny mirrors at their wrists, and a whole Babel of shouts and invective rises up as the day's cut-throat business begins. And as the baskets float across a sea of bobbing black heads, you can see that Bombay is a place where good cheer collides with enterprise, in a raucous defiance of every notion of propriety and order and a woman's place being in the home.

At such moments, I always feel I can see a Bombay that existed long before the Portuguese, the British, or the latest invasion of Coke and Colonel Sanders: a Bombay changeless as the sea, and one that still betrays its origins in its weatherworn surfaces, its skinny palm trees, the balconied apartments along the sweeping corniche of Marine Drive that is still known at night as the "Queen's Necklace." Like its kindred spirits, Hong Kong and Manhattan, Bombay is a street-smart, cash register–quick, anomalous hive—and an island; but for many Indians it has always been an island in a deeper sense, a beachhead for the modern, a multi-cultured port, and a haven of tolerance in a country too often torn apart by 1,652 dialects, more than 2,000 castes, several major religions, and all the extra divisions imposed by the East India Company and their successors.

Culturally, then, Bombay has always been a money-minded mix, where Christians called Coutinho, da Cunha, and de Souza have mingled with Parsees (from Iran) called Merchant and Engineer, in the company of Muslims, Sikhs, Jains, and an odd variety of cross-breeds (the hero of Salman Rushdie's last novel, *The Moor's Last Sigh*, is Bombay itself— depicted as a half-Catholic, half-Jewish Moor not unlike his creator, a Christian-educated, Hindu-surrounded, Muslim-apostate Englishman). Socially, the center of the subcontinent's bright-lights, big-city dreams— home to the strenuous fantasies of "Bollywood" and hunting-ground of mobsters and their molls—is at once the "Capital of Hope," to which hundreds of thousands of newcomers flock each year, dreaming of making their fortunes, and a decidedly ruthless place, where more visitors find jobs than homes. And economically, the country's capital of capital, responsible for nearly half of India's foreign trade, has always been no less extreme, as five million of its people live in slums or on the streets, while those above them recline in apartments more expensive per square foot than anything in Tokyo or New York.

In the '90s, however, all these quickening divisions have been intensified as all India has suddenly been released from forty years of socialist policies, and Bombay has suddenly found itself more than ever like some mythic creature in a Rushdie novel, experiencing dawn and dusk at the same time. On the one hand, the *masala* melting pot—India's Hollywood and Wall Street combined—has become the natural nerve center for a new "wired" free-market India, a time-worn Manhattan of the '80s, with its own insider scandals, runaway fortunes, and slightly precarious, self-exhilarated sense of being at the center of the universe. Yet even as— and largely because—it has been launching itself so eagerly into the future, some of its loyalists have been trying to tug it back into the past, and while Benetton and Web sites and long-banned multinationals have streamed into the "City by the Sea," the nervous right-wingers of the Shiv Sena Party, led by their cartoonist-turned-demagogue Bal Thackeray, have gone about setting off riots, bombing international buildings, and threatening to smash every Coke bottle in the country. Just over a year ago, they even managed to change the city's official name to "Mumbai," a way of telling the world that Bombay belongs to its original Maharashtrian settlers, and the outsiders who have helped to make it prosper— Parsees and Muslims and Gujuratis and Jews—should stay out.

Yet for me, the most recent agitations were set against a background

even deeper, and marked by the mingled origins that define the city at its
heart. For it was in Bombay that my mother and father (coming from
North India and South India, respectively) both grew up, and it is in
Bombay that most of my family still lives. It was in Bombay, on my first
visit, at the age of two, that I learned to walk. Yet Bombay remains as
alien to me as the street signs I cannot read and the names I can't pronounce. It is common these days to hear the city spoken of as a pressure
point for an archetypal global struggle between a multicultural future and
a tribal past, a place (like Hong Kong) where one kind of empire—
economic and postnational—is running up against another (Bombay is,
after all, the birthplace of Kipling as well as of Rushdie). But for me it
had a more complicated meaning, as the place where my parents imbibed
the eminent Victorians that sent them to an Oxford where I was born
(with the luxury of taking Victorians for granted).

When I returned to Bombay, therefore, on the eve of the country's
Golden Jubilee—its fiftieth year of independence—it was partly to see
the forces of nationalism and internationalism in collision. But it was, no
less, to look in on what I regard as my hometown once removed, in my
virtual stepmotherland. And it did not take me long to recall that some
things—especially in India—never change. On the flight coming in, the
man on my right, with typical Bombay pluralism, extended his cup for
coffee when the cabin attendant came around with that beverage, gulped
it down in a second, and then extended it again for tea when the next
woman came around. The man on my left, in equally typical Bombay
fashion, remained buried throughout in Leviticus.

As soon as we stepped out into the terminal, we were greeted by a list
of "Do's and Dont's for Security Officials" (beginning with "Be Courteous to Passengers," but quickly moving on to "Do Not Accept Any
Gift") and a crush of signs for "Car Hailer," "Liquor Permit," and even
one "Miss Rainbow." Ignoring a board that said: "Please Ensure that
Your Drawers Are Locked Properly," I pushed my way to a "Pre-Paid
Taxi" desk—and as soon as they saw me, the cashiers turned around and
began eating dinner. I got into the pre-paid taxi, and the driver closed the
door on me and walked away. I gave him a pre-paid taxi chit, and a fight
broke out. India's maddening charm was all around.

When at last we started up and began coughing into town, at a pace
only slightly slower than that of the passing autorickshas, I had a chance
to take in all the signs of a bright new city. The last time I had been here,
ten years before, nearly all the few cars I'd seen were aging, look-alike
Indian Ambassadors (copied from Morris Oxfords); now the streets were

swarming with cars, and they were Sumos and Marutis and Zens. The last time I was here, I had come upon exactly one Western-style coffee shop in all of India; now I saw ads for Pizza Hut, Baskin-Robbins, even a Mexican restaurant. And the last time I'd come, Indian television had consisted of precisely one government-run channel, broadcasting a few hours a day in black-and-white; now, as I checked into my hotel, I found seventeen different channels, blasting out *Batman* in Hindi, "The Top 10 Arabic Countdown" (from Dubai), and *Hard Copy.*

Yet my hotel, the celestial Taj, built almost a hundred years ago as a response to British rule, was a tonic reminder that India trumps every-thing—especially the normal, the foreign, and the new. The luxury hotel still offers an astrologer, and its bookstore (with *Jughead's Double Digest* on sale next to *The 99 Names of God* at the cash register) has a large sec-tion devoted entirely to "Erotica." Outside its ceremonial entrance, horse-drawn victorias still clop toward the ocean. And when I weighed myself on the scale in my room, it said I had gained fifteen pounds since the morning.


The next day, I set off to explore the city in earnest, a place that was origi-nally so far from England's sights that Lord Clarendon, upon its pur-chase, had pronounced it "within a very little distance of Brazil." Though the shrewd entrepreneurs of the East India Company had been the first to see the potential of the largest deepwater harbor on India's west coast, Bombay is essentially a product of the nineteenth century, when the British built a national railway network around it and local shipbuilders developed its position as India's chief port and link to the world. Bombay has long been a fragrant souvenir of the shotgun marriage of mercantile greed and imperial dreams.

I decided my first stop, therefore, should be a British cemetery marked on a map in my recent guidebook. I took a taxi down to Moscow Lane, at the very tip of Colaba Causeway, and began walking, past cannons and Connaught Barracks, past an "officers' mess" and "Single Officers Accommodation" bungalows—all the way down to an abandoned light-house. Not seeing any sign of English tombstones, I turned in to the Indian Institute of Geomagnetism, and asked a passing geomagnetist where they might be. He asked a passing nongeomagnetist, found out the cemetery was now a high school, and said, rather gallantly, "Goodbye, my dear," as I trooped off. Behind us, in the back of the old army school, a man was standing solemnly in khaki shorts, in the middle of a huge patch of empty grass, practicing "Reveille" on his trumpet.

Thus was I introduced to the first great rule of Bombay life, which is that everything goes wrong, and everything's all right. I never did locate the British cemetery, but when I turned around, there—as if by magic—was an Afghan War Memorial, complete with small weathered cross and plaques inscribed to "My Beloved Wife Lily Meek" and "Sarah Chandy." In the church behind the memorial, the reverend was sending birthday greetings this month to Mr. Christopherson Ebenezer and Bishop S. B. Joshua. (Names have always told the history of Bombay—or Mumbai—and the map is still a lexicon of bittersweet hybrids—Apollo Bunder, Cross Maidan, the J. J. Parsi Benevolent Institution. Mahatma Gandhi Road crosses Wellington Circle here, and the figure of Sir Dinshaw Manockjee Petit looks nobly out amidst a sea of Kemps and Wellingtons. Though the independent government tried to rename all the great British sites when the last imperial regiment sailed away, it was as quixotic a gesture as most things here: no one ever talks of Netaji Subhash Road when she's off to Marine Drive.)

For me, too, growing up half a universe away, the grand complications of Bombay had always been softened in my parents' reminiscences by the euphonious sound of their studies in Elphinstone College and their excited discoveries at the Royal Asiatic Library. Phrases that had long since lost their currency in England—"once in a way" or "alpha mind"—came down to me as the latest thing. And even now, when I asked my aunt how to get to her house, she told me to look out for V.J.T.I. (Victoria Jubilee Technical Institute), somewhere in the general vicinity of King's Circle.

The cathedral of this mildewed classicism—and a pounding reminder of the days when Bombay was the second-largest city in the Empire (after London)—is Victoria Terminus, the one-of-a-kind world-within-a-world railway station where the daily Indian madness plays out amidst the undecayed pillars of the Empire. Outside it, you will find a Palgrave's treasury of styles—stained-glass elephants, Progress atop its central dome, a British lion next to an Indian tiger, sculpted by students of John Lockwood Kipling, the father of the poet (and once principal of Bombay's school of art).

Inside, however, is a world even more polymorphously perverse. When I passed through the first door I saw, I found myself within a whirl devised by Lewis Carroll, and then translated by Jorge Luis Borges into Esperanto: booth after booth after incomprehensible booth, in room after room after hangarlike room, some offering "Manual Booking Refund on Pre-bought Ticket," some promising "Refund on Reserved Tickets for Trains Leaving on Same Day and the Following Day up to 0900 hours," some dealing only with "Freedom Fighters," others only with "Blind Persons," or those who might qualify for the "Military Quota." And all of them governed by a hundred rules both courtly ("Kindly Tender Exact Amount of Fare") and relentless (when informed of a seat's availability, you must say yes or no "in 20 seconds"). I imagined teams of men in tatty uniforms with stopwatches in hand, timing the responses of those who had so patiently observed the injunction to "Please Stand in Q."

Upstairs was a "Ladies Waiting Room," a "General Waiting Room" (which was, in fact, full of ladies), a sign for a "Housekeeper," and a pair of shower stalls. There was a "Superviser" on one floor, a "Supervisor" on another, and a set of rather gloomy rooms under the title "V.I.P. Suites." The second rule of Bombay life, I was reminded, is that anything one person can do, ten can do better—or, at least, more slowly.

Yet the biggest shock of all in VT is that somehow, amidst all the chaos, something works. Every morning, a small army of *dabbawallahs*— couriers in Nehru caps and khaki shorts—scatters around the city, collecting cylindrical stainless-steel lunch boxes, or *dabbas*, from housewives in the suburbs. They then bring the virtually identical containers to VT—more than 100,000 of them in all—and, with the help of nothing more than a simple color coding, deliver the right one to the right man at the right desk in the city. The third rule of Bombay is that its wonders are as beyond reason as its horrors.

Around VT and the General Post Office (a comparable labyrinth of 101 booths, with extra options—"Sattelite Money-Order Service" and "Speed-Post Complaints"—scrawled up on a blackboard), the city blithely continues to inhabit several different cultures all at once, so that past seems indistinguishable from present and future: the Catholic Syrian Bank is at the same circular intersection as the National Hindu Hotel here, and the Aladin restaurant nearby offers "Moghlai, Punjabi, Chinese, Singapore Fried Rice, Chicken American Chop Suey and Szechwan Fried Rice." Even the city aquarium has a fish with a line from the Koran on its back, and a crab with a Christian cross on it.

The epicenter of this eclecticism is in many ways the Oval—the stretch of grass built by the British at the center of the area still called "Fort." Along one side stand the proud buildings of the University of Bombay, and in its library, the card catalogues are still made up of handwritten index cards (the signs on the drawers saying, "Dictator," "Dynastic," "Economic Conflict," and "Family Saga," as if every book were about the Gandhi family). When I was seventeen, I spent a whole summer amidst its cobwebs, reading a small-print edition of the collected works of Shakespeare, and newly interested in India because Krishna and psychedelic posters were all the rage at my English high school. Now, when I returned, it was as if I had never left—and the British certainly hadn't. I walked through its beautifully landscaped gardens, of temple

trees and royal palms and noble Amherstia, past doors that said "Backward Class Cell" and "Institute of Distance Education"—and, more typically, "No Enquiries, Please"—and up into the library. As I picked out a
1969 copy of the *"Vogue" Book of Etiquette*, near a statue of Sir George
Birdwood, and read about how best to say goodbye to my hostess, birds
flapped above me in the rafters, and passed in and out of stained-glass
windows held together with rags and bits of cardboard.

Nearby, the Rajabai Clock Tower, which used to chime the sounds of
"Rule Britannia" on the hour, was closed now (too many disappointed
examinees having thrown themselves to their deaths here), but Matthew Thomas Titus had been awarded a First Class degree, I read, and
there were still signs for an "Intercollegiate On-the-Spot Fruit-Flower-
Vegetable Arrangement Competition" up on the bulletin board. Immediately outside the university gates, a palmist addressed such questions as
"Do I fall in love too easily?"

Across the street, the sidewalks teemed with bookstalls (selling *Time*
capsules from after the war, and dog-eared copies of *I'm O.K. You're
O.K.*), and in their midst sat ear cleaners and men selling free in-flight
magazines and coconuts, and another man, sitting calmly in the middle
of a busy sidewalk, typing out applications for Transit Visas to Kuwait. A
thousand cricket games were exploding all at once along the grass, and
sometimes the batsmen were facing two bowlers (cricket pitchers) all at
once, or a player in a soccer game turned around and made a cricket
catch. Everything was happening on every side, and loudly, and the sheer
energy and innocence of it all recalled to me that, more than a sage or an
old woman, Bombay most resembles a mischievous boy—irritating,
engaging, quick-witted, and eager to make good. Things were collapsing
all around him, yet still he could not keep a smile from his face.

What the pandemonium also brings home, with a vengeance, is that
the real sights of Bombay are the streets themselves, and though there is
not much formally to see here, you can have a great time not seeing it.
For it is—this metropolis as populous as Denmark and Costa Rica and
Iceland and Mongolia combined—all over the place, in every sense, and
though the buildings so carefully re-create Manchester, the life around
them contradicts it at every turn. When you drive through the shopping
streets in the suburbs, for example, at 7 p.m. on a weekday night, past
Lady Diana Tailors and Dreamers' Delight, threading your way between
the Eros Hair-Cutting Salon and the Clip Joint Beauty Clinic and
School, you may feel as if you're nosing through a rally or a parade. But
the rally in Bombay is perpetual, and the parade is held every day, in a
celebration of surprise and serendipity. There are few straight lines in

Bombay, and even intersections are often roundabouts, so that A gets to B via Z.

Flavoring your steps still further is the fact that nothing ever stops talking along the Bombay streets, and a trip down any sidewalk is like a journey through a bubble-filled cartoon strip, in which every building and car and little shop chatters away at you with the slightly too-confident volume of a man who's drunk too much at the office Christmas party. "Dark Glasses Make You Attractive to the Police," one hoarding cried at me. "You Can't Score with a Bat Resting on Your Shoulder," advised a large sign in front of the Virgin Mary. "Stress Is Coming Soon," piped the sticker on the back of a so-called Tourist Vehicle.

What this constant, compendious eventfulness also means is that rules are religiously observed only in the breach, and the charm of the city lies in its curlicues, its contretemps, the doodles that swallow up its main text: in the "Free Foot Service" at the tranquil Jain Temple at the base of Malabar Hill; in the trash cans like openmouthed penguins in the land-scaped Hanging Gardens; in the door at Balbunath Temple that adver-tises the Jayash Trading Company; or even in the little boy who comes up to you at a stoplight, flashes you a copy of *Naughty Boy* through the window, and, when you say no, comes back with a copy of *Chastity*.

Faced with a mass of such incongruities—all in a spiced version of English that might be called Bombastic—I decided just to surrender to the streets, and took to going each day, at sunset, to the clamorous riot that forms around the Gateway of India, where everyone assembles just to chat and gawk. Whirring toy helicopters skittered across the sky, groups of homesick Africans gathered where the sun burned the fishing boats golden, and old men paraded around with bags that said: "Smile. It Increases your Face Value."

After night began to fall, I continued on to Chowpatty Beach, where once the "Quit India" movement had held its rallies, and where now you can see flashing robots, flimsy merry-go-rounds, four-foot Ferris wheels, and men setting up shooting galleries made of balloons that spell the names of the latest hit movies. All around, at the Radio Club, along Marine Drive, and within the Indian Education Society, there were society weddings, and huge pavilions of orange garlands, the trees aglitter with fairy lights, and women in gold-brocade saris padding out from under lit-up tents. Such occasions, an uncle of mine told me at a cousin's nuptials, were increasingly like international cricket matches: they lasted five days, they were full of antiquated ceremony, and they generally ended (in all senses) in a tie.

In Hare Krishna Land at Juhu Beach—a whole minicity of the spiritual (appointed with its own six-story hotel, brand-new temple, and, as soon as you enter, branch of the Indian Overseas Bank)—I found myself in what could have passed for a pleasant tourist bungalow anywhere in India (though an electronic ticker-tape display beside the registration desk did flash unceasingly, "Hare Krishna Hare Krishna . . ." and among the young searchers in Gap T-shirts, there were ash-besmirched New Yorkers in orange robes and top knots). Behind it, in the shady compound where devotees live, billboards teach children the two Golden Rules ("Always Remember Krishna/Never Forget Krishna"), and a board depicts the history of basketball, just under one on "The Origin of All Culture" (in other words, Krishna consciousness). Another board offers tips on "Blooming Manners." Yet this curious tribute to the love affair of East and West is still renowned among canny locals as one of the finest places to stay, or eat, in the entire city.

Even when I went to visit the house where Mahatma Gandhi had lived for seventeen years, and first fashioned his campaign for *satyagraha*, or passive resistance, what struck me most, to my surprise, was what I saw outside: a "Suicide Prevention Centre" across the street, and, next to it, a poster for "Fun 'n' Fair with Funky Games." All Bombay, in some respects, resembles a suicide prevention center, and for all the extraordinary difficulties of life here—for all the 600,000 people squeezed into less than a square mile in Dharavi, the largest slum in Asia, and the infamous Falkland Road red-light district, where as many as 100,000 "cage girls" work in horrifying circumstances, Bombay is not a disheartening place; it has too much gusto for that, and too much crooked sweetness, and when you see the local stores called "Reliable" or "Honesty," or hear the tiny drinks stalls playing "Things Go Better with Coke" (in Hindi), you feel that something is invincible here.

Some of this is changing, of course, as the city speeds into a multinational future that brings with it new expectations and foreign hopes. When I opened the antique-seeming *Times of India* (which fills its editorial page with allusions to Bertram Wooster and quotations from G. B. Shaw, and offers, on its cover, "Invitation Price: 2 Rupees"), I found that page 2 was still given over to traditional "Matrimonial Notices"—but now these included some highly untraditional categories ("Multinational," "Green Card," and "Cosmopolitan"). One potential bride listed as a qualification that she "knows computer language," another was billed as "Girl with best of Indian and Western values having 8 figure personal assets, 7 figure personal income from property/shares. Heiress to large fortune." Nearby, a Mr. Iyer was advertising his detective services for cases involving "Data Leakage, White Collar Crime, Debugging, and Matrimonial Disunity'' (the link between data and dates becoming even more inscrutable!).

Still more vivid a sign of the coming times was the pub to which two recent M.B.A.s took me one lively Saturday night. Five minutes away, the illuminated buildings along the Esplanade looked like pieces of Oxford airlifted through the heavens. Inside the neon-lit boîte, however, Bombay's affluent young were sipping frozen banana daiquiris and cocktails called "Sexual Delight" that cost them 200 rupees a shot (traditionally equivalent for most Indians to $200). On TV screens around the place, they were watching Vanessa Mae, the teenage sex-kitten violinist, on MTV, and the Charlotte Hornets creaming the Denver Nuggets. Girls in University of Miami T-shirts, boys in tight 501s, sang along to Lionel Richie as they sipped their Long Island Teas, and took their leave of Victorian formalities.

A little later, on Valentine's Day, I got an even stronger dose of the new cutting-edge Bombay when I went out with Shobha Dé, the highly glamorous former movie-magazine editor and fashion model who has become the best-selling novelist in the country. Dé, a fountain of soigné energy and a mine of sex-and-shopping wisdom, moves through the city like its uncrowned queen, her white Mercedes (with its "3000" license plate) edging through backstreets and past bullock carts, with restaurateurs racing out to bow and salaam as soon as she appears and finding for her, out of nowhere, an empty table (or a fulsome compliment).

"Bombay is an evil city," the mother of *Sultry Days* and *Starry Nights* said to me over curried crabs, "but in a glamorous, romantic way. It's a ferocious city, but that's its charm." Around us, in the fashionable new Italian Trattoria, men were lugging in a twenty-nine-inch Trinitron, and stylish college kids were making plans for the evening—Valentine's Day being the latest commercial craze in this fashion-mad city. Tossing back her long, thick hair, Dé favored me with a whole anthology of rags-to-riches stories that commemorate the city's promise: about the former scrap merchant from Aden who's now perhaps the richest man in India; about the former fire-eater she recalls performing with Tomoko the Tomato (a professional ecdysiast) and now the boss of the chicest Chinese joint in town ("He has a thousand criminal cases against him," she purred approvingly); about the twenty-three-year-old villager who came to Bombay in his underwear and now owns stores all over the city and has "eight or ten" passports that he shuffles judiciously to facilitate his shopping trips to Hong Kong, Europe, the Gulf (the queen knows him because she goes in now and then to "bless his Levi's, his Giordanos, the lot").

Now, she said, slipping off her denim jacket, "the big thing is food criticism. And fashion. These saris today cost $6,000—who's going to buy them? I mean, here we are in Bombay, where there are only two seasons—summer and monsoon, hot and hotter—and these girls are modeling minks. Who's got the money? But that's the fashion." Some beautiful young things looked over at her and she threw a few kisses in their direction. A typical wedding, she went on, "costs $300,000. Even the trousseau, you're talking $100,000." But where, I asked meekly, did such money come from? "Oh, it's all funny money," she said negligently. "Smuggling and real estate."

Yet even as she kept talking, about "uppers" and audio books and "the ladies who booze," not to mention the 524-episode soap opera she was writing (at her kitchen table, surrounded by six children, working a hundred episodes ahead), the 524-episode megadrama of Bombay was continuing, unstoppably, all around us. I walked into the high court buildings nearby, after lunch, and instantly I was back inside the crazy, multifarious, completely unmanageable Bombay of old. Rows of ill-lit corridors stretched out in front of me, filled with petitioners sitting in the dark, or crowding into ancient courtrooms. Clerks clicked and clacked away on typewriters older than Lloyd George, like nothing so much as summa cum laude graduates of the University of Busywork. On every wall and bulletin board, lists and papers and requests and regulations fluttered hopelessly. Even in the parking lot there was a list of eight rules.

"Advocates" in tattered black blazers and white ties got up and talked and talked. The figures of Justice and Mercy presided immemorially from on high. Cases snailed ahead like badly translated versions of the opening chapter of *Bleak House*. And as I watched the Bombay free-for-all go on, tomorrow and tomorrow without end, I thought to myself, not sadly: Victoria really had not lived in vain.

(1996)

## The New World's New World:
## Making Itself Up and Over

Yes, yes, we've heard all the jokes: we know that "spacey" and "flaky" seem almost to have been invented for California, and that "California" in the dictionary is a virtual synonym for "far out." Ever since gold was first found in its waters, the Shangri-la-la of the West has been the object of as many gibes as fantasies: just over a century ago, Rudyard Kipling was already pronouncing that "San Francisco is a mad city, inhabited for the most part by perfectly insane people" (others might say "insanely perfect"); and more than forty years ago, S. J. Perelman was barreling down the yellow brick road to L.A., the "mighty citadel which had given the world the double feature, the duplexburger, the motel, the hamfurter, and the shirt worn outside the pants." Yes indeed, we know, all too well, that "going to California" is almost as proverbial as "going to Siberia" (except in the opposite direction)—tantamount, for many people, to going to seed.

And yes, much of the image does fit. Returning to California recently, I picked up the day's copy of the San Francisco *Chronicle* and, in the space of a single section, read about people attending a funeral in pinks and turquoises and singing along to Bette Midler ("Dress for a Brazilian party!" the invitation—from the deceased—had read); about a missing cat identifiable by a "rhinestone collar w/name and electronic cat door opener"; about women from L.A. hiring migrant workers to wait in line for them to buy watches in the shape of cucumbers and bacon-and-egg combinations. On Hollywood Boulevard, I saw a "Historic Landmark" sign outside the site of "The First Custom T-Shirt in California," flyers on the wall promoting a group called Venal Opulence, and, in a store across the street, "Confucius X-Rated Mini-Condom Fortune Cookies." No wonder, I thought, that when I tell people I live in California— worse, that I choose to live in California—they look at me as if I had decided not to get serious, or grow up; as if I had seceded from reality.

Part of the reason for all this, no doubt, is circumstance. For one thing, California wears its contradictions—its clashing hearts—on its sleeve: even its deepest passions are advertised on bumper sticker, T-shirt, and vanity plate. California is America without apologies or inhibitions, pleased to have found itself here, and unembarrassed by its pleasure. So, too, society in California is less a society than a congregation of subcultures, many of them with a membership of one: every man's home is his castle in the air here. In addition, California's image has been fashioned largely by interlopers from the East, who tend to look on the place as a kind of recumbent dumb blonde, so beautiful that it cannot possibly have any other virtues. Thus the California of the imagination is an unlikely compound of Evelyn Waugh's Forest Lawn, Orson Welles's Hearst Castle, every screenwriter's Locustland, and Johnny Carson's "beautiful downtown Burbank." Nice house, as they say, but nobody's at home.

By now, then, the notion of California as a wigged-out free-for-all has become a legend, and as self-sustaining as every other myth. If I had read about vegetable-shaped watches in the Des Moines *Register*, I would have taken it as a reflection not on Iowa but on humanity; California, though, has been associated with flakiness for so long that by now it is only the flaky things we see, or take to be Californian. There are all of five pet cemeteries in L.A. (versus eight in New York State), and exactly 138 health clubs in the Yellow Pages (versus 229 in New York City): but it is the canine mortuaries in L.A. that everybody mentions. When California is ahead of the world, it seems outlandish, yet when its trends become commonplace, no one thinks of them as Californian. Large-scale recycling, health clubs, postmodern enchiladas, all were essentially Californian fads until they became essential to half the countries in the world. And many people do not recall that such everyday, down-to-earth innovations as the bank credit card, the thirty-year mortgage, and the new-car loan were all, as David Rieff points out, more or less invented by that great California institution the Bank of America.

And as the California myth gains circulation, it attracts precisely the kind of people who come here to sustain it: many of the newcomers to the "end of America" are flat earthers, free speechers, or latter-day sinners drawn by the lure of a place where anything goes and where anyone can get away from everything (or *with* anything). And "California Dreaming" still has a magic to it, a talismanic ring that "Pennsylvania Dreaming" and "North Dakota Dreaming" and even "Florida Dreaming" do not. Frank Lloyd Wright once said that all the loose nuts in America end up in Los Angeles because of the continental tilt; Aldous Huxley, more imaginatively, suggested that the world resembled a head on its side, with the superrational Old World occupying a different sphere from the vacant, dreamy spaces of the collective subconscious of the West. California, he was implying, is the name we give our hopes and highest fantasies: an antiworld of sorts, governed by an antireality principle, and driven by an antigravitational pull. That is why he, like Thomas Pynchon and Ursula Le Guin and a hundred others, set his Utopia in California: with its deserts and rich farmland, and a valley (if not a sea) named after death, California has impressed many as a kind of modern Holy Land.

California, in short, doesn't stand to reason (or even a facsimile thereof). "The drive-in restaurant has valet parking," notes P. J. O'Rourke, and "practically everyone runs and jogs. Then they get in the car to drive next door." There's no beach at North Beach, he might have added, and *Sunset Boulevard* was shot on Wilshire. William Faulkner was arrested for walking here, and teenagers look older than their parents. "The tolerant Pacific air," in Auden's words, "makes logic seem so silly." And that air of unreality is only quickened by the fact that California is the illusion maker of the world: "Everyman's Eden" has made a living almost out of living up to other people's expectations. California is, quite literally, the landscape of our dreams—the movies and songs and TV shows of our youth were largely shot here: this is where D. W. Griffith built Babylon, and over there you can see the Bates Motel. Even now, "El Lay" in particular projects a sense of people leading faux lives in a world of Moorish towers and empty stage sets: of billboard-size faces against postcard-perfect vistas that might almost seem a kind of Magritte canvas declaring, *"Ceci n'est pas une place."* California is the home not just of recreation but of re-creation too: you can find Tomorrowland, Adventureland, and Fantasyland here, but Main Street is a replica.

What tends to get forgotten in all this is that the aerospace industry in Los Angeles brings in twice as much revenue as the entertainment industry: California is the sixth-largest industrial power in the world. The source of its wealth is that least dreamy, and most Realpolitik-bound, of industries, defense. Yes, Gene Roddenberry may have dreamed up *Star Trek* here, but he drew upon his experience in the L.A. Police Department. There are more engineers in the Los Angeles basin than in any other metropolitan area; and Nobel Prize winners live here not in spite, but because, of its amenities. When Jan Morris visited what she called the "Know-How City," she shrewdly concentrated not on the actors but on the sound technicians behind the scenes, seamless in their expertise. "Behind the flash and the braggadocio," she wrote, "solid skills and scholarship prosper." For every quaint, picture-book San Francisco floating in the air, there is an Oakland across the bay, gritty, industrial, and real; for every Zen-minded "Governor Moonbeam," there is a hardheaded Richard Nixon; for every real estate office in the shape of a Sphinx, there is a man behind the desk counting dollars.

The town in which I live, the pretty, sunlit, red-roofed Mediterranean resort of Santa Barbara, is typical. The town prides itself on being the birthplace of hot tubs, the first home of streaking, the site of the first Egg McMuffin. There is little or no industry here, and everyone seems to be working, full time, on his lifestyle. People from Melbourne to Marseilles tune in to the *Santa Barbara* soap opera, and in the Kansai region of Japan, women in "Santa Barbara" sweatshirts crowd into the Santa Barbara ice cream parlor. Yet there is a theoretical physics institute here, and there used to be a think tank, peopled by refugees from the University of Chicago. And it is in the nature of bright sunlight to cast long shadows: when Santa Barbara has hit the headlines recently, it has been because of an eight-year drought so severe that even showers were limited; a fire that destroyed six hundred houses, including my own; and one of the most poisonous homeless battles in the country. AIDS to the north, gang wars to the south; droughts interrupted by floods, mudslides down the coast that left ninety-one dead in 1969, earthquakes that bring in their wake bubonic plague (contracted by 160 people in San Francisco in 1906): California, as Christopher Isherwood saw, "is a tragic place, like Palestine, like every Promised Land."

The other thing to bear in mind is that the notion of an " 'I's have it," crystal-gazing California is based, for the most part, on an affluent, white, upper middle class that is increasingly beside the point in a state that will soon be the first to have a white minority. It is not the Beach Boys, or the Eagles, or the Grateful Dead, who provide the voice of California today; it is Los Lobos. Amy Tan novels and *Boyz N the Hood* are the artifacts of the new United States of California. And when it comes to the latest groups of immigrants—as with the settlers in Steinbeck country—few of the stereotypes apply: not notably self-indulgent, most of the state's Hispanics and Asians live a long way from attending hydrotherapy classes or sleeping with their therapists. The Filipino punk joint may be a symbol of the latest form of California strangeness—polyglot multiculturalism— but it seems hardly out of place in a state where tire stores are built in the shape of Mayan temples, and movies are screened in the replica of a palace at Thebes.

Not long ago, in Garden Grove, just two miles south of Disneyland, where Vietnamese *dentistas* ("Se Habla Espanol," say their windows) bump against Halal grocery stores—in Spanish-style malls—I paid a visit to the Crystal Cathedral. On first encounter, the area seemed a vision of the cacophonous dystopia of the future, in which a hundred California dreams collide and each one drowns the others out. Yet beneath the surface, there is a kind of commonness, a shared belief in all of them that the future can be custom-made. This faith is implicit in the immigrants' assumptions—they have voted with their feet in coming here; and it is made explicit, for longtime residents, by the Reverend Robert Schuller, who fills his Crystal Cathedral with hymns to "Possibility Thinking." Schuller's great distinction, perhaps, is not just that he pioneered the drive-in church (and his sermons are still broadcast, via a Sony Jumbo-Tron, to overflow parishioners in the parking lot outside), nor even that he has managed to erect a glittering monument to his "Be-Happy Attitudes," but rather than he has gathered a huge, nationwide following out of preaching what is, in effect, Californianism. For if you look at his books (*Your Future Is Your Friend, Success Is Never Ending, Failure Is Never Final*), and if you walk around his church, as airy and futuristic—and as free of Christian iconography almost—as a Hyatt Regency hotel, you can see that the heart of his scripture is simple optimism, hardly different from that espoused by New Age gurus across the state (in the Bodhi Tree bookstore, "Create Your Own Future" tapes are on sale, made by a professor from Stanford).

Faced by such unlikelihoods, one begins to see that California is still, in a sense, what America used to be: a spiritual refuge, a utopian experiment, a place plastic enough—in every sense—to shape itself to every group of newcomers. It is a state set in the future tense (and the optative mood), a place in a perpetual state of Becoming. Of course it's strange: it is precisely the shape of things to come, unexpected as tomorrow. Of course it's unsettled: it's making itself up as it goes along. Yet hopefulness itself seems almost a Californian native, and even the motto carved into the rotunda of the Los Angeles City Hall announces: "The city came into being to preserve life; it exists for the good life." The United Nations may do its dirty work in New York, but it drew up its idealistic charter in San Francisco. That, in a sense, is California's role, the part it has to play in the national pageant: to be outrageous, to go out on a limb, to make tomorrow's mistakes today.

All this gives the place something of the air of a child, innocent of time and care, asking questions so fundamental as to seem almost absurd (What is darkness? How deep is space?). Many outsiders look down on it as Thomas Gray did on the schoolboy he once was—"regardless of their doom, the little victims play!" And there is no doubt that its sunniness is often shallow, or selfish, or shortsighted. But it is never defeatist. And the place has a child's invigorating sense of wonder and reviving freshness. Convinced of its providential destiny, California never gets weighed down, as other places do, by last year's faux pas or the weariness of tradition. It even has the confidence to make jokes against itself. (How do you get a blonde to smile on Saturday? Tell him, or her, a joke on

Wednesday!) So let the wags from New York keep branding us with their satire (L.A. is "reality with a substitute teacher"). One thing we notice is that most of them—most of us, in fact, born-again and adopted and converted Californians—find what we're looking for here and, smiling as the jokes keep coming, stay.

(1991)

# New York:
## A City in Black and White

From my perch above the sea in California, New York seems a crepuscular place, Stygian almost, smoke hissing out of its manholes, long, dark streets narrowing one's horizons, infernal tremors rumbling beneath one's feet. Light is what gets lost in translation. The golden light slanting off the tall glass towers on early summer evenings; the leafy calm of October afternoons; the hush of first light after early snowfall, when even the avenues are deserted and still—all these are erased, in memory, or translated into Stieglitz monochrome. In memory, at least, and imagination, it is always 2 a.m. in New York, and you don't know what you're doing there.

From Santa Barbara, in fact, an escape as lazy and unreal as Helmut Newton's Monte Carlo, New York seems almost a Newtonian invention, made to illustrate Newton's three laws: that the world is a fashion show set in a jungle, peopled by creatures dark with a stalking glamour; that characters define themselves boldly against the landscape, staring back without apology at the camera's unsettling eye; that life, in fact, is theatrical, sinister, and a touch debauched. When Newton turns his eye on such polyester idylls as L.A. or the Côte d'Azur, it can be a shock almost to see what Pinter calls the weasel beneath the cocktail cabinet; in New York, though, his pictures feel like documentaries. L.A., after all, unrolls like a situation comedy, a life of no moment played out against the synthetic blue of sunny two-D backdrops; New York is cinema verité round the clock and in the round. "Londoners live *in* streets," as Peter Conrad notes, "New Yorkers live *on* them." And on every street in New York City, people are forever clamoring to push themselves forward from the milling masses, auditioning for a part in the city's nonstop drama, calling, "Take me! I'm different! I'm unpassbyable!" Seen from afar, at least, in the vicinity of Hollywood, New York is one nocturnal carnival of ashen faces and outré poses, lined up along an unlit, forbidding street, sometime after midnight, in the shadow of those dark satanic turrets that Barry Hannah likened to the fingernails of corpses.

From afar, indeed, in memory and imagination, all one's images of New York are negative: not just in the sense that they are unflattering, full of threat, shadowed by unease, but mostly because it is a city seen in black and white. The lighting is harsh, the contrasts are stark, and the effects are as loud as a tabloid headline in your face. When I think of New York, I think of people with an unearthly pallor, dressed all in black; of black jackets and white ties; black limos and white lies. New York comes to mind like grainy images on a contact sheet: dark tower blocks along the Great White Way; Art Deco buildings and King Kong; underground catacombs and Tom Wolfe–white suits. New York is the black and white of a Jules Feiffer cartoon, the black and white of the Great Gray Lady, the black and white of the editorial pages of *The New Yorker*, from which all color has been tactfully removed. It is also, in the end, the black and white of Warhol's sepulcher stare (so different from the cheery smile of that other pale blond artist, Hockney).

New York, in the mind, is the black and white of film-school projects, of *She's Gotta Have It* and *Sidewalk Stories*, of Jarmusch's arty squalor, and the skyline that inspired *Metropolis;* it is the black and white, in every sense, of Spike Lee. New York is the black and white of Lou Reed, Suzanne Vega, and the Talking Heads; the black and white, in fact, of all downtown (which in New York connotes not bright high-rises and municipal plazas but long sunless avenues and abandoned lots). New York is, above all, the black and white of Weegee photographs, clinical X rays of the naked body, entwined on park benches or caught in a post-mortem flash. New York, like Berlin, always suggests the dark: black and white and dread all over.

If black-and-white is the color of stridency and assertion, it is also, however, the shade of nostalgia, and it was the inspiration of that great anticolorist Woody Allen to compose his valentine to *Manhattan* in elegiac black and white. For all one's happiest memories of New York come from the era of black-and-white, when it was the world's bright promise. Allen chose to pay homage to the vanished elegance of George Gershwin and Willie Mays. But he could as easily have chosen other black-and-white mementos: Yankee pinstripes and the Stork Club; the Chrysler Building and the Cotton Club; newsreels, ticker tape, and Eisenstaedt's famous picture of the D-day kiss. What colors come to mind when one mentions Macy's? Or the Lower East Side? Or the South Bronx? Black and white and white and black. Say "Ellis Island," and the mind resolves into a framed snapshot done in black and white.

The only apartment I ever rented in New York—when I was doing time there—I rented because its proprietress rejoiced in the name Aida Descartes. Later, alas, I discovered that neither opera nor straight reasoning was her forte. That same apartment, when I fled New York, I left in the care of a thick-voiced, large-bodied pool player from the Bronx, who paid two months deposit in cash and looked, to my delight, like a recent refugee from *Prizzi's Honor*. In New York, though, things are often what they seem, and life seems determined to incriminate art. And so, sure enough, just a few months later, the picture-perfect gangster proved as bad as I had hoped. In New York, even the humor is black.

When I returned to my apartment, I found it laid waste amidst a blizzard of eviction notices. Unpaid bills were stacked inside the bookcases, and Polaroids of my sublessee, half naked, were displayed along the fridge. And yet, in the middle of the debris, there were piles of *Gourmet* magazines, and recipes carefully clipped; books on how to be slimmer, and books on how to talk better; a portrait of an elephant, inscribed, by "Barbara," "Come Back Soon." A miniature pool table rested on my shelf, and underneath my record player, twenty-year-old copies of Peter, Paul and Mary. A mobster, yes, but one with human aspirations. New York is the place where Horatio Alger stories come with afterwords, or dark twists at their conclusions; surrounded by unconquerable verticals two hundred times taller than oneself, one's body and one's dreams are brought quickly down to size. No one makes a mark on New York, and New York leaves its mark on everyone (where the accommodating, annihilating West is literally recumbent, a laid-back promise saying, "Do with me what you will").

New York, then, is also the black and white of screaming newsprint. Reality gets everywhere in New York. It pounds through the walls and seeps up through the gratings and tugs at one's sleeve and asks for a quarter. New York is a world unedited, unbowdlerized, with expletives repleted: not just Manhattans, but Bronx cheers and Bowery Bums. New York is a decidedly grown-up city, elevated in all senses of the word; I cannot remember seeing children there, or places for children to play, and innocence seems as implausible as solitude along its adult streets. "New York is too real," writes Don DeLillo in *Great Jones Street*. "It's just about the realest thing there is in the observable universe." New York is also, in fact, the terminal, hearse-polished sentences of DeLillo, with their slatted, venetian-blind effects, cold bodies arranged in cool positions.

Part of this, no doubt, is just because New York is such an angular place, geometrical and pointed. The city is a rationalist's conceit of sharp edges and straight lines, the 2,028-block grid that so obsessed Leger and Le Corbusier; a crossword puzzle of a place, its black-and-white blocks marked by numbers and letters. Alphabet City indeed. Skyscrapers sharpen to a point; Wall Street canyons foreshorten all perspective; the old subway maps are Mondrian patterns. New York seems often, in fact, like a city without curves. In memory, at least, it becomes a kind of boxed cosmopolis in the dark: office workers awakening in tiny cubicles, descending into the tunnels and compartments of the subway, coming up into their boxlike, fluorescent offices and then, after dark, descending again into the underground. A city on speed, as crowded in time as in space. And a mathematical diagram of a city, where quantities have a police-blotter precision—Jan Morris noting, ten years ago, that more cases of human bites were recorded each year than rat bites; the photographer Jacob Riis, one hundred years ago, remarking, of Baxter Alley, "I counted seventeen deeds of blood."

Much of this, of course, is what has made New York electric. It is the great man-made artifact of the Machine Age, a drawing board for every kind of absurdist utopian blueprint. Madmen have always had outsize designs upon the place, as Rem Koolhaas shows in his very mad, and brilliantly vertiginous, *Delirious New York:* Frederic Thompson's literally lunatic construction of Luna Park, studded with 1,326 snow-white towers and rewired each night with 1,300,000 lights; Senator William H. Reynolds's notion of a Dreamland, a huge water park complete with small boys dressed as Mephistopheles, reciting nonsense, and an experimental community of lascivious midgets, where terrain was to be defined by the absence of color; Henri Erkins's Dream Street, built on Forty-second Street, which sought, through mirrors, artificial moons, and a hidden orchestra, to re-create the splendor of Caesarean Rome, assisted by a "semi-nude female figure" blowing bubbles from a pipe; the Radio City of Samuel Lionel Rothafel, into which hallucinogenic gases were to be seeped to enhance the euphoria induced by its golden sunset arches. Plato's Retreat has a noble pedigree.

When Dalí was invited by Bonwit Teller to decorate a window on Fifth Avenue, he erected a nightmarish surrealist manifesto of naked mannequins shrouded in dust, and chaperoned by a bloody pigeon. Its theme was "Day and Night." Black and white again, in short. ("The lunatic asylum which I saw was perfect," observed Anthony Trollope after visiting New York. Perfect indeed, one thinks.)

Those of us who have escaped New York gather sometimes like semi-hysterical graduates of some internment camp and, amidst pastel greetings and crayon skies, blacken the city in our minds. Discussions begin, inevitably, with parlor-game dialectics. New York makes one hard, California makes one soft. California is about Being, New York about Doing. The East Coast is a race, the West Coast an exploration. Soon, though, the grievances strike deeper. New York, we say, is a place where day-dreaming is obsolete, an antitropic that condemns everyone it touches to a life of grime (New York has at least taught us sarcasm). New York never, even at break of day, we agree, feels like a city reborn. "In New York recently," wrote Emerson, "one seems to lose all substance, and to become a surface in a world of surfaces." In New York City, we commiserate, we could never see the stars.

And the only way to preserve this image is, of course, never to visit the place itself. For as soon as one does, one finds, to one's horror, that the city is much brighter than one imagined, looser than one recalled, marginally less evil. The museums, one sees, are flooded with images of light (even Hockney); the sidewalk cafés in summer almost feel like California; the music of the streets blazes with neon energy. And as the colors come flooding back, one begins, very slowly, to realize how many shadows are lost, how much dimension fades, in the bleaching, never-ending California sun.

New York, in memory and imagination, seems almost like a hallucination—a rush of strange faces, twisted shapes, flashes of the unexpected; a cultural pawnshop cluttered with bric-a-brac; a reality so exaggerated that it becomes a kind of surreality. And, from a porch above the sea in California, that can almost seem like something to yearn for.

(1990)

# A Hermitage in California:
## A Life Outside Time

It is hard to imagine that time—or anything else—exists, here in this silent hermitage above the California coast. No newspapers are delivered here, and no telephone ever rings. There is not even, really, an address. Days on end pass without the sound of a single voice. From where I sit I cannot see a trace of human habitation: just trees, birds, the sea beyond. Everything is resolved into absolute simplicities: blue sky, blue sea, and silence.

The monks who live here lead a simple, contemplative life, alone for the most part in their cells, reading, or thinking, or in prayer. They follow the rule laid down by Saint Benedict in the sixth century and extended by Saint Romuald five hundred years later ("Sit in your cell as in Paradise. Put the whole world behind you and forget it. Watch your thoughts as a good fisherman watches for fish"). There are no pious airs here, and most of the twenty or so monks in residence seem cheerful, friendly souls. They serve ice cream and cookies on Sundays, and talk, when they talk, of Raymond Chandler or a trip to Thailand. A Dead Head does odd jobs around the property, and a recluse comes down from the hills now and then to fix the water pipes.

The brothers are also catholic enough in the highest sense to see that everyone belongs here, and to keep nine rooms open to the public. All types assemble for a taste of silence—Buddhist nuns and Oxford scholars, sports-car drivers and even journalists. Each follows his own discipline in his cell, free to attend vigils and vespers if he wishes, free to spend all his hours with whatever he finds uplifting: the Bible or a Sufi text, Emerson or the memory of a love. The brothers let people of any (or no) religious background stay here because, I suspect, they know that everyone will come in contact with something high and pure.

Beyond even the grand extension of space, the great luxury of the monastery is that it takes one out of time: yesterday is tomorrow is next week. Is it 1631, or 2142? One doesn't know, and it doesn't matter. Time is suspended here, and with it, an identity formed by time: no longer John Doe, born in 1952, with a lunch date tomorrow, one is at some level essentialized. Time itself, one sees, the passing of all moments, is all momentary: it is only what is out of time that lasts. The bulldozer of the passing hours razes everything before it except what is belowground or invisible.

And where every moment is particular, so, too, is every movement: the skittering of a whitetail rabbit through the grass; the alighting of a blue jay upon that plant; the wisp of cloud that's curling round my terrace. For the monks, the day is marked out by the pattern of their worship; for the rest of us, only by the tolling of a bell. One learns to tell the hour as a mariner does, by the light above the sea.

It can, of course, be dangerous to live too long in so protected a retreat, so far removed from daily strife. Any serious monk does not seek to leave the world but seeks merely to step out of it awhile, the better to see it, and return with new strength and clear direction. Solitude is only as good as the compassion it releases. The monks here share the fruits of their reflections in counsel and in writings. For a visitor, though, the experience is not just regeneration but recollection: a chance, quite literally, to gather oneself again and recall what is important. Days spent within the code of chastity, poverty, and obedience feel sensuous and rich and free.

Occasionally, a car labors up the steep road that leads up from the narrow highway far below; occasionally, the lights go out. Yet the beauty of the monastery is that nothing ever changes, because there is nothing that can change. I have been here in all seasons and climates: in winter, when the rain hammers on the roof, in summer, when the flies are so thick you cannot sit; on misty mornings and on singing days. Yet what the monastery offers is simple enough, at heart, to seem inviolate: a jubilee of colors and, at night, a sense of the universe as a bowl of stars, rounded, protected somehow, and alight.

The clocks "moved forward" while I was staying in the hermitage this year, but I, like the fox who visits my terrace every night, knew nothing of it. The baseball season started, new governments were formed, presidential candidates came and went. But nothing disturbed the monastery, where white-hooded monks sing prayers at dawn as they might have done ten centuries ago. Many religious groups are approaching the end of the millennium with great apprehensions, fearful of the end of the world; in the monastery, every day feels like the birth of a new world—and a return to an ancient one. In that sense, it is an antimillenarian place, finding no meaning, or solace, or threat, in the arbitrary timing of calendars. The monastery will be here in the year 2000 and, one hopes, in the year 2092. And the mere presence of a sanctuary is as important as the voyage there: to know that bread is handy means one never need go hungry.

(1992)

# PEOPLE

*Norman Lewis: A Curious*
*Collector of Curiosities*

N orman Lewis is a dangerously easy man to idolize, if only because he lives so far from self-idolatry. A writer's writer and a traveler's traveler, in the very strongest senses of those words, he has quietly gone about his business for fifty years now, writing thirteen novels and, more famously, perhaps, ten works of nonfiction that mix beauty and irony in the most elegant of watercolors. Everywhere you go, in time and space, you seem to find Lewis: in Indochina, in the early '50s, negotiating over chrome-plated American cars in a Phnom Penh opium den, then meeting the Vietminh guerrillas through a taxi girl; in Cuba, at the outbreak of the revolution, amiably chatting with Fidel's executioner, an American who sports cuff links made of spent shells; in Togoland, being served on the veranda by "white-coated, whispering stewards who moved as stealthily as Indian stranglers"; in Naples, as a British intelligence officer, presiding over a scene of almost Dantean horrors, in which corpses of grown men were squeezed into child-size coffins and princes begged their sisters to become whores. His sunlit elegies of Vietnam and Burma (*A Dragon Apparent* and *Golden Earth*) were best-sellers in the '50s, and his novel *The Volcanoes Above Us* sold six million copies in the Soviet Union. His eerily knowing account of the Mafia (*The Honoured Society*) was serialized in six enormous parts in *The New Yorker*, and his report on the genocide of Indians in Brazil was at the time the longest article ever published in the *Sunday Times* of London. Lewis wrote about the destruction of the Amazon rain forest ten years before it became a fashionable issue, and his investigations into the elimination of indigenous peoples led to the creation of Survival International. Yet through it all, he has consistently written his seven hundred words a day in a state of "almost monastic calm" in the English countryside, far from the glamour of London's literary circles, far from the headlines. Norman Lewis is one of the world's last unguarded secrets.

Among his peers, Lewis has become a kind of surreptitious hero, and the connoisseurs of modern British writing have vied with one another in their eagerness to laurel him in praise. Cyril Connolly wrote that "Mr. Lewis can make even a lorry interesting," and V. S. Pritchett that "he really goes in deep, like a sharp, polished knife." Auberon Waugh, son of Evelyn, has called him "perhaps the best [travel writer] since Marco

Polo," and the British papers routinely describe him as "the doyen of our travel writers." In recent years, moreover, his reputation has enjoyed a kind of Indian summer, as his early travel books have been reprinted, while his newest pieces have been showcased in magazines like *Granta*. Yet perhaps the greatest compliment of all for this mild-mannered, self-effacing man with the scholarly air, now eighty, comes from the almost legendary British photographer Don McCullin, who has made a career of venturing where mortals fear to tread. "There was one writer who always brought out the best in me," writes McCullin in his recent auto-biography, *Unreasonable Behaviour*, "and in a way I became his disciple." The role model for the swashbuckling war correspondent turns out to be none other than the rigorously unshowy, self-denying Lewis, "the kind of man," as McCullin writes, "you could pass in the street without realizing anybody had gone by." In a tone of near reverence, McCullin describes Lewis, already in his seventies, wading waist deep through Venezuelan rivers, serenely hopping up and down while a tropical fish makes mince-meat of his groin; Lewis imperturbably sitting in a red-light hotel while peasants make rowdy preparations for a cockfight; Lewis visiting a local witch doctor—named Mary Skull—whom even McCullin cannot face.

So when I went to visit the retiring writer, on a drizzly winter after-noon, in his remote village in Essex ("the ugliest county" in England, as he gleefully calls it), I did not know quite what to expect: Lewis so shies away from the spotlight that the library records only two interviews with him over the past three decades, and his entry in *Who's Who* is as short as possible. I was somewhat taken aback, therefore, when a highly courteous man with a wistful smile, in thick sweater and sturdy corduroys, came out into the rain to greet me. As he led me into his four-hundred-year-old Tudor parsonage and graciously sat me down in a room full of African prints, Siamese angels, and Islamic miniatures, I felt myself in the presence of a kind of watchful, kindly owl, with a courtly military bearing. And when I brought out my tape recorder, Lewis peered at it with the same beady-eyed, amused attention that he clearly brings to all his subjects, wondering aloud whether this intriguing machine might save him from the hazards of scribbling down all his notes in the back of an aged car jouncing along unpaved roads, in a hand so unreliable that he cannot read his notes himself by the end of the day. Such delightful dis-comforts he had enjoyed most recently in India, where, typically, he sought out only the most blighted, unvisited, and undeveloped areas, and came back with a vision of pastoral idyll. India is "so glamorous," he said, "so civilized," choosing perhaps the last two adjectives that most travelers would use. The very next week, soon after his eightieth birthday, and just back from Barcelona, he was off, alone, to the wilds of primitive Irian

Jaya, buoyed beyond measure by having read that the local tribesmen had greeted some of their most recent Western visitors—missionaries—by "grabbing them all and executing them and barbecuing them! Thirteen of them! I've certainly got to get to this place!" he said with unfeigned enthusiasm. "Apparently, you've got to hire a helicopter at great cost, but I've got to go to this place and try to talk to someone who was involved in that great tribal meal!"

While awaiting his audience with the missionary-eaters, Lewis was tapping his fingers in an England that, in his idiosyncratic eyes, seems as alien as the Gobi. "Although I've spent most of my life in England," he confessed to me in his soft, rough voice, "I'm temperamentally totally, totally Welsh. I really find very little point of contact with the English temperament. The people I know here actually hunt!" He made them sound far stranger than cannibals. "People living in Wales are almost as different as the Chinese," he continued *sotto voce*. "They adopt a certain amount of natural color and polish, and often the right kind of accent, and *appear* like pukka English people"—his voice dropped to a conspiratorial whisper—"but they're really quite different." He made himself sound like a spy almost, an interloper investigating the strange ways of this tribe known as the English. "I'm probably trying to romanticize it, by the way," he offered cheerily, just as I was falling into the spell, but the Welsh did, he believed, tend to be more nomadic, more evangelical, more ready to cry in public. "I am absolutely an outsider," he concluded with quiet extravagance. "You could safely say that, apart from one or two people who come up from London, I've got no friends!"

Before long, in fact, everything in the house was beginning to take on the peculiar coloring of the Lewis world, and everything seemed fodder for his friendly self-deprecation. His very English-seeming wife came in with tea and scones. "Australian," he confessed as she went out, all but throwing up his hands in helplessness. "My first wife came from a Sicilian family! I don't feel I've organized or engineered this. It just happened." Then his twenty-year-old daughter appeared. "Samara," he explained, "which, as you know, in Arabic means 'dark.' But she is completely blond!" Then he effected an introduction to his retriever, Sheba. He paused for a moment, then added gloomily, "All the dogs in this area are called Sheba."

Lewis's whole life, indeed, as he tells it in his uncommonly strange and riotous autobiography, *Jackdaw Cake*, is one long brocade of fanciful absurdities. His father was a madcap pharmacist who would, claims Lewis, translate the prescriptions of his customers out of Latin, assure them that the prescribed goods were close to poison, and press on them instead a concoction of his own devising; his mother was greatly concerned with the children of Osiris. For part of his childhood, Lewis was sent to be raised by "three insane aunts" in a sullen, close, and incest-haunted Welsh village whose inbred little world of taboos and tribal curses he makes sound as alien as anything in Belize. One aunt was an epileptic, given to running screaming through the house once a day, and one cousin was a retarded boy who would walk with Lewis down shopping streets, hitting matchboxes with a golf club. The main highlight of his hometown, he writes, was "a rubbish dump smouldering incessantly like a pigmy Etna."

When he returned home, to the dreary London suburb that features (coincidentally) in the movie *Life Is Sweet*, it was, he writes, to find that his father had become a proleptic Buddha of Suburbia and now spent much of his time hypnotizing birds, wondering whether jellyfish had souls, and entertaining such professional contacts as "the shaman of the Blackfoot Tribe named Thunder Star, who in a fit of intense mental concentration had caused a small tributary of the Missouri River to run backward." Graduating during the Depression, Lewis saw his friends move on to become an assistant rat-catcher, a crucifix salesman, and a professional punter at the Tottenham Palais de Dance. He himself went into business bottling his father's elixir, taking pictures of weddings, and becoming what *Time* later called "a minor tycoon in photographic supplies." By day he raced motorbikes; by night he entered literary competitions in magazines such as *Titbits*. ("I can safely say that I never won a first prize," he assures me. "I probably won about two or three second prizes—over a long period—and innumerable third and consolation prizes." He could almost be talking of his life.) He also got into the business of buying and selling cars, the first vehicle he owned being a boat-shaped Bugatti whose dashboard was covered with "a pair of lovers in lascivious oriental intertwinings" and whose radiator cap was a representation of the elephant god Ganesha (the addition of its former owner, an Indian). Like all the details in his life, it sounds almost too good to be true.

By his mid-thirties, his circumstances were already irremediable tragicomedy. He married, almost without meaning to, a wild and mercurial Sicilian girl, whose father was a minor mafioso. When he took the Sicilians to meet his parents for the first time, he writes, everything was going swimmingly until his father suddenly started receiving messages from the Other World and began writhing and babbling uncontrollably. He took a message for his father-in-law to a bowler-hatted Italian count (married to a former Miss Italy) who promptly suggested wife swapping, and then he signed on as a photographer to go to North Yemen with Ladislas Farago ("an extremely charming villain," he remembers, who later became an adviser to Nixon and, after fabricating a story about meeting

Martin Bormann in South America, a millionaire). One day, not long after being stuck in the middle of a hurricane in Cuba and hearing about how voodoo dolls could be purchased at the local Woolworth's, Lewis learned that war had broken out in Europe. Hurrying back to Britain to enlist, he was dispatched to Algeria (because he spoke "Adenese bazaar Arabic"—as well, though he rarely mentions it, as Russian, Spanish, French, German, Italian, and even Welsh). His commanding officers in intelligence were—in this rare telling—an expert in Old Norse, an Australian obsessed with coal, and a man who chose to address subordinates while shaving off his pubic hair. His field security officer spent most of the time talking Latin. At war's end, he writes, his doctors told him he "should make no attempt to come to terms with a regulated and sedentary existence." Thus he embarked on the two most unstable of all occupations, traveling and writing.

Lewis assures me now that he had no training in writing. On the steamer to North Yemen, he found books by Somerset Maugham and Ernest Hemingway, and the latter quickly became his hero. (Many years later, he was sent by Ian Fleming to Havana to look in on Hemingway, arrived to find that his contact there, the man who was partially the model for James Bond, had just challenged Papa to a duel, and, when finally he saw the Nobel Prize–winning author, found him so sad that "it was hard to believe that he would ever smile again.") Not rich enough to buy books, he found his only other source of learning in the local library, which, through an eccentric bequest, had none of the English books Lewis wanted to read but an enormous collection of Russian novels, "shelf after shelf, with every Russian novelist, including all the obscure ones." So the young Lewis devoured them all. "I was dazzled by Chekhov, for example, and by comparison with the kind of stories that were being published in English magazines, they were extremely realistic. Even the people in Samarkand or Central Asia, in Chekhov, in highly exotic situations, struck me as eminently believable." And even now, he so loves good prose that he underlines fine sentences in the newspaper.

It is tempting, when first one enters Lewis's books, to see him as one of the last examples of that endangered species, the intrepid English traveler—he was, after all, a near contemporary of Robert Byron, Evelyn Waugh, Peter Fleming, and Wilfred Thesiger. Yet in reality, nothing could be further from the truth. Not just because Lewis feels so estranged from England, but more because he has always lived a universe away from the clubby small world of his traveling compatriots. Where most of them were Eton and Oxford boys who traveled the world with the imperial confidence of empire builders on vacation, and roamed around Ethiopia and Afghanistan safe in the knowledge that there would always be some school friend waiting for them at the next consulate with a gin and tonic, Lewis always traveled alone, grew up humbly, never went to university, and financed all his travels with his own implausible businesses. And where they customarily made their exotic destinations a setting for knockabout comedy or sportive digression, speeding through them in a mood of blithe urbanity, Lewis made foreign cultures his one and only subject. Settling down abroad, disappearing into the background, and unobtrusively living like a local—traveling Burma in a *longhi* skirt, eating food with his hands in India, going on dog-buying expeditions in Vietnam—he acts as if he were one of the natives' most eloquent spokesmen. He seeks not to rule the world but to give himself over to it. And in place of breezy, chatty entertainments, he produced books of lush and highly detailed beauty—textured, contextual, meticulous—in which amusement and affection play upon their subjects like sunlight off a stream.

Indeed, not the least striking thing about his romantic adventures is how little he seems to dwell on them. Lewis's books and travels are stuffed with almost impossibly colorful and curious happenings, yet none of them disturbs the stately and majestic flow of his rich and sturdy paragraphs. In his autobiography, he devotes exactly one and a half pages to the last thirty-five years of his life, and one paragraph to his divorce; burnished and polished till it shines, his prose simply rolls on, sonorous and imperturbable, through every event and emotion: in all the twelve books of his that I have read, I have never found a cheap or careless sentence (it is almost too fitting, in fact, that in the card catalogue, he is easily confused with another Norman Lewis, born just one year later, who wrote a book called *Power with Words*). There is something deeply settled about Lewis's persona and his level prose that underwrites all his wandering, and something old-fashioned about his ability (like Colin Thubron) to fashion the most dignified of sentences while traveling third class. Out of marvels he makes melodies.

If you read the books very carefully, you will notice that Lewis contracted malaria three times, fractured his skull in a car crash, and saw his skin and the whites of his eyes turn yellow. He saw men brain one another with the femurs of corpses and the howling procession of a bush devil. Yet none of this detains him for more than a sentence or causes his prose to lose its breath or poise. It is this almost implausible sense of reticence, together with his brush mustache and his air of gracious decency, that gives Lewis something of the sepia glamour of the strong, silent type in an old British war movie, tall, observant, good in an emergency, and full of sympathetic fortitude (one of the great ironies of his life is that this most implacable of Empire-haters embodies the very qualities of open-mindedness and honesty that made the Empire work: he is the kind of upstanding, understanding type who seems to belong to a Paul Scott novel). The most impressive thing about his knowledge of obscure places is how little he seems impressed by his own place in them: even the British reviewers, so suspicious of self-display, have sometimes complained that he is almost *too* modest. "I may be selfish," he told me matter-of-factly, "but I don't think I've got a normal, average ego."

It is this kind of stiff-upper-lip sangfroid that distinguishes Lewis's first two Asia books, which are still, in many ways, the best introduction to his work. Traveling to Vietnam and Burma in the early '50s, when both were still isolated and undiscovered (much as he is), he came back with what is still, forty years on, the definitive portrait of Indochina in all its sleepy, riverine languor, and Burma's unworldly charm (he completed a trilogy with his tour around a timeless India). Lewis has always seemed to have a soft spot for lazy, shady, spellbound lands—he still schedules his trips so as to escape the gloom of the English winter—and he seems to warm up to cultures that enjoy a kind of easygoing tropical morality, far from the puritanism and "joyless prosperity" of the north. Somehow, one always sees him in the sun, in some quiet rural setting, surrounded by people in festival mood (both the Laotians and certain Indians, he claims, regard it as ill bred to work). And everywhere he goes, he follows no agenda but the satisfaction of curiosity. When I asked him, for example, if he'd ever write on South Africa, he looked astonished. "To write well about a thing, I've got to like it. I'm not going to be infuriated all the time."

Those first books, moreover, lay out all the distinctive features of his universe: the stoicism, the delight in beautiful absurdity, the sense of sunlit requiem. Though he scarcely mentions it (three separate Indochinese rebellions "made traveling conditions sometimes arduous," he writes negligently), Lewis slept in rooms full of scorpions and rats, crouched like a hermit crab in a hole in the back of a bus, aware that if bandits attacked, he would be the first to be killed, and ventured blithely into war zones, encouraged in one instance by the advice of a man named Oh Oh, who assured him that he was in no danger of an ambush (but was very likely to get attacked). Over the course of his travels, I have noticed, Lewis has drunk black frog spawn, munched *qat* leaves, and eaten Belizean rodents, locusts en brochette, camel-hump fat, and lamb's testicles. In India, as a septuagenarian, he happily went to all the murderous areas that even Indians shun.

Lewis, in fact, is one of those even-tempered travelers who seem almost to relish things going wrong—the fact that the pilot scarcely knows what he's doing, or the maid barges in at dead of night, "bearing a raw potato on a silver tray." He is the most equitable of travelers, partly because he is the least provincial of souls (he actually apologized to me for having had to spend one night in a deluxe hotel in Calcutta). And so complete and omnivorous is his absorption in the world around him that he manages, understatedly, to assemble a mosaic of unlikely details. In Burma, a monk carrying around a "biscuit tin commemorating the coronation of King Edward VII, on which had been screwed a plaque with the inscription in English: 'God is Life, Light and Infinite Magnet' "; in Vietnam, a group of village children being taught to breathe, some local beauties putting on a version of *Oklahoma!*, and thirty-seven schoolchildren singing, under a ritually polished buffalo skull, "Auld Lang Syne," in French. The world he finds is at once utterly plausible and utterly strange, perfect material for his hilarious, deadpan wit. In Vietnam, for example, he is especially fascinated by the Cao Dai religion, which worships Buddha, Jesus, the Jade Emperor, Victor Hugo, and La Rochefoucauld, among others. At dinner one night, he finds himself next to a devotee who asks after Victor Hugo. " 'I am a reincarnation of a member of the poet's family,' the young man said. I congratulated him and asked if he also wrote." It is not hard, with his mix of dry humor and propriety, to see why his best friend (when he admits to one) was S. J. Perelman.

Yet however much he revels in the oddity of things, in the end Lewis catches most of all a sense of rural quiet, and of Eden. "A distant clock chimed sweetly an incorrect hour." "Sometimes, as the car passed a scarlet thicket of cactus and geraniums, a nightingale scattered a few notes through the window." "All day and all through the night the cool sound of gongs comes over the water from unseen Moi villages." His sentences take flight on lyric wings. Luang Prabang was "a tiny Manhattan—but a Manhattan with holy men in yellow in its avenues, with pariah dogs, and garlanded pedicabs carrying somnolent Frenchmen nowhere, and doves in its sky." "Down in the village," he writes of Ibiza, "life moved on with the placid rhythm of a digestive process," and his prose has this same almost vegetative calm, soaking up the cadences of the unhurried villages that to him have all the timeless rhythms of a paradise.

Yet all paradises are made to be lost, and if most of Lewis's travel books are love songs, they are also elegies, memorials to a purity threatened or already gone. All his books have this sense of dusk in them, of coming darkness; he went to Indochina and Burma, he wrote at the time, because he feared that their fragile cultures would soon be lost or else closed off to the world (and in both suspicions he was right). Cultures are often protected, he believes, by insurgency, pestilence, and bad government, and "progress" often marks the beginning of the end for them. Perhaps the strongest expression in all his books comes in the preface to a reissued collection of journalism, in which he sorrowfully, and unequivocally, repudiates his earlier belief that any place could ever remain unspoiled.

So intense is this sense of loss that he finds the same pattern even in England. He bought his present house thirty-three years ago, he tells me, in part because he saw a green woodpecker in the garden, "the only exotic bird in England," and in it he saw a way to cultivate his fondness for "plants and all growing things." To this day, he brings back samples from his travels and plants them in his garden, a third of which he has turned into overgrowth to "encourage the presence of the occasional fox, rabbits, birds." At its best, he finds himself still living in a kind of rustic paradise. "I like to walk around the countryside," he tells me. "If there are any birds or flowers, I make a note of them, and look at the scenery; think; and go home." And even in England he finds traces of the protected, medieval village that attracts him everywhere. "Even now there are people here whose surnames I don't know—incredible!" No one haggles, or worries about race, he says; "the people we deal with here are an extremely kind people," and best of all, most things in the village "are more or less as they were seven hundred years ago."

Yet here, too, he has seen the unfallen vision fade. When he arrived, he says, "wherever you went for a walk, there used to be hares gamboling around hedges. Now everything's gone. No flowers: they've all been sprayed out of existence." Worse still, the ancient rhythms of the place have been disrupted by "people from the city, with their different morality, and different standards, and the commercialism that goes with supermarkets. With every decade that goes past, the village is 25 percent uglier than the decade before." The area's new medical building, he says, "looks like a paramount chief's kraal in Zambesi. It's totally exotic, and it's the wrong kind of exoticism. Its unsuitability is extreme." Then, just as he's getting most passionate, he gives me his godfatherly twinkle. "Mind you," he says, "that's a typically exaggerated response."

Thus Lewis's primary role, in a sense, is that of a caretaker or protector of endangered cultures, practices, and peoples; more and more, this former photographer and camera salesman seems to be traveling to places to rescue them, or at least to bring back snapshots of a vanished world. While some travel writers ornament and structure their impressions around history (as Jan Morris, say), and others literature (Paul Theroux), or even personal and natural history (Bruce Chatwin), Lewis is closest to an anthropologist, a student of the human animal who loves its most pagan and atavistic forms ("backward" is for him a term of highest praise). Medicine men and superstitions are his thing, animist rites and secret societies (from Liberia to the Mafia). And where a writer like Morris, say, or even Theroux, is most at home in cities, catching the beat of dinner parties, buildings, and bright stimulations, Lewis is very much a pastoralist, drawn to the age-old rhythms of the village. (Part of the freshness of his Indian book comes from the fact that he never even visits Delhi, Varanasi, or Bombay, and never bothers, therefore, with the standard meditation on Indian energy and poverty; the India Lewis sees is not overcrowded but lonely, and the books he cites, living in his own untrendy world, are not those of Naipaul, Rushdie, or Chaudhuri, but authors like Ibn Battuta, in the fourteenth century, and seventeenth-century Portuguese travelers.) Like the best anthropologists, moreover, Lewis takes great pains to travel light, deferring to village customs (he always, one notices, uses local honorifics) and leaving his sense of right and wrong at home: in Naples, for example, he realizes that to refuse a bribe is to throw the system into chaos, and in India, to his delight, he finds tribal peoples for whom the ultimate sin is sexual fidelity. His gifts are not analytical; they are, rather, appreciative, those of an extremely patient, careful, tolerant observer who simply records details without passing judgment on them.

Indeed, if there is one flaw in all his writing, it is, I think, that he sympathizes so deeply and fully with aboriginal peoples, and is so put out by the threat of an air-conditioned future, that he comes close to creating an almost Manichaean struggle between "the gentle backward civilizations" and "shy primitive people," on the one hand, and the "juggernaut" of the modern world, on the other. The only people he seems not to savor are his own people, and, at times, one almost feels that he agrees with the Burmese (who regard foreigners as not quite human), or the Guatemalans (who think of tourists as nothing more than "ghosts"). At times, indeed, he appears so painfully aware of the dangers of "civilization" and so opposed to all forms of colonialism (not least the kind practiced by tourists) that the "poor, but supremely happy" natives seem almost too charmed to be true. When he writes, say, that Vietnamese armies used to carry lanterns at night to give their enemies a fighting chance to see them, or that cyclo drivers in Cambodia used to tip their passengers, one begins to suspect that his kindly eye can somehow see kindness everywhere, and that the other man's garden is always greener. Sometimes, in fact, slapping off "the bourgeoisie" like so many flies, roughing it at any cost, and finding ways to live in Ibiza for a few pesetas a summer, this most gentlemanly of Old World scholars sounds like a classic hippie.

The paradigm of this process is captured in his book *Voices of the Old Sea*, an account of three summers he spent forty years ago as a fisherman in a tiny Spanish village. The book is, in effect, a wrenchingly detailed autopsy on the ruins of a place he loved. It is the tale of a decent and good-natured man who tries to build up the unspoiled village into a tourist site, importing foreign guitars to a place that has never known their music, turning restaurants into Moorish cafés, and bringing in dancing bears—turning the village into a version of the Spain that foreigners expect. Soon the primitive, Chaucerian world that Lewis first entered (where there was a taboo against wearing leather, and the fishermen, he says, spoke in blank verse, and village enchanters could be found) becomes a replica of itself, the locals are learning about bikinis and public kisses from wealthy French holidaymakers, and fishermen are turned into bellboys, exiles in their own home. I happen to be one of those who believe that the horrors of tourism are all too easily exaggerated and that, in fact, the trade often brings benefits as well as sorrows, quickening an interest in customs that may have long lain dormant, and providing people with a sense of choice, and opportunity, as well as the facilities that we, in our comfort, would often wish to deny them. Nonetheless, it is almost impossible to resist the heartrending cadences of Lewis's lament, and his sadness as his second summer ends and he knows that the third can never be the same again. "The sun had crisped away the last of the stubble from Don Alberto's land . . . and the dry clicking of a water-wheel turned by a donkey sounded like the solemn tick-tock of a grandfather clock deep in the ears."

Not surprisingly, Lewis is the first to disparage this tendency in his own writing—"Every third Welshman would like the opportunity to get up in the pulpit, and I may be affected by that to some extent"—and frankly volunteers that he went through the whole of his manuscript on India, "cutting out numerous passages in which I thought I was taking a moral stance." Yet the fact remains that in recent years his traveling has assumed more of a crusading aspect, and as well as being an observer, he is more and more a kind of witness. As he grows older, his lovely, careless rambles have acquired a greater sense of moral urgency, and his sympathy for embattled peoples has turned into a quiet indignation on their behalf. The focus of this outrage has been very much the missionaries (the people most likely to affront someone who dislikes self-righteousness in any form and takes especial care not to impose on another culture's values). Lewis has always been a glinting-eyed opponent to religion (the result, perhaps, of being the one skeptic in a household of fundamentalists); and he can hardly conceal his delight when the cry of the muezzin in Tunisia, due to a technical malfunction, intones only, "There is no God," or when "God is Love" becomes, in tribal translation, "The Great Spirit is not angry." The fishermen of Ibiza, he notes admiringly, were "almost savagely anti-Catholic" and regarded it as an ill omen even to set eyes on a priest; and one of the things that seem to have won him over to his first wife was that she "despised religion." Lewis has always regarded missionaries as mercenaries of a kind, pledged to a conversion that is in effect corrosion, and so to a kind of ethnocide. And in his most impassioned works, he has conducted painstaking research to show how the very group set up to protect the Indians in Brazil went about exploiting—and even exterminating—them, while various American religious groups in South America have gone about conquering souls with the help of shirts infected with the smallpox virus and poisoned candies. Still, when I asked him about his literary influences, the one he singled out was the King James Bible. "I am probably one of the few non-Christians who has read the Bible through, most of it two or three times," he said, beaming. "Because it is superbly written, and the stories it contains are excellent."

In a sense, indeed, Lewis has so strong an attraction to the extraordinary, and is so drawn to life *in extremis*, that his writing often acquires an almost theological intensity, as if some of the places he knew were suspended in a state of Arcadian purity, while others were lost in a fury of hellish confusion. If part of his vision seems drawn from Poussin, part of it seems derived from Bosch. And as one goes through his writing, one finds horrifying accounts of cruelty and terror almost beyond imagining: teenagers performing decapitations, men biting one another's throats out, or (a typical Lewis irony) men who have eaten human flesh refusing liver on religious grounds. The epicenter of this can be found in his coruscating book about the war, *Naples '44*. In it, he registers imbecilities of war madder and more horrifying than anything in Heller or Pynchon, and the more terrible for their calm. Naples, by 1944, was in his account a city reduced to an almost medieval state of poverty and desperation, a place of exorcisms and evil eyes in which three out of every four young fiancées had entered a brothel, and a father of five was supporting his family on "just over one pound a month." Even the local aquarium was empty, looted by starving citizens. As he describes all this in his tone of clenched pity, Lewis develops a scene of almost unimaginable horror, in which glass-eyed girls try to sell themselves and lunatics roam the streets (there being no room in the town's asylum). Midget gynecologists ply their wares, and grown men work as professional mourners. "Churches are suddenly full of images that talk, bleed, sweat, nod their heads and exude health-giving liquors." And at the end of his twelve months there, he writes, as only he would do, "Were I given the chance to be born again and to choose the place of my birth, Italy would be the country of my choice."

The madness of war also provided him with plenty of material to satisfy his taste for irony. In the Jacobean chaos of a world turned upside down, lawlessness became the order of the day. The papal legate drove on stolen tires. The Allied command talked of using infected trollops to sap the enemy's strength. Soldiers were given guns they had never been shown how to use, and infantrymen raced into battle armed with mouth organs. While the innocent were hounded, murderers were set free. "In houses said to contain caches of arms we found nothing more lethal than unemptied babies' chamber-pots; while flashing lights in the night were always people on their way to the cess-pit at the bottom of the garden." The absurdity of war astonishes him even now. Just a week before I visited, he tells me, he picked up the *Sunday Times* and read about an aristocratic English armored unit in the Gulf commanded by a man who prefaced his orders with a blast on a hunting horn he'd inherited from his grandfather. "Can you imagine it?" he says in wonder. "This fellow with his hunting horn! He's got one hundred fifty tons of tank he's going to ride in, and he's facing Iraqis, who have a totally different attitude towards life, and what is he doing? He's back in Balaclava, he's about to indulge, essentially, in a Charge of the Light Brigade! It's grotesque!" He shakes his head. "A hunting horn!"

The final black irony of the Italian campaign, according to Lewis, was that, in the madness of a world turned into a death's-head mask, the Allied forces actually set about rehabilitating the Mafia (which Mussolini had almost succeeded in destroying); an illiterate mafioso was installed as mayor of Palermo, and half the cities in Sicily were given mayors with Mafia connections. This topsy-turviness became the occasion for Lewis's most fiercely reported book, *The Honoured Society*, in which he does for the Mafia what Margaret Mead did for the Samoans. Clearly, a world in which a criminal organization was called "the honoured society" and gangsters were looked up to as "men of respect" could hardly fail to appeal to a collector of anomalies like Lewis, and he was guaranteed to respond with relish to an island in which monks carried heavy automatics, became lira millionaires, and set up clubs for the exchange of obscene letters. The Mafia, for their part, rented out seats for confession, sold bloody relics of "stigmata," and produced sixty fingers belonging to Saint John the Baptist and forty heads of Saint Julian. In one town, he claims, every citizen wore black; in another, Mussolini was told that not a single man had died of natural causes in the previous ten years (Il Duce himself required Mafia protection). As one mafioso memorably put it, "We were a single body, bandits, police and Mafia, like the Father, the Son, and the Holy Ghost."

For all this, though, one feels that Lewis could not help being fascinated by the sheer bravado of the Mob, and I remembered his saying that he could not write about something that he did not like. "The prison of Palermo," he reports almost with admiration, "had in fact become almost a Mafia university where apprentice members received refresher courses in the latest developments in crime"; it also served as a kind of "rest home" in which killers would settle for a while, ordering in women and fine meals, firing wardens they didn't like, and, in one case, sauntering out again for a couple of years to conduct banditry in the hills. And Lewis, always ready to interpret foreign codes, found a backhanded order in their crookedness. The Mafia had become "a kind of beleaguered landed gentry," he writes, who still followed "the sacred law of vendetta" and had "an iron morality of their own." Only when some of them began to go to America, and grow more ruthless and rapacious, did they forfeit their sense of honor (even the Mafia, in his book, isn't what it used to be—having been corrupted by America!). Treating the Mafia as seriously as a tribe in Mali (which in many ways it resembles), Lewis excavates its rites with scrupulous vitality.

Yet for all the decline and depravity he's witnessed, Lewis does, in the end, seem the cheeriest of souls, as open to adventure as a boy, and as ready to give trust and sympathy as one who's never been betrayed. "I'm a sort of happy pessimist," he tells me brightly. "I don't believe anything's going to get better, but I'm fighting a rearguard action against absurdity and ugliness." Again and again, as he explained to me why Cubans are so handsome, or how he had once driven "a colossal Buick, a fireball, eight-liter engine, going about a hundred and twenty miles an hour," into a chicken-wire fence on his way to see Cesar Chavez in California, he returned to how "kind" people were, how "charming," how "the poor of the earth tend to be, to some extent, capable of such kindness!" When I asked if he'd still want to be reborn in Italy, he said, "They are very humanitarian still, the Italians, generally speaking," and told of how the Neapolitans had risked their lives to protect Allied soldiers from the Germans.

Even though he can hardly comprehend English pubs in Greece and *Bierkeller* in Phuket ("Alpine houses in the tropics, with sand and sea all around, and roofs specially designed to stand the weight of snow!"), when I asked him if he thought travel writing itself was on the verge of extinction, he gave a vigorous no. "I can think of all kinds of places where people have never been!" Even in Seville in 1981, he found "mystic carpet-baggers, 'cosmobiologists,' whirling dervishes, American fundamentalists howling for Armageddon, and sects dating from the pre-Christian era," and even there, in modern Europe, he could conjure up visions of Elysium—"Orange blossom bespattered the cobbles, and there was a champagne sparkle of May in the air." And though he does sound wistful about the fact that both Vietnam and Burma, which found their fondest and most utopian of voices in his books, have consistently refused him reentry (at the same time that Vietnam admits the very men who fought against it recently), he bears them no ill will. Travel, he says, "has become to some extent like taking an aspirin—you develop a certain degree of addiction." And it has also, he adds with characteristic modesty, taught him how to "develop a certain amount of vision. I learned from Don McCullin how beautiful the ordinary can be. Previously, the only things that attracted me were nonordinary things, exotic things. But traveling with him, I would see him suddenly spellbound by the beauty of rain drizzling down a mountainside."

After finishing his book on Indonesia, he suspects, he'll probably write a novel, very possibly one about English life. ("I hated the place so much previously, I couldn't bear to write about it. But I think I've come to terms with myself, and therefore I would probably be able to write a readable novel about England. But mind you"—he all but winks—"it would be full of fantastic characters!") One of the strange things about his career is that having written travel through the '50s, he spent twenty years more or less writing novels, and then, in the late '70s, went back to nonfiction, much of it devoted to events of thirty years before. His explanation of this was typically down-to-earth. "Whenever I go anywhere, I take an immense amount of notes, most of which I can't reread anyway. Then I come back, and instead of promptly filing them away, I chuck them in a cupboard. So possibly years go by before I find a notebook." The other strange thing about his writing is that his novels, though brisk and well paced, are to my mind more uniform, more everyday, and more obviously dated than his travel books, as if fiction put a bridle over his imagination, while nonfiction excites and expands it. One of the few ideas he ventures anywhere in his books is that humor is in inverse proportion to ambition.

The image of a writer sitting quietly alone, balancing memories and novels, is particularly apt, though, because in the final analysis, the one writer who most closely resembles Lewis is Graham Greene. Not just because both were intelligence officers during the war who wrote about the absurdity of British operations; and not just because both moved from Saigon to Havana to West Africa through the '50s, the decade that seems quintessentially theirs, and assuaged boredom by exposing themselves to so many dangers that they continue going strong even in old age. But more deeply because both men have fashioned the kind of sensibility that arises from prolonged exposure to the underdeveloped world: both have an instinctive compassion for the dispossessed or downtrodden, and both have a soft spot for the amiable crooks and quixotes who become one's friends in countries such as Spain; both have mourned the naïveté of U.S. foreign policy around the world and are firmly convinced that the

CIA is the root of all evil (Lewis's best-selling novel was based on the Greene-ish theme of U.S. involvement in Central America); and both, finally, have translated their sympathy for the individual into a full-bodied championing of embattled people and worthy causes. Lewis's name itself (an anagram, one notices, of "New is Normal") is so perfectly, redoubtably British as to seem to spring from Greene's imagination; and the missionaries he meets in Vietnam, "Mr. and Mrs. Jones," seem on their way to a part in Greene's novel *The Comedians* (as Mr. and Mrs. Smith). Even the titles of his novels (set in revolutionary hot spots from Algiers to Cuba, Siam to Italy) seem torn from one of Greene's notebooks: *A Suitable Case for Corruption, Every Man's Brother.* It is tempting, in fact, to call Lewis, in a sense, the secular Greene, or the unknown Greene, a Greene without the religion, or the anguished moral questioning.

It is doubly fitting, then, that some of the finest words on Lewis were delivered, as it happens, by Greene himself, praising, of all unlikely things, his attack on missionaries. "I have no hesitation," wrote the world's preeminent novelist three years ago, "in calling Norman Lewis one of the best writers, not of any particular decade, but of our century. His work, I hope, will be fully appreciated during the '90s." Certainly, the '90s are as good a time as any for readers to lose themselves in the gentle wonders of his world and the pleasures of his regal prose. When I left him that afternoon, he walked me out into a steady downpour. "Ah, a light rain," he said appreciatively, guiding me to my car. "In Sicily, in a rain like this, a man will always walk as slowly as possible, to show he isn't affected." And as the car pulled away, and I saw him standing in the driveway in the rain, on his way to Irian Jaya, I thought back to the line of Edgar's at the end of *Lear:* "we that are young / Shall never see so much nor live so long."

(1991)

Dogs bark in the Himalayan night. Lights flicker across the hillside. On a pitch-black path framed by pines and covered by a bowl of stars, a few ragged pilgrims shuffle along, muttering ritual chants. Just before dawn, as the snowcaps behind take on a deep-pink glow, the crowd that has formed outside the three-story Namgyal Temple in northern India falls silent. A strong, slightly stooping figure strides in, bright eyes alertly scanning the crowd, smooth face breaking into a broad and irrepressible smile. Followed by a group of other shaven-headed monks, all of them in claret robes and crested yellow hats, the newcomer clambers up to the temple roof. There, as the sun begins to rise, his clerics seated before him and the solemn, drawn-out summons of long horns echoing across the valley below, the Dalai Lama leads a private ceremony to welcome the Year of the Earth Dragon.

On the second day of Losar, the Tibetan New Year, the man who is a living god to roughly fourteen million people gives a public audience. By 8 a.m., the line of petitioners stretches for half a mile along the winding mountain road outside his airy bungalow—leathery mountain men in gaucho hats, long-haired Westerners, little girls in their prettiest silks, all the six thousand residents of the village and thousands more. Later, thirty dusty visitors just out of Tibet crowd inside and, as they set eyes on their exiled leader for the first time in almost three decades, fill the small room with racking sobs and sniffles. Through it all, Tenzin Gyatso, the absolute spiritual and temporal ruler of Tibet, incarnation of the Tibetan god of compassion and fourteenth Dalai Lama in a line that stretches back hundreds of years, remains serene.

In Tibet, he explains later, Losar used to be conducted on the roof of the thirteen-story Potala Palace, with cookies laid out for the masses. "Every year, I used to be really worried when the people rushed to grab the cookies. First, that the old building would collapse, and second, that someone would fall over the edge. Now"—the rich baritone breaks into a hearty chuckle—"now things are much calmer."

It was twenty-nine years ago last week that the Tibetan uprising against China's occupying forces propelled the Dalai Lama into Indian exile. Yet the spirit of his ancient, fairy-tale theocracy is still very much alive in Dharamsala, a former British hill station 250 miles north of New

Delhi. Here, attended by a state oracle, a rainmaking lama, various medicine men, body guards, and a four-man cabinet, the Dalai Lama incarnates all the beliefs and hopes of his imperiled homeland, much as he has done since first ascending the Lion Throne in Lhasa at the age of four.

Yet even as the "Protector of the Land of Snows" sustains all the secret exoticism of that otherworldly kingdom reimagined in the West as Shangri-la, he remains very much a leader in the real world. Since the age of fifteen, he has been forced to deal with his people's needs against the competing interests of Beijing, Washington, and New Delhi. That always inflammable situation reached a kind of climax last fall, when Tibetans rioted in Lhasa, their Chinese rulers killed as many as thirty-two people, the Dalai Lama held his first major press conference in Dharamsala, and the U.S. Senate unanimously condemned the Chinese actions. Yet even before that, the modest man in monk's raiment had found himself not only the spiritual symbol linking 100,000 Tibetans in exile to the six million still living under Chinese rule, but also, more than ever, a political rallying point. "The fourteenth Dalai Lama may be the most popular Dalai Lama of all," he says, smiling merrily. "If the Chinese had treated the Tibetans like real brothers, then the Dalai Lama might not be so popular. So"—he twinkles impishly—"all the credit goes to the Chinese!"

On paper, then, the Dalai Lama is a living incarnation of a Buddha, the hierarch of a government-in-exile, and a doctor of metaphysics. Yet the single most extraordinary thing about him may simply be his sturdy, unassuming humanity. The Living God is, in his way, as down-to-earth as the hardy brown oxfords he wears under his monastic robes, and in his eyes is still the mischief of the little boy who used to give his lamas fits with his invincible skills at hide-and-seek. He delights in tending his flower gardens, looking after wild birds, repairing watches and transistors, and, mostly, just meditating. And even toward those who have killed up to 1.2 million of his people and destroyed all but thirteen of his 6,254 monasteries, he remains remarkably forbearing. "As people who practice the Mahayana Buddhist teaching, we pray every day to develop some kind of unlimited altruism," he says. "So there is no point in developing hatred for the Chinese. Rather, we should develop respect for them, and love and compassion."

The fourteenth god-king of Tibet was born in a cowshed in the tiny farming village of Takster in 1935. When he was two, a search party of monks, led to his small home by a corpse that seemed to move, a lakeside vision, and the appearance of auspicious cloud formations, identified him as the new incarnation of Tibet's patron deity. Two years later, after passing an elaborate battery of tests, the little boy was taken amidst a caravan of hundreds into the capital, Lhasa, "Home of the Gods." There he had to live alone with his immediate elder brother in the cavernous, thousand-chamber Potala Palace and undertake an eighteen-year course in metaphysics. By the age of seven, he was receiving envoys from President Franklin Roosevelt and leading prayers before twenty thousand watchful monks; yet he remained a thoroughly normal little boy, who loved to whiz around the holy compound in a pedal car and instigate fights with his siblings. "I recall one summer day—I must have been about seven—when my mother took me to the Norbulingka summer palace to see His Holiness," recalls the Dalai Lama's youngest brother, Tenzin Chogyal. "When we got there, His Holiness was watering his plants. The next thing I knew, he was turning the hose on me!"

It was at this time, too, that the precocious boy first displayed his prodigious gift for things scientific, teaching himself the principles of the combustion engine and fixing the palace's generator whenever it went on the blink. To satisfy his insatiable curiosity about a world he was permitted to glimpse only through the silk-fringed curtains of his golden palanquin, the young ruler set up a projector on which he eagerly devoured Tarzan movies, *Henry V*, and, best of all, home movies of his own capital. Often, he recalls, he would take a telescope onto the palace roof and wistfully gaze at the boys and girls of Lhasa carelessly going about their lives.

In 1950, the isolation of the "Wish-Fulfilling Gem" and his mountain kingdom was shattered as the Chinese attacked from eight different directions. Suddenly the teenage ruler was obliged to take a crash course in statesmanship, traveling to Beijing to negotiate with Zhou Enlai and Mao Zedong. Finally, in March 1959, when a bloody confrontation seemed imminent as thirty thousand steadfast Tibetans rose up against Chinese rule, the Dalai Lama slipped out of his summer palace dressed as a humble soldier and set off across the highest mountains on earth. Two weeks later, suffering from dysentery and on the back of a dzo, a hybrid yak, the "Holder of the White Lotus" rode into exile in India.

Since then, his has been a singularly delicate balancing act, as the guest of a nation that would prefer him to remain silent and the enemy of a nation that much of the world is trying to court. Undeterred, the Dalai Lama has organized fifty-three Tibetan settlements in India and Nepal and set up institutes to preserve his country's arts, its scriptures, and its medical traditions. In recent years he has begun to race around the world like a Buddhist John Paul II—lecturing at Harvard, meeting the Pope, and attending to his flock, be they unlettered peasants or the American actor Richard Gere (a student of Buddhism since 1982). Always inclined to see the good in everything, he feels that exile has in some respects been a blessing. "When we were in Tibet, there were certain ceremonial activities that took up a lot of time, but the substance was not much. All those exist no longer. That's good, I think. Also, because we are refugees, we have become much more realistic. There's no point now in pretending."

Many young Tibetans would like their leader to be more militant. Angrily noting that there are more than 3,000 political prisoners in central Tibet alone and that Beijing has at least 300,000 troops on the "Rooftop of the World," they advocate violence. But the Dalai Lama refuses to be intemperate. "Once your mind is dominated by anger," he notes thoughtfully, "it becomes almost mad. You cannot take right decisions, and you cannot see reality. But if your mind is calm and stable, you will see everything exactly as it is. I think all politicians need this kind of patience. Compared with the previous Soviet leaders, for example, Gorbachev, I think, is much more calm. Therefore, more effective."

Pacifism, however, does not mean passivity. "Ultimately," he continues, "the Chinese have to realize that Tibet is a separate country. If Tibet was always truly a part of China, then, whether Tibetans liked it or not, they would have to live with it. But that's not the case. So we have every right to demand our rights."

The Dalai Lama spends much of his time reflecting on how Tibetan Buddhism can teach, and learn from, other disciplines. He believes, for example, that Buddhism can show Marxism how to develop a genuine socialist ideal, "not through force but through reason, through a very gentle training of the mind, through the development of altruism." He sees many points of contact between his faith and "psychology, cosmology, neurobiology, the social sciences, and physics. There are many things we Buddhists should learn from the latest scientific findings. And scientists can learn from Buddhist explanations. We must conduct research and then accept the results. If they don't stand up to experimentation," he says, beaming subversively, "Buddha's own words must be rejected."

Such quiet radicalism has at times unsettled followers so devout that they would readily give up their lives for their leader. In the draft constitution he drew up in 1963, the god-king included, against his people's wishes, a clause that would allow for his impeachment. Now he is considering new methods for choosing the next Dalai Lama—adopting an electoral system similar to the Vatican's, perhaps, or selecting on the basis of seniority, or even dispensing with the entire institution. "I think the time has come, not necessarily to take a decision very soon, but to start a more formal discussion, so that people can prepare their minds for it."

In the meantime, the exiled leader will continue to pursue a simple, selfless life that is close to the Buddhist ideal of the Middle Way—neither hostile to the world nor hostage to it. Buddhism's supreme living deity still refuses to fly first class and thinks of himself always, as he told the press last fall, as a "simple Buddhist monk." Though he is one of the most erudite scholars of one of the most cerebral of all the world's philosophies, he has a gift for reducing his doctrine to a core of lucid practicality, crystallized in the title of his 1984 book, *Kindness, Clarity and Insight.* "My true religion," he has said, "is kindness."

It is, in fact, the peculiar misfortune of the Chinese to be up against one of those rare souls it is all but impossible to dislike. Beijing has felt it necessary to call him a "political corpse, bandit, and traitor," a "red-handed butcher who subsisted on people's flesh." Yet everyone who meets the Dalai Lama is thoroughly disarmed by his good-natured warmth, and by a charisma all the stronger for being so gentle.

To an outsider, the life of a living godhead can seem a profoundly lonely one. In recent years, moreover, nearly all the people closest to the Tibetan ruler—his senior tutor, his junior tutor, his mother, and the elder brother who in youth was his only playmate—have died. Yet this, like everything else, the Dalai Lama takes, in the deepest sense, philosophically. "It's just like the days. An old day passes, a new day arrives. The important thing is to make it meaningful: a meaningful friend—or a meaningful day."

(1988)

*Peter Matthiessen:*
*In Search of the Crane*

W e'd heard from a Mongolian ornithologist," says the writer, and you
know there's only one major American novelist who could be speaking,
"that there were quite a number of cranes in the eastern part of Mongolia. So we spent two weeks exploring the river systems there. There are
only fifteen species of crane, and seven of them are seriously endangered.
And they're all very beautiful—the biggest flying creatures on earth—and
they seem to me a wonderful metaphor. They require a lot of space, a lot
of wilderness and clean water." They are symbols of longevity. "And
about half the population's on the mainland, the other half's in Japan."
He smiles. "They've probably been separated for millions of years. I like
that. It humbles one."

Peter Matthiessen is talking on a leisurely Sunday afternoon, in a
secluded sunlit space on the lawn of his six-acre Long Island compound.
His shaggy black yakling of a dog, Tess of the Baskervilles, is sitting at his
feet, and he is stretching out his long, strikingly lean—somewhat crane-
like—legs into the sun, picking up clumps of grass as he talks, and now
and then turning off the tape recorder with a desultory toe. Already this
week he's been to Idaho and Colorado, to attend conferences on freedom
of speech and the American novel. He's enjoyed a "very nice evening"
with Salman Rushdie, and turned in a 132-page manuscript to *Condé
Nast Traveler* on his recent trip to Mustang, in eastern Nepal, from
which he brought back photographs of prints that may support the existence of the yeti. He has two books just off the presses—on Siberia and
Africa—and in between working on the second part of his semifictional
"Watson Trilogy," he is preparing to lead a tour group into remote
Bhutan, for more investigations of the crane.

Not far away is the converted stable that is his meditation hall: after
twenty years of study, Matthiessen was, three years ago, formally accred-
ited as a Zen teacher. His Zen name—Muryo, or "Without Bounda-
ries"—seems inspired. For what other Zen-minded patriarch can claim to
be a founding editor of the *Paris Review*? How many other American
novelists have written whole books in Caribbean patois (and influenced
by the principles of classical Japanese art)? How many other *New Yorker*
writers have written of their LSD trips? And which other scion of the
eastern ruling class has devoted 628 pages and seven years of libel suits to

defending the name of a young American Indian charged with murder? While others pursue careers, Matthiessen has forged a path, and often it seems a high, chill path through what he calls "some night country on the dark side of the earth that all of us have to go to all alone."

The two words that friends invariably use when describing this rare bird are "Wasp" and "patrician," and Matthiessen's voice alone resounds with the kind of arrowhead sternness they hardly seem to make anymore. "Tomato" has seldom had a longer *a*, and visitors are handled with a reserve at once concealed and intensified by easy courtesy. Yet the other thing always said about him is that he has persistently tried to escape the comfort of his upbringing and to put himself in wild places where privilege has no meaning. At sixty-five, he's already spent a decade wrestling with his character Mister Watson, a fierce and accursed and untamable murderer who was, by all accounts, "a good husband and a loving father, an expert and dedicated farmer, successful businessman and good neighbor."

The story of Matthiessen's life sounds like a flavorful adventure tale. The son of an architect listed in the New York Social Register, he had already, by the time he graduated from Yale, studied at the Sorbonne, served in the navy, and sold fiction to the *Atlantic*. After a short stint teaching writing at Yale, he began working as a commercial fisherman to support his art. Then, separated from his first wife (he has had three, and four children), he loaded a few books, a gun, and a sleeping bag into his Ford convertible and set off to visit every wildlife refuge in the country; by the time he was thirty-two, this self-taught naturalist had produced the definitive guide to *Wildlife in America*. Already, too, he was showing that he needed a lot of space, and wilderness, and clean water. His early novel *Raditzer* is an almost allegorical tale of a restless, artistic-minded son of wealth—Charles Stark—who goes to sea, "unable to answer his own questions, and nursing ill-defined resentments," and finds himself irresistibly drawn to an orphaned ne'er-do-well who seems his shadow self. By the time of his next novel, *At Play in the Fields of the Lord*, the two sides are even closer—in characters whose names alone (Wolfie and Moon) suggest that men have murderous beasts in them, and pieces of the heavens.

From the beginning, in fact, Matthiessen has hewed to the same harsh, uncompromising path—nearly all his books are set in a primitive, almost mythic landscape where men are alone with nature and a lost spark of divinity. You will not find much that is contemporary in the books; and there is scarcely a mention of domestic relationships, or cities, or Europe. Nearly all of them simply trace the dialogue of light and dark. "One reason I like boats so much," he explains, "is that you have to pare everything down to the bare necessities, and there you are, the captain of a little boat, without a shelter, without a past, without future hopes."

That starkness seems to call to him like a bell in a forest clearing. "I longed for something very, very spare," he says of his favorite book, *Far Tortuga*, and he notes with pride that there's only one simile in all its 408 pages. "Simply putting down the thing itself was so astonishing," he says. "I often think of the antennae on a cockroach coming out from under a ship's galley, and the light catching these two extraordinary, delicate mechanisms—that light, and those things, to me is the echo of eons of evolution. What do you need with a simile or metaphor?"

The austerity of that approach gives the books something of the quality of redwoods—lofty, solid monuments invested with an almost classical presence. They can also seem unbendingly solemn. "I like to think I have a merry side," he says, almost wistfully, and in conversation he certainly talks often of "fun," his sonorous voice rolling up and down with command and theatricality, now mimicking a genteel old woman, now doing a Taoist sage. At the same time, he remains unflinchingly serious in his determination to speak for those who cannot speak for themselves.

In nonfiction, in fact, his principal role has been that of a warning bell and an elegist, trying to rescue traditional values and forgotten instincts from the ravages of progress ("Modern time, mon, modern time," runs the knelling refrain of *Far Tortuga*). "The world is losing its grit and taste," he says with feeling. "The flavor of life is going." And he rises to highest eloquence when talking of the loss of the stars he knew as a boy, and of the dark waters on Long Island Sound that used to terrify him. "I used to be able to count sixteen species of wood warblers here—all in a very short time," he says. "Now I'm lucky to see eight or ten warblers all spring—of any species." Matthiessen was an environmentalist before the term was fashionable (just as he was a "searcher" before it became a '60s job description, and an apostle of "male wildness" before Robert Bly got out his drums). Yet he has always been too tough-minded to dwindle into New Age pieties, and while offering a stinging denunciation of the Gulf War as "one of the great disgraces in our history," he concedes that police restraint makes this "a very easy country to be brave in."

In his nonfiction, especially *The Snow Leopard*, physical and meta-physical worlds have often beautifully conspired. His novels, however, can seem like mountain climbs—effortful, punishing, dauntingly ambitious mountain climbs that demand as much of the reader as of the author. Often, their virtuosity almost obscures their virtues. "Peter always takes the difficult way out," says one editor. "And the editor's job is to simplify." Matthiessen all but acknowledges this when he says that "I am really not in the least bit conscious of the reader. Maybe that's brag-gadocio, or flamboyance, but I really don't think that way. I think you're doing your best work when you're not even conscious of yourself. That's what's so thrilling about it—you're out of yourself."

That unsparingness may also begin to account for the fact that the sum of his parts—and of his books—sometimes seems greater than the whole. Here, after all, is a writer with all the gifts: an exceptional ear, an un-equaled eye, a ravenous soul, a committed heart, and a muscular radi-ance. While his more famous neighbors have ground out books every few years, he has completed six novels, as well as twenty works of nonfiction, all of them rigorously crafted, meticulously researched, and compen-dious. And yet, as his oldest friend, George Plimpton, says, "He's never been truly recognized." In part, perhaps, because so much comes easily to him that he has had to create his own challenges. "I think there's some sadness—not bitterness, but I know there's some sadness—about this," says Plimpton. "But Peter is determined to go his own way. He's made it difficult for himself."

It may also be that he juggles so many balls that it's hard for his audi-ence to follow the high, clear arc of any one. Nearly everyone seems to have a Matthiessen story or request, and with his generous blurbs, his name in the phone book, and his cordial manner, he may be one of the most overburdened writers in America, a natural ear for anyone con-cerned with Buddhism, Africa, American Indians, or any of the other topics on which he's written authoritatively. There are also other kinds of pressure. "Peter's a dream man in a certain kind of way," says a longtime friend, "handsome, adventurous, patrician, very well bred, and he's done all these things," and the small world of the Hamptons buzzes with tales of women who've given up everything just to live within sight of him. Yet in prose, at least, his remains a relentlessly male world—*Men's Lives*, the title of one book, might almost be the summary of his entire oeuvre.

After all his striving, there is a kind of fittingness in the fact that it was Zen, in a sense, that found him—in the form of three small Japanese masters he encountered in his driveway one day, invited by his late second wife. An aristocratic, solitary, exacting, elegant discipline that prizes immediacy, irreverence, and unanalytical attention to the moment, Zen might almost have been made for this practical rebel. ("We deserved each other," Matthiessen says with a self-mocking laugh.) His commit-ment to the discipline has never been halfhearted. "Peter is very, very serious about Zen practice," says Helen Tworkov, editor in chief of *Tri-cycle: The Buddhist Review* and author of *Zen in America*, and she recalls how he once took three months off from his "incredibly full life" to lead a Zen retreat. "Peter doesn't take himself for granted," she goes on. "Here he is, at the age of sixty-five, and he's still committed to exploring what life is about. There are very few people of his age, or accomplishment, or stature, who are trying so hard."

Trying for what? one sometimes wonders. Perhaps for the same simple thing that Mister Watson's neighbors seek: a good night's sleep. "Simplicity is the whole secret of well-being," he writes in *The Snow Leopard*. "The secret of well-being is simplicity," he writes in *Nine-Headed Dragon River*. His aim in life, he says now, is "to figuratively clean out my office. I've really said what I have to say, and I really would rather, if I could bring myself to a halt and stop traveling, fool around with fiction, maybe more experimental fiction." Maybe so, but seventeen years ago, in a talk with *Time*, he used almost exactly the same words. And so one is left with the noble, and slightly poignant, image of a restless, ambitious, complex man trying and trying for simplicity. "There's a line in Turgenev," he says, "that absolutely haunts me. It's a suicide note, and the entire note is, 'I could not simplify myself.' What an arrow through the heart!"

(1992)

# Peter Brook: Autumn of
## the Rebel Patriarch

Peter Brook is spinning out a vision, a vision of how the theater can change lives. "In some forms of theater—the very conventional theater—you'll find that people say, 'The best performance is in rehearsal. And once the audience is there, it's never any good.' That, I would say, is totally untrue." His hands move flowingly with his words; his voice, silken as Gielgud's, rises and musically falls; his whole body seems alive. "My own experience is that a small group senses there's a treasure some-where—on top of a mountain—and its members set off. And they come far enough to begin to get an impression that it's there. Then they go back and gather a large party, and because they are a large party, they can get across certain hurdles they couldn't get across before. So for me, the moment of greatest intensity is always within a performance."

At night, in the scrupulously dilapidated Bouffes du Nord, a funkily unreplastered shell of a Moorish cathedral that is Brook's theatrical home in Paris, the stage is bare, save for a pit of sand and a rock. A two-man orchestra tunes up in the wings. Bejeweled spectators take their places on the floor. Kids in jeans—sometimes Brook himself—show customers to their seats. Then four men all in black come out and sway to an imagi-nary wind. Unearthly Japanese music floats above their heads, as do strange, shamanic chants. In this French-language production of Shake-speare's *Tempest*, Prospero and Ariel are African, and Caliban is white; yet all are so transparent that they obtrude no more than notes within a score. Five curtain calls later (though minus a curtain), the audience spills out of a tiny front door—squeezed between a real estate office and a magic shop—and into the café next door to mingle with the actors.

Peter Brook's latest radically simple reinvention of a classic has, as usual, won otherworldly reviews: even the normally sober *Times Literary Supplement* described it as achieving "wonders quite beyond your dreams." Honors continue to rain down on the sixty-five-year-old sage of the theater—most recently an International Emmy for his TV version of *The Mahabharata* and an Honorary Fellowship from Oxford. Yet acclaim is one thing Brook can do without. Here, after all, is a perpetual boy wonder who, by the age of twenty-eight, had already directed Gielgud, Guinness, and Olivier; completed his first motion picture; and, as a director of the Royal Opera House at Covent Garden, staged *Salome* with sets by Dalí. Here too is a lifelong rebel who turned his back on the very Establishment he had mastered to go off on a more personal quest: staging a play in the unfamiliar language, partly of his own creation, of Orghast, above the ruins of Persepolis; leading eleven actors and a carpet on a 9,000-mile trek through Saharan Africa to improvise before bewildered villagers; and, most famously, taking his nine-hour production of *The Mahabharata*, in two languages, across four continents. Fully thirty-eight years have passed since Pauline Kael noted that Brook was the "grand old enfant terrible of the English theater," yet still he is doing what he has always done, turning expectations on their heads in his search for images that leave scorch marks on the soul.

Now, on a bright winter's day, sitting in his hideaway office above a cobblestone passageway in Paris, his Proustian answers flowing for five minutes or more—a running brook indeed!—Brook is throwing off metaphors like sparks. Shakespeare is like a worm, he says, or like a hologram; like a Hindu *rishi*, or like a compact disc. Again and again, he has returned to the Elizabethan classics, like a Zen monk devoting his life to drawing a single perfect circle. And each time he returns, he tries to eliminate more, to get to a core so essential and charged that the universe can, quite literally, be seen in a grain of sand. The first time Brook put on *The Tempest*, in 1957, he designed the sets, composed the electronic music, and had Gielgud as his Prospero; this time, the part is taken by a traditional storyteller from Burkina Faso.

Brook in conversation is a hummingbird in perpetual motion, whirring above positions, qualifying every utterance with "and yet," swiveling away from all fixities. The room around him is as unshowily eclectic as its owner: Persian carpets splashed across clean white spaces; books, in several languages, on Martin Buber, the Cabala, Buddhism; a plane ticket near some African ceremonial objects. Next to a bed on the floor, a volume, *Guerrillas & Spirit Mediums in Zimbabwe*; in front of it, a gleaming black tower of the latest audio and video equipment.

Though rigorously ideology-proof, Brook gives such poetic voice to his convictions—"A film is a passionate assembly of 'now's"; "Theater is always a self-destructive art, and it is always written on the wind"—that many seekers look to him as a kind of countercultural avatar. That role, like every other, he sees as a confinement. "Whenever anyone calls me a guru," he says, smiling merrily, with a hint of steel in his pale blue eyes, "I answer them by stressing that I look at everything from my own background in show business, and that for me what counts is show business values. If, on the other hand, I were dealing with a hardheaded Broadway producer, I would stress that whether people fill the theater or not is not in itself a criterion or a value."

Peter Sellers, whom some might call the Peter Brook of this generation, also sees the man whose work he once studied in decidedly practical terms. "Even his most far-flung productions have this razor's-edge, purely commercial effect," says Sellers. "A great sense of timing, and a sense of how to show the thing off at its best." Few yogis, one suspects, would have had the gumption to cobble together a small army of coproducers for *The Mahabharata*. Yet few show-biz types would have spent three years raising money to shoot a feature-length movie in Afghanistan about the wandering mystic Gurdjieff.

Thus the dialectic goes on, as Brook seeks out a course between the deadliness of traditional conventions and the dreariness of cutting-edge clichés. On the one hand, as he would say, a man fluent in seven languages and famous for his spellbinding monologues; on the other, one who aspires to a theater that is wordless. On the one hand, an omnivorous intellectual whose talk spins effortlessly from watchmakers' conventions to Hindu theology to John le Carré as a modern Balzac; on the other, a man of the people seeking a drama in which ideas are as beside the point as they are in lovers' talk, or prayer.

The story of Brook's shooting-star appearance has long been the stuff of theatrical legend. The son of a Russian-born drug manufacturer in London who patented the well-known laxative Brooklax, he was just seven when he put on a six-hour production of *Hamlet* "by P. Brook and W. Shakespeare," taking all the parts himself; while a teenager, he not only staged his first London production, of *Doctor Faustus*, but blithely eliminated the Chorus from Marlowe's play and had Mephistopheles take the part of all Seven Deadly Sins. By twenty the Oxford graduate was a professional director, and by twenty-two his productions at Stratford were already exciting every response but neutrality. The London papers of the day could not get enough of the whirlwind prodigy—physically strangely suggestive of the young John McEnroe—who dashed off ballet reviews, called in the black magician Aleister Crowley to advise him on Faust, and strode through the classical canon like a conquering Tamburlaine. Then, in the '60s, after roughly forty top productions, Brook embarked on what the British Information Services called "ultra-experimental" work, deconstructing himself and every work he touched; those who felt that his love of innovation could come dangerously close to art-for-artifice's sake exulted when his *Oedipus* (starring Gielgud) culminated in the cast's dancing around a giant phallus to the tune of *Yes! We Have No Bananas*.

And hardly had the curtain gone up on his greatest mainstream triumph—*A Midsummer Night's Dream* on trapezes—than Brook headed off to Paris in 1970 to form the International Center of Theater Research.

There, in secrecy, he resolved to follow drama back to its roots in myth. And so began a twenty-year pilgrimage through cultures and experiments, accompanied by a troupe drawn from a dozen traditions or more, as well as by his wife, Natasha, and two children, with the director himself no more than a "guide at night."

For some people, Brook's abandoning of the conventional theater represents an abdication of his strength. "Nobody else touches Brook in the interpretation of a text," says Robert Brustein, director of the American Repertory Theater and longtime drama critic for the *New Republic*. "But I'm a little oppressed by the fact that every piece must show how 'international' we are, how integrated." The other charge sometimes brought against Brook is that he has so powerful a vision that he cannot easily accommodate actors with strong talents of their own or plays that do not allow him to leave his imprint on them. Among the nicknames his actors have for him are "the Ogre" and "the Buddha"; generals, after all, wish to conquer the world as much as mystics do. Nonetheless, the fact remains that Brook helped discover Paul Scofield and Glenda Jackson and even now acts as witness to his actors' weddings, godfather to their children.

For a visitor, it is tempting to see a Shakespearean trajectory in the director's own life: from youthful virtuosity (his debut at Stratford was *Love's Labor's Lost*), through the darkness and anarchy of the middle years (when he staged and filmed *Lear*), to the reinvigorated and higher optimism of *The Tempest*. Brook admits to having mellowed a little. When asked if he believes that an audience should be "shocked into remembering" the better parts of itself, he answers softly, and with characteristic precision, "Not shocked—but drawn into remembering. There I've changed very much—into a feeling that there is something presumptuous about feeling that we are in a superior position to the audience. That, I think, is the failing of almost all political theater." Instead, he looks for actors who can mix "art with heart," and reflect his own wish to leaven discipline with passion. "Working in the theater or the cinema, one must try always to fight a never-ending battle—which can never be won— which is to bring together the need to be in the present, in a contemporary reality, a bridge to the audience—if it's hermetic, it isn't theater—and yet remember that the only reason for doing theater is to help those who are making it, and therefore those who are eventually spectators, in a search for something beyond the everyday."

Always the images of risk and adventure; always tales of exploration. If there is one constant in Brook's many lives, it is, perhaps, his belief in movement—and his loyalty to the principle he enunciated at nineteen: "I want to change and develop, and dread the idea of standing still." It seems fitting that his Paris theater is situated behind a railway station, and the theater where he works in Glasgow is a converted station; for years, in *Who's Who*, he has cited as one of his recreations "traveling by air."

His next trip, practically speaking, will involve taking *La Tempête* around the world, and already he is developing a new production based on Oliver Sacks's neurological sketches. Yet Brook acknowledges that there is a sense in which his search will never end. "What I'm looking for," he says, "isn't anything to do with the theater, in the sense that it's not about making a show, making a play right now. It's about trying to reach a point in the work"—he stops to choose the right word—"that's never reached. Suppose you're a sailor; you've gone through a storm, and you've arrived at the port. You don't think, artificially, 'Where's the next storm?' You just pause for a moment and then go back to sea." A little later, one of the world's more practical visionaries, Greek shoulder bag slung over his bulky duffel coat, gets out of a taxi and disappears into an elegant business office just off the Champs Elysées.

(1991)

# BOOKS

## Welcome to the Age
## of Tropical Classical

---

Many of us accept that we are living in a new kind of universe: an Information Age, for one thing, and a world of cross-cultural hybrids. Certainly, a unified field of multiculture. English is the official language in sixty-three countries of the world, and eighty-two different languages are taught in the Los Angeles school system. But what many of us are slower to see is that there are many different voices arising to articulate the features and possibilities of our age. It is easy to talk about a new kind of writer who mirrors the diminished attention span and image thinking of a video generation, and to cite Bret Easton Ellis, say, as the voice of the MTV era, a voice that sounds like a tape recorder picking up sounds issued from a video monitor; as it is easy to find in Don DeLillo's sleek and voiceless sentences unsettling premonitions of the future that awaits us.

It is not much harder to note that Salman Rushdie, for one, is the spokesman of a new, jangly, *pita fajita* world, with his chutnified London teeming with Indians, and his Anglicized India steadied by Old World leanings. His omnivorous voice is precisely that of the modern polyglot city, a ferocious mishmash of Bombay film talk, BBC English, and the lingo of pop culture. One postcolonial archetype was fashioned, appropriately enough, by James Ivory, in his early, personal film *Savages*, in which a group of "mud people," in loincloths and masks, take over a colonial mansion and, having appropriated the master's house (and voice), revert in time to savagery. Another, though, was given by Rushdie, in his *Satanic Verses*, when he gave that trope a spin and saw it in a more liberating light. Imagine, he wrote, if London were to turn tropical. Imagine how the Old World might be revived by the New, and how much brighter the city would become if some "savages" were brought in to educate the nobles.

Beneath all this, however, is another voice that is beginning to remake the contours of the global village, and it is one that I would call Tropical Classical. Three of its masters, in three different media, are Derek Walcott, in poetry, Michael Ondaatje, in fiction, and Richard Rodriguez, in the essay form. The revolution such individuals are enacting has gone largely unremarked, in part because they are so individual, and so various in their forms, that they exist without a group, without a school (even, sometimes, without a nationality). Yet what distinguishes one of them is what distinguishes all: the ability to season high classical forms with a lyrical beauty drawn from the streets and beaches of their homes. To learn from the tradition of Homer and Herodotus and Augustine, respectively, and yet to enliven and elevate those dusty forms with the rhythms of Saint Lucia, the colors of Sri Lanka, the love songs of the Latin South. To put sparkling new wine into cobwebbed old bottles, and shake the whole thing up to make it fizz.

Such writers are not merely bringing two worlds together, as migrant writers have always done; they are trying to put the realities of our multinational present into the established structures of the past; to link the tradition of our textbooks with the changing societies around us (thus Walcott likens Port of Spain to Athens, Ondaatje bases a love story on Herodotus, and Rodriguez thinks of Athens in contemporary Tijuana). Using their unique historical position—in a polycultural globe that enables them to range from Old World to New and back again—they produce effects closest, perhaps, to those of Wallace Stevens, the Yale man at the tropical tip of Florida, filling his formal and pillared stanzas with the sounds and scents of an imagined south. Plato in Key West.

Such writers are, moreover, showing us a new way of forging identities. Rather than simply rejecting the worlds into which they were born (or exalting them for their own sake), they try to find ways of having it both ways—of, in Walcott's terms, invigorating the classical forms he learned at school with his own West Indian words and names, while at the same time dignifying his beloved Caribbean with a classical high voice. Their most liberating assumption, in fact, is that identity is assumed and the self is what we make of it. Children of many cultures—born "multiculturalists," who do not need to use the word—they show us how we can create our own traditions, free of labels, in a universe of our own devising. Or make the old categories irrelevant by moving in and out of doors.

Imagine Henry James on the back streets of Tijuana. Kipling in the postimperial era. Aphrodite out to greet the tourist ships.


Consider Derek Walcott, for example, with reference to his contemporary, and his fellow writer of the Caribbean, the dean of the old postimperial debate, V. S. Naipaul. Begin with surfaces: Naipaul, stiffly immured inside his Wiltshire cottage, while Walcott shuttles back and forth between the islands and Massachusetts. Naipaul slamming the door on Trinidad, and keeping it locked up inside some dusty corner of himself, like the first Mrs. Rochester; while Walcott throws open the windows to West Indian light and lets it fall upon the pages of his Homer. Naipaul schooling himself in the way of his teachers, so that his prose is as chaste and formal—as rigorously English—as that of any Englishman; refining the West Indies (and the East) out of himself to write sentences that sound as if they have never seen tropical birds or island skies or hurricanes. A prose of discipline and clarity and order that always keeps its back straight and its shirt buttoned to the top; a prose that takes donnish pains not to dance. (Walcott, by comparison, cannot write even about Greenwich Village or London without admitting the music of his native island.) To be sure, some of our current liberation is largely the result of what the likes of Naipaul have achieved, now that students can devour copies of *Guerrillas* in Twentieth-Century English Literature classes. But where a Naipaul, on the right, tends to affiliate himself with the most traditional, conservative aspects of the Old World order, and where a Hanif Kureishi, on the left, merely reverses all that, allying himself with the radical anarchism of South London streets, a Walcott has made it his life's work to try to find a synthesis above and beyond received notions.

From the beginning, in fact, Walcott, a Dutch African born in British Saint Lucia, has been wrestling with what he repeatedly calls his "divided" heart: in only the second poem of his *Collected Poems*, he was already likening himself to John of Patmos, while affirming that "this island is heaven," and by the fifth (called "Origins"), he was struggling to resolve "the Greek and African pantheon." A typical Walcott poem conscripts the language and the landscape of an inherited England to enrich his own neglected islands, and their people:

> Below the bulb
> a green book, laid
> face downward. Moon,
> and sea. He read
> the spine. FIRST POEMS:
> CAMPBELL. The painter
> almost absently
> reversed it, and began to read:

> > "Holy be
> > the white head of a Negro,
> > sacred be
> > the black flax of a black child . . ."

Ever since boyhood, in fact, Walcott has been trying to revive the world he saw in Great Books—a world of theaters and trains and autumn leaves—amidst the sea almonds and spice laurels and shantytowns of the world around him. Sometimes, he chooses simply to inspect the colonial transaction from the other end of the telescope—Desdemona as seen by Othello, Crusoe as defined by Man Friday. Elsewhere, he finds Penelope in Martinique, retells the Bible in local dialect, sees Odysseus, the home-sick wanderer, in himself. Mostly, as he said when accepting the Nobel Prize in Literature in 1992, he has learned how to use the language of Shakespeare and Keats to perform the Adamic task of renaming his own unfallen world. He celebrates the cacophonies of self-made, self-respectful places like Port of Spain, "mongrelized, polyglot, a ferment without a history, like heaven," and he shows how an island, a self, an art, made out of fragments is one pieced together with deliberateness and love (the very word Rushdie finds missing from Naipaul's *The Enigma of Arrival*). The *tropiques*, he suggests, are not so *tristes* for those without alien eyes.

Much as Walcott makes music and poetry out of the liquid sounds of Antillean names (and Rodriguez rescues the Spanish meanings from California freeway titles), Michael Ondaatje, in his prize-winning *The English Patient*, takes us to a ruined villa in a Tuscan hill town at the end of World War II and fills the classic spaces with the names of distant places—"Ain, Bir, Wadi, Foggara, Khottara, Shaduf." Here, where the Renaissance legacy of northern Europe meets the lyric breezes of the south, he brings together wanderers from North Africa, India, and "Upper America," in a world in which nationality is irrelevant (and Englishmen are not English, while Indians often are). Surrounded by Piero della Francesca frescoes and memories of Michelangelo, his post-national souls fill the air with tales of "indigo markets" and a "street of parrots," of sensuous *souks* and desert winds. And even as the world around them is cementing its differences along national lines, they go back, in memory and imagination, to abstract spaces where distinctions are dissolved.

> There were rivers of desert tribes, the most beautiful humans I've met in my life. We were German, English, Hungarian, African—all of us insignificant to them. Gradually we became nationless. I came to hate nations. We are deformed by nation-states. Madox died because of nations.
>
> The desert could not be claimed or owned—it was a piece of cloth carried by winds, never held down by stones, and given a hundred shifting names long before Canterbury existed, long before battles and treaties quilted Europe and the East. Its caravans, those strange rambling

> feasts and cultures, left nothing behind, not an ember. All
> of us, even those with European homes and children in
> the distance, wished to remove the clothing of our coun-
> tries. It was a place of faith.

The quicksilver Ondaatje, a Sri Lankan of mixed ancestry with siblings on four continents, is clearly—and unapologetically—trying to subvert the classic British tale of exploration, to see *Kim* and Crusoe and Joseph Conrad in what he calls "translated light." His book is about the End of Empire—the characters are not map makers and bomb defusers for nothing—but instead of simply hijacking history, or burying the past, it seeks to chart the outlines of a new world order, like the desert, free of nation-states, removed from historical categories, in which "international bastards" and mock Englishmen and all the hybrid rest of us are free to recognize that we are "communal histories, communal books," made up of a hundred singing worlds.

Richard Rodriguez, too, in his most recent book, *Days of Obligation*, begins with the mestizo ideal and finds the redemption of our old and wasted ways in a new cross-fertilizing culture, wherein a Pakistani can talk to a Mexican in a Chinese restaurant and Native American moccasins are made in Taiwan. The son of Mexican parents, he feels himself "an Indian," an "Irish Catholic," an American, in a world made continuous and round. And more than just literally, he is speaking two languages at once when he cross-questions the high ideals of America's Founding Fathers in a light filled with the beauty of "the lemon tree in our mother's Mexican garden" and irradiated with the songs of doves and the sound of pealing church bells. Blessed with an outsider's freedom, he delights in mixing up high and low with an irreverent promiscuity, beginning an essay on modern San Francisco by citing both Saint Augustine and Liz Taylor (and then damning the Augustinian position in a Franciscan place). Thirteen years ago, in his first book, *Hunger of Memory*, the very subtitle, "The Education of Richard Rodriguez," announced that his intention was to bring Henry Adams into contemporary, multicultural California; and when he does so, he produces magically realistic effects that we have not seen before—finding Shakespeare's Jessica in a Vietnamese girl in Berkeley, seeing the Bill of Rights enacted in a waitress's wiping rag, and even (like Walcott) locating a character from Homer in the boy he knew in Sacramento, shouting from the front seat of his father's Chrysler.

The net effect of this cultural mixing and matching is that Rodriguez manages to address issues urgent as tonight—bilingualism and immigration and the tradition of American promise and AIDS—from a new and changeless vantage point: he counts the costs of self-creation by dismantling his résumé, and he talks about the drawbacks of American opportunity by measuring the silences around his family dinner table. Instead of joining the fray of editorial-page discussions, he tries to sit above it all, in a book-lined room, considering the headlines *sub specie aeternitatis*. Listen to the unaccustomed music with which he tells the age-old tale of assimilation in America:

> I am standing in my sister's backyard.
> They are away. The air is golden; the garden is rising green, but beginning to fall. There is my nephew's sandbox, deserted, spilled. And all his compliant toys fallen where he threw them off after his gigantic lovemaking. Winnie-the-Pooh. The waist-coated frog. Refugees of some long English childhood have crossed the Atlantic, attached themselves to the court of this tyrannical dauphin.
>
> *Asserín asserán*
> *Something something de San Juan . . .*
>
> I can remember sitting on my mother's lap as she chanted that little faraway rhyme.

As the blurb of his book puts it (aptly, for once), the closest parallel would be Jonathan Swift in a Mexico City nightclub (or, even closer to home, Oscar Wilde in Sacramento).

That they are doing something new can best be seen by the fact that one gropes in vain with these radical and elliptical writers for comparisons: whether one likes his abstract procedure or not, one is bound to admit that Ondaatje's novel is like no other. And Rodriguez, say, is so removed from traditional Mexican-American rhetoric on the one hand, and from the standard pundit's cool authority on the other, that he seems at times to be addressing an audience of one. People locked inside a single past must always define themselves in relation to what they have inherited; people with several pasts are absolved of this and so are free to create a "New World Order" (much as the New World itself did, more than a century ago, when Emerson and Melville and Whitman, choosing their fathers from among Shakespeare and the Bible and the *Bhagavad Gita*, "renovated English speech" with Whitman's "aboriginal names . . . Mississippi!—the word winds with chutes . . . Ohio, Connecticut, Ottawa, Monongahela").

Insofar as these writers are attempting a more difficult and lasting synthesis, insofar as they are trying to change the very terms of our discourse and forge a path beyond those of today's fads and ideologies, they have, of course, no shortage of detractors. Hispanic readers may claim that Rodriguez is too apolitical in his treatment of bilingualism (or simply too honest about the way his learning has removed him from his Mexican roots, and the more he succeeds, the more he feels he has failed—or betrayed—his parents); writers on AIDS are so used to approaching the topic in voices shaking with emotions—of sympathy or rage—that they may recoil from his note of dry, clenched sorrow and self-incrimination. Certain black militants may charge that Walcott is too tender toward the "Western Civilisation" in which he was raised and too reluctant to throw out the Shakespearean baby with the imperial bathwater. And Ondaatje's conscious determination to place his figures outside history—to explore love and identity and memory in Italy in 1945—may strike some geopolitical literalists as coy. Tens of thousands die in Hiroshima, and he is playing games with national name tags?

Yet for me it is in their very boldness, and their transcendence of trendy, op-ed thinking—their ability to show how political issues are personal, and too difficult for dogma—that these writers shine and liberate. Heir to many cultures, they refuse to be hemmed in by any one of them; fluent in many centuries, they cannot take too seriously the weather of the moment. They know that today's editorials go nowhere except into tomorrow's trash cans; and that a hundred years from now, the course catalogues of Duke and Stanford will be less important than how we teach ourselves, in private, with our histories, how to think.

They are also, I would posit, models of "affirmative action" in the highest sense, for all of them are affirmative and active. Why choose between Homer and Earl Lovelace—that is the burden of Walcott—when we are able to have both and, in fact, to see how Homeric patterns are played out in the world of Earl Lovelace? When we can bring Helen to life by finding her down the street in Saint Lucia, and when we can, in that discovery, give the calypso singer a new theme to incorporate? If the sins of the fathers need not be visited on the child, neither need they be simply compounded or replaced by the child's new and original sins. Why jettison either Confucius or Plato in a world in which the classroom in Sydney is full of immigrants from Taipei and Thessalonica, and the schoolgirl in Oakland may find herself in Confucian cultures, or in ones shaped by ancient Greece, after half a day's flying in the air? Derek Walcott's entire, noble career has been about making a peace, within himself, between the books he absorbed at school and the world he picked up under the sky and beside the sea. Richard Rodriguez writes—twice—in his recent book that the young have a wisdom from which the old can learn. And the nuclear explosion in Hiroshima, for Michael Ondaatje, marks not just the dying of the old order, but the dawning of a new. As we enter the new world that these writers are beginning to create, they— and a hundred others—show every sign of making the canon sing.

(1993)

# A Junglified Victoria

$T$*he Tempest* is the perfect paradigm for all postcolonial fiction. Who, after all, could resist
a tale of spirits and savages being

*Reef* BY ROMESH GUNESEKERA

tamed and taught by a fugitive European aristocrat (later joined by a
mixed-up band of drifters and dreamers and drunkards)? And who could
fail to see in it a metaphor for the way in which Western powers have
long tried to bring their native ways and speech to untutored paradise
islands? Shakespeare's experiment in magic realism offers an ideal proto-
type for the encounter between the civilized and the wild—or, as it
would more often be called today, between two different kinds of civilization, one drawn from nature and one from books. It not only acknowledges both the angelic and the bestial sides of the subconscious world but
also allows a visiting scholar to perform a kind of *mission civilisatrice*
before returning home.

Whether or not the inspiration for the play came from the islands that
have given us Derek Walcott and V. S. Naipaul, it is easy to see why
many ex-colonials have seized upon its images of Ariel crying out for
freedom; why the West Indian George Lamming, in his *Pleasures of Exile*,
dwelled on the mysteries of Sycorax; or why Walcott, in his poetry, not
only gives us Othello from the Moor's point of view but also describes
how "Caliban howled down the barred streets of an empire that began
with Caedmon's raceless dew, and is ending in the alleys of Brixton,
burning like Turner's ships."

When Romesh Gunesekera begins his first novel, *Reef*, then, with an
epigraph from *The Tempest*, we know that we are likely being ushered
into a new version of the age-old colonial transaction. And, moreover,
that it will probably be an example of what the voguish term calls "the
empire striking back," a shorthand for that increasingly visible phenomenon whereby much of the strongest writing in English—and especially in England—is coming from writers from the former colonies, who
are using the words they've learned at their masters' feet to turn their
masters' literature on its head. The kind of names to be found on the
shortlist for England's Booker Prize for Fiction—the clearest register of
British literary fashion—are Rushdie, Ishiguro, Okri, and Mo, and it is

more and more common to hear that, just as Spanish literature has been all but taken over by writers from Spain's former possessions (García Márquez, Paz, Allende, and Fuentes), so the new centers of English literature are Toronto and Sydney and Bombay. Gunesekera fits that description perfectly, if only because he is a creature of displacement, brought up on three separate islands (Sri Lanka, the Philippines, and England); he is published in England by Granta Press, long a sponsor of the highest-profile World Fiction; and his novel comes to us with the banner headline "Booker Prize Finalist." And when you read his perfectly weighted little gem of a prose poem, you see exactly how these young "foreign" writers are flooding the English mainstream with their alien colors and spices and sounds. In the course of this novel, Colombo comes to seem as close to us as Connecticut or Colchester.

On its surface—and it is an exquisitely sensuous and sweet-smelling surface—*Reef* simply tells the tale of Triton, a wide-eyed, earnest village boy, trained only in a "mud-walled school," who comes to Colombo to work in the junk-filled mansion of Mister Salgado, a quiet, rather dreamy amateur student of the sea. To Triton, Mister Salgado seems the last word in worldliness, though to us, as he sits on the veranda sighing over *The Mikado*, he seems dangerously unworldly. But between them, these figures of science and superstition combine to make their home a model of the island around them, and in every one of his exact details, Gunesekera acknowledges the mixed influences of an island in transition. Outside the house's entrance is a garden of "scarlet *rathmal* and white jasmine"; inside is a mix of "cane blinds, Formica surfaces and nylon mats." The master consumes soft-boiled eggs and plantain for breakfast, coconut cake and cucumber sandwiches for tea. And in perhaps the most revealing anomaly of all, the eleven-year-old boy confesses that such English as he knows he learned from a "poor, tormented schoolmaster, still under the spell of a junglified Victoria."

From the beginning, then, *Reef* presents us with an archetype of a master and his "boy"—a kind of tropical *Remains of the Day*, it often seems—and as in the Ishiguro book, the novel that unfolds is largely about the flatteries and follies of imitation (parrots and parrot fish flit through this novel). For while he registers some of the ironies of his mongrel home (it is only foreigners who are vegetarians here, and it is only Sri Lankans who speak of "Ivy League men" and Las Vegas), Triton is so unquestioningly devoted to his lord that he will not even eat until Mister Salgado has done so. Like Ishiguro's butler, he knows so little of the world outside that he believes his master to be omnipotent; and like Ishiguro's butler, he is not displeased when he is himself mistaken for a rich man on one of his rare forays outside his master's company. "I watched him, I watched him unendingly, all the time, and learned to become what I am," the boy says, in the voice of Ariel, with something of the straightforwardness of Caliban.

The book's own junglified spell arises from that very voice, one that we have seldom heard before—open, unlettered, eager to please—and from a perspective utterly unclouded by ambiguity or distance. For even on the outskirts of the Sri Lankan capital, the young boy is living in a world of spirits. He sleeps at night under a small round window and conjures demons out of the darkness. He rubs his "elephant-hair bracelet" for good luck and makes spells to hex his enemies. The whole island is alive for him—this junglified Pip—with "mischievous little godlings" and malevolent sorcerers like the elder servant Joseph (whose head is "shaped like a devil-mask"). This is very much Prospero's isle—"a jungle of demons," as Triton calls it—as seen by a local sprite.

And because the bulk of the book concerns Triton's spell as chef to the languorous Salgado, it allows him to immerse the reader in the bewitching smells and flowers and fragrances of his spice-filled, wind-softened home. The book is lush with the aromas of rose water, almond essence, and cardamom, with white flame trees and temple trees and lily pads, with "the perfume of cinnamon in pearly rice, or the hum of a hummingbird sucking nectar from a pink shoe-flower." And because the world of the artless boy extends no farther than the house, the reader's view, too, is circumscribed, and he mainly sees not an island of ethnic strife or social turmoil but, rather, an enchanted garden of "red-beaked parrots and yellow-eared *salaleenas*," where a boy freshens cupboards with drops of Moorish rose water and scrubs his hands with coconut hair and pink whalebone. Everything here is seen in local terms, the sea "like a Madras pancake. *Thosai* flat," and a woman's ears "curled in like the edges of a puppadum when it hits hot oil." Political tensions are no more than storm clouds on the far horizon.

The strength of *Reef*, in fact, lies in its absolutely unforced and convincing depiction of a self-contained universe ("I didn't know what happened much beyond our lane," the boy admits), one that takes the beauties of its elysian home for granted. Triton's work in the kitchen allows him to surround us with exotic flavors and seasonings, with *seeni-sambol* and *pol-sambol* and *pol-kiri-badun* curry; with *cadjan* fronds and *del* trees and *nelum* flowers. The first thing that hits one about *Reef*, especially when compared with Gunesekera's debut collection of short stories, *Monkfish Moon*, is that the pages here are lit up with italics, and every one of them seems to convey wild and unknown booty into our mother tongue. The second thing that strikes one is that Gunesekera deliberately chooses not to explain most of his Sinhalese terms, in much the same way that Vikram Seth, in *A Suitable Boy*, filled his pages with Indianisms and yet declined to include a glossary. Puppadum and sari and nirvana are English terms now, these writers are saying; or as Rushdie puts it in his more polemical way, "To conquer English may be to complete the process of making ourselves free."

The remarkable thing about this novel, indeed, is that it achieves nearly all of its effects silently, as it were, through almost imperceptible shadings of language and texture. The story it tells, of an island's fall from paradise, coinciding with a boy's fall into self-consciousness, is conventional enough; but the way it tells it, by showing how language itself is bitten by a snake and gradually falls prey to more and more of the outside world, is original and heartrending. Thus the early pages of *Reef* are luminous with local terms, like the central reef aglow with phosphorescent fish, and one feels, in Triton's inspired image, as if one is living "inside a conch"; when people speak, it is in the pungent, inimitable cadences of a village in Sri Lanka ("Big commotion was going on there with that Pando-*nona*"). But as the book goes on (and the boy grows up), more and more foreign influences start entering the sequestered house. The first comes with Mr. Dias, a friend of Mister Salgado, who speaks in the Wodehousean manner of the intellectual Anglo-Asian: "The rifle, you see . . . was resting like a fancy brolly on the tip of his shoe. In all the excitement, what with the din and all, the fellow pulled the trigger. Blew his own bloody big toe off!"

In the central scene of the book—again a little like the dinner party that is the centerpiece of *The Remains of the Day*—Triton faces his biggest culinary challenge as he cooks his first Christmas turkey (to be eaten near a plastic Christmas tree). Though a traditional bird, it is stuffed not only with raisins and liver but also with "Taufik's *ganja* and our own *jamanaran* mandarins" (much like the book itself). And though there is no apple in the bird, it marks the end of Eden. The first foreigners enter the book at this point, with their alien perspectives ("This extraordinary, I reckon, deeply *erotic* country . . . so uninhibited. Really wild"), and, even sadder, the first foreign attitudes enter the Sri Lankans, as they start to see themselves through foreign eyes (Mister Salgado tells Triton that the dinner is to begin "at nine o'clock. Punctually. None of this lotus-eating business"). Before we know it, Mister Salgado and his friends are trafficking in secondhand terms and Western platitudes, chattering about "haves and have nots," "conspicuous consumption," and the "Fifth Column," and trying on poses like the hangers-on from Alonso's ship.

One of them goes so far as to say, "Even before Kennedy we had a real modern assassination . . . we are not that backward." The reader hears the gates of Eden closing as Mister Salgado discusses "the thermodynamics of the ocean in the Age of Aquarius."

From then on, the trajectory *Reef* traces is, inevitably, an elegiac one, and the book, like its beloved island, fills up with engineers "trained in London and New England," "*nouveau* chefs," and references to Zeffirelli's *Romeo and Juliet* and "free love" in California. The government starts to plan inland seas and the diversion of enormous rivers, and the eponymous reef—the fragile system that keeps the ocean and forces of chaos at bay—is seen as a marketable resource. Marxists start burning buildings to purge the island, while pleasuremongers open "batik boutiques" and roar around on "fluorescent motorbikes." But the singular courage of *Reef* is to suggest that the corruption lies deeper than any ism or fashion, and that it is not death squads, nor nationalists, nor greedy developers, that are the downfall of Sri Lanka: all are merely symptoms of a deeper malaise, having to do with too-long horizons and foreign ideas. The flight from paradise begins when people start talking, too easily, of "the classic flight of capital."

*Reef* ends with Triton and his bewildered lord moving to London and setting up a home in a flat near the Gloucester Road, in an old Victorian house (every detail counts here). And like Ishiguro's butler, in a way, Triton comes to see that he has given his faith to a mage who is himself ineffectual and naive. But the loss of innocence is again most knellingly conveyed just through language. When Triton visits the British seashore, he finds a gray and cormorant-haunted place with none of the color and music he knows, and his prose hardens into a brittle and crabbed kind of Anglo-Saxon, as he describes how "the sea shimmering between the black humps of barnacled rocks, mullioned with gold bladder-wrack like beached whales, thickened into a great beast reaching landward, snuffling and gurgling. . . . In pock-marked, marooned rock pools speckled hermit-crabs and rubbery, red sea anemones dug in; limpets and periwinkles and bubble weed held fast waiting for the tide."

The procedure of *Reef* is so gentle and lyrical—whispering around us like a murmurous sea—that it is easy to overlook just how subversive the book is. For it allows, and even forces, us to see Sri Lanka from a local boy's perspective, as we have never seen it before (in English). For as long as those of us in the West have been reading of the island, it has been through the eyes of foreigners—and, moreover, foreigners highly aware of its alienness. "All jungles are evil," wrote Leonard Woolf, of the island where he made his home, and Edward Lear complained that "The brown

people of this island seem to be odiously inquisitive and bothery-idiotic."
And this was all before the great champions of global alienation, Paul
Bowles and D. H. Lawrence, hit the place (the latter with his talk of
"papaw-stinking buddhists").

Even the country's most famous contemporary writer, Michael Ondaatje, is himself a bemused half-outsider, a mixed-race product of Dutch
and even English forebears who has lived all his adult life far away and
who returns to his birthplace, in *Running in the Family*, saying, "I am the
foreigner. I am the prodigal who hates the foreigner." And the ancestors
that Ondaatje portrays in his memoirs, playing billiards, going to the
races, and "danc[ing] in large living rooms to the music of a Bijou-
Moutrie piano," are themselves the kind of deracinated cosmopolitans
who seem almost extraterrestrial to the likes of Triton (his father,
Ondaatje mentions in passing, was briefly engaged to a Russian countess
in Cambridge).

*Reef*, then, like more and more of its contemporaries, is radical
precisely in what it can take for granted: its very matter-of-factness
about Embilipitiya grass and frangipani is part of its sedition. And at
every turn, it performs a kind of counter-Orientalism, giving us the
island as it appears from the servants' quarters, and so replacing Western views of the East with Eastern views of the West. For Triton, after
all, it is not mynah birds or wizards that are exotic; it is copies of *Life*
and *Reader's Digest*, rumors of the Profumo affair and the Beatles. It
is England that seems the dark and frightening country where one cannot speak the language. And when he describes the world around him,
everything becomes transposed: he writes of "silver trays as big as the
moon," and one realizes that one is accustomed to hearing English
writers likening the moon to silver trays; he describes the sound of "onion
skin rustling . . . like trees blowing in a summer orchard," and one recalls that usually, from the other side, it is trees that are being likened
to books. The very terms of familiarity and strangeness are turned around
here, as in a photographic negative (just as, in Hanif Kureishi's *My
Beautiful Laundrette*, black and white are so reversed that it is the Paki-
stanis who are the bosses in England and the whites who are their
underlings).

This is, then, another example of the subversion enunciated so majesti-
cally by Derek Walcott. Here, after all, in the central episode of the
novel, the Sri Lankans not only assert that their island was the original
Garden of Eden but take the Bible itself—and the story of Noah's ark—
and turn it into a Sri Lankan folktale, of a "helluva bad monsoon" and a
"*baas-unnaha*—our carpenter with his boat." By the end of the scene, we

are seeing everything we thought we knew through the other side of the telescope.

In some ways, magic realism itself is nothing more than the conveying of everyday life to a world so distant that it takes realism for surrealism; as García Márquez discovered, the simple transcription of life in a superstitious and god-filled village will seem as otherworldly to us as our TV images and knickknacks seem to a Colombian villager: that is the *quid pro quo* of the modern imaginative trade routes. Magic realism is about transubstantiation—the turning of one man's water into another man's wine—and it adds to Kipling's famous line "The wildest dreams of Kew are the facts of Kathmandu" the rider that "The wildest facts of Kew are the dreams of Kathmandu." The lone, rather seedy American in Gunesekera's novel is described by the boy as a "film-star."

Though *Reef* is not strictly an example of magic realism, it is a glittering example of how Caliban is turning his master's speech upon him. A generation or so ago, V. S. Naipaul mastered the imperial voice, and attitudes, and trained them upon the third world he had taken such fastidious pains to flee; born fifteen years later, on the eve of Independence, Salman Rushdie simply celebrated the polyglot mishmash of our mixed-up cultures, in which Bombay is as full of pizzas as London is full of samosas. Now, though, even younger writers like Gunesekera are repatriating the skills and tactics they mastered in England to give new dignity and authority to their homelands. Ben Okri fills English with molue buses and Nigerian herbalists, all described in classic English sentences ("Under our intense gaze, he bit Mum's shoulder and pulled out a long needle and three cowries from her flesh"). The Caribbean-born Caryl Phillips writes a novel in flawless nineteenth-century prose and calls it *Cambridge*, to evoke not the bucolic English university town but a hideously mistreated black slave. And Gunesekera, like the Canada-based Indian Rohinton Mistry, looks back on the world he has left, from a Western perch, and concocts a new kind of English, in which he describes "some itty-bitty *koreawa* road" and characters dancing "the cha-cha-cha or the *kukul kakul* wiggle."

The ultimate point of *Reef,* about how the East was lost, and with it a certain rough magic, is nothing new. But the strength of the book is, in a sense, that it doesn't belabor that point and that it never lets its story dwindle into treatise or polemic. When Mister Salgado is asked, by a foreign journalist, how "the lifestyle in coastal villages is changing as a result of sea-erosion," he loses his composure for one of the only times in the book, simply because he loves his island too much to hear it subjected to op-ed clichés. In the same way, Gunesekera refuses tidy explanations or easy rhetoric, and simply shows us the eroding flavors of his sea-washed home. For me, this is the best novel from the subcontinent since Rohinton Mistry's *Such a Long Journey*, and for much the same reason. Calmly, in precise and measured prose, it gives us a new and unexpected world; and gradually, it makes it feel like home.

(1995)

# Jane Austen in Calcutta

In the house of English letters, Indian writers have often admitted us to the kitchen, with its hot spices and odd condiments *A Suitable Boy* BY VIKRAM SETH and strange terms; and to the bedroom, not only for its obvious seductions but also for the wild dream flights that it entertains. The event-infested city, the superstitious village, the polymorphous forms of Indian movies, are all by now familiar parts of the Indian scenery. But what Vikram Seth has tried to do, in his quietly monumental new novel, is to usher India into the drawing room, to make it seem as everyday and close to us as nineteenth-century Saint Petersburg, say, or Regency Bath. His is a novel of the parlor and the breakfast table, and one that passes like a long morning—and afternoon and evening—with the family.

*A Suitable Boy* is, on the face of it, simply a tale of a "nice, quiet girl" called Lata, nineteen years old, living in northern India in 1950 and trying to find a husband. Meanwhile, around her, the world's largest democracy is preparing for the first general election in its young history. At its heart a story of four intertwined families, and their universal anxieties and affections, the novel is also a portrait of India, three years after Partition, trying to find a suitable future for herself, and struggling to keep the customs that steady while shedding the ones that stultify. It is the story of the passing of an era, of the last strains of a rarefied world of *ghazals* and nawabs, and the first approaches of a new, industrial age; of how the elegant Rajput miniature, you might say, is being replaced by the news photo.

The distinguishing feature of the book, though, may simply be its uneventfulness, its surpassing dailiness, the way in which Seth catches a life-size, human, unextraordinary India. He sets the book, after all, not during the tumult of Independence but in the uncertain interregnum that comes after. And his purpose seems to be to rescue the country from melodrama and exoticism, and to show that if Dickens, with his volubility and humor and affection, is one natural chronicler of India, Jane Austen is another. As in Forster (another obvious precedent), traumas pass between the lines, and death is something that happens offstage. In that sense, *A Suitable Boy* could almost be said to be a novel about things not happening: when a drunken boy drives a car too fast late at night, he brakes *before* he hits a lamppost or a child; when a boy is rejected by his beloved, he does not kill himself but goes off to the country for a month; when a child is lost in a murderous riot, he is—somehow—found.

This benign refusal of block capitals is ideally suited to Seth's gentle pacing and to the admirable directness and lucidity of his prose. Nonetheless, the sheer bulk of the book comes as a surprise. For Seth's has always seemed a light, an almost glancing sensibility; his seems a kind of Noël Coward talent. Charm is his calling card, and sunniness his forte; playfulness is a large part of his attraction (evidenced here, before one even begins, in a rhyming Table of Contents, and two contradictory epigraphs from Voltaire about the longueurs of long novels). His last book—of poems—was one of the slimmest of the year; this one promises to be the longest. The question it raises is what happens to light comedy when it is extended across half a million words. Can an epic be built on charm alone?

There are, increasingly, two strands of Indian fiction, that of compassionate realism (exemplified by R. K. Narayan and, recently, Rohinton Mistry) and that of pinwheeling invention (the mode of Salman Rushdie, Shashi Tharoor, and I. Allan Sealy). Seth firmly allies himself with the former, and he attempts here what might be regarded as a counter-Rushdie epic: relatively secluded and old-fashioned where Rushdie is determinedly topical and international, somewhat conservative in style and temper where Rushdie is willfully radical (Seth writes a classic English prose, and the most tender and touching marriage of all in this book about marriages is an arranged one). Most of all, Seth is a peacemaker, where Rushdie is a belligerent, and there are those, of the Rushdie camp, who will find Seth's openness—"It is best to be on good terms with everyone," thinks one character, early on—too mild-mannered.

For me, though, the singular appeal of *A Suitable Boy* lies in its fondness, and in its evocation of an unhurried, gossipy, small-talking India as teasing and warm as every family reunion I've ever attended. His is the charmed world of the privileged middle classes, as Indian as their love of P. G. Wodehouse and Charlie Chaplin, as Indian as their college productions of *Twelfth Night* and boating trips on Windermere. Scattering movie ads, greeting-card jingles, and excerpts from lawbooks through his narrative, he catches something thoroughly and unmistakably Indian, in the soft spot for numbers, the riddles, the quips about "making hail while the sun shines." Here are absentminded professors, bored beauties, and feckless boys who say things like, "Nothing I've ever done seems to have happened." Here, too, are Dickensian processions of repetitious lawyers, stutterers, and eccentrics (and even a character consistently called Uriah).

It is in its characters, in fact, that the book lives; Seth clearly loves his people, and he passes that love on to us. He shows them selfish, quarrelsome, and idle, yet never without sympathy: indeed, much of the sweetness of the main plot comes from the fact that all three of Lata's shadow suitors are entirely engaging. Even a family that speaks largely in doggerel, composes poems to its dog, Cuddles, and keeps reminding one of how lovably eccentric it is, somehow becomes likable. There is in all this an occasional trace of self-delight, and not every reader will find himself won over by the boyish witticisms ("Curiosity is a curious thing" and "No fait is ever accompli until it's accompli") or the little jokes (characters called Dr. Matthew Evans and Sir David Gower). But it must be said that the only ill-tempered character in the book is the one called Seth.

Seth makes of his affections, moreover, a central point: the two strains running through the long narrative are a determination to see India through particulars and people, and a complete rejection of those besetting Indian vices, pomposity and abstraction. (In one bravura passage, Seth throws off a host of sparkling generalities—India is like the Square, like the Trinity, like a Duality, like a Oneness, like a Zero—so as, in effect, to show that anything you might say about this huge and contradictory place is true . . . and meaningless.) And at every turn he shows us—in the Forsterian way—how individuals can go beyond the divisions created by institutions, and friendship can conquer communalism. Thus a Hindu crosses religious lines to befriend a Muslim—and later stabs him, for reasons that have nothing to do with their religions. At the same time, Seth is worldly enough to see how idealism can undermine the people it would try to help; to show how undoing an unjust system can mean undoing the innocent people who are its beneficiaries; and to catch the heart of that age-old Indian riddle of compassion and corruption— that a man is damned if he tries to tamper with the law to save a renegade son, and damned if he does not.

Seth is at his finest, for me, in his portrayal of the people most unlike himself—such as Muslims, say, or women. He evokes with enormous sensitivity the plight—and strength—of women in the Austen-like space of a zenana and in an age when a man may say, "I had six children and six daughters too." One of his most powerful scenes is an episode of sexual threat, seen from the woman's point of view. He also writes of children—and dogs and parakeets—with an uncle's fondness.

By its end, in fact, the novel has found a place for almost every possible position: even that of the foreigner who finds Indians "face-flattering, back-biting, name-dropping, all-knowing, self-praising, power-worshipping . . ." (having lived half his life abroad, Seth can temper an insider's knowledge with an outsider's amusement). *A Suitable Boy* is, in its unobtrusive way, panoramic: it gives us Muslim festivals and Hindu ones, courtesans and courtrooms, villages and cities and towns. What he does not know, he has researched, and with his economist's training, Seth shows us all the details of how a Czech shoe factory in India works; just as, with his position as the son of a high court judge, he covers in commanding detail the debate about land ownership. He describes Nehru's coup against himself, and issues as current as Hindu temples in Muslim areas. And though these public passages occasionally seem a little tacked on—to give the novel epic status—there is not a detail that I found unconvincing or false.

But is it worth the weight? In *The Golden Gate*, as Gore Vidal saw it, Seth wrote the "Great California Novel," and his new one (handicapped, for some readers, by the Rushdie-like $1.5 million in advances it has received) is clearly an attempt to write the Great Indian one. In *The Golden Gate*, he was so much at home in his Pushkin stanzas that he made one forget (and so forgive) his virtuosity; here—attempting a 1,400-page novel on his first go at prose fiction—that is not so clearly the case. Over the course of the novel, he gives us any number of analogies for the book we are reading: it is like the Ganges, with its "tributaries and distributaries"; it is like a banyan tree, with its slowly exfoliating roots; it is like a musician's *raga*, starting slowly but picking up speed. The river affords the best metaphor. For if Rushdie is a furious, nonstop geyser, Seth is more like a placid stream, calmly taking in the scenery that passes. And even though I found myself thinking that Seth was more humane than Rushdie, and easier to take, I felt that Rushdie was the more inventive novelist.

Every single page of *A Suitable Boy* is pleasant and readable and true; but I found the parts better crafted, and so more satisfying, than the whole. At times, it almost felt as if Seth was following his story more than leading it, and I could not help but think of his alter ego, Amit (an Oxford-educated poet, and son of a high court judge, embarked on an enormous first novel), saying that the reason his book was so long was that it was "very undisciplined." At times, in fact, the book feels more like a serial than an epic, and it is not immediately evident that its 1,400 pages make it four times better than it would have been at 350. Indeed, its central love story is so compelling that I found myself thinking that inside this fat novel, a much stronger thin one was struggling to get out.

Its publishers—and many others—will liken the book, with its spacious realism, to Tolstoy and George Eliot (though this would be much truer if *Middlemarch* had been written not by Prospero but Puck). For me, though, *A Suitable Boy* is closest to Tanizaki, in his *Makioka Sisters*. For it is, like the Japanese novel, at its heart an elegy as well as a comedy of manners, about a traditional society in a time of change, and about a leisurely world of graces giving way to a new, more democratic time. Like Tanizaki, Seth locates these changes in the woman's curtained world of rituals, and uses a rich family's search for a husband as a way of making history intimate and human. Like Tanizaki, he writes winningly of everything domestic, especially women and their children. And like Tanizaki, he has given us that unlikeliest of hybrids, a modest tour de force.

(1993)

R. K. Narayan is India's literary grandfather—and has been
since his youth. Toward his country and his ragamuffin heroes he

*Malgudi Days* BY R. K. NARAYAN

is engagingly amused and indulgent; discerning their weaknesses, he
reveals in them strengths. Visiting writers (from Jhabvala to Paul Scott)
have earnestly expressed their bewildered mixed feelings toward India but
have never made their peace with her; those closer to the land (V. S.
Naipaul, archetypally, or Salman Rushdie) have interpreted her to the
West yet have, in the process, forsaken the East. Narayan, however, neither analyzes nor mythicizes; he simply stays at home and serenely documents the vagaries of a fictional, but typical, small town (Malgudi).
Where Naipaul addresses the mind and Rushdie takes off on the imagination, Narayan—like those around him—returns always to the heart.
And where Rushdie, and others, have suggested, terribly, that the ancient
land of fantastical legend is being transformed into an urban and relentlessly utilitarian dictatorship, Narayan's figures are, in their innocence,
too removed to notice or accept such developments.

It is fitting, then, that Narayan's new collection of old stories, *Malgudi
Days*, bears the same title as his first volume of stories, published in India
forty years ago. For their substance changes as rarely as their subjects:
Narayan neither attempts what he can't do nor elevates what he
can. Instead, likening himself to a village storyteller and relying only
on a trained eye, ear, and heart, he continues as chronicler (and caretaker)
of ageless rhythms and enduring problems. Almost all of his short,
swift tales describe small men confronting demands larger than themselves. To these overwrought situations Narayan habitually brings an
understated touch, an observant wryness, and a forgiving style discreet
enough to dazzle other writers more than readers. (Graham Greene, his
longtime literary chaperon and admirer, calls him the greatest prose
writer since Waugh, and Updike likens him to Dickens.) In story after
story, Narayan takes the India of fantasy and tradition—a place of
astrologers and arranged marriages, of tigers and gods—and brings it
gently down to earth.

He highlights people because, as he says, "it is personality alone that is unchanging." His characters, moreover, remain utterly uncontaminated by public and political realities. Indira Gandhi and a solitary hippie rear their heads in two recent stories, and one story, shockingly, tells of a simple old man forcibly sterilized. But the other tales invariably examine private rituals and domestic riddles, confrontations between men and slippery circumstances that swerve surprisingly. The crackle and static of Indian life hums in the background, but, ultimately, Narayan talks through his people; speaks in their (pungent, slightly askew) English cadences, communicates through their unexceptional actions and aches.

Uniquely, he understands both the feelings of his characters and the logic of their destinies. He likes—and trusts—the well-meaning good-for-nothings who act unexpectedly as his heroes: and yet, as a faithful Hindu, he accepts the caprices of the gods, whose sense of irony seems as refined and impish as his own. From these divided loyalties come his cheery skepticism and, in turn, the mingled sadness and sweetness of his stories. For each of them is hinged upon the workings of karma, of ineffable and inevitable divine laws Narayan neither tries to explain nor seeks to deny (hence, perhaps, his tentative endings). Some of his characters sustain themselves with guilt and kill themselves with joy; others are cursed for kindness and rewarded for chicanery; and still others come to lament their triumphs (a man wins in a lottery a road engine; it costs him more to maintain than his house). Nothing—and nobody—works as expected.

In this ironic world, burglars stop to pet dogs, and tricksters lie, only to find their fictions come true. One typical story describes a doctor faced with his dying best friend. He allows affection to compromise authority, deceitfully assures his patient that he'll live, and through force of will alone, saves his companion. Elsewhere, conversely, a thief steals a wallet containing a balloon meant for a motherless child. Crooked enough to keep the cash but not cruel enough to disappoint the child, he tries to slip the booty back into its owner's pocket, and is promptly caught and tried. No wonder the author of *Loser Takes All* found a kindred spirit here.

Westerners have traditionally tended to imagine India as a checker-board sprawl of otherworldly saints and underworld sinners. But Narayan realizes that both, touchingly, can be the same. It takes no great skill to find the folly in Western seekers, or the gurus who take advantage of them; but Narayan's skill is to look a little below the surface: in his world, when a hippie questions a village cobbler, each, in his innocence, takes the other for a god. The typical Narayan hero is a luckless, but affable, con man who inspires confidence and finally, to his surprise (and ours), deserves it; or a cunning fellow who grows desperate and finds in that desperation a sudden, transporting nobility. Such is Narayan's tenderness toward these vagabonds that their peccadilloes become as appealing as their improbable acts of heroism. In a peculiarly Indian way, his likable rogues are devious as only children are, and prompted more by mischief than by malevolence. None seems irredeemable.

So, too, Narayan suggests that India's fatal flaws—her inefficiency, indolence, and superstition—are, perversely, her saving grace. The Malgudi mailman takes so long to deliver letters because he also dispenses concerned advice; emotional loss may accompany practical gain; and schemers, if taken as saints, may become saviors in spite of themselves.

For despite his kindly tolerance, Narayan himself is also an artful dodger, a literary pickpocket whose puzzled shrewdness teases his readers out of their easy admiration (his memoir about being feted in America is called *The Reluctant Guru*). His fabled artistic innocence is at once studied and sincere. He includes in his books detailed maps, then chuckles to readers that Malgudi is near New York's Chelsea Hotel; he is compared with Faulkner and Chekhov, yet ventures few literary precepts more daring than "A short story must be short"; he is a quiet, orthodox vegetarian who seeks the company of his neighbors, yet is regarded by Garbo as, in Ved Mehta's words, "a specimen of the mysterious East"; his autobiography, *My Days*—the second word again betrays his priorities—begins with his pets and ends with his grandson. Like his heroes, Narayan failed exams persistently and lost his beloved wife at an early age.

Modern India has yet to find a literary voice for the new political identity she seeks. The most likely candidate (and the first novel to fashion out of India a modernist narrative as grand and gaudy as its subject) is Rushdie's *Midnight's Children*. At thirty-four, Rushdie did for his homeland what García Márquez had done for Colombia and Whitman for America: he wrote a book of a continent's voices, as loquacious and fabulous and extreme as the Indian temperament, a book that swallowed all the land's incarnations and contrarieties and chose as its hero the newborn nation herself. Rushdie's cacophonous marvel catches the clutter, the clamor, the claustrophobia of contemporary India. It reeks of the earthy streets and their spiced complications; it gives expression to the crowded, swelling, turbulent post-Independence cities. But of the old-fashioned, rather amiable rural heartland, the acknowledged laureate is still Narayan.

(1982)

It has, from the beginning, been a story much stranger than fiction: if a novel had been so riddled with ironies, it would have been condemned for implausibility. In Salman Rushdie and Ayatollah Ruholla Khomeini, the world has two master plotters, celebrated controversialists both, with unusually lively imaginations, each of them now in his own embattled hideout while the War of the Words rages on. Yet even Jorge Luis Borges—or Rushdie—could scarcely have dreamed up a scene in which a Muslim cleric vows to kill Salman Rushdie for a book in which the Prophet condemns an apostate called Salman for "polluting the word of God." When Khomeini issued a *fatwa*, or death sentence, on Rushdie last week, it became impossible to tell who was the prophet and who the victim—Rushdie, for predicting the confrontation in the first place, or the Ayatollah, for taking it upon himself to be the living embodiment of Islam. Life imitates art imitates life. . . .

Both scriptures and stories have always assured us that people create their own destinies, bring down upon themselves the justice they deserve. In this case, however, the justice could hardly be described as poetic. Both sides have, in a sense, got exactly what they wanted—only to find that perhaps they should not have wanted it after all. In banning the book, various wise bodies have ignored the truth that every parent knows: a prohibition is often an invitation in disguise. And in making his Valentine's Day call for massacre, Khomeini seems to have gone beyond overkill to hubris: unlike, say, the Christians who opposed the movie *The Last Temptation of Christ*, he appears unwilling to let God take care of ultimate justice Himself.

Rushdie, meanwhile, has all the controversy, and attendant celebrity, he has often seemed to crave—yet with a cruel vengeance. For years Rushdie has been one of Britain's most vocal polemicists, an agent provocateur who has delighted in mixing it up—even if "it" means politics and literature. His first great novel, *Midnight's Children*, about India, was successfully challenged by the Indian prime minister; his second, *Shame*, about Pakistan, was banned in Pakistan; now the last in his unofficial trilogy, about both India and England, has been banned in India and burned in England. As one who was born into the Islamic faith and studied "the Satanic verses" at Cambridge, he must surely have known that his skeptic's accounting of Islam was certain to offend; yet the very title of his book went out of its way to flaunt its hereticism.

Thus some of Rushdie's detractors can now say that a symmetrical justice has been served: those who court fame end up with infamy. The man who notoriously abandoned the longtime editor who backed him for more than a decade, in order to get a contract of roughly $1 million, has now got a $1 million contract on his head. And in the same breath as he became a household name, Rushdie has become a missing person. Almost worst of all, for a writer, his work of the imagination—and an exceptionally complex work of an uncommonly fertile imagination—is now being treated as if it were a heretic's pamphlet: *The Satanic Verses* has been turned from a book into a talking point. With the drama bringing more and more readers to a novel that most will find almost impossible to unravel, one is ironically reminded of the end of that classic discussion of faith versus doubt, Matthew Arnold's "Dover Beach," in which "ignorant armies clash by night."

Yet the saddest irony of the affair of the death, and the deadly sentences, is that the writer and the orator have somehow produced one of those rare situations—like the Iran-Iraq war—in which everyone is the loser. In vilifying the book, some Muslim extremists have promoted it much more effectively than Viking Penguin could ever have done, and condemned themselves, in some eyes, to blind intolerance much more convincingly than Rushdie could ever have done. Rushdie, for his part, becomes a man with a past, and a difficult future. Until recently, for example, it was not impossible to consider him a potential candidate, one day, for the Nobel Prize; now it seems hard to imagine the timid souls of Stockholm endorsing his vision. Most dangerous of all, he may become wary of himself, may be tempted to censor his own ravenously anarchic imagination—or else, perhaps, to forfeit the realm of art for the altogether meaner alleyways of argument.

At the same time, one's heart goes out to a man now marked for life, and hiding away in London like the Ayatollahish imam he describes in his novel. Khomeini's threat is a trick as old as Hasan-i Sabbah, the twelfth-century Iranian ruler who founded the order of the Assassins, based on the knowledge that the very threat of murder can be as disabling as its execution. A man who fears that he may be killed is often no stronger than a man already dead—and a good deal more unsettled. Now, as the British government rallies behind one of its most persistent critics, Rushdie, a connoisseur of dislocation, finds himself an exile in his own adopted home. In fact, ironically, he has ended up in much the same situation as the statesmen he has always attacked—the Gandhis and Khomeini himself—living under the perpetual shadow of assassination.

The final irony of the whole sad affair is that it has, in its perverse way, vindicated the power of the written word (even a writer can make nations tremble) and of the spoken word (even an aging foreign cleric can make merchants turn their back on Mammon). Whether or not the pen is mightier than the sword, both literature and religion have shown their strength. Yet who would want to assent to the darkest heresy of all: that he who lives by the word should die by the word?

(1989)

The great problem with Salman Rushdie, I have often felt,
is that he is simply too tal-
ented. And no writer I know has
seemed more captive to his gifts: his powers of invention and imagination
are so prodigal and so singular that he often gives the impression of not
knowing when to stop. Here is a man who has devoured films and soccer
stars and pop songs and TV, in India and England and many places in
between, till his puns and polycultural references and paralleling images
multiply to the point of overload. Rushdie can often seem like a one-
man, family-of-man orchestra, with a hundred virtuoso instruments
playing all at once—and sometimes one can almost long for the simple
clarity, and quiet, of a pause.

*East, West* BY SALMAN RUSHDIE

Thus the first great pleasure of his new, and teasing, collection of stories—more a series of *jeux d'esprits*, really, or imaginative jogs—is that so
many of them are un-Rushdie-esque: slight, straightforward, open-ended.
Indeed, the first two pieces in the book, set in folksy India, make one feel
as if Rushdie is rewriting Narayan, while giving him a spin. Their backdrops, to be sure, are dark—crooks and arranged marriages and steriliza-
tions; but the ironies are glancing, and the cadences are vivid, and there is
a tenderness toward both scene and style. In its opening pages, *East, West*
is written almost from an old man's perspective, and lit up with an old
man's sense of tolerant bemusement.

As the collection proceeds, inevitably Rushdie returns to a more con-
tentious mode, and to fables that have a satiric edge to them, a hint of
dark polemic; and one of the saddest ironies of his current plight is, of
course, that it has become almost impossible to read him innocently—
everything, willy-nilly, is taken to be a reflection of his unique predicament. Ever the impenitent gadfly, Rushdie does not try to discourage
such readings, and his parables about the media and the price of fame
invariably send echoes well beyond the pages ("What price tolerance if
the intolerant are not tolerated also?"). In what will surely be the most
controversial of these stories—"The Prophet's Hair"—a moneylender
finds a hair of Muhammad's and, keeping it for financial gain, turns into
a fanatic and finds his home has become a charnel house.

Yet the strength of this story, as of the serpentine ones around it, is that it renounces easy morals and piles irony upon irony until judgments all dissolve. In the same piece, a thief gives his sons a source of lifetime income by crippling them. And they, when suddenly released from their afflictions by a miracle, are outraged. In Rushdie's grown-up fairy tales, horrors become blessings where blessings are curses in disguise. And all these perverse twists have a special authority when coming from a man who discovered riches in the same breath as a death sentence, and acquired fame at precisely the moment when he could no longer enjoy it.

The second category of stories here, set in the West, is for me decidedly the weakest, if only because it is the most *voulu* and self-amused: a piece on Yorick, for example, allows the writer to show off his runaway linguistic skills with page-long sentences and lines about how Tristram is "neither triste nor ram, the frothiest, most heady Shandy of a fellow." There is something endearing in a writer of Rushdie's stature proving unable to resist lines like "Let sleeping bags lie,"and he is surely the jokiest, even the most uncontainable, of major novelists. There is also something invigorating in the notion of post-1952 India as a new Elizabethan Age, profuse with groundlings, evacuated princes, and urban energy. Yet the problem with many of Rushdie's contemporary, glossy pieces is that they abdicate the worlds he has made his own in favor of more standard *Granta*-ish devices. When he starts assembling lists of trendy props ("edible rice-paper panties in peppermint flavour"), he sounds a little like Martin Amis; and when he descends into virtual-reality dystopias ("She was at the far end of a long, dark, subterranean bar-room guarded by freelance commandos bearing battlefield nuclear weapons. There were Polynesian snacks on the counter and beers from the Pacific rim on tap: Kirin, Tsingtao, Swan"), we are reminded of Don DeLillo. Rushdie, more than any writer, is best when he sounds like no one but himself ("Since when he contacts me on official trip? Why to hit a telephone call when he is probably enjoying?").

What *East, West* demonstrates, in fact, is that this most current and *au fait* of writers has, even in his most casual mode, a genius for all the old-fashioned skills—language and storytelling and imagination. And the beauties of these pieces come often from their impenitent gift, and zest, for language: from the way *rutputty* and *khichri* and *funtoosh!* are smuggled into standard English; from the delight Rushdie takes in "hicksville" and "spooks" (as a verb) and the "hydravarious" sounds of our promiscuous pop culture; from his grasp of a sensibility that none of his London friends could muster ("Two mouthfuls are better to eat than wind"). *East, West* is, at times, a glorious Hobson-Jobson of postcolonial usage, the product of a man who is at home enough in any culture to bring equal-opportunity affection and irreverence to all.

In that sense, these stories really do underline what has been implicit all along: that Rushdie is the great postimperial Indian writer, bringing the sounds of India—*qua* India—into an England that has often sustained a more quaintly domesticated notion of the subcontinent. Though trained in England—perhaps because trained in England—Rushdie has greater ease with India than many Indians who grew up in India under English tutelage; his is, truly, the voice of an independent nation (and, therefore, of a polyglot global village). His is a world in which Indian boys in Kensington sing Neil Sedaka songs to baby girls called Scheherazade; and where diplomats from Asia play out the Captain Kirk fantasies they hatched in Dehra Dun. It is a world where Indians from Cambridge learn about gurus from mad Englishmen, and Jimmy Greaves meets Fred Flintstone, to the tune of Ravi Shankar. And when, in passing, he notes that "Home, like Hell, turned out to be other people," it becomes not just a witticism, but a touching cry of need.

Rushdie, in fact, is always strongest when leading with his heart. I have often thought that he is a more impressive writer than García Márquez, say, because his magic is so realistic, in a sense, and his symbols are so far from arbitrary; yet by the same token, he has often seemed a less transporting writer than García Márquez. His novels sometimes feel as if they're trained at the editorial page, and his imagination is often in danger of being let down by his intellect (which is why he is that rare writer whose fiction is much more accomplished than his nonfiction). More than almost any novelist I know, Rushdie is best when writing from somewhere other than his mind, quick and many-headed though that mind may be, and when he allows his sharpness to be modified by sympathy. In reviewing *The Enigma of Arrival,* he famously noted the absence of the word "love" from all of Naipaul's sentences; and sometimes that has seemed the problem with his writing too.

Here, though, much of that is remedied, in stories that, at their best, are plain tales from the after-Raj, simple scenes of daily heartbreak delivered without fireworks or special effects. In its final section, "East, West," the collection catches the realm that may be most his own, in autobiographical-seeming memoirs that turn bitterly on how all Indians look alike to the English and how all immigrants are socially leveled down, yet also show how sweetly discolored are the aliens' misreadings of their new homes. In the last of them, and best, a sixty-year-old Indian nanny, in London, is wooed by a courtly old East European porter, over games of chess, the two of them transforming "the great formalisation of war" into "an art of love." The ultimate virtue of *East, West* is that it shows this essential writer performing a similar kind of alchemy. Beneath all the elaborate images and ornate arabesques and imaginative somersaults, one can see a novelist who is living, and acutely feeling, the mixed rat races he describes. And instead of drawing them on broad canvases that can seem as noisy and tiring and overcrowded as the streets of an Indian city, here he gives us a narrow country lane into something vulnerable and true. That is why this is the first book of Rushdie's that I have liked as much as I've admired.

(1994)

*In Praise of Folly*

---

There is a world hidden within our own that knows no boundary or nationality or context, a
world of spiritual vagrants who
drift around the sacred places of
the East in their own kind of
traveling company—living out the gypsy ideals of Romanticism, keeping
the flames of the '60s alive, seeking out drugs or gurus or the highs that
both promise to provide. They move stealthily, these members of the
shadow jet set, traditionally from Istanbul to Kabul to Kathmandu, more
recently from Goa to Lhasa to Kashgar and Ladakh, picking up exotic
terms as easily as bangles, sustaining themselves on word of mouth, scav-
enging for whatever nourishment they can find in their secular scriptures:
Rilke and Bashō, Nietzsche and Henry Miller. And though many of the
people stranded in this vagabondage are shabby fugitives, traveling for a
living and living for traveling only because there is nothing for them at
home, many more are rich enough to afford renunciation—indigent
trust-funders, alimonied women, professional dilettantes, and dispossessed diplobrats in need of no resources but the inner. Many, in fact, are
privileged sophisticates in search of the innocence or simplicity they feel
sophistication has denied them. All they really want are the basics: father,
family, and home.

Ruth Prawer Jhabvala has long staked out this domain as her own.
Gita Mehta scored a few nice points against Western journeyers to the
East turning cultural exchange into the trading of illusions a few years
ago, and John Krich actually lived out the modernist quest with an anar-
chist's skeptical eye. But only Jhabvala has given this floating world all
the benefit of her cool and patient attention, laying dispassionate claim to
all its heartless and its homeless. Deracinated dowagers, flighty middle-
aged New Agers, mystically minded cosmopolites—all these people of
indeterminate nationality and uncertain profession are Jhabvala people.
Even the walk-on parts in a random Jhabvala party are reserved for such
soigné Bohos as "a German baroness who had been a skating champion
and taken part in the Olympics of fifty years ago, and an Italian countess
who had been first a fashion designer and then a Buddhist nun before

*Three Continents* BY RUTH
PRAWER JHABVALA
*The Web* BY ANDREW HARVEY

returning to the world and taking an apartment on Madison and Seventy-third."

On the other side of the equation, waiting to receive the openhearted seekers, is a motley crowd of locals veiled in its own kind of homemade exoticism—baby-faced Bacchus-like father figures, lush and languorous Indian voluptuaries sprung full-bodied from some Rajput miniature, and slightly effete, flashing-eyed young Krishnas. All three types are both god and men; all three are both charmer and snake. And the meeting of the two worlds is, in the end, a match made in pragmatist's heaven. People who want to give up the world meet people who wish to take it over; Westerners full of questions find Easterners all too full of answers; and men of confidence work their spells upon wavering souls ready to trust anything except themselves. By now, moreover, Jhabvala is unrivaled in the skill with which she can conjure up the delicate and enchanting haze through which the showman and shaman perform their emotional rope tricks, weaving together heart strings and purse strings, mingling the sensual and the spiritual, and playing with the different meanings of the "high" until their bewitched foreign visitors can do nothing but succumb. There is a sense, indeed, in which, for all their sophisticated motions, Jhabvala's novels are really just subtler, and more exquisite, versions of Harlequin romances. Shy, unloved schoolgirl, dreaming of romance in some gorgeous exotic setting, meets dark, handsome stranger who tempts her to stray beyond her better judgment. At that point, however, Jhabvala ventures where Cartland fears to tread; and where in Lawrence, say, or Forster, pallid Anglos are invigorated by their encounters with dark and primeval characters, in Jhabvala they are simply hollowed out by them, ravished in the worst sense of the word. Catlike man devours mousy girl.

By now, too, Jhabvala has been observing this dance of the seven veils so calmly and so shrewdly for so long that she has every last detail down cold. In her latest novel, *Three Continents*, a kind of compendium of all her worlds, nearly every particular is perfect (except for references to an "Old Etonian necktie"), and not a wicked phrase is wasted. The story she unthreads, moreover, is a distinctly familiar one, and not just from earlier Jhabvala books: rootless charge-card kids from a grand old East Coast family (called, with uncharacteristic crudeness, the "Wishwells") disinherit the parents who have both indulged and ignored them, in search of a little discomfort. Soon enough, one of them, Michael, finds the difficulty he has been seeking, amidst a group of vaguely Indian types anxious to change the world. Encountered first in an Indian flophouse and then in Berkeley Square, the unorthodox triad at the center of this movement is, of course, vintage Jhabvala: a fleshy icon of pampered idleness known

as the Rawul; his glamorously bejeweled companion, the Rani; and a
beautifully ambiguous young boy called Crishi. The story that follows,
told by Michael's nineteen-year-old twin, Harriet, is simply a tale of
the Indians' gradual and inexorable possession of the rich young Americans, first their hearts and then their homes. For all its intricate refinement, indeed, the story is best described simply by the titles of its three
sections: "Propinquity," "The Family," and "In the Rawul's Kingdom."
The title of the whole could be "I Was a Teen-Age Werewolf-Lover."

Almost every page in the novel, as in all of Jhabvala, is dense with
indelible detail. On a single page, chosen at random, she catches the
inside-out slogans of these underground men ("no discipline except self-
discipline"), the postnational rites of their consumer-wise sects ("a beer-
and-tacos party"), the ironies of their look-alike gestures (the Rawul
makes his followers doff their Indian clothes for a uniform of "blue shirt
and navy jeans"), and the hard details of their high-tech business (walkie-
talkie systems are installed, while disciples work on "the Xerox machines
and the teleprinter"). In every scene, from high to low, she is at home, be
it a cheap, loud room in Delhi ("everything was painted pink and with
fluorescent tube lighting and calendars of saints and film stars and not
much furniture except for string cots and steel trunks") or a soft-voiced
London gallery run by purring upper-class Brits ("The girls in the gallery
had a confident manner and were arrogant towards everyone except one
person—Rupert's partner Nicholas, who was sharp and sarcastic with
them though very deferential with potential clients . . . greeting many of
them by their first names and kissing the air near their cheeks"). Always
in control, Jhabvala unfurls stately portraits of stately houses, lovely lyric
tableaux of the dying light about the rolling lawns of country homes, of
wet and mulchy London afternoons, of elegant Indian hotels. Like many
an Old World writer, indeed, she takes her models not from rock music
or MTV or fashion magazines, but from the classical forms of landscape
painting.

Most important of all, Jhabvala also has a faultless nose for the rules,
the ruses, and the fluent self-deceptions of spiritual movements. So sure is
her command of details that she can describe Rawul describing himself as
descended from the moon, and make the claim sound plausible. She is
well aware of how the guru uses self-deprecation at once to preempt all
criticism and to persuade his disciples of nothing more than his detachment and self-knowledge (the charlatan in her previous novel, *In Search
of Love and Beauty*, wore a Mickey Mouse wristwatch, the perfect symbol
of his sense of irony, and of his practiced impishness). She also has the
agility to follow the twists and turns of countercultural reasoning: how

the guru strips his followers of goods in order to free them of materialism; how he tells them to exercise their desires as the only way to exorcise them; and how, whenever he is in trouble with the law, he simply invokes the precedents of Socrates and Jesus. If cults are partly families and partly armies, Jhabvala is also well aware that they are largely multinationals, most fittingly regarded in terms of property deals, takeover bids, and corporate mergers.

At the same time, she understands the confusions and inadvertent hypocrisies of all those lost and lonely children so keen to do the right thing that they crucify themselves on the cross of their good intentions. She sees their eagerness to convict themselves of being conventional if ever they long for togetherness or calm; their ardent hunger for the impersonal; their earnest determination to slough off family, society, and stability in search of communes that provide nothing more than family, society, and stability. Yet she is also wise enough to acknowledge that the transaction involves something more complex than surrender: the best perception in *In Search of Love and Beauty* was that followers of gurus are not "blank pages" but, rather, people "with such complicated personalities that they could no longer manage themselves and felt the need to hand themselves over to someone else." So, too, the best sentence in her new novel is a typically penetrating assessment of mixed motives: "[The young] need a future, like the middle-aged need to recover the past that didn't come up to expectations."

And yet, after a while, for all the meticulous craftsmanship, for all the impeccable observation, for all the steady balance, one begins to notice that there is something a little preconceived about the Jhabvala vision. To begin with, there are never—never—any normal relationships in her books, never any regular parents or happy marriages. That is partly a reflection of the times, perhaps, but it is also a reflection of something else. For it is the basic assumption of all her work that everyone is on the make and every relationship is one of exploitation. In her film scripts, Jhabvala is rightly famous as the chronicler of sugar daddies and gigolos, of camp followers and charlatans; of predators, in short, and parasites. Yet her ability to see manipulation wherever she looks can sometimes seem developed to the point of self-parody. In the only scene in *Three Continents* in which Harriet manages at last to steal away from her captors, she goes for a walk in a rainy London park and is instantly accosted by an exhibitionist. She is rescued soon enough from that threat—but only at the hands of a slimy Arab, who promptly sets about raping her. Every single one of Jhabvala's people is, as Harriet says of her mother's friends, "utterly, utterly selfish and self-centered, and yet with a

nervous fervor to improve themselves," and while Jhabvala is right, perhaps, to see that power is more central than love in all these settings, she
is less convincing when she omits love altogether.

At the same time, she is so smooth and accomplished a craftsman that
it is easy to overlook these tics in print; on celluloid, however, in movies
like *Quartet* or *Roseland,* one can more easily detect, beneath all the
decorum, an elaborate kind of kinkiness that politely embraces every kind
of perversity. If ever one manages to disengage oneself from the spell
of her flowing, perfect sentences, one gradually comes to see that in
the novels, too, aberrancy is the norm. *Three Continents* has an air of
documentary-like fidelity to fact. Yet Michael and Harriet's mother is a
lesbian, their father is involved with a fluffy blonde less than half his age,
their guru is a bigamist, and his wife and son are themselves lovers who
add to the somewhat joyless fun by sharing their lovers with one another.

This sense of incestuousness doubtless contributes to the other curious
feature of Jhabvala's world: its claustrophobia, and its inescapable fixation
on suffocation (the Rani has only to stroke the narrator's cheek for Harriet to take off, half hysterically: "I was beginning to feel smothered. She
was too close to me, too large and smooth, too creamy and perfumed: a
fleshy flower of too strong a scent"). This is, of course, an inevitable
response to India, the most intense, intrusive, and inquisitive of lands,
where all barriers are dissolved and privacy is unknown. Besides, Jhabvala
has made her name, and rightly so, as the ultimate Western laureate of
the terror of its charms. Yet at times her fear of being possessed seems
almost a nervous habit, and just as Joan Didion seems to take her anxiety
wherever she goes—she can sense death and danger as quickly in a California shopping mall as in El Salvador—one feels that the similarly small,
equally detached, and slightly wallfloral Jhabvala would feel agoraphobia
wherever she travels (a suspicion hardly dampened by her famous reputation for never leaving her home in Delhi and for cooping herself up in
the same New York building as her collaborators, Ivory and Merchant).
It is, in fact, remarkable how much of *Three Continents* takes place
indoors: in stuffy hotel rooms, in undersize bedrooms, in damp London
cells, and in cosmic worlds that are always small and closed. At the end of
the novel, in a sudden burst of movement, Harriet and her surrogate
grandmother flee their hotel rooms and race through India in a train. But
of course they are shut up in an "ordinary first-class compartment" with a
barred window—"a little box of a compartment" with "the window
tightly shut"—and when they get out, they are thrown into a waiting
room where "the atmosphere was fetid, because of the crowd of poor
people waiting with their babies and bundles of food." Yet after at last
they arrive at their destination, a ruined palace, Harriet "drew the cur-

tains shut again; it was so much nicer that way, the two of us in the room together with the air-conditioner on." That, in a sense, is the perfect image of Jhabvala in India: inside a tiny railway compartment, with the country flashing past, "a country shrouded in dust, a region of invisibility which we had traversed encapsulated with our own thoughts and fears." And Harriet's response to her terror of the open spaces—shutting herself in—gets quickly to the paradox at the heart of Jhabvala: that having desperately shut out the awful, encroaching pressure of reality, she begins to feel stifled at being shut in. It is as if she quite literally felt herself squeezed between Scylla and Charybdis—the threat of being hemmed in and the fear of being swallowed up—and so, by avoiding the one terror, commits herself to the other. And if it is her sensitivity to the terror of losing one's soul that enables her to visualize with unfeigned urgency the horrors of being caught up inside a cult, it is that same sensitivity that confers upon her novels their sense of strangulation, of locking their readers up inside a dank and airless space. Like Didion again, Jhabvala seems captive to her own insecurities.

This it is, perhaps, that accounts for the third strange disability of Jhabvala novels: that for all their effortless fluency, they nearly always lack drive. Her sentences flow beautifully in a swift and easy current, yet in the end they seem to go nowhere. This is, once again, a quality most often remarked in her movies: that with the exception of *Shakespeare Wallah* or *Room with a View*, say, they are all so paralyzed by tastefulness and tact that they become coffee-table pictures, beautiful to eye and ear but lacking in all the vital fluids (as most notably in *Heat and Dust*, where beautiful people sit on lovely verandas moaning melodiously about the madness and suffocation of the heat and dust, when in fact it is precisely heat and dust that are most evidently lacking). Yet it is also a tendency apparent in her novels: the most shocking thing about a scene from *In Search of Love and Beauty* in which a child observes her mother making love to a fat old man is not that it happens but that it moves us so little. And as Jhabvala's novels grow longer and weightier and more compendious, taking in more and more of the worlds that she has mastered, they increasingly leave one with nothing more than a series of perfectly composed and perfectly motionless scenes.

In part, perhaps, this is because Jhabvala is much too sophisticated to let her characters simply degenerate, yet much too circumspect to let them grow. And that, perhaps, brings us closer to the problem. For if the folly of Jhabvala's people is to believe that they are always regenerating themselves, when in fact they are merely changing clothes, the folly of Jhabvala herself is to believe that they are terminally unregenerate. She is so adroit at exposing the perils of indiscriminate hopefulness that she

is wont to go to the other extreme. Nobody is better at catching susceptible hearts and treacherous minds; yet when it comes to the soul, to all
that is numinous or invisible, Jhabvala invariably shies away. From her
strategic vantage point along the distant sidelines, there is no way she can
perceive self-abandonment or wonder or faith—or if they are perceived,
they can only be taken as something else. Thus her vision comes to seem
as closed to hope or transformation as her characters are dangerously
open to them.

This may begin to explain why Jhabvala has never really come to terms
with the central puzzle of the whole guru scene: namely, that the bulk of
its votaries—or victims—are not just anchorless teenage waifs or fluttery
upper-class matrons but well-educated professionals in their mid-thirties
who have everything to lose by giving up the world. Jhabvala tends
to simplify the issue by remaining aloof from it. And she is so good at
reading manipulation that she tends to read everything in terms of manipulation. Thus, in some sense, she writes always from a position of
strength. And by keeping her distance from the events she records, she
virtually guarantees that neither she nor her reader will be surprised. Like
other champions of the clinical detail—Didion, Shiva Naipaul, and even
his brother—she assembles data with an irreproachably cool and clean
hand, remaining quietly in the corner, simply taking notes. Yet as with
them, by hazarding nothing of herself, she is certain to change nothing of
herself, or of her reader. And as with them, her caution can often seem
close to cowardice, a nervous refusal to be touched, let alone transformed,
by the world around them. None of them, it seems, is strong enough to
hearken to the radiant reminder afforded by Emerson, in his beautiful
essay "The Poet," that "The poet knows he speaks adequately, then, only
when he speaks somewhat wildly . . . not with intellect alone, but with
the intellect inebriated by nectar." And none is in a position to appreciate
what Andrew Harvey says of India in his new novel, *The Web:* "The
horror is easy to see, easy, even, to react to, to despise or to pity. What is
harder is to see the wholeness, the health that survives within it, despite
and beyond it."

Harvey's is an instructive counterexample to Jhabvala simply because
he is dealing with almost exactly the same themes and locations. Indeed,
*The Web,* the second in a trilogy that began with *Burning Houses,* has at
its center a classically Jhabvalian unholy Trinity, here described by one of
them, a silk-scarfed movie director turned drag queen, as "God the
Father, an aging transvestite; God the son, a Garbo-eyed Possessed One
with a penchant for ephebes; God the Holy Ghost, a gauloise-voiced
demi-mondaine." All these mandarin wanderers, moreover, are bound
for Jhabvala's three continents: India, Europe, and New York. Yet

Harvey comes at the subject from exactly the opposite angle: where Jhabvala is the perpetual outsider, telling her story in the voice of a nineteen-
year-old girl worlds away from herself, Harvey is a born-again mystic,
ready to give himself up to the world he describes, making every character
an aspect of himself. The result, of course, is infinitely less orderly, less
mature, and more peacocked than the whiter-shade-of-pale classicism
practiced by Jhabvala. Harvey is definitely an esoteric taste, and many of
his epicene aperçus and flights of cosmic fancy could be labeled, like
Harry Haller's Magic Theatre in *Steppenwolf*, "For Madmen Only." But
Harvey knows this himself, and knows that this is the price he must pay
for challenging his perceptions and leaving himself open to surprise
("How hard it is," he writes in *The Web*, "to speak of the absolutely beautiful without sounding ridiculous"). He knows, too, that only by risking
himself can he balance the view from without with that from within.
Thus Jhabvala's self-effacement comes, in the end, to seem like a kind of
self-protection, and Harvey's vanity like a kind of valor.

Certainly, there is much in Harvey that is almost willfully insufferable:
all his characters are indistinguishable, and all are preening self-infatuates
who revel in a brittle cocktail-party tinkle of epigrams and "darling"s ("I
knew a swami with the most delicious eyebrows," coos one of them, and
"One does so want to be radiant in one's coffin, doesn't one?"). Promis-
cuously flinging together high culture and high camp, chattering away in
an insider tongue compounded of Callas, Shakespeare, and Lao-tzu, all of
them are so much in love with themselves, and with their wits, that they
raise the unquiet spirit of Oscar Wilde, not just in their willy-nilly
Parisian mysticism, but also in their weakness for poses and dinner-party
paradoxes ("The thought of suicide has cheered me up so often in my life
I wouldn't actually do it"). Yet if it is the first feature of a Harvey character that he is too full of himself, and of *bons mots*, to resist such asides as
"Nothing serious, old bean, just death," it is the second to find a deeper
truth beneath the glibness: death, after all, need not be quite so serious.

And Harvey, for all his archness and his showy affections, manages to
go one step further than Jhabvala—far enough, that is, to see the fraudu-
lence of accepting ready-made beliefs, but then still further to see the
shallowness of skepticism. On the one hand, he is experienced enough to
know that religious institutions are often more institutional than religious and quickly congeal into bureaucracy, materialism, and even a kind
of totalitarian division of the world into Us and Them. He is also discerning enough to acknowledge that renouncing the world may just be a
way of renouncing a sense of responsibility, or a sense of humor: "Spirituality must not be otherworldly," says one spiritually minded quester in
*The Web*, "we have no time any longer for the whitewashed sanatoria, the

flower-gardened mountain retreats." Yet as one who was an Oxford don at the age of twenty-one, Harvey is also in a perfect position to register the limits of common-room wisdom, and the hollowness of that "sophisticated core of ignorance that invents every reason for disbelief, irony and safety." If he is too shrewd to be credulous, he is also too shrewd to be taken in by a cynicism that is as easy as credulity and often a good deal more costly. He is, in fact, one of those rare souls intelligent enough to see through the follies of the guru scene, yet thoughtful enough to see it through; more rigorous than the typical seeker, he is also more adventurous than the typical professor, able therefore to recognize that the blind pursuit of gurus discredits neither the gurus nor the pursuit, but only the blindness. Jhabvala rightly criticizes her characters for their simplistic reasoning—the West is all wrong, so the East must be all right. There, however, she stops. Harvey, by contrast, sees that if drifting around the third world on the cheap is the easiest thing in the world to do, the second easiest is finding fault with it. Thus he presses beyond the confining poles that Jhabvala erects to attempt a third and more exacting position, of honesty leavened with irony, innocence guided by intelligence. Open-eyed idealism is his aim.

Like Jhabvala, Harvey knows full well that nothing may be more foolish than the pursuit of enlightenment or self-transcendence. But he also sees that nothing is more necessary. He is wise enough, that is, to be foolish, and strong enough to lose himself. When one of his alter egos finds herself in India, she instantly sees all that Jhabvala sees from the window of her railway compartment. But she goes on, with a recklessness one can hardly imagine in Jhabvala: "I forgot myself in the misery and splash and scent and noise around me. . . . I even conquered my fear of street food, and ate fistfuls of samosas—probably, god knows, stuffed with dog meat." Self-forgetfulness, in fact, is what Harvey is all about, and therefore self-transcendence: in all his books, beginning with the starlit travel journal, *A Journey in Ladakh*, he displays himself the better to chastise himself. Thus in *Burning Houses*, a character just like Andrew Harvey reads out a dewy-eyed novel that sounds just like Andrew Harvey, only for another character to tear it ruthlessly apart; and in *The Web*, Harvey's fictional self writes moony letters agonizing about his love, only for his respondent to tell him firmly that he is in love with nothing but his sorrow and his guilt. Harvey has the courage, moreover, to present his beliefs and even his visions naked, to mock the awkwardness that nakedness involves, and then to show the shallowness of mockery. Discretion here is the lesser part of valor. " 'Into this matter, this transfigured matter, no death can enter,' " cries a Tibetan monk in a Parisian café, announcing the coming of a new order. " 'Or, rather, death and life are two sides of the same golden vibration and one enters and re-enters one and the other a thousand times a second.' The Vietnamese waitress came and stood sulkily by the table. 'Anything else?' " In the end, it seems to me, it is precisely this willingness to attempt to describe wonders that cannot be explained, to mingle irony with confidence, to make a strength of vulnerability and so to essay a compassion that cannot be rationally defended, that distinguishes such redeeming artists as Graham Greene, R. K. Narayan, or Isaac Bashevis Singer from such professional observers as Jhabvala, Didion, or the Naipaul brothers.

To appreciate *The Web*, then, the reader need only defer to the credo set down by one of its characters: "Don't be superior and don't judge on externals. Sometimes they are just a screen, a sort of wonderful absurd smoke a self throws up to hide behind and get on with its real work." For once the smoke has cleared—such is the wonder of the novel— self-regard has indeed turned into self-awareness, and the characters are indeed shown to be "precious" and "divine" in ways deeper than they know. That is the kind of achievement that Jhabvala, for all her artful- ness, has yet to attain. In one of the most damning lines in all her fiction, a wide-eyed believer tries to silence a skeptic by spitting out, unanswer- ably, "You're just being subjective." The sorrow of Jhabvala, and of others like her, is that they cannot see that the opposite is just as true.

(1987)

# The Spiritual
## Import-Export Market

Finding a guru is famously
like falling in love, and both
experiences are as irresistible to
many writers as they are notori-
ously difficult on most readers: part of the delight, and definition, of such
transports, after all, is that they place you firmly beyond the reach of
reason and of other people (even, in fact, of your usual self). And writing
about such raptures cannot be done in stages, or in measured tones. Thus
the lure of the guru poses the same challenge as any other affair of the
heart: if you're under the spell, you are, almost by definition, too tongue-
tied and perhaps shortsighted to render it credibly; and if you're not,
you're immune to its power. As Robert Capa said in a different context
(the making of photographs in war): stand too far away, and you don't
get the picture; come too close, and you're dead.

*Journey to Ithaca* BY ANITA DESAI

The best position for regarding this mating dance, then, may be the
one that generates such surprising successes as Jeffrey Moussaieff Masson's *My Father's Guru*, his disarmingly lucid and fair-minded account of
growing up with the tiny, rather suspect, but generally likable Englishman whom his parents followed around the world. In Masson's book, the
guru is seen from a liminal position by a boy half in, half out of his orbit
and at one remove from his fascination (and coercion), and to that extent
able to see him as a regular guy with irregular longings. Precisely because
the thirteen-year-old Masson couldn't think of Paul Brunton as a god (or
demon), he was able to see him as an excellent companion, a compelling
storyteller (with his exotic tales of journeys to Tibet and astral travel)—
and, in fact, the perfect diversion for a boy to have around the house.

Anita Desai seems likewise to be in a perfect position to address the
ancient themes of spiritual imperialism, if only because she grew up in
Delhi as a mixed outsider, able, she has said, to see the land of her birth
through her mother's (German) eyes, even as she felt it with her father's
(Bengali) heart. More than that, Desai has shown herself to be a connoisseur of illusion and imprisonment—the hopes with which men ensnare
themselves—and if her novels have often been about the frailty and mortality of the seemingly dignified, they have been no less about the struggle
for nobility in the face of that mortality. Most of her principals have been

dreamers and poets and hopeful young men, at loose ends often, or in flight, but set on a quixotic search for dignity (in art, in music, in the elegant old court language of Urdu), while the traffic outside brings them rudely back to earth.

The relationships in her books are less between men and women, then, than between individuals and their dreams—and she has traditionally turned a stern eye on these often passive and self-deluding men (her women, by comparison, tend to be pragmatists, and so survivors). Thus in even a relatively small walk-on part, the interestingly named Dr. Biswas in *Clear Light of Day* turns out to be a weak drifter, hostage to nostalgic memories of Germany and a desperately feckless love of Mozart—the only forces that can take him out of the pettiness of his life. In his romantic reveries, he seems more pitiful than poignant, a fool, really, who inflicts his folly on others. And so, for all the brilliantly colored vividness of her scenes, Desai has mostly given us rather dark and chastening stories about people in a loveless world, trying to make their pinched lives grand. Animals, you might say, dreaming of the stars.

At the same time, with quiet authority, she has gradually closed in on what is her distinctive domain. She began her career with relatively traditional novels like *Bye-Bye, Blackbird*, telling the now familiar tale of Indians arriving in a less than friendly England, and then moved on to richly textured, highly poised, and sometimes slightly housebound tales of middle-class India—*Fire on the Mountain, Clear Light of Day, In Custody*—all of which centered on people seeking a refuge from the world, or some kind of imaginative sanctuary (as with the old woman in *Fire*, who retreats to the mountains, only to have her peace disturbed by the visit of a headstrong great-granddaughter, who "walked about as the newly caged, the newly tamed wild ones do"). Far from the clamor of the Indian streets, far from the suffocation of most Indian families and books, her characters were generally displaced, "shipwrecked and alone," without much contact with the world around them (as Desai herself, growing up in Delhi without ever seeing Germany or Bengal, must have been), and feeling closest to worlds that are now gone (the elegance of princely India, the rites of prewar Germany, the exquisiteness of Urdu culture). That sense of alienation may begin to explain her curious fascination with zoos (ways of suggesting that, in the clear light of day, all of us are in custody); at any rate, it brought her to her last book, *Baumgartner's Bombay*, which is for me her most moving (because most mobile and energetic) work. In Baumgartner, an only child, a prisoner of war, and a hemmed-in victim of the world—a Jew in Nazi Germany, a German in British India, and then just a European in postcolonial Bombay—she found her perfect image of the perennial outcast, and the

perfect forum for drawing together the disparate worlds of her own heritage. *Baumgartner* revealed her great and signature strength to be the evocation of a European who has spent so long in India that he is almost part
of it (while always remaining apart from it); and in the driving intensity
and sympathy with which she made us feel his loneliness, she showed
how someone like Baumgartner could almost long for the strictures of his
internment camp, because there at least he was not alone.

All this would seem to lead perfectly to *Journey to Ithaca*, which traces
two overlapping and parallel stories (not always perfectly joined) about
two generations of Western seekers in India—the first the generic Euro-
travelers of the mid-'70s, who went to find enlightenment (or enthrall-
ment) in distant ashrams, the second arising out of that electric moment
between the wars when the moneyed bohemian women of the West first
came into contact with the sinuous wise men of the East (a *folie à deux* by
no means extinct). In dealing with the search for truth, Desai gets to
handle, once more, disconnected souls always estranged from their surroundings (in the eclectic collection of sources she cites at the end of her
novel, she includes not just the paintings of Nicholas Roerich, the Russian mystic, but also those of Edward Hopper). At the same time, she gets
to exercise the qualities that make her a persistent candidate for what I
would call the Somerset Maugham Award: namely, the ability, and even
the eagerness, to sympathize with spirits very different from her own (as
evidenced in the support this most tactful and restrained of writers has
given to writers as exuberant as Salman Rushdie and as heedlessly uninhibited as Andrew Harvey).

The story here begins, essentially, with Matteo, a lonely, dreamy
Italian boy, raised mostly by women, in a grand fountained villa near
Lake Como. In the sunwashed Italian lawns, the epicene English tutor
his parents bring in to teach him English, and the tapestries and silk
screens that fill his house, Desai shows us why she is a sometime colleague
of Merchant-Ivory (the producer Merchant, indeed, made his directorial
debut with her *In Custody*). And in such particular details as a peacock
sewing box and a mysterious apparition in the garden, she also shows us
she has read closely in Andrew Harvey's *Hidden Journey*. For hardly has
the tutor exposed Matteo to Shelley and *Journey to the East* than the boy
senses something lost in his soul, and finding a fellow refugee from affluence in Sophie, a sensible, "square-shouldered" German girl, he takes off
with her for the East (the two of them, as Desai rather incriminatingly
writes, "in identical blue jeans . . . carrying identical rucksacks").

They are, in fact, more types than souls, and soon enough they are
bumping into other figurative shadows, who join them in donning
Indian clothes, going to visit yogis who haven't slept in twenty-five years,

and gathering on the beach in Goa to swap tales of rape and revelation. Their wanderings through the swarm and animation of the Indian streets allow Desai to give us some of her matchless atmospherics, for by this stage in her career she is able to evoke color and sound and even fragrance almost effortlessly, at once perfectly at home in India's "heat and dust" (the terms recur often in her work) and yet still able to feel, keenly, how they shock and often crush even the most well-meaning of visitors. Whenever her prose falls into long descriptive passages, it comes into the sharpest focus:

> It was noon before they had left behind them the cotton mills and warehouses and workers' shanties and emerged into the straggling outskirts of the city where dwellings made of battered tins and plastic sheeting stood by pools of city sludge and effluents, and palm and drumstick trees made smudges of green upon a landscape otherwise uniformly grey. Finally even these shanty towns dwindled and ran out in flat fields of mud that stretched as far as the horizon.

The laughing children traveling through these vital backdrops are, however, somewhat more schematic. In Matteo and Sophie, Desai has a tidy dialectic in motion, the boy eager to find wisdom wherever he looks, the more skeptical woman (a journalist by training) longing only for a clean room. Desai brings the right kind of wryness to the cultural import-export market ("Pierre Eduard was busily collecting saints as earlier travellers had collected gold, spices or shawls"), and she certainly catches the horror and meanness of the spiritual bargain basements in which the travelers' wanderings deposit them ("his disgust infected her as if it were a disease"). And yet her young seekers never feel quite real to me, with their earnest cries of "You need to learn, man, and meditate," or "Are you all blind? The divine manifests itself in everything, everybody." They probably don't seem entirely real to Sophie, either, because she takes to going off alone each day, in flight from the ashrams, to the zoo. This is an ideal metaphor, of course, for a world in which everything is seen as a bestiary—in the space of three pages, we see Westerners living "like animals," a man who is "bestial," and Sophie herself "looking like an animal about to spring"—but it does rather load the scales.

And then at last, just as the two are close to breaking, they stumble upon the Mother's ashram, which sounds like a *Lost Horizon* vision of cleanliness and calm, its huts (somewhat to Matteo's disappointment) named not "Truth" or "Knowledge" but, simply, "Welcome." The disciples here are, true to form, seen "in the postures and attitudes of forest creatures," living in "lairs," cavorting "like young goats," and stumbling around "like ants," but still, with its carefully lettered signs, its friendly non-Indian guru, and its cool landscape of trees and hills, the place feels to Matteo like the home he has somewhere lost.

The Mother herself, "a small, aged woman . . . shrunken and somewhat hunched," of indeterminate calling and nationality, preaches a cheerful and practical kind of truth that sounds rather like old wives' wisdom ("If there is God or not, I cannot say, but there is Evil, I know"). Distributing bananas because they make one "happy as a monkey," donning "baggy white pyjamas" to play badminton, and discoursing on the "honey made from spiritual nectar" (one thinks of the teenage Masson portentously declaring, "A bee in search of honey has no prejudices"), the Mother blends a kind of Rajneeshee spirit of "Don't worry, be happy" with a Krishnamurti-like line in telling us that she has "no wisdom at all, no Knowledge" (and, with her simple affirmations of awareness and hard work and awakening to joy, this resident of the "Abode of Bliss" even sounds a little like the denizen of "Bliss Road," Dr. M. Scott Peck). Her teaching, in fact, lies less in her words than simply in her soothing, kindly voice, as she tells her disciples they should be "kittens" cared for by herself as mother cat.

To Matteo, of course, this figure seems like "a manifestation of the Divine," while to Sophie she seems like just another transplanted granny: he reaches for abstractions while she tries to bring him back to the realities of home and food and family. Their discussions are not helped by the fact that Matteo is clearly in love with the Mother ("Any time spent away from the Mother, without her, was wasted time, empty time, dead time"), while Sophie is ill and in hospital, giving birth to their first child (which, with her characteristic detachment, she sees as "a rat, or monkey"). Finally, feeling herself as confined as an animal, Sophie leaves the ashram with her two children—only to find, as Desai's earlier books could have warned her, that all the world is "a zoo, or prison" (Deven, for example, in *In Custody*, resembles "a caged animal in a zoo . . . a trapped animal," and even his hero, the great poet Nur, lives in "a cage in a row of cages"). As she fends off the lechers in Indian hotels and endures the dogmas of her family back home, she comes to see that the real world is as full of superstition and delusion as the ashram, but without its innocence or hope. She also cannot get out of her mind the memory of a stray moment in which she saw the Mother coax a whole flock of peacocks out of the wilds and realized that this "aged, solitary woman with sparse hair and a faded nightdress" had something not quite ordinary about her.

In the second half of the book, Sophie leaves her children with their grandparents (children in Desai are nearly always raised by surrogate parents) and sets off to find the real story of the Mother's early life. At this point, the book becomes the story of Laila, a rebellious young half-French, half-Egyptian wanderer (much like Sri Aurobindo's consort), who moves through a handsome series of exquisite scenes, in Cairo, Paris, Venice, and New York. And given the pointillist immediacy of Desai's prose (this part of the book might almost be called *Journalist to the East*), the narrative here picks up conviction and momentum.

We see the restless young spirit breaking out of her parents' scholarly home in Alexandria and going off to Cairo. We see her picking up some Islam there, fleeing to Paris, finding a copy of the *Rig Veda* in a musty, secret bookstore, and beginning to express herself in dance. And mostly we see her, in her adventurousness and defiance, tracing the same path as her later followers: she gives up meat, as Sophie does; she runs away from bourgeois comfort, as Matteo does; and most remarkably, she spends her idle moments as Sophie does, in a zoo, and there becomes transfixed (as Sophie does) by a single noble cat.

Then one day, almost inevitably, she finds her dreams of India come to perfect focus in a visiting dancer called Krishna, who strikes her as a shimmering embodiment of the mystic East and an image come to life from a hundred Indian paintings. Playing the role of the Divine Lover, surrounded by a group of *gopis* and appearing onstage in a "crown of peacock feathers," Krishna impresses the susceptible girl as "god-like," his proud and enigmatic face "celestially calm, powerfully noble, the eyes half closed and dreamily smiling." Beneath his eyelids, writes Desai, "the eyes seemed both mysterious and mischievous, playful and elusive as fishes in a pond."

It must be said here that Krishna may strike many readers as a somewhat familiar figure, and that the Suzie Wongs and Miss Saigons who have become the staple of every Western male's account of the mysterious East post-Loti and -Puccini have their counterparts on the distaff side. Nearly always, these lithe, androgynous objects of female fascination are called Krishna (though in Ruth Prawer Jhabvala's *Three Continents* he is called Crishi and in Rumer Godden's *Coromandel Sea Change* he is Krishnan), and nearly always they are surrounded by women of shifting name and nationality (in Jhabvala it is Rani, née Renée, in Godden it is Leila, and here it is Laila, who wants to style herself Lila). The image of the seductive god who takes on mortal form and mortal loves offers, of course, an all but ineluctable shortcut into the age-old confusion of sacred and profane stirrings. Even Tom Stoppard, in his latest play, *Indian Ink*, cannot resist having his Englishwoman in India say, "I wasn't sure of whether Krishna was a god or a person."

Desai's handling of this Orientalist trope is characteristically discreet, and her Krishna never becomes more than the languid, spoiled prima donna he first appears to be, but nonetheless, in the interests of equal opportunity, this Indian male would like to suggest that a moratorium be declared on these male Kissy Suzukis. For those who want to see the paradigm of the type, the best specimen is in *Coromandel Sea Change*, where, again, the reigning Krishna is perceived (by a neglected English wallflower) as a god, again (as in *Three Continents*) he is bent on collecting supporters for a cause, and again he seems to offer a divine blend of Western sophistication and Eastern innocence. At one point in Godden's novel, Krishnan "wore a well-cut European suit of fine linen, a shirt of palest blue that set off his good looks, a public-school tie—Harrow, wondered Mary," although, at another moment, "she could see, in the firelight, how the muscles moved with rippling ease, almost like a great cat's, under the dark skin." This puckish, insouciant charmer got a First at Oxford and can, as he boasts, speak "Tamil, Telegu, Hindi, English, French, even a little Russian" (though mostly he says things like "I am everyone, everything, just as everything, everyone is me"). And once the smoke clears, the pale girl is, of course, undone (even though, like Desai's Laila, she actually enacts the part of the god's consort Radha), the divinity is shown to have a slippery relation to truth, and we see again that "all Krishnan did was to play tricks on poor girls." In Jhabvala's *Three Continents*, for variety's sake, the guru is the product not of Harrow and Oxford, but of Harrow and Cambridge.

In any case, Desai's Krishna, true to form, lives off the attentions of fluttery Western women, and Laila joins his troupe and learns from him how in India "dance is worship, it belongs to the temple." The dancers proceed to their next rich patron, in Venice, a powerful symbolic zone for Desai's cast-off loners ("It was so strange," says Baumgartner, "it was both East and West, both Europe and Asia. I thought—maybe, in such a place, I could be at home"), but Laila remains as much an outsider there as everywhere, watching lavish tableaux of balls and bangled dancers and English dilettantes (Merchant-Ivory, take note). The scenes in Europe are as bejeweled and romantic, in *Journey to Ithaca*, as those in India are pockmarked and intrusive.

By the time the troupe moves to New York, however, its luck runs out, and Desai has some savory moments with snappy, unimpressed theatrical managers and breathlessly incomprehending headlines ("Snakes and Peacocks from East arrive"). Though Laila has indeed mastered a dance called *The Peacock*, she is soon performing onstage amidst sword swallowers, trained poodles, and a "pyramid of cages." Krishna, "the godly flute-player, the darling trickster," cuts his losses by fleeing back to India, and Laila seizes the opportunity to do the same and then cuts him to go off in search of "Eternal Knowledge and the Supreme Light."

Like Matteo, again, Laila is quite unprepared for the clutter and squalor of the land she imagines to be her home, and is shocked to find the Easterners she meets as preoccupied with worldliness and profit as any Westerner (this is by now a familiar conceit: even Boy George, in his recent autobiography, *Take It like a Man*, notes of the grabby Indians in his Indian hotel, "I've come seeking spiritual enlightenment and they want a Gucci handbag"). Broken, and reduced, like many foreigners, to her bed, she comes to long for nothing more than peace and quiet (and India, in that sense, is a perfect Desai locale, as its very cacophony and vulgarity excite a longing for sanctuaries). And then, just when we least expect it, in the shadow of the Himalayas, Laila has a blinding, blazing mystical experience, quite the equal of anything in her reading, or in Andrew Harvey ("I was on fire, the tree was on fire, light blazed and the whole sky was illuminated"). And on this ringing and radiant vision of being found and transformed, the book more or less ends. Laila finds her Lord, "[standing] there in the light of that lantern of love, golden as a rose, golden as a lotus," and with a stirring visionary daring, Desai carries us into the poems and exaltations of a sobbing, transported ecstatic.

This is in many ways a remarkable conclusion, especially for one who has written (in *Clear Light of Day*), "That was life—a snail found, a pearl lost. Always, life was that." And it establishes *Journey to Ithaca* as very much Desai's bravest and most exploratory book, as well as her longest and most ambitious. (It is also, it should be noted, the first book she has written on the move, not while stationary in India, and to that extent her most itinerant and international, as well as perhaps her most scattered and least focused, lacking at times the stillness that often lies at the heart of her work.) Roaming across continents and generations, and laying claim to worlds very different from her own, she takes structural risks here (with a very long, and somewhat circuitous, prologue) and substantive ones (trying to make credible a woman who says things like "Lead me out of the hell of hate into the paradise of love").

For me, the book's most inspired moments come without doubt through its guru. Selecting a female teacher is, I think, a particularly wise choice, and not only because such women are more or less invisible in fiction even as they become more and more ubiquitous around us (the Divine Mother, Guru Mai, and Mother Meera all have considerable followings in the United States). And using a female teacher allows Desai to show us the emotional needs a guru can satisfy without getting into the philosophical complications (it also frees her from some of the hoarier clichés of seduction and manipulation). The great charm of the Mother here lies in her humanity, her whimsy, her down-to-earthiness—her freedom from guru sagacity, in a sense—and even her teaching is, by her own admission, not the "way of knowledge" but the "way of love." She really is a kind of all-smiling, all-forgiving mother offering her followers the luxury of a new and chosen kind of family.

The other brilliant move here is to make the guru an artist, and so to change the very terms of the discussion. For throughout her work, Desai has not only accorded a certain glamour and even regality to artists but also reminded us again and again how "guru" in the Indian context means only "mentor" or "instructor"; many "gurus" are simply dancers or musicians or even poets who are presumed to have attained a high level of expertise in their disciplines and so can exact unquestioning obedience from their students, much as a piano teacher in Vienna or New York might exert absolute sway over his pupils' musical careers. In India, a music student may stay in his guru's house, cook for him, sweep his room, and lay himself entirely at his feet. And in certain contexts, a spiritual teacher may be seen as little different: an artist of the self, so to speak, who has developed particular skills that may dazzle, and even transport, the rest of us and so act as a kind of inspiration. Just as Bob Dylan's words or songs may have a talismanic charge for his fans far beyond the confused nature of the man himself, and just as we can acknowledge Mozart to be possessed of a seemingly divine talent, even as he remains a promiscuous adolescent, so a guru, a Rajneesh or a Chögyam Trungpa, say, may be a fallible man with a real gift for imparting enduring truths. In Desai's scheme, it becomes ever harder to tell the dancer from the dance.

Her central figure, moreover, is no figment of the imagination: as her notes suggest, she is a close cousin, it seems, to characters such as Ruth St. Denis, the New Jersey farm girl (with a shifting date of birth) who somehow rose from being the so-called mother of striptease to becoming the "First Lady of American Dance," performing before the doyennes of New York society, sketched by Rodin, and identified in the pages of the *National Geographic*, no less, as "East Indian." St. Denis was especially famous for her portrayal of Radha ("a dramatic, symbolic example of man's search," she once said, "for contact with the divine") and the piece *Egypta*, in which she sought to incarnate Egypt itself ("without knowing it," she asserted, "I must have been half-Oriental"); and flourishing amidst the vaguely spiritual currents in vogue at the turn of the century, her Dance of the Delirium of the Senses and Dance of the Sense of Touch prompted newspapers to headline reviews of her work: "Founds New Cult." The great—and useful—thing about St. Denis was that she dwelled in that shadowland between the secular and the spiritual (she was once called "half-mystic and half-mick"), and dancing for eight hours at a stretch even in her eighties, she made no bones about planning a Church of the Divine Dance that would blend the "motivations of the church with the instrumentation of the stage." In such celebrated pieces as *Legend of the Peacock*, she was inspired, she felt, by her faith in herself and in an unknown god (though "sometimes," as her husband wisely remarked, "she confuses the two").

Yet if Desai catches compellingly the older figures in her book (including Sophie's surrogate mother, the kindly British nurse who tends to her and is named, almost too fittingly, "Dr. Bishop"), she is less successful with their charges. Throughout her work she has evinced an impatience with the young, in part perhaps because they are the most irresponsible captives of illusion and in part, no doubt, because she is by temperament more at home with chamber music than with the Grateful Dead. None of her characters mourns her youth. "I'm so glad it is over and we can never be young again," Tara says in *Clear Light of Day*, to which her thoughtful sister, Bim, adds, "I would never be young again for anything." Nanda Kaul, in *Fire on the Mountain*, asked explicitly if she would like to be young again, answers, "No. No, I don't think I would. I don't think I'd find it—quite safe." In *Baumgartner's Bombay*, the action specifically closes in on a confrontation between two generations of Germans in India, and if we sympathize fully with the older man, the younger one ("like a sick cat") seems merely a parasite and even a murderer. In Desai, the young are more often rebuked for their confusion than admired for their enthusiasm, and it is not always easy to see a higher purpose behind their wanderings.

Here, this becomes something of a liability. The young devotees she describes feel a little secondhand to me (as if taken more from books than life) and are not always seen from within. I don't quite believe it when they say things like, "He has it bad: all that searching and meditating can drive you crazy if you haven't a guru to guide you," or, "It was full of snakes and scorpions but she stood there, man!" And I don't buy it when, in one loose-jointed discussion, "Pierre Eduard began to tear his hair at her cynicism," and, eight lines later, "Pierre Eduard flung himself forward and beat at the table with his fists." Sophie assumes that her husband's whole downfall comes out of "reading Hesse" (to which he replies, "Why do you say it leads to my death when it is to my awakening I go?"). Yet I'm not convinced that Hesse alone could ever precipitate such a move, and when Desai describes the disciples in an ashram as resembling "figures in an etching, or a tapestry," she may be speaking truer than she knows. The emptiness at the heart of Matteo cannot be written off just to mystery.

Yet to get a fuller sense of what Desai has achieved, it may be best to place her beside her longtime friend, neighbor, and partner in Merchant-Ivory dramas, Ruth Prawer Jhabvala. In many of their writings—the European sections of *Journey to Ithaca,* for example—their themes and scenes are so similar that one cannot help but feel that they've been sitting in the same rooms. And this is hardly surprising given that both lived on the same street in Delhi and are quiet, watchful daughters of German mothers, wives of middle-class Indians, and frequent travelers among what Jhabvala has called *Three Continents.* Desai's early novel *Fire on the Mountain* was actually dedicated to "Ruth and Jhab," and her new one might almost have been given the same title as the early Jhabvala collection, *How I Became a Holy Mother.*

When one picks up Jhabvala's new novel, *Shards of Memory,* one may be forgiven, then, for feeling it's déjà vu all over again. Her epigraph about memory sounds like the epigraph about memory in *Clear Light of Day.* Her young Indian poet, Kavi, dreaming of becoming a Byron, sounds like Desai's young Indian poet, Raja, dreaming of becoming a Byron. And the whole Merchant-Ivory aesthetic—slow, meticulously detailed, and sometimes more concerned with curlicues and textures than with drama—links the two still more. Here, besides, is a skeptical young woman trying to restrain an unworldly young man. Here is a boy (having been neglected by his idealistic parents) being raised by a grandmother. Here are rich women giving up their houses to vague gurus.

Yet when one looks more closely at the two, one sees that they could not be more different. For Jhabvala's stories take place almost entirely in their characters' heads, where Desai's are set in precisely described gardens and streets and homes. Jhabvala's concerns, that is, are primarily social and psychological, where Desai's are more sensual—she describes the ironies that Jhabvala diagnoses. And where Desai's characters are mostly victims of circumstance or delusion, Jhabvala's are nearly always victims of manipulation. For Jhabvala's protagonists are predators, where Desai's are idle dreamers. Jhabvala's often seem soulless, where Desai's are merely spineless. And Jhabvala, ultimately, is about people using others, where Desai is mostly about people misusing themselves.

One curious feature of Jhabvala's work, in fact, is that she is consistently less interested in the guru figure than in the projections and delusions his followers spin around him. And she tends to interpret the guru world almost exclusively in terms of this world: not as a spiritual endeavor, but rather as a political order—generally of the one-party kind—and a business proposition involving transfers of assets and real estate and trust funds (with the emphasis on "trust"). This is certainly sensible, but it is highly limiting, and for all her metaphysical settings,

Jhabvala's are among the least philosophical (or inquiring) novels around: in *Three Continents*, she coins a wonderful name for the guru's movement—Transcendental Internationalism—and then more or less leaves it at that; in *Shards of Memory*, she reduces the Master's message to a nebulous slogan of "one step higher" (easier, I suppose, than twelve steps). Jhabvala's *tricoteur* gaze is trained upon the politics of the drawing room, and the guru-disciple transaction for her is mostly a way of staging neo-Jamesian dramas of innocence and experience, in which Old World cats devour New World mice (and then dissolve often into catfights). To that extent, all her books are relatively straightforward tales of possession and repossession—*Invasion of the Out-of-Body Snatchers*, they might be called—and play on the familiar ways in which Eastern supply meets Western demand when young people eager to be taken in meet older ones eager to take them. Though Jhabvala is unfailingly shrewd ("as usual, when surrounded only by his adoring followers, the Master was bored, and eager to see other visitors"), she is content to shrink her gurus into terms she can comprehend—so the Master in *Shards of Memory* becomes part "psychologist" and part "political leader" and "really rather sweet."

One result of this reductionism is that *Shards of Memory*, to a disarming extent, reads like *Three Continents Revisited*, with the same cast of philandering fathers, sapphic mothers, bodiless young men, and confused young women, and a plump, inoffensive, and accommodatingly vague guru at their center, talking of truth. In both novels there are strange, afterthought marriages and canny, capable grandmothers. And in both novels, the guru is just a fat, jolly, somewhat self-mocking figure who sits among his supporters like a blank screen. The claustrophobia that is Jhabvala's theme and tone causes both novels to shrink into ever smaller spaces instead of opening out onto new perspectives—and though she does leave the door slightly ajar at the end of her latest book, the chink of light is not very persuasive given the emptiness of the Master's "message."

In that context, Desai's daring seems all the more impressive, as does her readiness to live with mystery. In an odd way, her somewhat downcast vision of the world actually gives her sympathy with the quest for something better (her epigraph from Cavafy, after all, suggests that it is better to have sought and lost than never to have sought at all). And in the guru she has given us, she presents someone who does not exploit needs so much as meet them, a Mother Teresa for the New Age. Yet oddly, even as she catches what is hardest in the equation (the appeal and value of the guru), she does less well with what seems easier (the psychology of the followers).

For the great conundrum of the guru scene is not, in the end, how it attracts the lost and lonely and directionless, but rather how it attracts those who have everything to lose by joining it. That is the insistent burden of Frances FitzGerald's study of Rancho Rajneesh (included in her *Cities on a Hill*), one of the most searching and careful accounts of ashram life we have. "They were not kids but adults," she writes of the Rajneeshee, "and many of them well-educated professional people: accountants, doctors, lawyers, even professors." Far from being a spaced-out flower-child commune, the ranch is an efficient and well-organized society most reminiscent to her of "Camranh Bay in the mid-sixties." And as she runs into ex–city planners, Yale doctors, clinical psychologists, and former IBM systems analysts, she comes to accept the truth of what one of them who has studied the group concludes. "By and large," he explains, "the people here on the ranch are people who have had success in worldly terms." They are not dropouts, they joke, but "drop-ups."

This is not of course true of every spiritual group (Jim Jones appealed mostly to the poor), and such an orderly and self-enclosed retreat cannot fail to gain its share of the strung-out and confused. But that is no more than to say that an Edenic beach may attract rogues. More interesting by far is the fact that these groups, like a certain kind of lover, attract precisely the kind of people who might seem to know better—in part by showing them the limitations of their knowledge (in Japan, the horror attending the Aum Shinrikyo attacks derives in large part from the fact that its members are not just the hopeless and the dispossessed but, in fact, the best and the brightest graduates of Tokyo University, who might otherwise go on to rule the country). The guru scene becomes interesting at precisely the point where it appeals to those who are skeptical of gurus (like the Rajneeshee FitzGerald meets who are scornful of "weird gurus and Westerners on strange trips of one sort or another").

Desai senses this, I think, and in her Mother (though not in her seekers) she begins to suggest how it is that someone like Andrew Harvey, who is billed on the back of his books as "the youngest fellow ever elected to Oxford," could sit for sixteen years before a relatively young, mostly uncommunicative Indian peasant girl (though now he has violently repudiated her). As FitzGerald notes, "The Rajneeshee education program struck me as surprisingly unintellectual given the number of Ph.D.s in the community," and one women in charge speaks, "like the house-mother of a boarding-school dormitory." (Desai reaches for the same image—"the atmosphere was rather like a boarding school," she says of one ashram, and, of another, "It sounds like school, like a British boarding school.") It is, one assumes, precisely by virtue of being non-verbal and nonintellectual that Mother Meera could give Harvey something he couldn't get at All Souls, just as it was apparently the simplicity and clarity his Indian guru opened up in him that struck Christopher Isherwood as tonic after the complications of Cambridge and Berlin. Desai gets at much of this with her admirable willingness to understand (and not to do so), and her evocation of warmth as a kind of wisdom, as well as transport, takes her further, I think, than almost any of her predecessors. Yet motherly care alone (as she knows) is not the whole of the mystery. Or as Boy George puts it, rather memorably, "Religion is like a beautiful flower with sharp teeth."

(1995)

I t seems only appropriate, perhaps, that of all the books tumbling off the foreign presses
purporting to explain Japan to
the West, the most revealing

*The Remains of the Day*
BY KAZUO ISHIGURO

one so far is not, in fact, set in Japan, has nothing to do with Japan, and,
as it happens, is a novel about six unexceptional days in the cloistered life
of an English butler in 1956. Yet the author, Kazuo Ishiguro, is one of
those lucky individuals with one foot on either side of the widening gap
between Japan and the world at large: born to a samurai family in
Nagasaki but resident in England since the age of five, he is as Japanese as
his name and as English as the flawless prose he writes. Janus-mined, he is
perfectly positioned to see how one island of shopkeepers, bound by a
rigid sense of class and an unbending sense of nationalism, can shed light
on another; how one monarchy, bent on keeping up appearances, in part
by polishing nuances, is not so different from another; and, in fact, how
the staff of an English country house, with its stiff-backed sense of "self-
training," its precisely stratified hierarchy, its uniforms and rites and
stress on self-negation, might almost belong to Sony or Toshiba. No man
may be a hero to his valet, but every valet is a samurai hero to his man.

*The Remains of the Day* is, as its title suggests, written in that favorite
Japanese form, the elegy for vanished rites: it is a vespers novel, set in an
England made more lovely and more lulling by the late-afternoon light in
which it is seen, dark shadows lengthening across the empty rolling
lawns. And to all appearances, the novel, which recently won the Booker
Prize, is nothing more than a depiction of a certain kind of man, reflected
in the elaborately formal diary of a butler as he takes himself on a
motoring holiday through the English countryside, doing nothing more
dramatic than looking in on a former colleague, peering, in some
perplexity, at the ways of the ordinary world and wondering what "dignity" in a butler truly means. *The Remains of the Day* may seem just a
small, private English novel done to—Japanese—perfection: a *vale* from
a valet. To anyone familiar with Japan, however, the author's real intention slips out as surely as a business card from a Savile Row suit.

For Ishiguro's butler is so English that he could be Japanese, in his finely calibrated sense of rank, his attention to minutiae, his perfectionism, and his eagerness to please; his pride is his subservience, and his home is only in the past. Stevens has no self outside his job, and no thought for anything except his job; he even—like a good company man—gives "military-style pep talks" to his staff and surrenders now and then to "wishful thinking of a professional kind." His is the gentleness of innocence as well as self-delusion.

In smaller ways, too, he reminds one of a *salariman:* solemnly practicing witticisms in the hope of putting his new employer at ease, and deriving his great—his only—emotional excitement from agonizingly impersonal daily chats over cocoa in the pantry with the housekeeper. Sometimes, when he addresses his dying parent as "Father" (and never "you") or when the woman who is closest to him delivers sentences like "Is that so, Mr. Stevens?," his narrative might almost be translated from the Japanese; and sometimes, when he reveals, in all naïveté, the discriminating assumptions on which his life is based—"But life being what it is, how can ordinary people truly be expected to have strong opinions on all manner of things?"—one can almost hear the unconscious snobbery of Sei Shōnagon, or a hundred other ancient Kyoto courtiers.

Yet part of the skill of Ishiguro's plot is that by placing us inside the butler's voice, and mind, he makes his most distant qualities accessible to us, and almost touching. He lights up the Japanese mind from within, and then shows how it is all about us: the rococo periphrases, euphemisms, and litotes, the life so provincial it could be almost prelapsarian, the unfailing self-surrender that seems so alien, so Japanese to us—all are alive, and not so long ago, in the quiet hills of Oxfordshire. When Stevens reminds a colleague, "Our professional duty is not to our own foibles and sentiments, but to the wishes of our employer," it sounds perfectly natural, even normal, in the context of their lives; and when he reminds himself, "There was little to be gained in growing despondent," his stoicism makes all the practical sense in the world. Seen from afar, he might seem cold or prudish; seen from within, he is a profoundly decent man trying to do his best. In perhaps the novel's central scene, the bespoke butler dutifully goes about his job, tending to the feet of a distinguished guest, while his own father dies of a stroke upstairs. In most lights, this kind of self-denial would strike us as unnatural to the point of heartlessness. But in the context of Stevens's high-minded code of service, it becomes the crowning achievement of his career—grace under the intensest pressure—and one can almost see how he can recollect the night of his father's death "with a large sense of triumph." Here is the heroism of Benkei at the Bridge, here the self-transcendence of Shinji Hasegawa at the Seoul Olympics, robbed of a gold medal after four years of practice, yet refusing to indulge himself in protest.

Stevens's life, as he sees it, has no meaning save in self-subordination. He is only as great as the man he serves, and he can best serve king and country, he believes, by waiting, quite literally, upon history, keeping the silver polished on behalf of the ministers and ambassadors who visit his house to change the world. "A 'great' butler can be only, surely, one who can point to his years of service and say that he has applied his talents to serving a great gentleman—and through the latter, to serving humanity," he opines (not so different from "I work for Mitsubishi, therefore I am"). And as befits a classic retainer, Stevens does indeed shine in the reflected glory of his lord: on those infrequent occasions when he ventures outside the manor gates, he is taken by nearly everyone he meets, with his perfect manners, his well-cut suit, and his posh address, as a gentleman himself. Yet it is one of the sad ironies of his sheltered life that he never fails to be disarmed, even intimidated, by the very people who look up to him; Stevens is never more moving—or more Japanese—than when he earnestly meditates on the virtues of "bantering" and realizes, to his sorrow, that he will never be able to speak the language of the world.

For while Ishiguro can create an utterly convincing Japanese from the inside out, he is also far enough away from Japan to be able to count the cost in fashioning so limited a self; and to see that meticulously sticking to decorum is a way of staying at a safe distance from warmth or wit or risk. Not for Stevens the bold inspirations of Jeeves—he is a man who lives entirely by the book, permitting himself neither opinions, nor curiosity, nor even, really, self. And in the end, it is his very virtues—his loyalty and diplomacy, his self-restraint—that leave him high and dry. His unquestioning fidelity to his master's voice leads him to defend a man who fraternizes with Nazis and dismisses two housemaids on the grounds of their being Jewish. And his insistence on self-control at any cost, and in any context, prevents him from admitting, even to himself, any softer feelings to sustain him—such as love, perhaps, or hope. For all his command of subtleties, Stevens is, in some ways, emotionally deaf, trying with reason to fathom the logic of the heart. "Why, why, why do you always have to *pretend*?" the woman who loves him finally cries out; to that, he can answer only that it is his duty, his self. The dying light that casts a valedictory glow on all the fading houses of his world finally includes the protagonist himself.

The great skill of Ishiguro's book—the grace of his position, perhaps—is that he lets us sympathize with both the lover's impatient cry and the butler's perfectly dignified response. In that sense, he shows us

how unreasonable it is for us to expect those trained—or even hired—
to be self-annulling to act otherwise; and how unreasonable for them to
expect us to renounce impulse or emotion. In the process, he begins
to explain how the Japanese can be highly sophisticated, yet innocent as
toddlers; refined, yet seemingly by reflex; extraordinarily considerate and,
in spite—indeed *because*—of that, apparently unfeeling. Translating the
most Japanese of virtues into terms we recognize as our own, he brings
their most foreign features home to us.

Without a doubt, the thirty-five-year-old author owes a great deal to
his background. The atmosphere of all his books is set by the title of the
first, *A Pale View of Hills*, and all three of his novels have that same ink-
wash elusiveness, an ellipticism almost violent in its reticence; all three,
moreover, are exquisitely fashioned miniatures, miracles of workmanship
and tact that suggest everything through absence and retreat. His books
are all as delicate as antique vases, and sometimes just as cold. Occasionally, in fact, his craft can seem almost too well designed, too careful in its
calculations: it seems almost too symbolic that Stevens's English country
house be taken over by a crude, straight-ahead American, and too allusive
that a couple mentioned in passing, just before an Indian anecdote,
be called "Mr. and Mrs. Muggeridge" (as if to summon up Malcolm
Muggeridge, who famously—and appropriately—claimed that Indians
were the last great Englishmen). Yet all this can be forgiven so long as
Ishiguro shuttles with such discretion between his motherland and his
mother tongue, making close to us the quiet heroism that is the other,
unacknowledged side of Japanese "inflexibility." There is a nobility to
Stevens's uprightness, and a pathos too, only compounded, perhaps, by
his awareness that all the world will interpret it as folly. In the end, *The
Remains of the Day* is a perfectly English novel that could have been
written only by a Japanese.

(1989)

# A Martian in
# Mittel Europe

"I can produce something pretty strange and weird now," Kazuo Ishiguro told me, in an interview three years ago, of the way *The Unconsoled* BY KAZUO ISHIGURO

that winning the Booker Prize might liberate him; he longed, he said, to break through the veil of expectations and constraints that both his success, and his readers' stubborn determination to take him absolutely literally, imposed. He could appreciate himself, he said with typically wry detachment, the drawbacks of an "overperfect novel," like *The Remains of the Day*, a book, he said, that had been almost too easy to write, "a bit like pushing a button all the time"; now he wanted to try something wild and even frightening, which would prevent him from ever being taken as a realist again.

In *The Unconsoled*, his first novel in the six years since his Booker victory, he has surely succeeded beyond all expectations, for even though every sentence and device and theme is recognizably his, he has written a book that passes on the bewilderment it seeks to portray. *The Unconsoled* is an odd, sepulchral, mazelike journey through a nameless European country with no point of reference save the North Road, the South Road, the Old Town. It tells of Ryder, a celebrated pianist, who arrives in the haunted town to give a concert and finds himself led, like a silent witness, through a never-ending sequence of unexplained mysteries, old wounds, and vicious rivalries, none of which he (or we) can begin to understand. Before he has even arrived at his hotel room, he is being lectured at by a porter who is old, ill, and full of embattled pride (Stevens the butler in a new disguise) and who pours out his life's sorrows and frustrations in a three-page monologue.

Everything in this penumbral shadowland passes, in fact, like a dream. Old friends from the past suddenly appear, and cause has no relation to effect. Time and space are weirdly exploded, so that the first night in town alone takes up 148 pages. And as in a dream, everything is so without context that one does not know whether to laugh or to weep. ("Surely there's no doubt about it," a woman says, drying her eyes. "He was the greatest dog of his generation.") Some of it is sad, some of it is zany, much of it is obscure—a Kafkaesque horror story made to play like social comedy. And though Ishiguro evokes this lightless, claustrophobic world with wonderful economy, conjuring up mists and dead ends and look-alike housing estates, the real proscenium is the mind itself: this is the human tragicomedy as seen from a Martian viewpoint.

Readers familiar with Ishiguro's earlier novels will feel themselves at home here: the beset narrator is forever saying things like, "Suppressing a sense of panic, I set about formulating something to say that would sound at once dignified and convincing"; the overall tone is one of nostalgia with an edge—nostalgia tinctured with self-delusion; and the stiff, excruciatingly formal, and secret-filled town is, like all his protagonists, more concerned with the past than the future (is, you might say, Stevens writ large). The whole murky book is about being in the dark, about being a foreigner in an ill-lit minefield, and the protagonist's air of baffled politeness, when confronted with the unknown, acquires at times an almost Paddingtonian air—"It's quite all right, Miss Collins . . . Please don't worry. I wasn't really upset at all."

Yet beneath the formality, the book's signature tune is oddness. Sometimes, without warning, we enter other characters' heads and rooms; sometimes Ryder becomes privy to what other people are saying about him. Nearly everybody speaks in the same studied, almost disembodied voice (even a little boy, asked how his day has been, answers, "Somewhat tiring"). And as in a Lewis Carroll fantasy—this is an abstract *Alice*—the main character is almost entirely passive, and the events that jump out at him are almost nightmarishly funny (suddenly, out of nowhere, someone will pop up and say, "Is Henri right in believing we can't at any cost abandon the circular dynamic in Kazan?"). At the end of 535 pages, one realizes that one still doesn't know the main character's first name.

There is only one writer whom Ishiguro resembles, and that is Harold Pinter: both have a knife-edge eye for English lunacies and hypocrisies, and both have an uncanny ear for the threats within requests and the coercions in civility. Ishiguro, perhaps because he is (like Pinter, in his way) a foreigner to the rites of the English middle class, has a wicked way with nuance, seeing the menace in "You will come, won't you?" and hearing how "Very understandable" can often mean "Absolutely unforgivable." Here, of course, he is in his perfect element, in the wings and corridors of a posh hotel where people are putting on their best faces to try to impress a distinguished guest (and his eerie, dreamlike ramblings through the back corridors of the hotel are a perfect metaphor for what the book is about). In one typical scene, the obsequious manager is so anxious to make Ryder more comfortable that he forces him to change rooms—his kindness itself an intrusion, and ultimately a kind of selfishness.

Much of the book, in fact, reads like the harried, disoriented report of someone who has just been on a book tour (Ishiguro spent eighteen months touring with *The Remains of the Day*) and whose discomfort at all the demands made on him is only compounded by his inability to say no. The book is in large part about assumptions and presumptions, about being put out and put upon (and putting on a face of obliging acquiescence). Part of the sad horror of Ryder's visit is that, ricocheted like a pinball from request to obligation to life story, he comes to see how much these strangers have staked their lives, their loves, their hopes on him; how much he is an unwitting pawn in other people's incomprehensible dramas.

Yet even sadder is his dawning realization that nothing he can do can help them: in one extraordinary scene, Ryder actually sits next to two women who keep talking about how much they'd like to meet him. The desolating import of *The Unconsoled* is that everyone is ultimately locked inside his own concerns, deaf to everyone else, and doomed to shout his sorrows to the wind. And what is touching in Stevens, say, when seen from within, when seen from without can seem petty or self-deluding or irrelevant. One recurrent trope here is of hearing screaming behind closed doors; and when an old man confesses at length (at huge, imposing length) his wish to make love again to a long-ago sweetheart, there is disgust and absurdity mixed in with the pity.

The real theme of this profoundly lonely and harrowing book is disconnection, and nearly all of its incidents are about misunderstandings and missed understandings. Everyone is speaking a different language, in some sense, and so everyone ends up unheard and unhearing. As the title suggests, the book gives us a vision of humanity so abject in its self-enclosure and its vanity that there seems to be no hope: everyone is waiting for a savior whom all of them would be too blind to see even if he were in their midst.

One of the distinctive features of Ishiguro's world is that it is an overwhelmingly social one: his milieu is a relatively formal, civilized, ritualized kind of interaction in which people seem to have no existence outside the way they are perceived by others. All life is a performance for him (as befits, perhaps, a writer who learned to speak English by copying the sounds of the five-year-old English boys around him)—all of us are butlers, in that sense—and that notion takes on a literal meaning in this book as Ryder is forever about to mount a podium to make a speech. Thus, in a device characteristic of Ishiguro, he is habitually planning "at least one spontaneous witticism" or repeating things like, "The task was to strike the correct balance between the sorrowful and the jovial" (the natural response of a foreigner suddenly set down in a society he cannot read), and every effect is planned, every emotion made up. It is this almost crazily self-conscious eagerness to do and say the right thing that can make his dialogue sound like some old joke about a Japanese man saying, "Honorable sir, very sorry to be bothering you with my suicide" (and though he would not like to hear it, the way people here refer solemnly to "Father and Mother," their constant use of honorifics seldom heard in contemporary Europe, their relation to grandparents and their answers of "Is that so?" all could be translations from the Japanese).

What distinguishes *The Unconsoled* from his earlier books, though, is that much of the action takes place backstage, as it were, and we are pushed back and forth between the practiced public selves that people present before the world and their sudden expression of hidden aches and sorrows and rage. We see here both the weasel and the cocktail cabinet (no wonder Pinter bought the film rights to *The Remains of the Day* with his own money). "They'd go out of their way to be kind to you, sacrifice all sorts of things," says a woman, reminiscing, "and then one day, for no reason, the weather, anything, they'd just explode. Then back to normal again." The strangeness, the manic comedy, and the chilling sadness of this novel come from the movement back and forth between people keeping up appearances, and then letting their feelings crash through.

In that sense, the book is a natural extension, and grand amplification, of *The Remains of the Day*, presenting us with a whole world made up of Stevenses, a whole society that wonders if it has missed the point and missed the boat, and comes to see that perhaps, at some critical juncture, it was too timid, too accommodating, too dutiful, to stand up for its real needs. And in the end, when Ryder himself, the helpless audience to other people's problems and regrets throughout the book, breaks down, we see that he, too, is burdened with pressures he hasn't been able to confess to anyone; that he, too, has been the victim of his own eagerness to please and self-suppression; that he, too, in honoring little obligations, has missed out on the biggest ones of all. Like Stevens, he is forced to acknowledge that in his very readiness to be manipulated, he has cheated himself out of a life.

In many ways, *The Unconsoled* marks a return to the Ishiguro we knew before *The Remains of the Day*, whose first two novels were haunting, and entirely enigmatic, and notable for their control of tone. For despite its perfect lucidity, this book is transparently opaque. Every detail of its craftsmanship is, as ever, seamless and unimpeachable, and Ishiguro is so polished a storyteller that he leads us with smooth self-effacement through a series of set pieces that are, in their content, suffocating and unyielding and very heavy going. Yet sometimes the effects are so calculated and careful (in the book as much as in the characters) that I felt as if

I were hearing about sadness rather than feeling it; that the pathos of the human condition was coming to me at one remove, analytically rather than emotionally. *The Unconsoled* is a humane and grieving book, as well as one of the strangest novels in memory. But as Ryder congratulates himself on feeling "rather pleased by the tone I happened to strike, perfectly poised between seriousness and jocularity," one can almost sense how a master of tone might find his own effects heartbreaking.

(1995)

# A Small, Bewildered Foreigner

Although Paddington cele-brates his twenty-fifth anniversary this year, he seems no older than when first we met him. A hopeful gleam ever in his eye, he

*Paddington's Storybook*
BY MICHAEL BOND

is still tumbling down the manholes of propriety, spinning around the revolving doors of language, and bumping his head against all the baffling vagaries of British life. Yet however often Paddington loses his balance, he rarely abandons his equilibrium. Through all the blandishments of multimedia fame—grasping toy makers, television makeup men, translations into twenty tongues, and imitators neither sincere nor flattering—the little bear manages, as ever, to land on his paws, with good nature and politesse intact. His misadventures have left him a little wiser, perhaps, but no sadder.

Paddington's gift for survival springs, I think, from his happy, evergreen mixture of naïveté and maturity. For he is no ordinary bear, no idle plaything to be cuddled, cosseted, or kept, cobwebbed, in the children's closet. He is, rather, a fully rounded character zestfully moving in grown-up circles: his best friend, after all, is that other kind and elaborately courteous émigré Mr. Gruber, his persistent foe the Shylock of Windsor Gardens, Mr. Curry; neither Jonathan nor Judy enjoys so close an understanding with their buoyant and bewhiskered houseguest as the eminently prudent Mrs. Bird. Small wonder, then, that Paddington's discovery in a railway station echoes Jack Worthing's in *The Importance of Being Earnest*, while his spirited declarations are delivered, on television at least, by Sir Michael Hordern.

Just so, the universe through which Paddington bundles is neither whimsically personal (like Pooh's) nor idyllically pastoral (like Toad of Toad Hall's). Its wonders and excitements are simply and authentically familiar: Paddington's "Aladdin's cave" is Mr. Gruber's antique shop, his land of enchantment the City of London in which Mr. Brown works. The villains Paddington faces are not monsters but small-time crooks, the rewards he enjoys not pots of gold but mugs of cocoa. Although Michael Bond teases many ineffably funny visual and verbal effects from his protagonist's bearhood, his plots invariably turn upon the bear's everyday humanity: Paddington is fundamentally a small foreigner doomed to accident-prone bewilderment. Indeed, the very innocence of his assumptions exposes him to anomalies that he in turn exposes to us, for in his alarm Paddington reveals, and often reverses, inequities that we tend to take for granted: the mysteries of instruction manuals that assume the reader to be brilliant and the world to be compliant; the hypocrisies of snooty garçons who would rather stand on ceremony than wait on tables; the treacheries of an idiom in which the same word carries very different meanings.

But even as he tilts against such sophisticated foils, Paddington remains an eager and intrepid ingenue who regards the world as we did in those days when we were old enough to be intrigued by its complexities and young enough to be puzzled by them. His is a life at once charged and, ultimately, charmed: he, and we, can relish all the glamour of exhilarating treats and all the danger of dizzying perils in the knowledge that our hero will at last be rescued and returned to a comfy armchair at home. Michael Bond himself has allowed that Paddington "goes back to a slightly pre-war world which is fairly safe," the world, one assumes, of Bond's own youth. Paddington will always, it seems, be current precisely because he lives in a changeless past: reading of his escapades is like revisiting the pre-fallen, never-never land of remembered innocence, rich with such cozy, but thrilling, pleasures as special outings and scrapbooks, pocket money and buns.

And yet, after all the winning features of his universe are mentioned, it is to the bear from Darkest Peru that one returns, and to the awareness that he remains close to us because, at heart, he is so amiable and well-meaning a soul. Even while tripping over baroque puns and banana peels, Paddington is a resolute little fellow of strong principles and few prejudices, full of resourcefulness and free of rancor: at once the bear next door and something of a role model. Throughout *Paddington's Storybook*, a greatest-hits album of ten routinely splendid stories culled from eight of the eleven earlier volumes and escorted by Peggy Fortnum's inimitable full-color illustrations, Paddington is, of course, in trouble. He tugs at an innocent bystander's beard, executes an unorthodox *pas de deux* with a Russian prima donna, and, at an expensive restaurant, pours water over an omelette *flambé*. But on every occasion, before they can chastise him, authorities are disarmed and dignitaries quite charmed by the modest, duffel-coated figure whose only, and original, sin is innocence. Whether administering hard stares, gallantly raising his hat, or fishing for emergency sandwiches from his battered suitcase, Paddington, with his friendly optimism, guarantees his own resilience, and moves one to hope that by the time of his golden anniversary, it may seem that the station was named in honor of the bear.

(1983)

The *Misalliance* is not a novel, really, so much as a portrait of a lady, a handsome miniature of a certain kind of woman, of a certain age, childless, alone, and

*The Misalliance* BY ANITA BROOKNER
*Persian Nights* BY DIANE JOHNSON

adrift in her own private universe. Blanche Vernon's husband has recently left her for a flighty young computer programmer, called (too fittingly, perhaps) Mousie, and in a larger sense, the whole world has left her, too, for the flashy novelties that Mousie represents. The setting of *The Misalliance*, and almost its only subject, is the curtained life of an elegant, intelligent, self-possessed woman, alone at her window on long summer evenings, looking out on the world from which she is excluded, and wondering to herself, without anger or self-pity, what it avails her to have prudence, patience, and forbearance in an age when all are out of style.

For Blanche is a model of old-fashioned goodness and Old World breeding in a time that appreciates neither, a kind of noble Hermione in a video arcade. She is one of those eminently civilized women who can use words like "behoove," "volage," and "noisome" with scarcely a trace of self-consciousness and who consoles herself on lonely nights by taking Plato to her bed. Yet all her strengths are liabilities in a modish world that cannot take her on any terms except its own: because she is uncomplaining, she is seen as unfeeling; because she is strong, she is regarded as tough; because she is learned, she is deemed to be odd. Blanche's greatest sin is to be irreproachable.

*The Misalliance* explores this predicament not so much by putting Blanche into the world as by putting the world into Blanche. For Blanche, like many a solitary person, lives mostly in her own head, organizing her perceptions into the tidiest of patterns and inhabiting a private mythology. Considerably closer to art than to life, she gradually comes to see her world through the lenses of the neoclassical painters she so admires in the National Gallery—divided, that is, between the brilliant, charmed, amoral gods who frolic careless in the clouds, and the well-intentioned, martyred souls below who are forever struggling to do the decent thing. The relevance of this scheme to her own life is almost

painfully apparent, as sensitive, sensible, selfless Blanche is again and
again confronted, and conquered, by a new breed of pretty young things
who cannot imagine a world outside themselves. The simple, sadly per-
plexed question that the novel keeps asking is why men so often abandon
good women for impossible ones.

Brookner herself obviously feels a strong sense of kinship with her
heroine. For she, too, is a subtle classicist in an unsubtle pop-star age,
bringing to the brittle surfaces of contemporary London a ceremonial fluency and an unfashionable sense of irony. And she, too, an art historian
when not engaged in writing novels, seems most at home amidst the
settled verities of still life. Her loveliest effects are painterly: "She saw the
park at Versailles, always deserted in its farthest reaches, golden leaves
settled in drifts around the bases of the statues, the water in the stone
basins still, undisturbed by the fountains, and mirroring the slow clouds
in their lofty movements." Mirroring the slow clouds in her lofty movements, Brookner excels at decorative domestic touches, at catching
flowers and curtains, fabrics and china, the play of light on lusterless
London evenings. "A shaft of sun struck through the window, as an
almond biscuit, essence of bourgeois sweetness, crumbled into sugary
dust on Blanche's tongue." Such is a Brookner epiphany.

In a sense, indeed, Brookner has the style and sensibility of a collector
of antiques: her prose gleams with a burnished vintage elegance, and her
weighty, beautifully carpentered paragraphs resemble Chippendale desks,
in which the sentences are arranged like impeccably organized drawers,
each of them aglitter with bright jewels. Socially, too, Brookner moves
almost exclusively within a rarefied Jamesian domain of minute observations and fine discriminations, the small dinner-party world of the
English upper middle class, untouched by anything needy, and un-
changed since the age of Bloomsburials. As a well-bred heir to the Grand
Tradition, Brookner is habitually loath to raise her voice. Indeed, the discretion of her novel, and its distance from all vulgarities and headlines, is
announced in the very first sentence: "Blanche Vernon occupied her time
most usefully in keeping feelings at bay." The ambiguity about where the
emphasis should fall (on "most" or on "usefully"?), the nice use of "usefully" to dissociate narrator from character, the scrupulous vagueness of
"feelings" (which kind of feelings are being kept at bay, and whose?)—all
usher the reader into the most decorous of drawing rooms.

In its procedure, then, *The Misalliance* itself ends up becoming very
similar to the plush, exquisitely appointed, somewhat narrow room that
Blanche inhabits: it is as lovely, as shuttered, and as sad. And much in
keeping with the Woolfian tradition, very little really happens in the
book: its plot is as impalpable as the shift from spring into summer; its

moods develop as subtly as the changing light in Monet's studies of the Thames. Blanche is never haunted by the wild spirits that trouble her counterparts in Bowen or in Woolf; nor does she even share very much, except for her costly innocence, with the tea-cozy spinsters of Pym. Indeed, Blanche moves in almost no circles except her own mind, and her mind, like that of anyone alone, tends to move in circles of its own. At times, therefore, the book returns so often to its central contrast between women of no substance and excellent women that the point, for all its understated delicacy, may come to seem a little overstated.

In the end, though, Brookner's modest, flawless chamber is largely redeemed simply by the fact that it is wonderfully *inhabited*. In Sally Beamish, the languidly imperious temptress who reclines in her unmade life, treating the world as her personal plaything, Brookner has fashioned an unforgettable image of the kind of young beauty who captivates people stronger than herself and masters life by mocking it, a perfect '80s Rosamond to Blanche's Dorothea Brooke. And in the attractive composure of Blanche herself, weak only in her dreams, Brookner invokes all the pathos of a passing age, knelled by the knowledge that "time misspent in youth is sometimes all the freedom one ever has; that is why the gods are always young." Over the course of a few short chapters, Blanche gradually becomes so real as to be sympathetic, and so sympathetic as to seem downright heroic. So when at last she resolves to throw aside her duty and presume for once upon the world, one almost feels like cheering. Without a hint of strain or fuss, Brookner has somehow moved from asking how a woman can please a man to wondering how a woman can please herself, and yet she has posed the issue with a subtlety too fine to be simplified by doctrine, and a civil grace that marks the distance between feminism and a feminine position.

Diane Johnson's novel begins at almost exactly the point where Brookner's leaves off, with a self-determined, intelligent woman, in early middle age, embarking on a trip alone, into the unknown, and so into an unknown self. Chloe Fowler, the heroine of *Persian Nights*, is, as her name suggests, a somewhat ingenuous and Victorian woman, old-fashioned enough to enjoy tatting, cooking, and childbearing, yet shrewd enough to recognize herself as "the most unliberated woman she knew." Like Blanche, she is sufficiently proper to conceive of adultery only with her husband's old friend, and like Blanche, she looks on with wry bemusement as men of her age throw over their wives for thoroughly unsuitable young girls. Like Blanche above all, Chloe "regretted this curse of reasonableness, and longed to be, but knew she could never be, flamboyant."

Unlike Blanche, however, Chloe gets the chance to take a holiday from self, if only, perhaps, because as an American, she occupies a much more open and emancipated world. Where Blanche only walks through museums, Chloe actually works in one, and where Blanche comes almost to resemble an ageless and bodiless figure locked in some mythological frieze, Chloe is, for all her bookishness, an active contemporary woman living in a world of sex, of politics, of sexual politics. In a sense, indeed, Blanche and Chloe do not inhabit different worlds so much as different ages, as different in their way as England and America. One might almost say that the Anglophile Chloe, who wishfully likens life in an American compound in 1979 Iran to the "life of an eighteenth-century village, say, in England," is the kind of woman who longs to be an Anita Brookner heroine but is doomed by circumstance to inhabit a much more modern world.

All of which is another way of suggesting that Johnson's settings are more banal than Brookner's impressionistic landscapes, yet also more exciting. For although Chloe is a modest housewife, with quaint habits and PBS tastes, she is also a decidedly Californian woman, a peroxide blonde who shuns red meat, sticks to diet drinks, and frankly expresses her admiration for male bodies. Enthralled by the Islamic veils that she sees as both a refinement and a repression of the sexual urge, she is more of a feminist, and less of one, than Blanche could ever be, at one moment maintaining, rather stridently, that "to the eye of a guard, all women are interchangeable," at the next wondering dreamily "how Muslim men were in bed. Maybe they were terrific, intense, insatiable; you heard of men with harems who had to do it ten times a day."

Chloe brings to Shiraz, in short, both a mind overstuffed with rose-colored images of pavilioned sensuality, torn from some unexpurgated copy of *The Arabian Nights*, and a highly realistic openness to romance quickened by the last-minute disturbance that has kept her husband at home. For more than two hundred pages, *Persian Nights* is little more, in fact, than a matter-of-fact account of Chloe's unsettled and exhilarated impressions of her strange new home, spiced up with thoughts of dysentery. In true soap-opera fashion, the American couples in the medical community in Shiraz swap partners, gasp at poverty, discuss their therapists, and long for egg creams.

*Persian Nights* is saved from becoming just another story about analysts and adulterers only by the menacing, fleetingly glimpsed presence of Iran in the background. For if the Americans in Shiraz are more interesting than they would be at home, that is only because they steal into different selves abroad, gathering secrets and prompting speculations. In the helter-skelter confusion of Iran in 1979, everyone is strange to everybody else, and everyone is suspect. Iranians watch Americans watching

Iranians, none of them knowing who is SAVAK and who CIA, all of them assuming only the worst. By day, the Americans move through a prefabricated world of coffee and gossip; by night, they are alone again, and uncomfortably aware of shadowy presences at the edge of their vision—a figure at a window, a corpse in the dust, wild dogs howling in the dark.

With these penumbral shapes seeping across the Americans' vision, as ineluctable as blood across a Kleenex, the novel slowly gathers momentum until, very suddenly, in an extraordinary twenty-five-page scene at the ruins of Persepolis, the Iranian world once and for all blots out the American. Suddenly the lights go dead, and the American sightseers who have come to watch a sound-and-light show are lost, separated from one another, alone in the dark. Through the long and vertiginous hours that follow, the tourists can only cower in the desert, listening to footsteps, distant calls for help, the occasional sound of gunfire. By the time the light has returned, unknown local forces are shooting it out down below, while the visitors remain crouched behind their rocks, guiltily aware of how much they should be doing and how little they really can do.

And suddenly, by the end of this wild and remarkable scene, *Persian Nights* has been transformed from a mild Forsterian comedy of manners into a palpitating drama. Suddenly the Islamic revolution is no longer just an exciting topic for faculty club discussion but a deadly political struggle with stakes far deeper than the visitors can fathom. And suddenly the blithe illusions that the Americans have smuggled in through customs are exploding in their faces, as their casual inability to distinguish one Iranian from another becomes a terrifying inability to separate good from bad.

All the visitors, then, undergo their own kind of revolution. Chloe, for example, has until now grown steadily more Iranian—slower, more sensuous, dense with secrets; she has even taken to wearing a veil. After Persepolis, however, she is newly aware that the veil is not just an exotic kind of sexual aid but also a set of blinders; it makes her unseeing as well as unseen. And as she is swept up in the country's turmoil, in Tehran, for the first time, surrounded for the first time by everyday Iranians, and out in the streets, she is forced for the first time to recognize—like Sarah at the end of the "Raj Quartet"—how deeply she is implicated. In the final, clamorous scenes of the Americans' inglorious flight—fighting and fretting over boxes of caviar to take away with them—Johnson slyly notes how their destinies for the first time reflect those of the people around them. And the violence in the Iranian streets is more than matched by the turmoil in the American hearts, as they struggle with the mixed feelings of leaving danger behind. For the saddest goodbyes of all, as Johnson knows, are those we say to ourselves, at foreign airports, as we shed the daring and irresponsible selves we have come to acquire abroad, and re-collect our normal working lives.

*Persian Nights* becomes, therefore, a penetrating meditation on Abroad, and on the price we pay for seeking unrealities. Abroad eroticizes us, pro-pelling us into a heightened state of sensation, but finally our flirtation with the unknown makes claims on us we did not seek. Abroad, we have the luxury of imagining ourselves heroic, able to change every life including our own; but in the end, as Chloe learns, the thrilling cloak-and-dagger schemes that she dreams up to help out various Iranians are mostly ways of helping her image of herself. Abroad, we are free of iden-tity, but in the very same breath we are also loosed from every kind of certainty. *Terra incognita* is seldom *terra firma*.

Diane Johnson has none of the gorgeous finish of Brookner, nor the chamber-music beauty. Hers is an altogether looser style, with nary an ugly sentence and nary a striking one. When her characters thrash out "penis envy" on the streets of Shiraz, one winces, perhaps, as Blanche might do, and when she heads her chapters with quotations from FitzGerald's Omar Khayyám, one senses the literary critic hijacking the novelist. The dazzling scene at Persepolis is almost blocked out by the wealth of its symbols (the outbreak of violence coinciding with the coming of Chloe's period, for example, and the final struggle centering upon the all-too-relevant image of an American archaeologist selling arms to rebels in exchange for artifacts, precious pieces of their past). As their occupations might suggest, Johnson is the more literary of the two authors, and Brookner the more artful, for better and for worse.

In the end, however, the distance between the two is best measured, perhaps, by the different kinds of English that each applies to her title: Johnson's describes, with straightforward irony, the romance of the visi-tor who finds in her Persian nights more mystery and more darkness than she bargained for; Brookner's passes an altogether more detached and ambiguous kind of sentence. That may be because Johnson is using her slightly flimsy characters to point up a breezy moral lesson on the deceits and seductions of being a tourist at a revolution; Brookner is crafting a much more private elegy for the kind of woman who is a tourist every-where, even, and especially, at home.

(1987)

# The Meek Inherit No Earth

I f self-consciousness is one pre-requisite of worthy fiction, its opposite—the play of the un-conscious—is surely another. Art cannot exist without some degree of artlessness; no amount of calculation can produce an

*Grace Abounding* BY
MAUREEN HOWARD
*No Fond Return of Love* BY
BARBARA PYM

epiphany. But in an age when we are reminded on all sides of critics and criteria, when the nature of good writing—and good reading—is publicly defined again and again, novelists must often be tempted to listen more closely to the mandates of pundits than to the secret urges of the imagination. Novels these days are more and more often written by the book, dictated not by the Muse but by a sense of what Great Literature ought to be.

In two recent books, two highly accomplished novelists, Maureen Howard and Barbara Pym, address the tricks and treacheries of the wanton unconscious. Yet Howard's artistic method is as self-conscious as Pym's is self-effacing. And, perhaps not coincidentally, Howard, apparently a cosmopolitan writer *au fait* with today's approved fictional strategies, spins an absorbing tale whose virtues run ahead of its achievements; while Pym, whose mystique lies in her relative indifference to literary trends, writes an appealing novel whose whole is more distinguished than its makeup.

Howard's *Grace Abounding* reads, in a sense, as if it were designed to be put together or taken apart in some school of creative writing: all its themes are capitalized for easy digestion, all its symbols spelled out for trouble-free dissection. Every motif is placed just so, every irony comes thoughtfully gift wrapped, every metaphor has been laid out as precisely and tidily as hors d'oeuvres at a fashionable cocktail party. For all its melodious fluency, its metropolitan refinement, its impeccable manners in entertaining grand American themes (the loneliness of the imagination, the encroachment of the prim upon the primitive, the barbaric yawps of the Genteel Tradition, and the need to balance loves both sacred and secular, and so to find a religion that is a form of love and a love that is a form of sacrament), *Grace Abounding* seems, in its subtle way, to be anything but subtle.

Such schooled artfulness and calculated helpfulness are disappointing, I think, given Howard's distinct gift for evocation and ellipsis. She seems intent upon presenting the lovely sylph of her prose in the one context—a hermeneut's seminar—where its elegance and grace will be least appreciated. For there is no disputing that the novel's plangent phrases fall just right. Its incantatory, cloistral rhythms both advance the story and cast shadows on its surface. Lullaby and threnody chime in its clean cadences; church bells toll through its moody sentences. Yet it is precisely the knelling eloquence of Howard's opening—a kind of spinster's Song of Songs—that makes redundant her portentous references to the Bible. Her beautiful conjuring of the noiseless, weightless swirl of a snowstorm in which movement and silence fall together makes gratuitous her begged-for comparison with Mrs. Dalloway. Her intermittent astuteness—in noting her heroine Maude's realization, for example, that with her mother's death she has lost a pet name and therefore a kind of identity—puts to shame all the studied subtleties of calling the heroine "I" and "Maude" and "Bert Lasser's wife" to show how everyone presents different selves to the different souls she meets.

There is no denying that Howard is a conscientiously observant writer who registers with wonderful precision the details of commuter lifestyles, intellectual trends, and social postures. Many of her interiors have the bright, clean spaciousness of *New Yorker* covers. She records tone-perfect exchanges ("Out with those boys until this hour?" asks a concerned mother. "We went to Dunkin' Donuts," answers her sullen daughter), coins trenchant phrases (one couple had become "Christmas Card friends"), and even catches fugitive sorrows ("What Bert Lasser never got was how deeply his wife feared purposeless days"). Thanks to the density of its prose and the shrewdness of its choices, *Grace Abounding* does manage to cover a large amount of ground in a small amount of space. And yet in spite—perhaps because—of her self-consciousness, Howard often does little more than trick up a melodrama in the season's latest literary fashions. Her shortcomings, moreover, seem the result not of too little thought but of too much; of plotting not wisely but too well. She confuses the stylish with the stylized. And so, at heart, and beneath all the palpitating prose, her novel enjoys little of the tranced and transporting mustiness of a real American original like Marilynne Robinson's *Housekeeping*, nor even quite the cosmopolitan poise of Shirley Hazzard's *Transit of Venus*. *Grace Abounding* has, in the end, too little witchery and too much craft.

To say that Howard's book comes to resemble the envelope that

Maude finds, "written so nicely and evenly it might be penned by a schoolmarm or nun," makes it sound as if it were written by the relentlessly unfashionable (though currently voguish) Barbara Pym. Yet for all their convergences, the two are actually worlds apart. For if Howard's characters and devices are unflaggingly sophisticated, Pym's people and prose are above all else straightforward. Both novelists favor dank, close chambers, but Howard searches for infinite riches in the little room, where Pym prefers to dwell on—and in—its smallness. If Howard is grand (and very American) in her ambitions, Pym remains deliberately circumscribed (and very English) in hers, and where Howard's women entertain visions that are gaudy, shocking, and chic, Pym's country-mouse females enjoy the most modest, even moth-eaten of dreams. (It is noteworthy, too, that the American heroine is young at forty-three; the Englishwoman aging at twenty-seven.) Pym's patient, diffident women—blue of stocking, not of blood—treat life as if it were a book they were not writing but reading. So, too, Pym is determined to have almost no designs upon the reader, no great expectations, no intricate patterns except in her plot. Her charm lies in her innocence of literary fashion, her willingness to sew together a series of shrewd observations into nothing more, nor less, than a solid, old-fashioned entertainment.

From the deflationary title of *No Fond Return of Love* to its benevolent conclusion, Pym restricts herself to the narrow imaginative limits occupied by her unprepossessing heroine. Like the rest of Pym's fiction, this novel resembles nothing so much as a cramped, somewhat lonely little bed-sitter complete with floral wallpaper, well-made bed, and pot of strong tea. Psychically, the weather forecast always calls for mild drizzle; the menu generally offers up macaroni and cheese, tomato soup, and boiled potatoes, with Nescafé for pudding; the dramatis personae include nobody except timid scholars, spinsterish researchers, and bachelor clergymen. And all the excellent women are, of course, themselves vicars—unrewarded consolers and confession takers who choose to live vicariously.

Pym catches the tiny tremors and shy sorrows of these women *manquées* with such glancing precision, balancing amusement and sympathy so evenly (and instinctively), that every incident becomes, as the heroine regards a friend, "at once comic and pathetic." Pym's eye infallibly alights upon all the humble objects that are, as she puts it, "mean" unless or until they are transfigured by sentiment. Above all, she expertly calibrates the gradations of embarrassment, regret, and disappointment. "Life," she ventures, "is often cruel in small ways." The sentences that stick here, and the sentences that sting, are always spoken softly: "It is sad, she thought, how women longed to be needed and useful and how seldom most of them really were," or, "Perhaps it is sadder to have loved somebody 'unworthy' and the end of it is the death of such a very little thing, like a child's coffin."

The transforming grace of Pym's measured compassion is that she brings to her sheltered characters the same strict wistfulness they bring to the world, yet treats their lackluster good nature no more kindly than does the world. Many of her heroines are as polite, well-meaning, and earnest as any foreigner; their element is innocence and their natural environment a schoolgirl's world of crushes and mild-mannered schemes, lessons and secret treats. They are still guileless enough to regard a librarian as glamorous, compare an old professor to Rupert Brooke, listen with beating hearts to a lecture on "the terrors and triumphs of setting out a bibliography correctly." And in the end, their deepest sorrow is that they are unable to abandon this sweet naïveté, yet much too sensible to allow themselves the luxury of foolishness or hope. The absence of glitter from their lives is only made the sorrier by the absence of illusions; the inalienable sadness of Pym's forgotten characters lies less in the drabness of their lives than in their steady and unsentimental acknowledgment of that drabness. Both of the quotations that conclude the previous paragraph are placed in the person of the heroine; elsewhere, she asks, almost rhetorically, "Do we all correct proofs, make bibliographies and indexes, and do all the other rather humdrum thankless tasks for people more brilliant than ourselves?" Beyond making sympathetic those characters who seem charmless from the outside, Pym manages to convey the ache of their knowledge that they will never by themselves win sympathy from outsiders.

Pym's women are, in addition, much too practical to linger on their disappointments: they recognize that these must be borne bravely, and alone. And their sadness is tenacious because it involves no bitterness and no prospect of epiphany. Their lives, the heroine thinks, have "the inevitability of Greek drama." But in reality, of course, her life proves to be all inevitability and no drama, all sorrow and no sweep. It is not a dark star that hangs over such destinies, just a very dim one. Howard's characters fly on the wings of reverie to a Brontëan heath; Pym's women visit that magic place fleetingly, but are doomed to awaken almost immediately, aware that theirs was an unattainable dream and that they must attend instead to the daily round.

Though Pym's devices are certainly as careful as Howard's, they refuse to draw attention to themselves. Pym is content to allow features to remain features without becoming themes. Thus the names in her novel are by no means carelessly chosen, nor are they transparent: the still pretty but entirely unromantic heroine is called "Dulcie" (though she does in a moment of panic seize upon the alias Miss Lamb).

When the brave, goodhearted, lonely heroine is seen through the eyes of her sweet eighteen-year-old niece—as a bland, joyless dullard—we do not see so much as feel her hurt. And though Christianity is a constant presence in Pym's novels, their matter-of-fact moral is that the meek, however blessed, will not inherit the earth.

Pym takes trouble all the while to observe the rules of storytelling. She organizes her fiction with brisk aplomb and drives her story forward at a smart, sprightly pace. Every strand of plot is assiduously tied together with an economy and a reliance on coincidence that make her universe a small world as well as a world of small horizons. Although she indulges herself cautiously by obliquely defending her art ("People blame one for dwelling on trivialities . . . but life is made up of them," muses Dulcie, while a housekeeper assures her elsewhere, "Oh, I know it's a trivial detail, but these are the things that make up life, aren't they"), she tells her story and, when it is finished, stops. She does what she can do, and nothing more.

This can, on occasion, make her universe almost suffocatingly cozy (even when the protagonists repair to a seaside resort, they meet nobody there save schoolteachers and clergymen, and even when they board a train, their fellow travelers are—what else?—a clergyman and his maiden sister). It also means that one of her books is almost indistinguishable from another and that her entire oeuvre can be—as a Pym character might put it—quite pleasant but a little tiresome.

Of the two novels, *Grace Abounding* is undoubtedly the more daring, more exciting, more important; but its knowledge of its own importance and its anxiety about it tend to obscure its intrinsic power. And where *Grace Abounding* disappoints only because it delivers much less than it promises (or even pretends), *No Fond Return of Love* satisfies because it provides exactly what it claims. On reflection, the pleasures of glittering soirées may prove less durable than those of teatime chats in modest quarters where words are more innocent and lines less rehearsed.

(1984)

# Richard Burton in
# the Peace Corps

Charm is one of the easiest
ways to sell a travel book, and
making oneself seem agreeable,
or one's destination Arcadian, is
a surefire way to attract a reader-

*The Happy Isles of Oceania*
BY PAUL THEROUX

ship. One of the peculiar charms of Paul Theroux, by contrast, is that he
makes no attempt to ingratiate. He simply presents things the way he sees
them and himself entirely in the raw—often prickly and superior and
unfair—and he tosses off his chapters without frills or fuss. His narratives
race past with the quick immediacy and apparent candor of a diary unexpurgated, and one seldom feels that he is looking in the mirror to see
what impression he is making. He is, in fact, unembarrassable. Which
other writer would go out of his way to endow a fictional protagonist
with all the details of his own life (in a book teasingly entitled *My Secret
History*) and then portray his alter ego as mendacious and exploitative
and self-centered? And how many other travelers, after meeting the
governor-general of New Zealand, would simply pronounce that she
is "silly and shallow and unimaginative, as well as bossy and vain and
cunning"—and then, the *coup de grâce*—"but principled in a smug and
meddling way"?

At the same time, Theroux's new book, which finds him paddling
alone in a collapsible kayak through fifty-one islands of Oceania, reveals a
much more sensitive soul than the bogeyman of legend. Perhaps because
he is more vulnerable than usual—traveling in flight from a painful
divorce and the threat of cancer—he seems almost eager for delight, and
the title of the book is not ironic. The close reader, in fact, will find
Theroux, all but inadvertently, fretting about the "fragile ecosystems" of
Tahiti, railing against nuclear testing, and delighting in islands free of a
"money economy." He always sides with the aborigines, hates "anyone
who killed animals for sport," and even admits to being a fish-eating
vegetarian. Drinking green tea in his tent, and marveling at the sight of
romping dolphins, Theroux sounds at times like just another healthy
outdoorsman from Cape Cod. (At one point, he gets so moved by the
starry firmament that he includes exactly the same description, word for
word, in both Chapter 15 and Chapter 16). Again and again one finds

oneself recalling that Theroux began his wanderings as a Peace Corps vol-
unteer—part of the most liberal and idealistic group of the '6os.

Like many travelers, Theroux is readiest to find good in those people
most removed from himself and is harshest on other white sophisticates, whose lies and delusions he can see through. Certainly, he has no
patience for prudes or pseuds, and turns a pitiless eye on anything
approaching the high and mighty. Throughout his trip, he rants against
missionaries and never mentions the Japanese without making a joke of
them. "Ignorant" and "stupid" and "sluttish" are three of his favorite
adjectives.

Yet what this sometimes obscures is the fact that he is an uncommonly
literate and inquisitive and hardworking traveler, drawing locals out
about their past, collecting thirty indigenous words at every island he
visits, making sketches of canoes. His tastes are nothing if not varied (he
listens on his Walkman to Kiri Te Kanawa, Charlie Parker, and Chuck
Berry), and at every stop, he burrows exhaustively into some theme, be it
the "semiotics" of Honolulu's class divisions or the perfidy of Thor Hey-
erdahl. His curiosity is endless—it is incuriosity, indeed, that most riles
him—and it throws up fresh curiosities at every turn. "Guadalcanal," he
informs us, is derived from the Arabic, Wadi el Ganar, the hometown of
the area's first Spanish explorer. Tonga does a roaring trade in Tongan
passports (Imelda Marcos bought one for $20,000). Frenchmen buy their
teenage Tahitian mistresses sets of false teeth, which the men remove
whenever they return to France. And nearly all these odd epiphanies are
enlivened by a rapid vitality—the king of Tonga, lecturing him on the
Franco-Prussian War, has a voice "exactly that of someone protesting as
he swallows his mashed potatoes."

The great charm of his book, in fact, comes from an unhesitating
irreverence that Theroux shines often upon himself. He dispenses with
the obvious Pacific ironies fairly quickly—that beaches are used as toilets,
that islanders eat their fish out of cans, and that the greatest sailors in the
world, the Polynesians, all boast of getting seasick. But what he develops
is a much wider line in mischief, subversively urging a Solomon Islander
to get his own back by setting up a business in Japan, and scouring the
Bible to find quotations with which to flout fundamentalists. At one
point he meets a woman who says, "You must write Paul Theroux–type
travel books" (and elsewhere a Chinese Mimi Theroux, who turns out to
be married to a relative). He also gives us tantalizing glimpses of the suffering man beneath the quick facade, weeping when he sees a happy
family, imagining himself dying abroad, and feeling his loneliness
mocked and underlined by the extended families all around.

Theroux is at his best, then, when he is furthest from his own opinions. His evocation of Easter Island as a dark chill place of whistling winds and bolted doors is extraordinary, and made me want to reserve a seat on the next flight there. At other times, one can feel him growing tired and tiresome—especially in his passage through Tonga and the Samoas. Tongans, he asserts, are "usually late, unapologetic, envious, abrupt, lazy, mocking, quarrelsome, and peculiarly sadistic to their children." Western Samoans are "gloatingly rude and light-fingered." American Samoans are "oafish, and lazy, and defiant and disrespectful." It is not so much that this is wrong—though I confess to having found Western Samoa fairly idyllic—as that he devotes ninety-five very long pages to an area in which he can find little to like, and so turns what could have been the richest travel book of the year into a tome that feels as overweight and exhausted as the people he mocks. There is, I think, something almost unhinged about his glee in vituperation at times, and as the adjectives pile up, almost out of control ("The French are among the most self-serving, manipulative, trivial-minded, obnoxious, cynical and corrupting nations on the face of the earth"), one can feel him drawing dangerously close to the disturbing hatreds of his half-genius brother, Alexander, author of *Three Wogs*.

Yet just when the storm clouds are blackest, he will rebuke his own intolerance, or acknowledge that he is merely visiting his moods upon the places he visits. ("No sooner had I made my mind up that these people were brutes than I met a person who was decent and restrained, dignified and helpful, among the most hospitable I had ever met in my life.") And in his impenitent political incorrectness, as in his unvarnished directness, he has something of the vigor of a classic Victorian explorer, calling spades spades and fools fools, yet always with an arcane volume at hand, and a compendious interest in everything around him. He is certainly unabashed about sounding supercilious ("I could not remember having seen a people so bereft of enterprise, so slow of speech, so casual in manner, so indifferent to a schedule, so unable and unwilling"). Yet he is equally unafraid of talking pidgin to the locals, sharing megapode-egg omelettes with them, or portraying himself, in borrowed clothes, as resembling "a mentally defective bum." This Everyman's Naipaul is as full of surprising affections as of raving annoyances.

In the end, in fact, the author he most resembles—traveling alone, strapped within his headphones, a perpetual outsider at the communal feasts of the Pacific—is another untamed New Englander with a French-derived name, an affection for Cape Cod, and an aversion to all finery: Thoreau. Here is the same unassimilable crankiness, the same rage at bigotry, the same quirky erudition (Theroux has even written an introduction to Thoreau). And here is the same exploratory isolationism. One cannot help noticing how he looks with envy at a beachcomber he meets and admits that "My ideal island would have a sandy beach, and coconuts, and jungle, and no people." And as he ends his trip—forsaking a $2,500-a-night suite in Hawaii for the luxury of camping under the stars, at $2.50 a night—one begins to sense that his fifteen-foot boat is, in a sense, his cabin in the woods. His Walden Pond is the whole Pacific.

(1992)

# An Englishman in Paradise

If Christopher Hudson didn't exist, David Lodge would have had to invent him—or at least that side of him that the former chooses to explore in his tender and searching new book. For the story that Hudson examines is archetypal to the point of being allegorical: a bookish and reserved young Englishman, in the mid-'70s, wins a fellowship to write on paradise, and elects to do so in the California Eden of Santa Cruz, where the notions he is writing about are dancing in the sunlight all around him. Before he knows it, intellectual thesis and sensual reality are entangled between the sheets, and the scholar is trying to tap out his research in the midst of naked young girls (who find him as exotic as he does them). Even the modulated lyricism of Hudson's evocations of juniper and pine and sweet-scented nights is strikingly reminiscent of Lodge's descriptions of Berkeley and Honolulu—and a reminder of the fact that the Venice the nineteenth-century Romantics sought is now to be found in the American West.

*Spring Street Summer*
BY CHRISTOPHER HUDSON

Yet that rough outline does scant justice to the weight and resonance of what turns out to be a beautiful and risky meditation on memory and Elysium and loss. As Hudson returns to Santa Cruz to seek out the enchanted boy that he once was, and the seven housemates who shared his lost, forgetful summer, thirteen years before, he finds, not surprisingly, that everything is changed, and he ends up with a generational study that might almost have been called *42-Up*. The Maoist gardener is a lawyer now, and the drug-taking Don Juan a high-tech businessman. The "University of Arcadia," as he calls it, is negotiating to set up an industrial park. More than that, the returning prodigal sees how much he didn't see before, and how much what he didn't see combined with what he didn't remember to make his paradise plausible. He also finds that California is hostile to memory (which is, of course, what drew him there in the first place).

To that extent, *Spring Street Summer* is a parable of returning to the place where one started and knowing the place for the first time. In retrospect, Hudson can better understand why he fled to California, in flight from the smooth diminishments of English cocktail parties and the pinched injunctions of Methodist grandparents who taught him that duty was preferable to love and that pleasure was a shortcut not to heaven but to hell. In California, he could learn about a paradise that was not lost but about to be regained. In California, he could round out the classical forms he absorbed in the shadows of King's, Canterbury (also, by curious chance, the alma mater of the definitive English pagan in California, Alan Watts, and of our foremost contemporary explorer of anti-Englishness, James Hamilton-Paterson).

Yet as he listens to his old friends' very different versions of the past, Hudson comes to recall how skepticism in California is "just another word for emotional withdrawal." And as he sees them hankering after the very stability that he was trying to escape, he acknowledges that paradise is best appreciated in the context of its absence. Shuttling back and forth between the Christian notion of paradise as a transcendence of earthly temptations and the Californian notion of paradise as a garden of earthly delights, intercutting his readings in Augustine and Aquinas with his romantic interludes among the lemon trees, he begins, in fact, to learn the lessons that strike many an Englishman in California: that paradise is often a conspiracy of memory and innocence; that golden ages, in time and space, are as equivocal as childhood; that paradise is best known only when it is lost.

Rarely, however, have these conclusions been developed so thoughtfully or feelingly, and with an honesty deeper than mere commonplace. Though Hudson is open and sensitive enough to lose his heart to Santa Cruz, he is also alert enough to see how much it is taking out of him, in terms of irony and energy, and a sense of responsibility, and to note how close it comes to Ariosto's Garden of Alcina: "its danger lies not in what it does to you but in what it allows you to do to yourself." And if he is provisional enough to seem quaintly English to his Californian housemates, he is passionate enough, one suspects, to shame his former colleagues at the *Spectator*. *Spring Street Summer* involves a treacherous amount of self-examination, yet one that Hudson handles with such tact and grace that his experiences become ours. And as the narrative goes on, it ripens into a much wider and deeper cross-examination of the costs of paradise, and its consequences, especially for the orphaned dreamers of the '60s. Christopher Hudson has written a lovely book, and one that will be deeply moving to anyone who believes that the real tragedy of consciousness came when paradise was expelled from Adam and Eve.

(1992)

# Private Eye, Public Conscience: The Works of Raymond Chandler

I lit another cigarette and looked at the dental-supply company's bill again. The minutes went by with their fingers to their lips. Then there was a small knocking on wood. It was a blonde. A blonde to make a bishop kick a hole in a stained-glass window. She smelled the way the Taj Mahal looked by moonlight. She gave me a smile I could feel in my hip pocket. "Cops are just people," she said irrelevantly. "They start out that way, I've heard."

The lines above come from four different novels by Raymond Chandler. Yet all of them seem to issue from our memories or dreams, or at least the ones in which we picture ourselves, alone in the office, dreaming of cool blondes and stiff whiskeys (or cool whiskeys and stiff blondes). Raymond Chandler was ghostwriter to the sound track our lives so often imitate. The figure of the tough but tender hero cracking wise to cover up his soft spots, the lethal blonde, and the flick-knife dialogue on which the movies (and so the rest of us) still feed—all seem to have been copyrighted by the onetime oil executive who began writing at the age of forty-five. In seven novels and in the screenplays he wrote for Billy Wilder and Alfred Hitchcock, Chandler scripted much of the unshaven poetry and arsenic idealism that form us now, and haunt us still, in Mickey Spillane beer ads and smoky urban videos, from Jack Nicholson's Chinatown to Joan Didion's Malibu.

Chandler is not, of course, the only American writer with a centenary this year who worked in a British bank, steeped his writing in the classics, and explored the breakdowns of the age in cadences so memorable that he seems to have taken up a time-share ownership of Bartlett's. But T. S. Eliot was an American who found his voice in England, and in books. Chandler, by contrast, was an honorary Brit who smuggled two foreign substances into Hollywood—irony and morality—and so gave us an unflinchingly American voice, the kind we hear in the rainy voice-overs of our mind. Few would suggest that Chandler is a more significant literary figure than Eliot. But quality and influence are mysteriously related, and Chandler has inspired more poses and more parodies, perhaps, than any other American writer of the century save Hemingway. Eliot merely articulated the deepest spiritual and emotional issues of the times; Chandler put them on the sidewalk.

Chandler's most immortal creation—coproduced by Humphrey Bo-
gart—was the quixotic figure of the gumshoe: Philip Marlowe, private
eye and public conscience, sitting behind his pebbled-glass door with an
office bottle and a solitary game of chess. What made Marlowe special
was simply the fact that he was nothing special, no genius like Sherlock
Holmes, no *Connoisseur* model like James Bond. Just an underpaid
drudge with, as one mobster says, "no dough, no family, no prospects, no
nothing"—except a habit of making other people's worries his own, and
a gift for walking in on corpses he knows just well enough to mourn.

Chandler's greatest invention, however, may well have been Marlowe's
constant adversary, California. Nobody has ever caught so well the smell
of eucalyptus in the night or the treacherous lights and crooked streets of
the L.A. hills. In Hollywood, city of false fronts and trick shots, Chandler
found the perfect location for investigating artifice, and with it the
shadow side of the American dream of reinventing lives. The one time
Marlowe enters a Hollywood stage, it is from the back, and that, in a
sense, is his customary position: seeing glamour from behind, inspecting
illusions from the inside out, a two-bit peeper spying on the rich man's
costume ball from the service entrance. His is a Hollywood filled with
missing persons, bit players who are living a long way from the lights:
gigolos, gold diggers, and snooping old women, remote-controlled punks
and "the kind of lawyers you hope the other fellow has." Chandler found
gurus, juju addicts, pornographers, and abortionists before most people
knew they existed.

It is no coincidence, then, that Chandler's most famous weapon was
the simile, the perfect device for describing a world in which everything is
like something else, and nothing is itself. And the unrelenting sun of
California only intensified the shadiness. By the end of his career, in fact,
Chandler was pulling off a series of bitter twists and brilliant turns on the
paradoxes of illusion: the prim secretary from Manhattan is, in truth,
from Manhattan, Kansas, and turns out to be a tight little chiseler, while
the movie-star vamp has a fugitive innocence the more theatrical for
being real. Chandler's greatest technical flaw—his way, ironically, with
plots—arose from the simple fact that he felt the only real mystery worth
investigating was morality, and why only the innocent confess, while
murderers are brought to no justice but their own.

There was, of course, an element of romantic sentimentalism in much
of this, as Chandler well knew—it was no coincidence that he called his
first detective Mallory. Chandler identified all too closely, perhaps, with
his "shop-soiled Galahad," struggling to maintain a code of honor in a
Hollywood that had never heard of the Marquis of Queensberry rules.
And he certainly knew the sting of being typecast as a small-time opera-

tor. ("The better you write a mystery," he complained, "the more clearly you demonstrate that the mystery is really not worth writing.") Yet what he knew most of all, as one of Hollywood's great theoreticians, was that a writer cannot afford to be too removed from the streets, and that what the public needs is a shot of romantic realism. T. S. Eliot was a civil man, and a public-minded writer, and so it is only right that his anniversary be marked in public ceremonies; Chandler was the laureate of the loner, and so his admirers recall him now in quieter ways, alone, unnoticed, with a light on in their darker corners.

(1989)

In Japan, as in many places, America is still regarded as the home of optimism. But nations, no more than individuals, are often negligent of their blessings. This year marks the centenary of one of the republic's most bountiful and boundless founts of optimism; yet the occasion is more likely to be marked abroad. Henry Miller—his middle name was Valentine—was born the day after Christmas, one hundred years ago, and spent the next eighty-eight years as a professional enthusiast, making a living out of pleasure and a music out of saying yes. Where an Old World master, like the peerless Graham Greene, could write elegant circles around doubt, hedging belief in with a knot of moral ironies, Miller just went straight to faith. From the first page of his first book—"I have no money, no resources, no hopes. I am the happiest man alive"— through fifty-odd books about finding ecstasy in squalor, he simply sang of life and love as if the two were interchangeable. His guiding star was Rabelais's "For all your ills I give you laughter."

In the days when Miller was growing up, the Genteel Tradition was in its prime: so much of America was so captive to European proprieties that it might have seemed the Revolution had been fought in vain. A writer like Henry James, for example, in transporting a nuanced country-house sensibility to England, was, almost literally, carrying coals to Newcastle; Miller, by contrast, brought to Europe things it was less accustomed to seeing—naked appetite, hopeless high spirits, French spoken with a Brooklyn accent. And what he brought back was something even richer: the great French passions—of love and talk and food— translated into a rough Anglo-Saxon vernacular. *Joie de vivre* made American.

For however much he tried to school himself in foreign masters of despair—Mishima, say, or Céline—Miller could not help remaining a fearlessly joyous soul, "100 percent American," right down to his repudiation of America. No one ever embraced life, liberty, and the pursuit of happiness more lustily. An Emersonic boom was his, and Whitmanic energy. For like Emerson, he saw the Greek roots in "enthusiasm"—the word means divine possession—and knew that life is a festival for the wise; and like Whitman, his fellow rhapsodist of Brooklyn, he sang only of himself—in that great American form the comic-romantic monologue—but found in the self everything he needed ("If we have not found heaven within, it is a certainty we will not find it without"). Celebration, not cerebration, was his thing: even in old age, he was young enough to set about listing all the books he'd ever enjoyed, to fill his pages with reminiscences of his friends, to dash off fifteen hundred letters to a starlet named Venus. And even when inspiration failed him, he simply kept writing and writing till he broke into epiphany. No one who ever wrote so badly wrote so well.

But more than his art, it was his life—the only subject of his art—that served to inspire millions. By now, it is easy to forget how many of our myths of youth were all but patented—or lived out most whole-heartedly—by Miller. The college dropout devouring dictionaries while working as a messenger for Western Union. The would-be writer heading off to Paris with ten dollars in his pocket. The self-anointed artist collecting his mail at American Express, while living off his crooked smile. The underground man going back to nature, and living—in his fifties—without telephone or electricity. Carloads of Europeans still make pilgrimages to the Henry Miller Memorial Library in Big Sur, California. There they can find his legacy all over: in the "Question Authority" bumper sticker on the van in which a wandering Englishman sleeps beside the road; in the "How to Be an Artist" poster on sale on the front porch; in the young man practicing his juggling on a sunlit lawn amidst the redwoods.

Miller was so spendthrift with himself, and so loud in praise of folly, that he laid himself open to every charge. Yet to return to his books is to find him much more shaded than the goatish orgiast of stereotype. Those who would brand him as an irresponsible apostle of hedonism must explain why he grew so censorious when it came to drugs. Those who would call him a male chauvinist pig must account for his fervent championing of Gloria Steinem and Germaine Greer. Those who would write him off as a pornographer must tell us why he spoke out against the sexual revolution (in which he found more signs of jadedness than love). Even his ardent worshiper Anaïs Nin confessed some disappointment that he kept so clean and "monastic" a home. Besides, the one person who called him "monstrous" was himself.

For many Americans, Henry Miller is still a slightly embarrassing presence, the unruly bumptious country cousin who makes a display of himself at the dinner table. At the age of sixty-nine, he still had not seen his first book published in his homeland. And even now, eleven years after his death, he is still a tireless troublemaker (the movie about his love affair with Nin prompted a new kind of X rating). Yet all this is precisely what endears him to the visitors. It is why he is the envy of many an Old

World sophisticate (George Orwell called him "the only imaginative prose-writer of the slightest value who has appeared among the English-speaking races for some years past"). And it is also why the perennial schoolboy from the streets of Brooklyn—a New World Rabelais—is still, one hundred years on, one of the great American exports, unlikely to be eclipsed even by the Japanese.

(1991)

# Searching for America

Jim Harrison is one of that renegade band of drifters and dreamers—including Sam Shepard, Thomas McGuane, Jack Kerouac, and sometimes Norman Mailer—who are sick with longing for America and regard their homeland with all the tenderness and solicitude of lovelorn swains. Like Shepard's monologues or Mailer's jeremiads or Kerouac's solos, Harrison's lyric flights are, at heart, songs of innocence and experience, chanting his country's praises or mourning its losses. These vagabond visionaries are not so much flag-waving patriots as votaries of America as symbol, promise, and ideal; they are afflicted not so much with parochialism as with a Romantic's expanded sense of boundary. And all these freethinking hoboes constantly yearn to rescue and recover their country's lost youth—its vanished pastures, its Indian relics, the clear-cut rituals of the West, and all the other customs that grounded and ordered the land once upon a time. All, in the end, lust after innocence and are hungry for a state of grace, a home.

*Sundog* BY JIM HARRISON

In Harrison, this longing becomes a search for the natural sanctuaries he knew as a boy—a time, and a place, of certainty and calm. He is forever in quest of a green thought in a green shade, a clearing illuminated by shafts of clean, unfallen light. Glades and streams are most often his protagonists, and silence and light. Yet for Harrison, as for any self-respecting Romantic, nature is more a golden means than an end in itself, not only a constant symbol but also, and more important, a symbol of constancy. Thus, among the detritus of the disorderly world around him, visions of woods and wolves and fish gleam like a cool silver stream. And in the midst of confused wanderings and strung-out aspirations, his characters invariably long to return, in reverie or reminiscence, to the sylvan places that were their boyhood haunts ("In the woods," writes Emerson, "we return to reason and faith"). Harrison's fiction is drenched in nostalgia, in wistful memories of fathers, first loves, and discoveries in the woods (and in a sense, all these roles are played by America: it seemed most grand when he was small).

In Harrison's novel *Sundog*, two such voyages dovetail: the physical pilgrimage of a brittle Manhattan journalist to a homestead in the wilds

of Michigan inhabited by an old wanderer named Strang; and the weathered ancient mariner's account of his own hegira. Dwelling in a cabin in
the woods not far from a running stream, the curmudgeonly former engineer has fashioned what amounts in Harrison's world to a lease on the
Garden of Eden: he is attended to by a loyal dog and a lovely Costa Rican
nymph, is treated to hearty home cooking and Stravinsky all around.
Settled within this Henry Millerish shrine, Strang spends most of the
novel rambling along the byways of his memory and imagination, collecting en route, as if they were wildflowers, a few flashes of beauty, some
glimpses of perfection, a handful of stories both short and tall. And as
befits a Romantic vision, the return to boyhood becomes a kind of religious revival—a reawakening of possibility, a rehearsal of a leap of faith.
Strang is the lay preacher in this natural religion; his reminiscence is its
prayer, his retreat its chapel. "Of all beautiful things, I take to rivers the
most," he admits in a typical moment. "They give me that incredible
sweet feeling I once got from religion."

Naturally enough, the patron saint of any such faith is the household
god of woody cabins, the guru of all craftsmen, isolates, and pioneers, the
yogi who turned common values on their heads, Thoreau. It was he, after
all, who first forged a way of living at an angle to American society—and
there is no more ardent angler than Jim Harrison. It is no coincidence,
then, that Harrison and his characters go fishing with Thoreauvian ceremony and deliberation. For they approach rivers in much the same spirit
as the Transcendentalist once reflected, or meditated, on his pond: to
plumb silence and solitude, to find a concentrated calm, to take the
depth of their nature, and of a nature that will never be theirs.

Like Thoreau too, Harrison observes nature not only with a believer's
eyes but also with a painter's care and a scientist's precision; he carpenters
his prose, building its constructions as a beaver might his dam (to invoke
a favorite Harrison prop). His sentences, like Thoreau's, are sturdy
and sound and sometimes sly ("I'm sure that Eulia made a practice of
saving her soul by giving it up," he writes in a turn of phrase and paradox
that almost reprises the finest sentence of another Thoreauvian disciple writing about the master, Stanley Cavell: "One earns one's life by
spending it; only so does one save it").

Most important, perhaps, in devoting his novel to hero worship and in
turning Strang's life into his art, Harrison is following firmly in the footsteps of the Sage of Walden, whose grand mission was to rehabilitate the
very notion of heroism by making himself its central example. For Strang
consistently embodies both the theory and the practice of Thoreau: in his
craggy self-definition and gruff self-sufficiency, in his catholic collection
of natural scriptures and his refusal to keep purity and scatology apart, in

his habits (he "gets up at first light when the world begins again") and in his premises (according to his theory of nonviolence, "Vengeance is commonly thought of as satisfying, where forgiveness is an intellectual effort"). Above all, most of the homespun homilies in the Gospel According to Strang are taken from the Noble Savage Handbook that Thoreau first translated into American: veils must be torn away, eyes must be opened, consciousness itself must be elevated and expanded. "The only aristocracy," Strang likes to repeat, "is that of consciousness."

Yet Thoreau's greatest legacy to Harrison and the rest of America's unkempt and homeless anarchists may well be his gift for dropping out of society without dropping into chaos. Searching for foundations and first principles, all these wanderers have a fondness—a weakness, perhaps— for holy fools. They are all, in a way, rebels with a cause, fugitives for justice: their rebellion springs not from cynicism but idealism, not from a contempt for reality but a commitment to possibility. They wish to overturn contemporary America and its established practices only so that they may discover instead an America of the imagination governed by more thoughtful values. Thus they hate puritans only because they cherish purity; they condemn educational institutions only because they care about learning. Determined to cut through "the apparent contradiction between intelligence and optimism," Harrison forgives the same souls that society condemns so long as some radiance still flickers within them: "The woman was known to be a bit of a drinker," begins Strang in a typical reminiscence, "but she once invited us [two little boys] into her house for a Coca-Cola and played the piano for us."

And though they are often devil-may-care outlaws, the rebels' imaginations fly on angels' wings. Though their social status may be low, their moral and aesthetic standards are never anything but high. Thus Harrison's shyness and his swagger—his willingness to write with a lump in his throat and a challenge in his eye—go hand in hand. Sure, he is prepared to brawl if innocence is compromised, but he is just as ready to sing lullabies to keep it intact. No, he does not stand on ceremony, but he maintains a touching respect for civility. Yes, he may sometimes seem a tough-talking redneck whose love of girls and indifference to etiquette betray an excess of animal high spirits, but he is also a purist of elevated habits and erudite tastes. In *Sundog*, he admires boys who quote Lorca and civil engineers who compose poems. He revels in Beethoven, quotes "the Danish malcontent and humpback Kierkegaard," discusses Saul Bellow, and extols Agassiz's essay on the bluegill. Like his sporting buddy McGuane (who favors a Renaissance frame of reference and elaboration of syntax), he is partial to discretion and verbal decorum. Strang tenderly recalls brushing his sister's hair while she read to him from Romain Rolland's *Jean-Christophe*. And the narrator specifically rejects David Bowie's "China Girl" in favor of "monks in cool, soundproof monasteries" singing Bach chorales.

Harrison is driven, then, by a quintessentially American openness of heart and innocence of spirit that enable him to glimpse and then to chase ideals. Yet that same simplicity often disqualifies him from assessing realities. For those who write in the American grain seem always to issue blessings more naturally, and more effectively, than curses. Perhaps it is because they belong to a relatively unworldly society predicated on idealism. Perhaps because it is the young nation's prerogative to be liberated from the burdens of history, and therefore exempted from its lessons. Perhaps because the country has its head in the clouds of pure abstraction, where goodness works best but evil lacks the complexity and concreteness that make it so strong. Whatever the reason, American literature excels, it seems, at the dizzy, tricky task of creating heroes, yet falters when it comes to creating villains. While Gary Gilmore, Billy the Kid, Charlie Starkweather, Jesse James, and a hundred others are enshrined as models, it is hard indeed to think of an American Iago (and it seems almost laughable when Harrison, for example, likens all journalists to Iago because—significantly—they choose to demean and not to exalt their subjects). For the same reason, the best American writing specializes in the erection of ideals, not the execution of satire. Whitman, Miller, Shepard, and the rest may hymn their country's greatness, but the dirty work of adroit and cutting social observations is best left to sophisticated aliens—Nabokov, perhaps, or Waugh.

Harrison fits this model all too well: the part of his writing that explores possibilities, scouting new ground and scanning the horizon, is irradiated with a remarkable glow; the part that would expose social shortcomings is callow, jejune. He has a boy's unguarded gentleness with his idols, but that same boy's unrefined coarseness around his enemies. With his starry eyes go stumbling feet. Here, then, is a craftsman who takes fastidious pains to sketch exquisite pictures of harmony and idyll, yet resorts to condemning all oilmen because of "their utter greed and the direct venality of their business," writing off all congressmen as "a bilious clot of lawyers," and twice in eleven pages calling politicians "swine." Worst of all, perhaps, Harrison's caricature of the Cynical New York Writer is broader than the Grand Canyon and not a tenth as deep. This so-called sophisticate shows no qualms about blithely condemning himself out of his own mouth, announcing, "I crave the topical, the ephemeral," advertising his yearning for "an embittered career woman with whom to exchange caresses," and, apropos of nothing, exalting the delights of snobby New York shops. Suspending disbelief is not, perhaps, the best way to anatomize the real world.

Keeping his senses more about him than his wits, Harrison therefore has little taste for argument, and no talent for it. But his miscalculations seem only typical of his breed. Unable to embrace the private world without reviling the public, Thoreau squandered much of his fathomless dignity when he took to railing crankily against the society he had so nobly transcended. Mailer, so electric and fresh when pursuing wild theories, never seems more foolish than when flogging the dead horse of plastics or totalitarian architecture. Shepard, so transporting in his riffs, often remains transparent in his poses (counteracting the mystery of his drama with sulky complaints about his own success). Though the desperadoes' points are well taken, their polemics are often ill chosen. In the end, perhaps, they are great casualties of an age that would exalt the man before his work.

Harrison also brings to mind those writers like Henry Miller and his spiritual descendant Charles Bukowski, who boast voices so strong and compelling that they can speak in no voice except their own. In *Sundog*, he tries to disguise this by switching back and forth between the writer's narration and Strang's *apologia pro vita sua* and the narrator's taped diary. But all three blur into one indistinguishable sound, and the characters develop no more than trees. By the same token, Harrison's portrayal of his girls is terrible, even as his portrayal of a man's lustful, lyrical longing for a girl, driven by an avidity that is at once reproved and refined by tenderness, is quite wonderful. "We love before we know how to protect ourselves—pure and simple," he writes. Beyond the pure and simple, Harrison himself, like much of America, seems unprotected and lost.

More fundamentally, he has yet to find a way to fuse the two impulses he describes. All his books swing between gypsy narrative and tranquil meditation, adventure and reminiscence, Kerouac, in a sense, and Thoreau. In his first novel, *Wolf*, Harrison placed himself in the woods, and there recalled his wanderings; in his next novel, *A Good Day to Die*, he drove across the country while dreaming of the calmness of the woods. Now, in his sixth novel, he divides the two forces into two characters, seeker and sage, jaded skeptic and settled pundit—much as Shepard has begun to do in treating divided loyalties between the head's urge for adventure and the heart's longing for a home. But still he can find no unity. Harrison's novels are often hailed as "poet's novels," and that may be their problem: they amount in effect to nothing more than generous anthologies of sweet visions and sunlit epiphanies and lyrical tableaux. Since their highlights are still lifes, their climaxes are often stillborn.

Sometimes they seem as serene, and as motionless, as the beautiful Russell Chatham watercolors that grace their American covers.

And yet for all their lack of momentum, Harrison's novels are never unmoving: there is no denying his strong, luminous—even numinous—talent. Such men, rough-handed yet soft-hearted, should supply America with its dreams. And with its elegies. For Harrison is an unusually heartfelt chronicler of loss and departure, of all those moments, endemic to adolescence, when the agent of our growth lights out, leaves town, and takes away forever something of our hearts. Suddenly, in the novel's final rites of passage, all its limitations are swept away by force of sensibility alone. "There was an odor of lavender, her scent, and I felt congested as if I were about to cry," writes the narrator as the girl he longs for boards a bus heading south. But before the tears can come, there he is, in the book's closing paragraph, in his element again, in flight: racing downstream with the current, hearing the cries of owls, listening for the baying of wolves, hurtling into the unknown, alive with all the fearful wonder of a boy on the move, not knowing whether he will ever come back home.

(1984)

# A Connoisseur of Fear

Writing of death, Don De-
Lillo takes one's breath away. A
private man issuing a strangely
private kind of fiction, he is the
closest thing we have to an Atomic Age Melville. That rarest of birds, a
novelist on fire with ideas—and an outlaw epistemologist to boot—he
uses his fictional excursions as occasions to think aloud in shadowed sentences, speak in modern tongues, plumb mysteries, fathom depths. In
book after cryptic book, DeLillo circles obsessively around the same
grand and implacable themes: language, ritual, breakup, death. How to
make sense of randomness or piece together identity. How, in a cen-
trifugal world of relativity, to steady oneself with absolutes. How, in the
end, to get across the untellable.

*White Noise* BY DON DELILLO

The DeLillo universe is an ordinary world transfigured by extraordinary concerns, a quotidian place seen in the terrifying white light of eternity. Thus *White Noise* is furnished with all the suburban props of the
all-American novel: an amiably rumpled middle-aged professor, his
plump earth-motherly wife, bright children from scattered marriages, a
nuclear family in a pleasant postnuclear home. Their story is unlikely,
however, to be mistaken for a '60s sitcom. The academic, Jack Gladney,
teaches Advanced Nazism at the College-on-the-Hill; the matriarch leads
adult education classes in posture; Gladney's three ex-wives all have
ties with the intelligence community; and the fourteen-year-old eldest
child of the household, Heinrich Gerhardt, has both a receding hair-
line and a philosophical bent—on his first appearance in the novel, he
solemnly proclaims, "There's no past, present or future outside our own
mind. The so-called laws of motion are a big hoax. Even sound can trick
the mind."

Nothing in DeLillo's world is casual, nothing free of occult significance. Dark forces swirl around the bright, plastic artifacts of Anytown,
U.S.A., and the country seems nothing but a gleaming library of por-
tents. Bills, bank statements, the brand names of cars, are recited as if
they were mantras; tabloids are read as fragments from an American
Book of the Dead; the television is consulted as a mystic oracle in the

dark. The very title of the book, we learn, refers to death: the static of our lives is thus the sound track of our dying.

Yet of all the subversions of the everyday this nightmare turns on the American Dream, the most unnerving comes when the Gladneys pile into the family station wagon and head off on what resembles a picnic. It is in fact a nuclear evacuation. The huge cloud of escaped poison gas that drifts through the novel's central episode as symbol, prophecy, white whale, and man-made black death all in one seems at first to be the stuff of routine sci-fi apocalypse (though, in a harrowing, but not unexpected, irony, this book came out at the same time as the Bhopal disaster). Yet the effect of the rogue chemical is almost entirely internal. In the wake of the fugitive cloud, Gladney brings up pulsing stars on a computer. What does that mean? The poison has entered his system; he has come to incarnate death.

It is said that DeLillo is funny, but his is the funniness of peculiarity, not mirth. It is, more precisely, the terrible irony of the lone metaphysician, rising to a keening intensity as he registers the black holes in the world about him. In *White Noise*, as in all his novels, DeLillo absorbs the jargon of many disciplines and reprocesses them in a terminal deadpan. His is a hard-edged, unsmiling kind of satire. It is not user friendly. And where Thomas Berger, for example, trains the same kind of heightened sensibility on low-down Americana, setting loose an antic concatenation of events that unravels the world and triggers a resistless cycle of repercussions (this is what happens when Archie Bunker makes a pass at Clytemnestra), DeLillo has no time for anarchic pratfalls, Aristophanic gambits, non sequiturs. His humor is pitch black. The National Cancer Quiz is on television. The local college offers courses on "The Cinema of Car Crashes." On family outings, Gladney reads *Mein Kampf* in the neighborhood of Dunkin' Donuts.

Just as DeLillo's characters are often not people so much as energies or eccentricities with voices, just as his suburbia is a crowded set of signs fit for a moonlighting Roland Barthes, so his speech is not normal discourse as much as a kind of rhetoric pitched high, a collection of phantom sentences, a chorus of texts without contexts. And his (charnel) house style has the cool, metallic sleekness of a hearse: it is all polished angles, black lines, sunless planes. No wasted motion. No extraneous matter. No scraps of the regular world. Words in DeLillo-ese are stripped dry, sheared clean, given a deadly precision:

> "Am I going to die?"
> "Not as such," he said.

"What do you mean?"

"Not in so many words."

It is this stark tonelessness that accounts for the terrible beauty of much of his writing. DeLillo does not put spin on his words; he leaves them hanging—weightless, somber things full of density and gravity. Disconnected, theirs is the kind of bare, brooding blankness that suggests not numbness so much as mystery, a world not empty of meaning, but too full of it, electrically supercharged. The most conspicuous tic in a DeLillo novel, indeed, is to end chapters with a paragraph consisting of nothing but a single sentence:

"Pansonic."

"I am the false character that follows the name around."

"Who will die first?"

Grist for a paranoid or a nihilist, the words simply stand there in space, mute, momentous, eerie as the pillars of Stonehenge.

DeLillo's other characteristic device is to put together words and rhythms into patterns, sequences, escalating cadences, that build a mood and gather momentum and pick up in time a hypnotic and heart-stopping intensity. They turn into riffs, disquisitions, revved-up harangues. They move with the even, pounding purposefulness of footfalls down an alleyway.

This dazzle of Promethean language is largely consecrated to a single driving theme: the rising struggle between tribalism and technology. DeLillo's novels worry and worry at humanity's fight with science; DeLillo's characters are caught between the spirits of their ancestors and the gods of their computer world. The courses in "Eating and Drinking" he satirizes are no idle joke: in Gladney's world, primal instincts are threatened by a conception of progress that would transform men from animals into machines. "The greater the scientific advance, the more primitive the fear," Gladney tells his wife. Science and fear, those are the antagonists in *White Noise*; we need our fear to defeat a science that tries to conquer fear. And the most potent instrument in that contest, the original—the aboriginal—martial art, is language. DeLillo is fascinated with the ways in which language creates and re-creates the world. Names nail down slippery identities; chants mass together crowds into forces stronger even than technology; language is a way, perhaps the only way, of making connections, an ordered system that can withstand the entropic pressure of the world at large. (Like Pynchon, DeLillo every-where seeks out networks, circuits, codes, connections; and like Pynchon, he knows that the man who finds connections everywhere is a paranoid.) Words, in the end, make up the fabric of our being (and so the assurance that Gladney is not dying "in so many words" knells with particular plangency).

Above all, language, for DeLillo, is like fear: it is all we have of certainty, and humanity. In this novelist's (largely verbal) universe, words are treated as archaeological fragments that can help us recover something of a more primitive and so more human past. Words are runes, atavistic relics, talismans with something of the sacred about them. Language is ritual; language is liturgy. It is no coincidence that the scenes from DeLillo's fiction that hum in the memory are virtuoso set pieces fashioned out of nothing but syllables: the conquest in *The Names* in which the protagonist makes love to an uncertain woman just by mouthing words to her in a crowded Athens restaurant; the episode in *White Noise* in which two professors deliver, simultaneously and in the same room, lectures on Elvis and Hitler, their words and ideas chiming and separating as in some verbal stereo system. At his most reverberant, DeLillo at once explores and embodies the power, the fear, of sound: recitation, repetition, incantation; words as rough magic, a way of making spells.

At times, perhaps inevitably, DeLillo's rhythms overpower him, acquire a life of their own, race so fast that they overthrow the meaning they are meant to carry. The minute Gladney is given a gun, he thinks of it as "a secret, a second life, a secret self, a dream, a spell, a plot, a delirium." Also concealed in the runaway rhetoric is the deeper liability of seeing eternity in a grain of sand: DeLillo and his characters are so eager to read the world, to invest it with significance, that they come on occasion to seem overanxious. Hardly has Gladney begun to rummage through the trash than he is off again: "Is garbage so private? Does it glow at the core with personal heat, with signs of one's deepest nature, clues to secret yearnings, humiliating flaws? What habits, fetishes, addictions, inclinations? What solitary acts, behavioral ruts?" His atmospherics stronger than his aphorisms, DeLillo occasionally builds up menace without meaning, is about profundity rather than full of it, becomes—in a word—portentous.

The other surprising affliction of his books is that for all their preoccupation with plotting, they are themselves ill plotted; portraits of a mind as searching, driven, and ceaselessly vagrant as the narrator of a Beckett novel, they have trouble with resolutions. Such, perhaps, are the treacheries of a Melvillean course. For DeLillo is determined to take on inquiries that cannot be concluded, to make challenges that cannot be met (just as Gladney resolves to wrestle with the riddle of the Holocaust while his colleagues content themselves with deconstructing detergent jingles, soda bottles, and bubble gum). Writing of the unspeakable, DeLillo is fascinated with the unanswerable. "Is a symptom a sign or a thing? What is a thing and how do we know it's not another thing?" "What is electricity? What is light?" "What is dark?" "How does a person say goodbye to himself?" The questions keep coming and coming, pushing the reader back to metaphysical basics, mocking the answering machine, refuting artificial intelligence, mimicking the manner of a child who goes instantly to the heart of the matter, and with it the heart of darkness.

Next to DeLillo's large and terrifying talent, most modern fiction seems trifling indeed. A connoisseur of fear, he leaves a steady chill in one's bones. At the same time, however, it is always difficult to tell what he is about, beyond fear, emptiness, the dark. He knows his data cold; he addresses the great themes with uncommon courage (and so, at moments, heroic presumption and folly); his skills are astonishing. But where is he going, what can he do, with them? Imprisoned, it sometimes seems, within the four walls of his obsessions, he keeps on, in a sense, writing the same book, simply carrying his medicine bag of tricks and themes into a different genre, a new language, with every novel: college football or rock 'n' roll, science fiction or international business or the academy. Thirteen years ago, his second novel, *End Zone*, sounded many of the same notes of foreboding that toll through *White Noise:* film clips of hurricanes and tornadoes; some all-American boys with names like Hauptfuhrer, others burdened by an obscure need to master German; the consoling, earthbound magnetism of the fat; classes in "the untellable."

For all that, however, *White Noise* remains a far greater book than *End Zone*, in large part because it is something more than cold and curious reason; it offsets its existential shivers with a domestic strength that is touching and true. In the midst of all the Pandoran currents and forces that pulse through the dark is a family that is vulnerable, warm bodies that turn to each other for shelter. Gladney wards off the power of the unknown by holding on to his adored wife at night; his unquiet mind is grounded, and uplifted, when he gazes upon the simple calm of his off-spring—"Watching children sleep makes me feel devout, part of a spiritual system. It is the closest I can come to God." The professor's fears for his children as they move through a world of dangers are reminiscent, perhaps, of John Irving's Undertoad. But where Irving was coy and ingratiating, DeLillo is serious and moving. It is a shock to learn after reading his book that DeLillo has no children. All his terrors, his affections, are imagined.

(1985)

# Black-Magic Realism

At the beginning of Cormac McCarthy's new novel, *The Crossing*, a sixteen-year-old boy, Billy Parham, is haunted by a wolf—

and, even more, by an old man's solemn words that the wolf knows a higher truth than is available to men: "that there is no order in the world save that which death has put there." A little later, as Billy leads the she-wolf into Mexico, her eyes burn "like gatelamps to another world. A world burning on the shore of an unknowable void. A world construed out of blood and blood's alcahest and blood in its core and in its integument because it was that nothing save blood had power to resonate against that void which threatened hourly to devour it." (Quite a gaze!) And only five pages later, the reflections in the wolf's eyes are "like some other self of wolf that did inhere in the earth or wait in every secret place even to such false waterholes as this that the wolf would be always corroborate to herself and never wholly abandoned in the world."

Great daring or unconscionable hubris? A writer driven by his unconscious or one all too conscious of his literary effects? High consistency or mere repetition? Those are the questions that go round and around as one makes one's way through this powerfully heightened, defiantly unvarying work, which seems, from the outset, determined to present itself as a masterpiece. Taken out of context, much of this writing is so weighted down with portent that it all but keels over; taken in context— the context of an uncommonly lucid and lapidary prose that spins an almost hallucinatory spell—it can seem like the product of an imagination unvarnished, and all the purer for its distance from the real world. How you read these kinds of sentences, and how much you surrender to the incantatory grip of McCarthy's writing, will largely determine whether you regard him as a latter-day Melville, better able than any writer in memory to confront darkness (and to conjure it into light), or just another overheated Southern crank. Thirty pages after the last description, a wolf's eyes have "that same reckonless deep of loneliness that cored the world to its heart."

McCarthy's is a cold, dry, barren landscape, so shorn of particulars and redundancies that it seems an almost abstract frontierland of the soul. It is a place of the elements, so bare that it doesn't have room for apostrophes or question marks or digressions, a world that comes to us with the transparent immediacy of a vision (or a film). Thus places are defined in terms of north and south and east, and time is measured typically as "two hours past dark." Page after page proceeds without a single adjective or adverb; and the first date in the book appears on page 389. And always we feel we're in some archetypal, not-quite-real zone where details are so scant that they reverberate across the page: "moon" and "wolf" and "mountain."

His is, in fact, a world halfway toward myth, and one in which every literal question acquires metaphorical meanings ("De quién es?" people keep asking. "Adónde va?") If half the book reads like a dream, half reads like a rancher's manual. This is, you might say, a kind of black-magic realism: magic realism with an ungolden and unsettling core.

For every action in this novel's world is shadowed by some distant sense of justice that looms behind the characters like the outline of blue mountains; again and again, there are intimations of a higher order behind things, an ageless system or a forgotten wisdom, framed against a universe as cold and distant as the stars. Men are often animals here, or objects in a landscape more eloquent than they. (The fact that the main character speaks to his horse, and a wolf, as much as to the people round him tells you a little about how McCarthy regards animals, and a lot about how he regards men.) Indeed, if McCarthy resembles anyone, in his clean, lunar prose and the unflinchingness of his vision, it is Paul Bowles, and the sere landscape around the Mexican border becomes his version of Bowles's Morocco, a theological black hole where young Americans come into contact with death and antiquity and the prospect of annihilation. His is a spooked land, of bones picked dry and bad dreams; a prehuman order, where things are reduced to a biblical simplicity: trees and huts and cool blue silences. But where Bowles has one foot in civilization, and shows the slow passage toward alienation, McCarthy is entirely out in the wild. And where Bowles has a sense of social and emotional nuance, McCarthy starts where society ends. Bowles, in fact, is so detached from his universe that he is content merely to record it; McCarthy, by contrast, cannot stop trying to peel the surface of the world back to find its metaphysical core.

For the odd truth of it is that McCarthy, for all his bare-bones authenticity, is never shy about his aspirations; he seems less innocent of literary tradition than almost any writer I know. When young Billy rides over the border accompanied by a wolf and a horse, it does not take a graduate student to find images of civilization and the wild; and the border itself, which exists mostly in his mind, is as linear and schematic a symbol as any exegete could want. Mexico is antiquity, Mexico is death, Mexico is fate, we are told again and again: "we are close to the truth here," a Mexican says, as if he's just stepped out of a Richard Rodriguez essay. America is the place where all pasts can be healed, says one obliging oracle met on the road; Mexico is the place where the past is past.

It was this kind of promiscuous generalizing that gave D. H. Lawrence, in a very different vein, such a bad name. And there is a persistent sense of hollowness behind McCarthy's claims. Yet the case to be made for him is, in an odd way, the same one I would make for Lawrence: that he is absolutely committed to his vision and utterly unafraid of making utterances that could be taken as unhinged. Unlike many writers, McCarthy does not try to satisfy our expectations; he simply takes us into the heart of his belief and—caught in his strange seclusion (he seems to live out of time as well as place)—makes fewer compromises than any writer around. Sometimes, when I chafe at the sheer weight of his ambitions, I remember that Tolstoy might almost have been running interference for him in *War and Peace:* "One step beyond that boundary line, which resembles the line dividing the living from the dead, lies uncertainty, suffering and death. . . . You fear and yet long to cross that line."

At the same time, to this English-born reader, McCarthy seems a profoundly American writer, deeply physical in his attentions and heavily metaphysical in his implications, impatient, in fact, with anything but absolutes: God and Fate and the passage of the soul. For all his extraordinary precision writing about a wolf in a trap and a boy in a private medical operation (and the way one resembles the other), his is an impenitently theological book, about the secret design of the world and the nature of preordination. It is littered with young girls who do not speak, and blind sages who see everything. And though some of McCarthy's strongest passages are about all-American Boy Scout activities—ranching and hunting and traveling—he never lets us forget that two orphaned boys on a road to nowhere are a metaphor for just about everything.

At times, in fact, I felt that if shaken out of its momentous cadences and claims, his book would merely read like a standard cowboy tale: a typical, almost romantic B movie Western story of a boy on a horse in an alien world. If you pull yourself free of the magic of his sentences and actually look at the characters, they are mostly pretty fourteen-year-old *señoritas* and wise old *brujos* on their beds (straight out of *La Bamba*); silent, kindly women serving tortillas by the road, and laconic cowboys offering folksy wisdom. If you were to make an outline of the story, it would largely involve duels in cantinas and dark riders from the mountains, women in doorways in the twilight and Yaqui sages announcing, "The soul of Mexico is very old. Whoever claims to know it is either a liar or a fool." Besides, a landscape made up of dogs and horses and wolves can be a landscape without emotion.

Richard Eder, in the Los Angeles *Times*, has pointed out, with some impatience, that much of the Spanish in the book is either unidiomatic or wrong; and certainly most of the Mexicans on hand are knowing, superstitious peasants, or champions of machismo. A train here is even pursued by a "long lonesome whistle." Yet at his best, McCarthy takes the dustiest clichés in the land and makes them fresh simply by the power of his writing.

And what writing it is! I cannot remember reading a book with such sustained beauty of prose, or such virtuosity: a whole page with only a single comma; declarative sentences that rise to the level of chant; single words—usually "cold" or "dark" or "blue"—that stretch like shadows across the empty landscape. Twelve sentences on one page begin with "He," and ten more on the next; no italics, no proper names (save for "God"), nothing to relieve the clean, inexorable procession of words across the page. McCarthy alternates, more or less, between the Faulknerian orotundity of counterbiblical prophecies and the Hemingwayesque plainness of *ranchero* dialogue (though he is, I would venture, more mythic than Hemingway and more lucid than Faulkner). There is no book I know that might more profitably be read, and reread, and read out in its entirety aloud.

And so I found myself in a frenzy of mixed feelings about this novel. Sometimes I would read it, and find moments of Melvillean hugeness, of darkness and intensity and vision, that have the demoniac power of the pamphlet by Plotinus Plinlimmon from *Pierre*. There are passages here that seem to come out of a wildness and silence and madness of which there's no explaining; passages that are almost the equivalent of Dostoevsky, and that seem to come from some dark, unhallowed core that is far beyond our reckoning. Much of McCarthy's prose is as black as Bartleby and heavy with Melvillean doubleness ("I seen it rain on a blacktop road in Arizona one time, he said. It rained on one side of the white line for a good half mile and the other side bone dry. Right down the centerline"); I felt at times the same terror and raptness I felt when reading *Moby Dick*, the terror of being possessed by a man possessed, in thrall to some terrible vision.

Sometimes, too, I saw only the strain of cadences that fall roughly on the ear ("Those too drunk to travel were shown every consideration and room made for them among the chattels in the carts"). I wearied of reading things like, "The world which he imagines to be the ciborium of all godlike things will come to naught but dust before him" (or, in the same paragraph, "Somos dolientes en la oscuridad"). And sometimes I didn't know whether to regard with awe or impatience a novelist who can write, of a teenage boy, "He looked fourteen going on some age that never was. He looked as if he'd been sitting there and God had made the trees and rocks around him. He looked like his own reincarnation and then his own again."

Toward the end, as the boy rides his horse he knows not where, on a quest for something in the desert, McCarthy begins to leave realism entirely behind and to move into a universe of signs. Everyone becomes a symbol or an oracle, and, as in DeLillo, everyone speaks in the same high voice, an odd, disembodied voice that suggests some post- (or pre-) human wisdom. A blind man in touch with "the true and ageless world" pronounces, "The world was sentient in its core and secret and black beyond men's imagining." A woman by the side of the road reads Billy's palm and says "that while the rain fell by the will of God evil chose its own hour and that those whom it sought out were perhaps not entirely lacking of some certain darkness in themselves." Even a traveling actress opines, "The road has its own reasons and no two travelers will have the same understanding of those reasons. If indeed they come to an under-standing of them at all. . . . The shape of the road is the road. There is not some other road that wears that shape but only the one. And every voyage begun upon it will be completed." (Lucky she doesn't work for Triple A!)

Five pages after that, an old man is declaring that "the ox was an animal close to God as all the world knew and that perhaps the silence and the rumination of the ox was something like the shadow of a greater silence, a deeper thought," and when Billy meets a Mexican in a bar, "what he saw was that the only manifest artifact of the history of this neg-ligible republic where he now seemed about to die that had the least authority or meaning or claim to substance was seated here before him in the sallow light of this cantina and all else from men's lips or from men's pens would require that it be beat out hot all over again upon the anvil of its own enactment before it could even qualify as a lie."

In many books, this kind of prose would be held up for ridicule, or worse. If McCarthy's is not, it is only because his is so dazzling and eerie a narrative gift. His very pretension—in short, his high ambition—is what makes him rise above the world and offer unflinching proclama-tions about good and evil that almost no other living writer would attempt; he's wonderfully unabashed about laying his philosophy cold and bare before us, and shooting for the stars. When McCarthy's charac-ters dream, they dream of the Day of Judgment ("He crouched in the sedge by the lake and he knew he feared the world to come for in it were already written certainties no man would wish for"). This is a man who doesn't deal in half measures.

And when one looks at the field of American letters these days, it's not easy to find signs of redemption. Pynchon can work wonders, when he looks in from his other world, and DeLillo impresses with his uncanny consistency. Updike and Roth keep turning out books with inexhaustible eloquence, and younger writers like Jane Smiley and Richard Ford bring hoary myths into the American grain. But there aren't many novelists of true individuality and power, driven forward by a style and vision all their own and willing to lay claim to desperate heights. In that context, it is something of a miracle to come upon someone of McCarthy's audacity and concentration. In the end, perhaps, *The Crossing* may be nothing more than a *corrido*, an age-old folk song handed down by horsemen ("The *corrido* tells all and it tells nothing," says one Indian sage, obligingly). Yet even as I was reading, again and again, that wolves' eyes are "like footlights to the ordinate world," and even as I was coming upon yet another gypsy saying, "in those faces that shall now be forever nameless among their outworn chattels there is writ a message that can never be spoken because time would always slay the messenger before he could ever arrive," and even as McCarthy's night was "harbor[ing] a millennial dread panoplied in feathers and the scales of royal fish," I felt shaken as I have seldom been before, and came away thinking that this really might be the first novel since *Vineland* (or, before that, *Beloved*) that did, in however self-conscious a way, belong somewhere in the canon. McCarthy is so anxious to stand up on his tiptoes that sometimes, I think, he really does touch the heavens.

(1994)

# In the Shadow of the '60s

$T$he *New Yorker* has long seemed to be written for, by, and about those who lead lives of quiet desperation. In its discreet, fearfully subdued stories the usual milieu is peripheral suburbia, the usual mood penumbral regret. Indeed, many of the magazine's most celebrated contributors—Salinger, Cheever, and Updike among them—are best known for coolly chronicling the sad eccentricities, plaintive longings, and quiet frustrations of their generation. The newest inheritor of this tradition, speaking for a new and peculiarly displaced generation, is Ann Beattie.

*The Burning House* BY ANN BEATTIE

The surface details of Beattie's stories so strikingly resemble Cheever's that one might almost read them as a sequel ("Son of Cheever," perhaps). For although her characters swallow pills instead of booze; although they flee to California instead of Europe; although their hassles are those of cohabitation instead of marriage—they might well be the progeny of Cheever's well-heeled lonelyhearts, raised on expectations they frequently let down. Like their literary forefathers, Beattie's well-educated vagrants might be mistaken for the charmed and witty creatures who inhabit television ads, save that their urbanity protects their lives, like their words, from all the obvious clichés. They often reside in Connecticut and pursue moderately successful careers. They know how to drop the right names and dabble in chic tastes. And most of them are haunted by a cool shadow, a listless despair.

For Beattie is perhaps the first and finest laureate of that generation of Americans born to a society built on quicksand and doomed to a life in the long, ambiguous shadow of the '60s. The characters in her stories are left over from that abandoned decade, hung over with its legacy, saddled with hand-me-down customs that have gone out of style. Usually in their early thirties, they stand for all those who were neither incapacitated by Vietnam nor unhinged by drugs, but unsettled only by their innocence of both extremes. Sprung loose from certainties without being swept up by revolution, old enough to have witnessed turmoil, yet too young to have joined or beaten it, they find themselves stranded in that famous space between two worlds, one dying, the other powerless to be born. Yes, they

routinely—if not religiously—smoke dope, crash on sofas, sing along to
Dylan, shack up, and hang out; but they also think of ardor, passion,
change itself, as cobwebbed anachronisms. For there is resolution in revolution; and if the '60s were a time of decisiveness, however reckless or
wayward or violent, the '70s recoiled into hedged bets and hesitations. In
the world of Beattie's people, conviction has followed convention into
premature retirement; commitment is a dirty word.

The natural element of these dropout *manqués* is therefore a kind of
limbo, a no-man's-land. Their scruffily hip dwellings are not in the city,
but not entirely out of it. With-it enough to know what they can't stand,
they are not steady enough to know where they can stand. And so they
are always moving, but rarely going anywhere, in flight—from reality,
responsibility, normality—without a destination. Their secession from
the world is more a silence than a statement. And their lack of control—
they less make their lives than fall into them—is registered in the blankness, the glassy blandness of their world. As one character admits, "I'm
exhausted from sitting all day, drinking, and doing nothing." Beattie's
people are single mothers, would-be artists, veterans of one-thousand-
night stands; they are returning to nature, enduring a midlife crisis,
sifting through the bric-a-brac of past lives, unthreading the tangle of
children, lovers, friends, and, above all, hoping not to dissolve. All of
them are, in every sense, between engagements, forever commuting
between one another's homes and lives, both of which they enter and
leave with casual frequency.

There is, in short, nothing holding them down or keeping them in
place. Unsituated, they are unstimulated, and driven to seek not answers
but anesthetics—therapy, TV, Valium, joints. Their main activity is
refining inactivity; they space out into a druggy ether world of thought-
less, self-enclosed oblivion. As one nameless figure remarks, "Everybody
who doesn't take hold of something has something take hold of them."
And Beattie evokes this atmosphere of dangling conversations between
people deaf to one another's griefs with characteristic compression: her
figures are constantly calling each other up, answered by machines, and
left to whisper their secrets or endearments into thin air.

Beattie has always crafted metaphors that precisely reflect such off-
balance lives slipping out of control. One of her latest novels is titled
*Falling in Place;* stories in *The Burning House* are called "Learning to
Fall," "Gravity," "Waiting," "Afloat," and "Like Glass." They are preoccupied with weightlessness and drifting, with water and air. Characters
do not sink or swim; they float or—as the modish phrase has it—they go
with the flow. It is the unspoken irony of the title story that nothing
seems to be "burning"; on the contrary, Beattie marked out the frosty

and fragmented terrain that has become her own with the title of her first novel—*Chilly Scenes of Winter*. Her stories are archetypally set in winter, when snow eradicates color, contour, and contrast, when fingers and lives seem numb, when people, shuddering, can claim to be cool. Hers is not, to be sure, the anorexic pallor of Joan Didion's cardiograms of stunned or shattered nerves. Nor is it the overheated whiteness of Emily Dickinson, staring so intensely at a single spot that she grows dizzy. Beattie's is the white of hospital sheets and muffled December fields; not neurosis but paralysis.

Her parched, exhausted stories themselves seem numb. She reads them in a plain, flat, utterly toneless voice that suggests deadened feelings or, on occasion, a determined effort to fight back tears. Her wan sentences and neutral cadences follow one upon another with sharp, chill clarity. Wandering like their characters' days, her anodyne stories have no resolution—in part because their people can't make sense of life, in part because nothing ends in any case. As if to invert the eventful frenzy and clamorous manic swings of the world according to television, a Beattie story is naked of explosions or emphases. It has neither strain nor looseness; neither lyricism nor radiance nor rhythm nor hope. Reading it is like driving for mile after mile down a straight road through a snow-covered desert.

One of Beattie's deftest narrative tricks is to catch the blur of personal relations in today's America by plunging her reader, without introduction or reference, into a chaos of first names (uninterested in the public world, she rarely mentions surnames). Upon beginning one of her stories, one always takes a while to determine the relations between the floating soap bubbles; a child can easily be mistaken for a boyfriend, a gay lover for a brother or a son. For the family circle of middle-class America has apparently imploded, and its domestic structure has been distorted and distended. People change spouses, disguises, even sexual preferences at random; thus children do not know their uncles, girls are older than their stepmothers, fathers are in love with other men, and many need calculators to count their siblings. Everybody cares about "relating" to everybody else, in part, perhaps, because relatives are unknown. Nothing is quite as it seems or as it should be: in one Beattie story, a woman shares roller-coaster rides, confidences, and a joint with her husband's gay brother; in another, the narrator must try to win over her lover's teenage daughter; and in a third, a woman commiserates with her husband's live-in male lover, as all three try to cope with separation.

Elsewhere, again and again, we see men boyishly wooing their children. For it is the dark and perverse paradox of this country's broken families that adults and children have effectively changed places (a phenomenon touchingly noted in the recent film *Shoot the Moon*). While all too many adults still lust after adolescence, all too many kids are thrust into a precocious maturity. Forced to fend for themselves, to walk a tightrope between the sins of their fathers and the vices of their peers, more and more children are hustled by privilege and negligence into a hard wisdom they must reluctantly assume. (The ubiquitous figure of the sage ten-year-old in current American movies is, alas, no exaggeration: one need only contrast the recent Scottish film *Gregory's Girl*, in which a gangly and good-natured fifteen-year-old, wryly mocking his own growing pains, spends the entire film in unarticulated adoration of a girl whose hand he longs to hold, with *Fast Times at Ridgemont High*, in which a group of Californians of the same age languidly deal with abortions, hard drugs, and jaded sexual appetites.) In Beattie's stories, children are knowing before they are discriminating: a six-year-old refuses stories with morals, dismissing them as "kid's stuff"; a parent reads her child R. D. Laing instead of Andrew Lang; one nine-year-old carries around a copy of Samuel Beckett. Even as these children are turning into tough little realists, their parents are tumbling into stolen romances and irresponsible rites, belatedly courting an innocence they had earlier squandered. We see them dressing up as bears, playing with Frisbees, devising quirky surprises for their lovers, and running with dogs. And we come to see that their prankish charm is only another face of their affliction, a refuge and a mask. "If the birds could talk," announces one nonchalant narrator, "they'd say that they didn't enjoy flying." It is sad that the children of Beattie's world are afraid, confused, disenchanted; it may be sadder that their elders are no wiser and no better off.

It cannot be denied that Beattie's stories are perfect mirror images of the protagonists and predicaments they describe. But that may be their problem. They surrender to diminished expectations; they change location and little else; they loiter and go nowhere. Because her theme so rarely varies or evolves (save for one gay and giddy *jeu d'esprit* called "Happy," an exception to prove the rule), Beattie's tales seem almost mass-produced. One can say that first-person narratives suit her dispassion better than third-, that she seems at sea in those segments set in Los Angeles, or that stories like "Playback" have occasional epiphanies. But nearly all the offbeat tunes she plays are in the same (minor) key, and after reading a few, one feels that one could write a few. Collect some characters and name them Jason, say, or Hilary or Barrett (not Tom, Dick, or Harry—Beattie people invariably wear slightly upper-middle-class, faintly original names midway between Zowie Bowie and John Smith). Give them trendy occupations and engaging idiosyncrasies. Place their homes in the woods, and supply them with shaggy dogs, coffee, and conversations around the kitchen table. Make it a gray day in winter. Let there be a phone call from a former lover, a child from a sometime marriage. Ensure that someone takes Valium and someone refers to a gynecological operation. Write in a withered present tense and end before the conclusion.

This is not to deny or disparage Beattie's commanding talents. Her spare, soft-spoken prose is singularly observant: she can conjure up a dog without a single physical detail, so keen is her sense of gesture. She clearly knows the very pulse and heartbeat of her dreamless drifters—indeed, with her long fair hair, air of seraphic funkiness, and apparently itinerant, makeshift lifestyle, she seems to belong in their midst. She performs many narrative tasks with unrivaled skill: conveying the weary braveness of children who secretly long to be children again, or the poignancy of the grown men, equally eager and equally desperate, who long to entertain them; pinning down voguish tastes, brand-name allusions, and aimless dialogue; sketching pale, lead-colored skies. The harsh transparency of her unblinking, unstinting realism is almost photographic.

And ultimately these stories may best be regarded as a collection of photos in an album: each records a situation, revives a memory, and redeems nothing. Considering them is like consulting a doctor's X ray of contemporary America. But unless he is impeccably sterilized, a doctor is vulnerable to the very diseases he treats; just so, the closeness of Beattie's manner to her matter can be dangerous. Privy to anomie, her stories become party to it; faithful to the details of the world, they seem treacherous to the energy and heroic idealism that are her country's saving grace. Her disciplined, levelheaded realism—exemplary of the meticulous tradition she upholds—finally passes on to the reader, as if by contagion, a melancholy torpor that suffocates. And so, having paid one's respects to the tasteful and well-ordered room of her fiction, one yearns only to escape, or to fling its windows open and admit the wild, fresh air of possibility.

(1983)

# A Waiting Room for Death

In August 1991, the writer Gretel Ehrlich was struck by lightning, flung across her road in Wyoming, and left for dead. She had been struck before—

*A Match to the Heart* BY GRETEL EHRLICH

had even written about being struck before—but this time it was a fatal blow, and even when she was nominally brought back to life, she felt as if she were a posthumous soul of sorts, living in a kind of limbo: alone, the only patient, in an understaffed Wyoming hospital, her recently separated husband away buying cattle in a distant part of the state, while she passed in and out of consciousness like a refugee from the afterworld. Writing from that penumbral state—the *bardo* of Tibetan Buddhism—in the spirit of a person halfway across the River Styx, she has produced a wry and haunting and dreamlike book about what it means to have one's heart stop, and what exactly is this self that's here today and gone tomorrow.

It would be easy, and probably tasteless, to say that if anyone should undergo this death-in-life experience it ought to be Ehrlich, for she is one of those writers—Annie Dillard and Wallace Stevens are others who come to mind—whose very being depends on frequent commutes between a world described with almost scientific precision and the more lyrical, abstract speculations of the mind. The connection between two different kinds of nature, within us and without, has always been her subject, and the way seasons pass inside us and we find in the world a mirroring, or a guide, for our own inner geography. Blending a highly distinctive sense of physical movement with an almost theological interest in metaphysical movements—seeing her body, typically, as an illuminated manuscript, and a hill as a "woman lying on her side"—she is always writing, metaphorically, of how bodies take in fire, and how tides are a "form of breathing." There is, then, at the very least a kind of poetic justice in the fact that of all writers, it was she whom nature chose to inhabit and possess.

Yet the pull of this narrative, for me, lies mostly in its utterly strange location, as written by one who seems the ultimate transit passenger in a waiting room for death. *A Match to the Heart* seems to take place in some liminal, almost twilit zone where all borders are dissolved and all bets are off: where the curtains between different states of consciousness are drawn back, as between a dead person and a barely living one sharing the same hospital room, or between a waking dream and a dream of wakes. (For six months after she "dies," Ehrlich has no dreams, and then she dreams of death.) But where the more sanguine explorers of after-death states ascend to the best-seller lists with tales of redeeming lights and light redeemers, Ehrlich comes back with something more difficult and demanding: shadows and shadow states and a sense of keen uncertainty. Her souvenirs from the distant shore are not answers but more questions. And years of Buddhist training make her toss and turn and toss on all the questions, until she seems like a modern-day version of Chuang-tzu—is she a dead person dreaming she's alive, or a live one dreaming she's dead? Or, as she more eloquently puts it, "I wondered if light had invented the ocean and my hand dragging through it, or if memory had invented light as a form of time thinking about itself."

On the surface, *A Match to the Heart* proceeds like a matter-of-fact journal about the chemistry of people, and the process of loss and recovery: Ehrlich takes us meticulously through all the scientific causes and effects of her injury. She also gives us plenty of empirical lightning lore (including the fact that lightning, contrary to superstition, loves to strike twice in the same place). She tells of lightning entering the hole in the throat of a man who's had a tracheotomy; of lightning striking an entire baseball team; of a boy hit by lightning who lets out an orange ball of fire that comes out through his mouth, flies through the air, and kills a cow. She attends a Lightning Survivors Conference, and she follows her own doctor through all his hospital rounds. Here is one writer who, when her heart stops, resolves to plumb every meaning of the heart, and even dons surgeons' clothes to watch the dynamics of the vital organ.

Yet the singular strength of Ehrlich's book, for me, lies in its inwardness, and its acknowledgment of more mysterious, moon-driven currents within: if she is wise enough to see how far knowledge can take one, she is wise enough, too, to see where knowledge must give way to uncertainty or wisdom. The real question of the book is what relation, if any, lightning has to enlightenment, and to what extent it can be a kind of shadow *satori*: a blow to the self so shattering that it forces you into a radical reevaluation of the self. And to answer that, Ehrlich turns herself inside out—or, more precisely, makes herself a kind of empty vessel for forces and elements to pass through ("I felt like a river moving inside a river," reads one typical sentence). Reading her book, one has relatively little sense of Ehrlich the rancher, the writer, or the woman, yet an uncannily powerful sense of Ehrlich as an archetypal mind of sorts, exploring underground passageways and labyrinths in her consciousness. She makes herself impersonal, even universal. And the protagonists of the book are, in some sense, images, of fog and lightning and water, of moonlight and crosses and fire.

Ehrlich is constantly aware that 78 percent of the world is water and 70 percent of the brain is water; and the drama of the book lies in the interplay between the fire that entered her body and the water that's already there ("bodies of water," in fact, begins to acquire all kinds of resonance here). Always attuned to the hidden continents of the heart, she becomes a kind of scientific wanderer through states both luminous and foggy. Torn open by the lightning, and stripped, amnesiac, of past and future, she finds herself in a place where different states of being merge: "The sea looked like time, and time was water and tides, the heart's ardent tick and the sea star's flip." Or, "The rivers were layers of grief sliding, the love of open spaces being nudged under fallen logs." Meanwhile, all around her, fire breaks out in the hills of California; there are eclipses and meteor showers and sudden rains; lightning forks before her in the desert. In this way she is a true inheritor of all the Transcendentalists, who looked inside and saw the world (or, their enemies would say, looked outside and saw themselves).

The other thing that intensifies her book is her poet's awakened eye. Every page here is strewn with images, a sky like "tattered book pages" and lightning "fingering" the heavens on a single early page, and literal meanings merging with metaphorical, as when she finds herself alone by the sea, a foghorn sounding through the dark. More than that, she has a poet's ear for language, and the inner meanings that dwell in seemingly casual turns of phrase. She has suffered, she learns, an "electrical insult" that damages her "sympathetic system"; a fisherman's coworker is a "tender"; and her inbreathing is known as "inspiration." "Tender" and "inspiration" become, of course, words crucial to her healing. And when she describes the moon on the water "like a tapering path" and then likens it to a candle, you know that "taper" is not accidental.

Thus images link with words, and words with the myths—rich myths of dogs and afterworlds and owls—that she weaves through the fabric of her narrative: Arctic lore and Buddhist beliefs and the consequences of thunder entertained by Pliny. What finally gives the book its poetic texture is the way her uncommonly close-knit mind is strung along a web of images, and though nothing is included that is not relevant, relevance can be found in even the smallest thing. For in her heightened consciousness, everything acquires meaning: she returns to her hometown of Santa Barbara, and learns that Saint Barbara is the patron saint of those threatened by thunder, lightning, and fire; a friend sends her a scepter from Nepal, and it turns out to be a Vajra, or thunderbolt; she settles by the coast, and finds that the Chumash regarded the area as a gateway to the afterworld.

This highly elemental book—a lunar, submarine book lit by fire—proceeds less like a story, in fact, than a tide, coming back, again and again, to the same images and forces, the same places and stories: to her cardiologist, Blaine, to her dog, Sam, to the books of Walcott and Heaney she reads in her solitude. She returns to the town where she was born—to die, it seems; she goes back to the beach where she first touched love—to taste loneliness; the very friends and dogs she has nurtured all her life come back to nurture her. Everything circles back, and returning to the places she has known, she knows them for the first time (the ash-gray, sepulchral incandescence seems, indeed, to echo the Eliot of the *Four Quartets*).

I am, I confess, a friend of Gretel's, but that does not inhibit me from saying, as disinterestedly as I can, that this is a subtle and searching book that put me, at least, into a state of consciousness I cannot remember visiting before. As a longtime Buddhist, Ehrlich is well placed to meditate on formlessness and form, and to think about how every life is, in a sense, a death sentence, and existence itself a joke with a death's-head mask. Yet what pulls her through, finally, is company and fortitude and flinty humor: once gravity has no pull on her, she learns the necessity of laughing. In an age of twelve-step recovery programs and Enlightenment While-U-Wait, it is refreshing, even redeeming, to read about someone who is prepared to live with doubt, and to forgive others before herself, and to see things in the long perspective. Ehrlich does not shy away from giving us a rigorous and detailed accounting of how lightning leads to cardiac arrest; but—more impressively, perhaps—she also does not shy away from accepting that a doctor can cure as much with his optimism as with his instruments, and a dog can help her as much as any doctor. Within and without are as inextricably linked as above and below, or spirit and flesh. And in the end, the only thing that can cure a heart is—of course—another heart.

(1994)

# THEMES

*In Praise of the
Humble Comma*

---

The gods, they say, give breath, and they take it away. But the same could be said—could it not?—of the humble comma. Add it to the present clause and, of a sudden, the mind is, quite literally, given pause to think; take it out if you wish or forget it and the mind is deprived of a resting place. Yet still the comma gets no respect. It seems just a slip of a thing, a pedant's tick, a blip on the edge of our consciousness, a kind of printer's smudge almost. Small, we claim, is beautiful (especially in the age of the microchip). Yet what is so often used, and so rarely recalled, as the comma—unless it be breath itself?

Punctuation, one is taught, has a point: to keep up law and order. Punctuation marks are the road signs placed along the highway of our communication—to control speeds, provide directions, and prevent head-on collisions. A period has the unblinking finality of a red light; the comma is a flashing yellow light that asks us only to slow down; and the semicolon is a Stop sign that tells us to ease gradually to a halt, before gradually starting up again. By establishing the relations between words, punctuation establishes the relations between the people using words. That may be one reason why schoolteachers exalt it, and lovers defy it ("We love each other and belong to each other let's don't ever hurt each other Nicole let's don't ever hurt each other," wrote Gary Gilmore to his girlfriend). A comma, he must have known, "separates inseparables," in the clinching words of H. W. Fowler, king of English Usage.

Punctuation, then, is a civic prop, a pillar that holds society upright. (A run-on sentence, its phrases piling up without division, is as unsightly as a sink piled high with dirty dishes.) Small wonder, then, that punctuation was one of the first proprieties of the Victorian Age, the age of the corset, that the modernists threw off: the sexual revolution might be said to have begun when Joyce's Molly Bloom spilled out all her private thoughts in thirty-six pages of panting, unperioded, and officially censored prose; and another rebellion was surely marked when e. e. cummings first committed "god" to the lower case.

Punctuation thus becomes the signature of cultures. The hot-blooded Spaniard seems to be revealed in the passion and urgency of his doubled exclamation points and question marks ("¡*Caramba!* ¿*Quien sabe?*"), while the impassive Chinese traditionally added to his so-called inscrutability by omitting all directions from his ideograms. The anarchy and commotion of the '60s were given voice in the exploding exclamation marks, riotous capital letters, and Day-Glo italics of Tom Wolfe's spray-paint prose; and in Communist societies, where the State is absolute, the dignity—and divinity—of capital letters is reserved for Ministries, Subcommittees, and Secretariats.

Yet punctuation is something more than a culture's birthmark; it scores the music in our minds, gets our thoughts moving to the rhythm of our hearts. Punctuation is the notation in the sheet music of our words, telling us when to rest, or when to raise our voices; it acknowledges that the meaning of our discourse, as of any symphonic composition, lies not in the units but in the pauses, the pacing, and the phrasing. Punctuation is the way one bats one's eyes, lowers one's voice, or blushes demurely. Punctuation adjusts color and tone and volume till the feeling comes into perfect focus: not disgust exactly, but distaste; not lust, or like, but love.

Punctuation, in short, gives us the human voice, and all the meanings that lie between the words. "You aren't young, are you?" loses its innocence when it loses the question mark. Every child knows the menace of a dropped apostrophe (the parent's "Don't do that" shifting into the more slowly enunciated "Do not do that"), and every believer the ignominy of having his faith reduced to "faith." Add an exclamation point to "To be or not to be . . ." and the gloomy Dane has all the resolve he needs; add a comma, and the noble sobriety of "God save the Queen" becomes a cry of desperation bordering on double sacrilege.

Sometimes, of course, our markings may be simply a matter of aesthetics. Popping in a comma can be like slipping on the necklace that gives an outfit quiet elegance, or like catching the sound of running water that complements, as it completes, the silence of a Japanese landscape. When V. S. Naipaul, in his latest novel, writes, "He was a middle-aged man, with glasses," the first comma can seem a little precious. Yet it gives the description a spin, as well as a subtlety, that it otherwise lacks, and it shows that the glasses are not part of the middle-agedness, but something else.

Thus all these tiny scratches give us breadth and heft and depth. A world that has only periods is a world without inflections. It is a world without shade. It has a music without sharps and flats. It is a martial music. It has a jackboot rhythm. Words cannot bend and curve. A comma, by comparison, catches the gentle drift of the mind in thought, turning in on itself and back on itself, reversing, redoubling, and returning along the course of its own sweet river music; while the semicolon brings clauses and thoughts together with all the silent discretion of a hostess arranging guests around her dinner table.

Punctuation, then, is a matter of care. Care for words, yes, but also, and more important, for what the words imply. Only a lover notices the small things: the way the afternoon light catches the nape of a neck, or how a strand of hair slips out from behind an ear, or the way a finger curls around a cup. And no one scans a letter so closely as a lover, searching for the small print, straining to hear its nuances, its gasps, its sighs and hesitations, poring over the secret messages that lie in every cadence. The difference between "Jane (whom I adore)" and "Jane, whom I adore," and the difference between them both and "Jane—whom I adore," marks all the distance between ecstasy and heartache. "No iron can pierce the heart with such force as a period put at just the right place," in Isaac Babel's lovely words; a comma can let us hear a voice break, or a heart. Punctuation, in fact, is a labor of love. Which brings us back, in a way, to gods.

(1988)

# Excusez-moi!
## Speakez-vous Franglais?

The best way to deal with a foreigner, any old-school Brit will tell you, is to shout at the blighter in English until he catches on. If he professes not to understand, just turn up the volume till he does. A man who doesn't speak English is a man who isn't worth speaking to. Robert Byron, the great traveler of the '30s who wrote so feelingly on Islamic culture, treated every alien as an unintelligible buffoon; and his John Bullish contemporary Evelyn Waugh all but enunciated the Blimp's Code when asserting that no man who knew more than one language could express himself memorably in any (take that, Nabokov! *Et tu*, Samuel Beckett!).

To speak or not to speak—it is a question at least as old as moody Danes delivering English couplets. And every year, as summer approaches, we face the same dilemma: whether to try, when in Rome, to speak as the Romans do, or to rely on Italian cabbies speaking English (with brio, no doubt, and sprezzatura). In some respects, it comes down to a question of whether 'tis better to give, or to receive, linguistic torture. The treachery of the phrase book, as every neophyte soon discovers, is that you cannot begin to follow the answer to the question you've pronounced so beautifully—and, worse still, your auditor now assumes you're fluent in Swahili. Yet sticking to English, it's easy to feel that you've never left home at all—and are guilty, to boot, of a Waugh-like linguistic imperialism.

In recent years, of course, the spreading of the global village has made cross-purposing a little easier. We think it only natural to ask for hors d'oeuvres from a maître d'—as natural, perhaps, as discussing Realpolitik and the Zeitgeist with a Hamburger. And as English has become a kind of lingua franca, all of us are fluent in Franglais and in Japlish. It really is possible for *un self-made man*, arriving in Paris, to ask a *mademoiselle* for a *rendezvous*, and then to take her for *le fast food* and *le dancing* and even, perhaps, *le parking*. But then she may call him *un jerk*, and he may get upset if he doesn't know that the term, in French, means an expert dancer.

The problems are most acute, in fact, when both parties think they're speaking the same language: Shaw's famous crack about England and America being "two countries separated by the same language" is thirty times more true now that sixty countries claim English as their mother—

or at least their stepmother—tongue. An Australian will invite you to a hotel, and you may be shocked if you don't know that it's what you know as a bar. An Indian will "prepone" a meeting, and only if you're quick enough to calculate "postpone" in reverse have you any chance of showing up on time. Above all, as English has become a kind of prized commodity—and a status symbol—in many corners of the world, those of us born in possession of it are apt to feel as vulnerable as a bejeweled dowager on a dark back alleyway. There's always someone waiting to jump out and mug us with his English—before we can try out our Bahasa Indonesia on him.

And yet, and yet, there is to all this another dimension. For in speaking a foreign language, we tend to lose years, as well as other kinds of time, to become gentler, more innocent, more courteous versions of ourselves. We find ourselves reduced to basic adjectives, like "happy" and "sad," and erring on the side of including our "Monsieur"s; and we are obliged to grow more resourceful and imaginative in conveying our most complex needs and feelings in the few terms we remember (like a child rebuilding Chartres out of Lego blocks). Think of how English sounds as spoken by Marcello Mastroianni—romantic, suggestive, helplessly endearing. Might not the same be true in reverse? Peter Falk appearing in a German movie (*Wings of Desire*) seems as exotic as Isabelle Adjani in an American one.

Speaking a foreign language, we cannot so easily speak our minds; but we do, willy-nilly, speak our hearts. We grow more direct in another tongue, and say the things we would not say at home—as if, you might say, we were under a foreign influence. Inhibitions are the first thing to get lost in translation: *je t'aime* comes much more easily than "I love you." Small wonder, perhaps, that spies are gifted linguists by nature as well as by training (John le Carré was one of the most brilliant language students of his day); entering another tongue, we steal into another self.

And even when we're not speaking Spanish, but only English that a Spaniard will understand, the effect is just as rejuvenating. Reducing our own language to its basic elements, we find, of a sudden, that it becomes new to us, and wondrous. How vivid the cliché "over the hill" sounds when we're explaining it to an Osaka businessman! How rich the idiom "raining cats and dogs"! Speaking English as a second language, we find ourselves rethinking ourselves, simplifying ourselves, committed, for once, not to making impressive sentences, but just to making sense. English is the official language of the European Free Trade Association, none of whose six members has English as its mother tongue. Why? Well, says the secretary-general disarmingly, "using English means we don't talk too much, since none of us knows the nuances."

Besides, whether we inflict our French on the concierge or not, many of our transactions will come down, in the end, to an antic game of charades. English may be the universal language, but it's still less universal than hands and eyes. So even as we become unwitting James Joyces—coining neologisms by the minute—when we essay a foreign language, we also become Marcel Marceaus: asking the way to the rest room with our eyebrows, sending back the squid with a paroxysm of mock pain. Ask a man in Tierra del Fuego to point you to *The Sound of Music*, and he'll instantly reply, "No problem!" (which means—in every language—that your problems are just beginning). Then he'll direct you to the Julie Andrews musical that the Argentines call *The Rebel Nun*. And when you say "thank you" to him—in Spanish—it can almost sound like a kind of grace.

(1990)

T
he whole of Japan is a pure invention," said Oscar Wilde, who should have known, since he was a pure invention himself. What he meant, of course, was that Japan, as much as anywhere, is a product of our imaginations, and the country we see is only the one we have been trained to see. Life imitates Art. Yet in a deeper sense, even after a hundred years, anyone who would understand that land of cultured surfaces can do no better than to turn to Wilde, who kept up appearances as if they were the only reality he knew. His championing of masks, his preference for style before sincerity, his unfailing conviction that there was nothing wrong with reality that a little artifice couldn't fix, might all be prototypes of a certain kind of Japanese aesthetics (the Japanese *Book of Tea* reads almost like a pure invention of Wilde's, with its "cult founded on the adoration of the beautiful among the sordid facts of everyday existence"). Yet Wilde also saw that silver generalities conceal basic copper truths: "The actual people who live in Japan," he wrote, "are not unlike the general run of English people."

The issue is, of course, an increasingly urgent one: are the Japanese really different from you and me (and not just as the rich are)? Wilde certainly brings many Japanese cultural positions into the living room. But culture, you will say, is not the point: it is Japan's one-party democracy, its corporate monopolies, its patriotism, which amounts to protectionism, that exasperate; it is Japan's trade practices, in fact, and economic strategies. But trade practices are in some respects the product of cultural values, and no country pursues policies in which self-interest plays no part. The Japanese system *is* different from ours; so, too, are the French, the Chinese, and the South African systems. And when it comes to competition, all those powers go with their strengths. Yes, you will add, but the Japanese keep telling us they're different; indeed they do, and try to make it a self-fulfilling prophecy. But Americans, who start many of their sentences with the words "Americans . . . ," may not find this so alien.

Inevitably, it is never hard to find differences across the sea and to say that we cannot possibly make our peace with people who put their verbs at the end of their sentences, say "yes" where we would say "no," read their books back to front, and take their baths at night. Just as easily, we could say that there is nothing much that need separate us from a race that likes to eat at McDonald's, listens to the Walkman on the train home, watches baseball on TV, and takes its honeymoons in Hawaii (some Japanese children, indeed, are surprised to find that there are McDonald's outlets in America, too, and that foreigners play *besuboru*). Recently, as though relocating in Berkeley, Japan's most prominent gangsters reportedly complained that laws to curtail their activities were "a violation of their human rights."

It may be, too, that every nation acquires certain habits at certain moments of its growth. One of the best descriptions of Japanese "conformity," as stereotype conceives of it, was given by William Manchester in *The Glory and the Dream*. Believing, he wrote, that "leadership came from the group, that progress lay in something called problem-solving meetings, [they] had no use for drive and imagination. Above all, they distrusted individualism. The individual sought prestige and achievement at the expense of others. He was abrasive; he rocked the boat; he threatened the Corporate One, and they wanted no part of him." The only trouble is, Manchester was describing Americans there, in the "silent generation" '50s.

Yet an even closer kinship links Japan, ironically, with the country that many Americans feel closest of all to, and regard as their second—or cultural—home: the country with which we enjoy our "special relationship." The affinities between England and Japan go far beyond the fact that both are tea-loving nations with a devotion to gardens; far beyond the fact that both drive on the left, are the world's leading overseas investors, and are rainy islands studded with green villages. They go even beyond the fact that both have an astringent sense of hierarchy, subscribe to a code of stoical reticence, and are, in some respects, proud, isolated monarchies with more than a touch of xenophobia. The very qualities that seem so foreign, even menacing, to many Americans in Japan—the fact that people do not invariably mean what they say, that uncertain distances separate politeness from true feelings, and that everything is couched in a kind of code in which nuances are everything—will hardly seem strange to a certain kind of Englishman.

Perhaps the best illustration of this can be found in the best-selling novel about six days in the life of an English butler, *The Remains of the Day*. The book reads almost like a handbook of traditional Japanese values: a samurai-like loyalty to a master, a rigid sense of duty, a quiet and impenitent nationalism, a sense that self is best realized through self-surrender. Many of the scenes—in which the butler speaks to his father in the third person, refers to "military-style pep talks" to his staff, and solemnly resolves to practice "bantering"—might almost be translated from the Japanese. Yet here are all these values, in the midst of an instantly recognizable England, in 1956! The book's author, Kazuo Ishiguro, who came to England—from Nagasaki—at the age of five, grew up simultaneously as a Japanese and an English schoolboy, and so can see that the two are scarcely different. "I think there are a lot of things about the Japanese way of communicating, and of discussing problems, that I don't know about," he says, "simply because I don't know my way around the codes. But the actual Japanese method, the actual approach, I think I'm quite at home with—because I've been brought up in middle-class England." Japan, as Wilde might have said, is only as alien as ourselves.

(1992)

---

A hundred years ago this summer, José Martí, the great poet, orator, and freedom fighter of the Americas, died trying to liberate his native Cuba from Spanish colonial rule. For Martí, the Spanish-descended and Madrid-educated patriot who was jailed in Havana at sixteen and lived abroad for twenty-four of his forty-two years, a death in his first battle, near the town of Dos Ríos ("Two Rivers"), was only the last in a series of heroic quixotisms. El Apóstol, as he was called, had agitated for the freedom of Cuba mostly from a New York that he found a model of both independence and oppression.

Now, therefore, the self-styled "son of America"—O fatally ambiguous phrase!—is a hero of both the Cuban exiles who long to rescue their lost homeland from the tyranny of Fidel Castro, and the Cuban government, which sees in him a great precursor to Castro's liberation of the place from foreign domination. Thus Havana fills the island with slogans, memorials, and busts of Martí (whose books still often top the local bestseller list), while Washington responds with anti-Castroist propaganda on Radio Martí and TV Martí. Martí is the most equivocal symbol of a looking-glass war in which two bitter enemies pelt each other with the same all-purpose icon.

As President Clinton moves to ease travel restrictions to Cuba—and José Martí International Airport—in the coming weeks, he seems sure to effect another halfway compromise guaranteed to antagonize both left and right. But on a deeper level, he will be honoring the great tradition of paradox and ambiguity that governs the hip-hop syncopation of U.S.-Cuba relations. Even now, Cuba's latest "liberator" is busy turning his home into precisely the kind of Babylon he overthrew thirty-six years ago, a prostitute-filled shopping mall for imperialist consumption where the goal of every young Cuban is to be a foreigner; while on the other side, Washington sedulously contrives to help, with its embargo, the one person it is trying to hurt (Castro), while hurting the eleven million (Castro hostages) it is claiming to help. A black ironist could not have devised things better.

Such ill-starred topsy-turviness is the abiding fate of a claw-shaped island that seems always to be nipping at North America's toes. When first he arrived in Havana, Ernest Hemingway (another amphibious symbol, thanks to his scrupulous no-comments about the revolution) stayed at the Ambos Mundos ("Both Worlds") Hotel; his most memorable treatment of the Cuban-American transaction was called—what else?—*To Have and Have Not*. Modern Havana is still a hauntingly allegorical place, in which people with names like Jesus, America, and Charity walk through streets called Virtues, Hope, and Loneliness. The strongest woman on the island, Castro's onetime sister-in-law, Vilma Espín, is a Vassar girl, and the building at the center of Havana is a replica of the U.S. Capitol. When he was just a teenager at the Colegio Dolores (or "School of Hard Knocks," as it might be translated), young Fidel wrote a letter to President Roosevelt, requesting an autographed ten-dollar bill. He got only the autograph.

The cynical dreamers of contemporary Cuba have learned to savor such ironies—especially when their free-market Communism offers them little other nourishment to enjoy; the party-loving Cuban spirit is forever rebelling against the Party-loving Cuban system. Habaneros note that the former Soviet Economic Mission is now an office dedicated to foreign exchange; that the brightest Yummies, or young upwardly mobile Marxists, pay their Party dues in dollars; and that one of the island's flashiest streets—a memorial to its future—is called Calle Ocho, as if in honor of the main street in Little Havana, Miami, which is a memorial to its past. *Perestroika*, in local parlance, becomes *la espera stoica* ("the stoic wait").

Thus Cuba comes to seem as slippery a symbol as the great exiled hero—Martí—who was once derided as a "useless Christ." Though it's common to hear that one man's freedom fighter is another's guerrilla, in Martí, Washington and Havana have an idol in common, whose main legacy was his death. And even as both sides aspire to the same goal—a free and prosperous Cuba—both continue to find new ways of making it impossible. In the crazy logic of their tired rivalry, they come to resemble Tweedledum and Tweedledee, arguing about whether the new flag should be red with black stripes or black with red stripes.

In John le Carré's depictions of the cold war, both sides were mirror images of each other, divided by all they had in common. And even as that bipolar disorder is now elsewhere discredited, in the context of a *Cuba libre*, both sides continue to lock each other into old Us Against Them projections. Bill Clinton, more than any U.S. President since Kennedy, surely, is Castro's kind of man: the two thinkers and talkers could charm each other all night. But instead of acknowledging their common aims, they insist on flinging allusions to Martí back and forth. And failing to recall that the fallen idealist's most plangent nickname was a sad one: "Cuba Weeps."

(1995)

# The Rise of
## Minority Terrorism

When Actors Equity briefly decided, some weeks ago, that the part of a Eurasian in the play *Miss Saigon* could not be taken by a European, its board members provided some of the best entertainment seen round Broadway in recent months. It was not just that they were asserting an Orwellian principle: all races are equal, but some are more equal than others. Nor even that they were threatening to deprive thousands of playgoers of a drama that promised to shed some light on precisely such cross-cultural nuances; nor even that they were more or less ensuring—if the principle was to be applied fairly—that most Asian-American actors would have to sit around in limbo and wait for the next production of *The Mikado*. They were also raising some highly intriguing questions. How can John Gielgud play Prospero when Doug Henning is at hand? Should future Shakespeares—even future August Wilsons—stock their plays with middle-class whites so as to have the largest pool of actors from which to choose? And next time we stage *Moby Dick*, will there be cries that the title part be taken by a card-carrying leviathan?

The quickly reversed decision, which effectively proclaimed that actors should do everything but act, was a short-running farce. But when the same kind of minority terrorism is launched offstage, as is more and more the case, the consequences are less comical. Jimmy Breslin, long famous as a champion of the dispossessed, speaks thoughtlessly, and finds himself vilified as a "racist." Spike Lee, an uncommonly intelligent filmmaker whenever he remains behind the camera, maintains that films about blacks should be directed by blacks (what does that mean for *The Bear*, one wonders, or for *Snow White and the Seven Dwarfs*?). Lee in turn becomes an irresistible target for charges of anti-Semitism. And others contend that Marion Barry is being hounded because he is black, as if to suggest that he be excused because he is black.

The problem with people who keep raising the cry of "racism" is that they would have us see everything in terms of race. They treat minorities as emblems, and everyone as typecast. They are like the man who tells us, "Don't think of purple elephants. Clear your mind of purple elephants. Whatever you do, don't think of purple elephants." And in suggesting that a white cannot put himself in the shoes, or soul, of a half-white, or a black, they would impose on us the most stifling form of apartheid, condemning all of us to a hopeless rift of mutual incomprehension. Taken to an extreme, this position can lead to a litigious nation's equivalent of the eye-for-an-eye mentality that has brought about a never-ending cycle of tribal vendettas in the Middle East (and Sri Lanka, and Northern Ireland, and . . .). You did my people wrong, so now I am entitled to do you wrong. A plague on every house.

Almost nobody, one suspects, would deny that equal rights are an entirely laudable goal, and that extending a hand to the needy is one of the worthiest things we can do. Reserving some places in schools, or companies, or even plays, for those who are less privileged seems an admirable way of redressing imbalances. But privilege cannot be interpreted in terms of race without making some damningly racist assumptions. And nobody stands to gain if decades of oppression are replaced by decades of condescension. And rectifying the injustices of our grandfathers is no easy task, least of all in a country made up of refugees and immigrants and minorities of one, many of whom have lived through the Holocaust, the Khmer Rouge, the unending atrocities of El Salvador. Sympathy cannot be legislated any more than kindness can.

The whole issue, in fact, seems to betray a peculiarly American conflict and conundrum: the enjoyment of one freedom means encroachment on another; you can't school all of the people all of the time. Older, and less earnest, countries, like Britain, or France, or Japan, live relatively easily with racial inequalities; but America, with its evergreen eagerness to do the right thing, and to impose freedom, even by force, tries to remedy the world with an innocence that can become more dangerous than cruelty. All of us, when we make decisions—which is to say, discriminations—judge in part on appearances. All of us treat Savile Row–suited lawyers differently from kids in T-shirts, give preference to the people that we like—or to the people that are most like us—and make differing assumptions of a Texan and a Yankee. To wish this were not so is natural; to claim it is not so is hypocrisy.

But state-sponsored favoritism is something different. As an Asian minority myself, I know of nothing more demeaning than being chosen for a job, or a position, or even a role, on the basis of my race. Nor is the accompanying assumption—that I need a helping hand because my ancestors were born outside Europe—very comforting. Are those of us lucky enough to be born ethnic to be forgiven our transgressions, protected from insults, and encouraged to act as if we cannot take responsibility for our actions (it wasn't my fault if I failed the exam; society made me do it)? Are we, in fact, to cling to a state of childlike dependency? As an alien from India, I choose to live in America precisely because it is a place where aliens from India are, in principle, treated no better (and no worse) than anyone else. Selecting an Asian actor, say, over a better-qualified white one (or, for that matter, a white over a better-qualified Asian, as is alleged to happen with certain university admissions) does nobody a service: not the Asian, whose lack of qualifications will be rapidly shown up (thus consolidating prejudice); not the white, whose sense of racial brotherhood is hardly likely to be quickened by his being the victim of discrimination himself; not the company, or audience, which may understandably resent losing quality to quotas.

Affirmative action, in fact—so noble in intention—is mostly a denial: a denial of the fact that we are all born different; a denial of a person's right to get the position he deserves; a denial of everyone's ability to transcend, or live apart from, the conditions of his birth. Most of all, it is a denial of the very virtues of opportunity and self-determination that are the morning stars of this democracy. People around the world still long to migrate to America because it is a place, traditionally and ideally, where people can say what they think, become what they dream, and succeed—or fail—on the basis of their merits. Now, though, with more and more people telling us not to say what we think, and to support everyone except the majority of Americans, the country is in danger of becoming something else: the land of the free, with an asterisk.

(1990)

In his new novel, *Vineland*, Thomas Pynchon, that disembodied know-it-all hiding out somewhere inside our nervous system, performs an eerie kind of magic realism on the McLuhanite world around us. His is an America, in 1984, in which reflexes, values, even feelings, have been programmed by that All-Seeing Deity known as the tube. Remaking us in its own image (every seven days), TV consumes us much more than we do it. Lovers woo one another on screens, interface with friends, cite TV sets as corespondents in divorce trials. And the children who have grown up goggle-eyed around the electric altar cannot believe that anything is real unless it comes with a laugh track: they organize their emotions around commercial breaks and hope to heal their sorrows with a Pause button. Watching their parents fight, they sit back and wait in silence for the credits. History for them means syndication; ancient history, the original version of *The Brady Bunch*.

All this would sound crazy to anyone who didn't know that it was largely true. As the world has accelerated to the fax and satellite speed of light, attention spans have shortened, and dimension has given way to speed. A whole new aesthetic—the catchy, rapid-fire flash of images—is being born. Advertising, the language of the quick cut and the zap, has literally set the pace, but Presidents, preachers, even teachers, have not been slow to get the message. Thus ideas become slogans, and issues sound bites. Op-ed turns into photo op. Politics becomes telegenics. And all of us find that we are creatures of the screen. The average American, by age forty, has seen more than a million television commercials; small wonder that the very rhythm and texture of his mind are radically different from his grandfather's.

Increasingly, in fact, televisionaries are telling us to read the writing on the screen and accept that ours is a postliterate world. A new generation of children is growing up, they say, with a new, highly visual kind of imagination, and it is our obligation to speak to them in terms they understand. MTV, *USA Today*, the PC, and the VCR—why, the acronym itself!—are making the slow motion of words as obsolete as pictographs. Writing in *The New York Times* not long ago, Robert W. Pittman, the developer of MTV, pointed out just how much the media have already adjusted to the music-video aesthetic he helped create.

In newspapers, "graphs, charts and larger-than-ever pictures tell the big story at a glance. Today's movie scripts are some 25 percent shorter than those of the 1940s for the same length movies." Even TV is cutting back, providing more news stories on every broadcast and less material in each one.

There is, of course, some value to this. New ages need new forms, and addressing today's young in sentences of Jamesian complexity would be about as helpful as talking to them in Middle English. Rhetoric, in any case, is no less manipulative than technology, and no less formulaic. Though TV is a drug, it can be stimulant as well as sedative. And the culture that seems to be taking over the future is a culture so advanced in image making that it advertises its new sports cars with two-page photographs of rocks (though the Japanese, perhaps, enjoy an advantage over us insofar as their partly ideogrammatic language encourages them to think in terms of images: haiku are the music videos of the printed word). Nor would this be the first time that technology has changed the very way we speak: the invention of typography alone, as Neil Postman writes in *Amusing Ourselves to Death*, "created prose but made poetry into an exotic and elitist form of expression." No less a media figure than Karl Marx once pointed out that the *Iliad* would not have been composed the way it was after the invention of the printing press.

Yet none of this is enough to suggest that we should simply burn our books and flood the classroom with TV monitors. Just because an infant cannot speak, we do not talk to him entirely in "goo"s and "gaah"s; rather, we coax him, gradually, into speech, and then into higher and more complex speech. That, in fact, is the definition of "educate": to "draw out," to teach children not what they know but what they do not know; to rescue them, as Cicero had it, from the tyranny of the present. The problem with visuals is not just that they bombard us with images and informations only of a user-friendly kind, but also that they give us no help in telling image from illusion, information from real wisdom. Reducing everything to one dimension, they prepare us for everything except our daily lives. Nintendo, unlike stickball, leaves one unschooled in surprise; TV, unlike books, tells us when to stop and think. "The flow of messages from the instant everywhere," as Daniel Boorstin points out, "fills every niche in our consciousness, crowding out knowledge and understanding. For while knowledge is steady and cumulative, information is random and miscellaneous." A consciousness born primarily of visuals can come terrifyingly close to that of the tape-recorder novels of the vid kids' most successful voice, Bret Easton Ellis, in which everyone's a speed freak and relationships last about as long as videos. Life, you might say, by remote control.

If today's computer-literate young truly do have the capacity to process images faster than their parents, they enjoy an unparalleled opportunity—so long as they learn to process words as well. They could become the first generation in history to be bilingual in this sense, fluent onscreen as well as off. We need not, when we learn to talk, forget to communicate in other ways. But only words can teach the use of words, and ideas beget ideas. So just as certain tribes must be taught how to read a TV set, we must be taught how to read the world outside the TV set. Much better, then, to speak up than down, especially when speech itself is threatened. Nobody ever said that thinking need be binary. Nobody, that is, except, perhaps, a computer.

(1990)

I t is increasingly common to hear how the visual media are usurping the
world of books, giving us a sound-bite attention span, splicing off the
conventions of narrative, making the very process of reading seem as
archaic as traveling by horse and buggy. If the camera famously turns the
eye into a viewfinder, the video image reduces the imagination to a
twenty-one-inch screen, all too easily turned off.

Yet there is another way in which the imagination is being eclipsed by
the image—or the private eye by the collective—and that is when words
are given flesh. All of us know how difficult it is to read a novel once we
have seen it on the screen: the parts have all been cast for us, and the
ghost images of this rival production intrude on the one we're staging
within. The characters are no longer ours, but someone else's. And seeing
a movie after you have read the book is scarcely any better: suddenly the
lovely Dorset peasant girl who kept you company since youth is a
German sex kitten whose offscreen liaisons you know all too much about.
Even the author is often helpless before this tyranny: John le Carré has
said that after seeing Smiley played by Alec Guinness, he could not see
him in any other terms. His creation had been snatched away from him,
his imagination blocked out by the BBC's.

Now, though, it is not just the book that is abducted from our minds,
but the author too. Has anyone noticed how many books now come with
full-cover photos of the author, more and more of them in living color?
And has anyone considered what the costs of this might be? One of the
pleasures of reading has traditionally been that we construct an author as
we imagine him to be; he becomes, in a sense, a figment of our imagination. Thus every foreign correspondent—in the mind's eye at least—is
tall and lean and flak-jacketed, and every romance novelist has tumbling
auburn tresses. Laurence Sterne is your uncle Toby, or the man down
the street, or just an empty page: Madame Bovary, *c'est moi!* In the
past, readers have created their authors as much as authors have created
their readers—or their characters; we make them up to be the people we
would like.

These days, however, this is increasingly difficult: the author's face is
everywhere. On video screens, on dust jackets, on posters, and on cable
channels—his face looks up from a three-foot display, his voice is on the

Walkman, and his talking head is being broadcast Live at Five. Even when books do not show his face, notices of books do. Thus almost every reader today can conjure up Joyce Carol Oates's look of owlish intensity, or John le Carré's veiled urbanity; some authors' faces are as ubiquitous as cans of Campbell's soup. And inevitably, however much an author protests that he is not the "I" of his narration, it is easy to read as much into his picture as his words; in the absence of any other information, the face becomes the one to which we attach the disembodied words. The book takes on its maker's image. At best, this is merely another kind of editing, or coloring, no worse than bringing the memory of an author's previous books to his latest one; at worst, though, it can have a kind of proleptic effect, robbing us of the special thrill of reading, which is to plumb, page by slowly turning page, the mystery of another's self. It is like reading the last page of a detective story first.

The dangers of this process are especially great, of course, when a book involves a first person, and greatest of all when that person is fictional. Yet even in the most distant of texts, it is hard, for example, not to see Robert Caro's sober, besuited form shadowing Lyndon Johnson across the fields of Texas. Bret Easton Ellis appears next to the description of the American Psycho. Paul Theroux and Philip Roth have given characters so many of the details of their own lives that we inevitably complete the picture by giving them their creators' faces. The only escape, it would seem, is for a Jay McInerney to write in the voice of a twenty-year-old girl. But even that hardly guarantees immunity for the writer: I always see John Updike's face attached to Harry Angstrom's lanky body, and I would have pronounced Pat Barker male—till I saw her picture on the dust jacket.

Some readers, perhaps, claim absolute impartiality—just as some examiners protest that they are not affected, or predisposed, by the names on the blue books in front of them. Yet just imagine, for a moment, that a mischievous Puck transposed the photos of Joyce Carol Oates and Danielle Steel, or John le Carré and Alan Dershowitz: Would that not have a wickedly subversive effect on our reading of all four? And does not the invisibility of the authorial presence in *Vineland* account for a large part of the novel's eeriness and breadth? And what do photos do to the very notion of negative capability, the assumption that an author's highest task is to make himself something other than himself? This isn't just a matter of promiscuous celebrity, or the demystifying impulse of the age, in which we domesticate the rich and famous by devouring the small print of their lives. It is, rather, something more mysterious, even primal. Graham Greene shied away from the camera, one senses, not just because he did not wish to be associated with his self-indicting narrators; but more, perhaps, because he felt that the camera would, in some obscure way, catch his soul, or catch the uncertainty where his soul should be. The opposite fear is even greater: that the lens will catch not the soul but everything but. Our reading becomes viewing.

With some authors, of course, this is fair enough—indeed, it is precisely what we ask of them. We pay celebrities to present us with a certain face—to play themselves—and they professionally oblige: a Brian Bosworth book without an author's photo would be as out of place as a William Wharton novel with one. If many people now become celebrities because they are authors, just as many become authors because they are celebrities. Others, whose faces are, quite literally, their fortunes, are duty bound to show us the looks out of which they made their living (as in any book of beauty tips, say, or Pamela des Barres's confessions of a groupie). Even movie stars with literary aspirations are, more often than not, moonlighting celebrities: Joan Collins's novels sell partly because of the aura of the author's name and photo, and partly because of the associations we bring to them. Many readers, in fact, might almost be happier if the books of Suzanne Somers or Hank Aaron had more pictures than accounts of high-school traumas.

Real-life authors, too, can occasionally emerge intact. Some, after all, look exactly the way they are supposed to look: Tom Wolfe has, in the Wildean fashion, constructed a cream-suited public self perfectly matched to the persona behind the books. Somerset Maugham's face was as invisible to most readers as his narrative "I"s (until, at least, Anthony Burgess re-created him in novel form). Don DeLillo is protean enough to look just the way we imagine him to be—a shadow man on guard against the camera's intrusions. As for literature's dandies, like Mishima and Whitman, they could not get enough of trying on selves for the camera, and doubtless felt that the postures they fashioned in real life were as creatively satisfying as the ones they fashioned on the page. In some books, moreover, the face scarcely matters: we hardly see Ursula Le Guin in the otherworldly realm of Earthsea. And Hamlet, for all his literary heroics, will never speak quite like Mel Gibson.

Yet even those authors who know how to play the image game become its victims. If Truman Capote helped to launch his career with the (in)famous photo on the cover of his first book, he also served to limit it; and in keeping his face always in the public eye, he diminished it too, till people thought of him more as a talk-show feature than as a serious craftsman. More often, reality cannot keep pace with the imagination. Hunter Thompson's weedy bald-headed figure on the cover of his recent books has surely reined in, as much as it has filled out, our sense of the self-abusing wild man within. Christopher Isherwood's later books were all about egolessness, and a purposeful self-erasure: bringing his image to them begins to defeat their purpose. The reader can, of course, perform some touch-ups of his own: Samuel Johnson always gains a few pounds before the mind's-eye camera, and Oscar Wilde loses some. Yet still the fundamental point remains: a large part of Shakespeare's power would be lost if we could visualize his smile; and Homer would be the poorer if we could hear him speaking in a Michael Jackson falsetto. That is one reason, perhaps, why university presses tend not to run pictures of their authors: their absence makes the words seem more dispassionate—impersonal expressions of imperishable truths. I never knew what Northrop Frye looked like, and his words were deathless for it.

For the heart of the issue is that an author has a self out of which he writes, a private self, a self that no one sees and he keeps jealously to himself. It is a self, by definition, very different from his public face, just as my face, lost in this sentence, is different from the one I put on as soon as someone enters the room. Everyone knows how writers "in person" are seldom the persons we imagine them to be. But an author's photo defines a self, and it is generally the self that didn't make the book. Besides, the very taking of a photo can itself make alterations in a writer's image—the visual equivalent, perhaps, of believing your own press. Often, in fact, authors' photos commemorate nothing but a writer's poses—so unless he is Oscar Wilde (or Quentin Crisp), the highest part of him is being sold by the lowest.

None of this would matter, really, except that we can all feel the process accelerating, as images proliferate, and "novels" like *Havana* and *Dances with Wolves* fill the shelves, and an author's voice reads us his words along the Hollywood Freeway, then explains them to us on Channel 4. Nowadays, not even the dead are safe: Virginia Woolf's pale and swan-necked form is so familiar that it haunts her every paragraph. And even the dead are moving now: Proust, so numinous and disembodied a consciousness in his books, speaks today in Alan Bates's cadences (after the TV movie *102 Boulevard Haussmann*). It may take Mozart decades to recover from Tom Hulce.

As this suggests, musicians, and painters, and the rest of us, are all equal victims of this phenomenon: but those working in the visual media are by definition in the business of producing images strong enough to efface the outline of their maker. And Beethoven will never occupy a symphony quite so insistently as James Joyce accompanies us through the twenty-four hours that it takes to read *Ulysses*. The dead, moreover, have solved the other curious aspect of this process: that we want all our authors to be Dorian Gray. Having been fixed by a photo, they should remain obedient to it. When Annie Dillard recently appeared with suburban glasses propped up on her hair, some of her admirers reacted as when Dylan went electric: the flower girl had sold out. And Barry Lopez, in appearing without his beard, looked like Samson without his hair, divested of shamanic authority.

Is there any way out of this hall of mirrors? Probably not, in an age when publishers' contracts oblige authors to promote their books, and the author video seems only a micro–brain wave away. Some writers may refuse to be photographed, or use pictures that give nothing away (as Thomas Berger does); some, like the famous novelist-recluse in DeLillo's *Mao II*, may choose to mass-produce photos instead of books; some may turn their pictures to their words' advantage (both Mary Gaitskill and John Burnham Schwartz probably gained extra exposure for their first books with their striking portraits). Jan Morris, by changing gender, confounded our sense of her so well that the face behind the sentences grew fuzzy. But that may be a little radical. Perhaps the best idea, in these Milli Vanilli days, when so many celebrities hire ghostwriters, is for writers to hire ghost celebrities. Could any first novelist with Rob Lowe's face, or Greta Scacchi's, on his cover fail?

(1991)

Browsing in a bookstore not long ago, I came, by happy chance, upon "the scientific discovery of the century, if not of all time" (as no less a dignitary than Stephen Hawking called one recent book); nearby was a volume, with sex and spirituality in the title, that was described (by a doctor, on the front cover) as "one of the most significant books ever published." I let my eye stray farther: "Imagine Vladimir Nabokov and Anne Rice collaborating to produce a historical novel in the tradition of Mary Renault." (Imagine!) "If a manic J. G. Ballard and a depressed David Lodge got together," I read, they could produce something to sit on the same shelf as the first novel of another author, who "writes like some pixillated offspring of a secret liaison between J. D. Salinger and Isabel Allende." Everywhere I looked, such literary paternity suits and unlikely coproductions seemed to be the order of the day. "If Thomas McGuane, Bob Marley, and Jimmy Buffett collaborated on a novel . . ." (it would read like melodious gibberish, I completed the quote, unasked); "a shrewd and magical story-teller sired by García Márquez," another advised the doubtless surprised García Márquez. "Imagine Evelyn Waugh reincarnated as an angel, or Ronald Firbank returned to earth with a passion for *shih tzus* . . ."

Such feats of the imagination abound these days, if only on the covers of books. Turning to the Yellow Pages, I half expected to see them described as "the most compendious catalogue of American lore to spring from the loins of Walt Whitman." And I could hardly believe that a copy of the 1996 Department of Motor Vehicles handbook did not come with an encomium from some Cal Tech scientist calling it "an unprecedented look at issues that concern us all."

The trend began, I surmise, in the '60s, when someone in a publicity department had the bright idea of taking a quote from an article or interview and splashing it across the cover of a new book (this, I imagine, is how W. H. Auden's praise of Firbank—not returned to earth yet—got such wide circulation: "Any person who dislikes [the novels of Ronald Firbank] may, for all I know, possess some admirable quality, but I do not wish ever to see him again"). And from excerpting a sentence of Graham Greene's, say, in praise of one of the writers he tirelessly championed, it could not have been a large step to actually writing to Greene, asking if he might lend a word to this attack on U.S. foreign policy or that new Catholic novelist. And from there, it was surely an even smaller step to the self-addressed, stamped envelopes, "endorsement forms," multiple-choice boxes, and follow-up letters inviting one to join the company of "Pulitzer Prize–winning Plump" and "best-selling author Benign" that I, and thousands of others, receive in the mail every day. A publisher has little to lose by sending out early versions of a book in the hope of snagging blurbs; and he has everything to gain—or, at least, the prospect of hearing that the author's "synthetic, fortified, irradiated, robotically processed genuine New Jersey guacamole may be a disturbing hue of green, but it's zeitgeist frappé, babe, and addictively zesty."

One result of all this is that even a relatively fledgling writer like myself gets five or six bound galleys a week, often, some misspelling my name, some congratulating me on books I haven't written, some with five blurbs already assembled for a work that's still in manuscript. Not long ago, almost simultaneously, I received tomes on Hasidic children, wine-making impresarios, and the whorehouses of Saigon (who do these people think I am?).

The other result is sheer inflation: if once a blurb served to distinguish some genuinely remarkable first novel from the two hundred others that appear each spring, now the cottage industry of "puffs" (as the British nicely call them) has reached such a pitch that anything without testimonials from four Nobel laureates is bound for the remainder bin. Even *The Oxford Book of Women's Writing in the United States* sails on the wind of four separate eulogies.

Thus seasoned book-lovers, and people who simply recall that "blurbing" is an anagram of "burbling," come now to relish the art of judging a book by its cover. Blurbs themselves have become a wonderfully coded subset of literature, rich with as many subtexts as a Derrida anthology: works of fiction, often, compressed into the space of a haiku. We learn to look for comments that damn all the praise they're giving with a simple preposition ("I have read in *Such and Such*, and found it fascinating"), or laurelers who scrupulously avoid passing any judgment on the book at hand ("A modern-day *Little House on the Prairie* gone mad," is the ambiguous verdict of one, and another writes, "As though some gorgeous neo-Ballardian eco-catastrophe had been rear-ended by a Steve Erickson novel on its way to the Viper Room," which makes one feel even sorrier for the now rear-ended, as well as manic, Mr. Ballard). We look for indirect confessions of prior interest when the blurbist refers to the author by first name or even nickname (as in Willie Nelson's *ne plus ultra* assessment, "Kinky is the best whodunit writer to come along since Dashiell What's-his-name"). And mostly, we scan the pages to see what the hidden connection between blurbist and blurbee might be—do they have the same editor, the same alma mater, the same hometown, even the same sexual orientation? Occasionally, one can find a blurbist mentioned in the acknowledgments; sometimes, even better, one finds the blurbist blurbed by the blurbee on one of her own books (a practice *Spy* magazine chronicled in its "Log-Rolling in Our Times" column). At the very least, they often live in the same state (the Montana writers, for example, are habitually generous in praise of one another's work) or write in the same uncommon vein (Latina writers invariably appear on the cover of one another's books, with colorful effusions dipped in a Tex-Mex salsa: "a *chismosa* par excellence . . . a story told *con ganans*").

We also learn to make complicated calculations depending on the status of the blurbist. We subtract one point if she puts a degree after her name (a sign, perhaps, of lack of confidence) and subtract a few more if she is identified (the classier houses tend not to say, " 'Brilliant'—William Shakespeare [author of *Othello*]," on the reasonable grounds that if you have to ask who the commender is, the commendation is unlikely to have much sway over you). And we add a host of bonus points for any names we haven't seen on other covers (thus a Thomas Pynchon is worth five Salman Rushdies, the almost posthumous cry of William Burroughs on one recent book—"A page-turner!"—struck me as a veritable coup, and a J. D. Salinger would be enough to merit a four-color headline).

Blurbs, in fact, offer an unrivaled glimpse into the literary pecking order. For one implicit assumption behind them is that people blurb others only on their own level or below (I'm not sure, that is, that Saul Bellow needs me to say, "He reads like J. G. Ballard on helium," and one sign of making it is to be above all blurbs—a Norman Mailer or Harold Robbins is likely to come with huge photos of the author, and his own name printed in thirty-point bold). A few years ago, Robert Olen Butler was a fairly infrequent visitor to the back covers of books; now that he's won the Pulitzer Prize, he's everywhere. Thus the art of reading blurbs becomes as absorbing as that of reading excerpts from reviews (subtracting points for *Publishers Weekly* or *Kirkus Reviews* and adding points in proportion to the length of the commending sentence—since a bare "remarkable" may be taken from a review that read, "Remarkable in its loathsomeness"). Once the paperback edition of a book comes out, the number of blurbs (favors apparently from a friend) should be exceeded by the number of review quotes (praise ostensibly from a stranger), and the quality of the book can be gauged by the relation between the two.

I must confess at this point that I am no innocent bystander on this issue: I have given blurbs, quite often, to both friends and strangers; I have solicited them; I have even been mentioned in some of the shotgun weddings they arrange ("St. Augustine meets *Raging Bull* via T. S. Eliot"). I have also seen my unfortunate blurbists grossly plagiarized. On the cover of my first book, a kindly elder wrote: "the best writers of travel seem to invent the places they bring to life. This is why I am certain that Pico Iyer invented modern Asia. No other explanation could account for his producing so shrewd, so funny, so dazzling a book." Recently, seven years later, I picked up a brand-new volume in the travel section of a bookshop and read the following—with a different name attached: "The best writers of travel seem to invent the places they inhabit. That is why I am certain that Brian Alexander invented the rain forest. No other explanation could account for his producing so shrewd, so lethally humorous, so expressively sympathetic a book."

And until I first began contributing blurbs, I never realized that it is, in fact, a sorry occupation. The average book buyer, in her innocence, may imagine that people long to give blurbs—to see their names on the back of 7,500 new copies of a novel; to get to show off their prose in the company of J. K. Galbraith or Stephen Hawking; or even just to secure their future by inspiring a sense of gratitude. A blurb, after all, is often as much thank-you note as critical assessment, as much IOU as I ♥ you; and if reviews (which often read like blurbs) are sometimes ways of settling accounts, blurbs (which often read like reviews) may be seen as ways of paying off debts.

What is harder to realize, though, is that blurbing is an extremely hazardous task that requires advanced degrees in politics, economics, and just plain manners. At the very least, it involves some of the terrors that assault one before a dinner party (what *does* one say to the hostess about her sixth marriage? how does one respond to her six-year-old's "Pollack-inspired" drawings? and how does one dress when one doesn't know who's going to be there)—a blurbist, after all, seldom knows whether he'll be sharing back-cover space with Zbigniew Brzezinski or William Gibson. Imagine the horror of blurbing Indrani Aikath-Gyaltsen as "bringing to life a vision of India which mocks stereotypes and replaces them with something much more vivid and enduring," only for her India-set book to be revealed as plagiarized from a provincial English novel. Imagine the mortification of the person who recently praised a novel by proclaiming, "*Hard Copy* meets James M. Cain meets white trash with a vengeance," when someone else, on the same cover, came up with the untrumpable: "If Hannibal Lecter were in the market for a mate, he would look no further." And imagine the sorrow of seeing a close friend become an ex-friend because you have praised his book in the wrong terms, or less glowingly than you praised his ex-wife's book.

And if giving a blurb is difficult, soliciting one is even worse. Asking a friend to turn into a Madison Avenue salesman on one's behalf is much harder, say, than requesting a letter of recommendation (which is generally private, and aimed at an audience of four); it is, in effect, a form of fishing for public compliments. The process is made a little easier by the fact that it's often one's editor who sends out the letter of appeal, but while some editors go no further than saying, "I'd be interested to know what you think of this," others actually insert a blank space on which the recipient can inscribe his mail-ordered praise. And even if you do receive the plaudits you seek, you can't help feeling that they constitute more of a kindness to you than to the unwary reader.

Thus giving a blurb is often an act of generosity and self-sacrifice—which is why, I think, many of the writers who appear most often (and with the most self-effacing sentences), from Graham Greene to Peter Matthiessen, are those generally associated with a sense of social conscience. To give a blurb means putting aside the unread Musil and Proust on one's bedside table in order to plow, unpaid, through 650 pages on the life and thoughts of Enver Hoxha, simply to send a bouquet that may explode in one's face.

No wonder many writers have an unbending policy of just saying no.

The trouble is, though, that blurbs, like amoebae, can only multiply. By now, they have reached far beyond the mere literary domain (I have seen Bob Dylan, the coach of the San Antonio Spurs, and David Byrne—twice!—on the backs of recent books; and Martin Scorsese, perhaps unaware that his *Raging Bull* has "met St. Augustine via T. S. Eliot," appears on a novel by Shūsaku Endō). If moviemakers are eager to show they know their scholars of the Cabala, scholars of the Cabala are eager to show they know some movie stars. Even magazines have blurbs now, and movies too—ads for *Il Postino* have quotes from John Updike, Isabel Allende, and Kurt Vonnegut—though the fact that movies and records rely so little on them shows that they have evolved well beyond the cap-in-hand desperation of books. And with more and more "books" extending our notion of "writers" and "readers," their ads look more and more like "We Are the World" congregations of all-star cronies. Berry Gordy's *To Be Loved* lived up to its schmoozy title with quotes from such literati as Smokey Robinson, Dick Clark, Diahann Carroll, and Diana Ross ("A supremely loving book"); from Barry Diller, Mike Ovitz, Lee I. Iacocca, and David Geffen ("An astounding story not only of a great artist but a great visionary"); and (wondering, perhaps, what they're doing here) from Sidney Poitier and Coretta Scott King. "This book is empowering," pronounced Calvin Klein of Deepak Chopra's *Seven Spiritual Laws of Success* (to which Peter Guber, then CEO of Sony Pictures, added, "A Virtual Reality toolkit for the 21st century spiritual traveler"). What is a publisher to do if he's about to bring out *Hamlet*, when even *The Kid Stays in the Picture* features blurbs from Jack Nicholson and Faye Dunaway?

None of this is to deny the virtue of blurbs (which helped to bring about the breakthrough success of such classics as *All the Pretty Horses* and *My Traitor's Heart*), nor their entertainment value. Some self-destruct heroically (I came upon one half-page ad for a book that Arthur C. Clarke, the Dalai Lama, and Harvey Cox had all allegedly enjoyed: further down, there was a lukewarm sentence from "Arthur C. Clark" [*sic*], a note from the secretary to the Dalai Lama, a not very ringing message from Harvey Cox, saying, "I think you are on to something," and a quote from an unnamed "Educator in Boston," who, in lauding the book's "refusal of all pretentiousness," succeeded in misspelling "its"). Some are simply comical ("The twenty-first century literally has three choices," I read. "Aristotle, Nietzsche, or Ken Wilber"). Sometimes they show a different side to an author (Paul Theroux's comments on *The Snow Leopard* reveal a much more gentle soul than the travel books acknowledge); and sometimes they have the lure of gossip-column items in disguise ("Marianne has always been cruel, especially to herself. This is a delightful book," writes fellow Stone-woman Anita Pallenberg, of Marianne Faithfull's autobiography). I admire the mischievous way one techno-best-seller has quotes from Arthur C. Clarke, Rupert Murdoch, George Gilder, and an associate of the author's identified as a "sixteen-year-old Internet user," and I like the way the blurbs on the back of *The Primary Colors*, by Alexander Theroux, match the mad compendiousness and baroque eccentricity of the book itself: John Updike writes of "omnidirectional erudition and an omnivorous poetic instinct"; Robertson Davies refers to "apophthegmatic" essays, "vagarious adventures," and Sacheverell Sitwell; and James McCourt, identified as "Author of *Mawrdew Czgowchwz*," calls it, "Humane-letters essay-writing of the most beguiling *perpetuum mobile* sort." The book itself begins to seem an afterthought.

And that, in fact, is precisely the problem. Given the riskiness of writing blurbs at all, given the attempt to keep up with one's neighbors (on the cover) by writing something memorable that zings, given the fact that the names, and often the sentences, in blurbs are more compelling than the ones inside—and given our accelerating culture of the sound bite, the boldface name, the browser, the virtual reader, and the capsule review ("11 on a scale of 10!" "Three thumbs up!" "Oscar better polish his statue!")—can the day be far off when every book will be read only on its cover?

(1995)

$F$orty years ago, Graham Greene wrote what with every passing season feels increasingly like a definitive account of cultures clashing and colluding. Pyle, in *The Quiet American*, is an almost too perfect embodiment of American innocence abroad, so full of good intentions and treatises on Democracy that he steps from Harvard Square to Indochina without breaking his stride, determined to make the world better, whether the world wants it or not. Yet the man who remarks on his folly—the English journalist Fowler—is, in his way, no less captive to self-delusion, hiding behind an indifference he likes to call "detachment" and failing to acknowledge, even to himself, how deeply he is implicated in the world around him. Where Pyle unseeingly embraces the world, Fowler prides himself on his distance from it. And through it all, at the heart of their struggle, sits enigmatic Phuong, the Vietnamese girl who so gracefully bends to their every need that she seems certain to come out ahead.

The novel is, of course, in part a parable about faith, and the costs of idealism weighed against those of defeatism. Yet in a deeper sense it is about the contagion of innocence, and how innocence awakens its shadow in everyone it touches. However much he is opposed to Pyle in love and war, Fowler cannot help but take pity on his guileless vulnerability. And the very innocence that proves so debilitating in foreign policy becomes, in the private sphere, almost impossible to resist.

The visitor to Vietnam today may be surprised to see how much Pyle's innocence has wrought, and how much it has won, in the hearts and minds of one of the last of America's official enemies. He will find a country that, in most cases, is praying for American intervention, and a people who look down on no one but the Soviets, whom they deride as "Americans without dollars." He will find crowds of citizens in Hue, in waterside cafés, desperate to get a glimpse of Meryl Streep on video, and among the illuminated lanterns and crooked streets of old Hanoi he will find rooms full of faces lit up by the unearthly glow of new Nintendo screens. At night, in Dalat, he will hear every last word of "Hotel California" floating across "Sighing Lake." And in the War Crimes Museum in Ho Chi Minh City, once the U.S. Information Office, and not far from the Ca-li-pho-nia Ham-bu-go restaurant (rather freely translated as

"California Fried Chicken Burger King"), he can inspect a whole display case given over to the diabolical weapons of "Cultural Ideological Sabotage": a "Dracula for President" T-shirt; some Black Sabbath memorabilia; and a shirt bearing the legend "Ozzy Osbourne: Sympathy for the Devil."

Apparently, no one has told the Politburo that Ozzy Osbourne hails from the British Midlands. Yet that is only the first of many unsettling ironies. The one Russian product that I found popular in Vietnam this spring was an all-girl pop group—called, perversely, The Originals—whose MTV gyrations, synchronized with four bikinied dancers, held the locals in awe. The former Vietnamese platoon commanders I met wore "Atlanta Placons" baseball caps and spent half their savings on showings of *Hamburger Hill* and *Platoon*. And nothing in Vietnam seemed more popular than a group that could perform note-perfect renditions, in English, of Bruce Springsteen's anthems for the Vietnam Vet.

All this, of course, is hardly surprising, and hardly new: pop culture makes the world go round, and America makes the best pop culture. By now, indeed, such products represent the largest single source of America's export earnings, even as America remains the single most popular destination for immigrant visas. The more straitened or shut off a culture, the more urgent its hunger for all the qualities it associates with America: freedom and wealth and modernity. Thus poor countries around the world still hold themselves hostage to *L.A. Law*, and Communist countries everywhere seek to make contact, if only in their minds, with a place that has never outgrown its image as the Promised Land of Opportunity. It is not just hard currency that most nations want; it is a deeper kind of "currency"—the sense, however limited, that they are in tune with the coming thing, in step with what is happening in the capital of the American Century. That is one reason why Václav Havel, as soon as he became president of Czechoslovakia, lost no time in inviting Lou Reed to the palace and in appointing Frank Zappa his unofficial cultural ambassador: they were the *samizdat* heroes of his youth, whose strength had little to do with power chords. And it is also why the kids on the streets of Moscow famously yearn to buy not just jeans, but *used* jeans: that is, quite literally, the closest they can come to putting themselves in American shoes.

Nowadays, though, the world that we grew up with is turning on a carousel of dimes, and America may be coming to seem increasingly redundant. Now that Communism is disintegrating, the allure of capitalism will surely begin to dissolve too: America can no longer be seen as the lesser of two evils. Besides, there is a genuine sense in many parts of the world that the disciplined efficiency of a unified Europe and of the new East Asian powers is leaving America far behind. The largest debtor nation in the world, where ten million blacks alone live in poverty, whose capital was run by a cocaine addict, and whose capital also had a murder rate, during the '80s, higher than that of Sri Lanka or Beirut, seems an unlikely model for emulation. And yet, I think, America's hold on imaginations will remain secure. In the cultural realm, the emphasis on "New World Order" will still fall squarely on "New World." The British make better music, the Japanese are far ahead in efficiency, the Europeans have a stronger and more self-conscious sense of their aesthetic heritage, yet in the world of movies and songs and images, America is still, and long will be, the Great Communicator. The capital of the world, as Gore Vidal often says, is not Washington but Hollywood. And however much America suffers an internal loss of faith, it will continue to enjoy some of the immunity that attaches to all things in the realm of myth: as much as we—and everyone else—assume that the French make the best perfumes, and the Swiss the finest watches, the suspicion will continue that Americans make the best dreams.

In some ways, indeed, the domination of American pop culture is only increasing as communications speed up and the world continues to shrink. More and more of the planet now is wired for sound, and marching to the beat of a single satellite drummer. In the past year alone, I have seen CNN in Beijing, Buenos Aires, and even on Cubavision; MTV is sending out its images from Mexico City to Moscow. And if *Batman* could claim 100 percent name recognition before the movie even came out, it is hardly surprising that within a few months of its release, I was seeing bowler-hatted Indian women in Andean villages phlegmatically selling Batmobiles. In some respects, the impact of America is nowadays instantaneous: in Bhutan, where televisions are unknown, and high-rises are scarcely dreamed of—in Bhutan, perhaps the most tightly closed country in the world, which has never seen more than three thousand tourists in a single year—the pirated version of Eddie Murphy's *Coming to America* was on display well before the video had ever come to America.

The reasons for this process are not hard to explain. For one thing, the explosion of technology's most powerful media coincided almost exactly with the flowering of American political strength: America began to rule the world at the same time that movies, and TV, and pop songs began to rule our minds, so that the two came to seem inseparable. And the sense that America was the home of promise—and the latest, brightest news—quickly became so entrenched that everything that was promising was taken to be American (even if it was Ozzy Osbourne, or Nintendo, or the enchilada). Success begat success, and before long the notion of American preeminence was self-fulfilling. When an English fast-food joint wants to make a killing, it simply slips "Texas" or "Tennessee" into its title and watches its profits soar (a Chicago Steak House in central London proudly asserts, "Famous since 1987").

To us, much of this may seem inexplicable: even as people in Honduras, or Melbourne, or the country houses of England, are still tuning in to *Dallas*, after all, a few stalwarts in Cambridge, Massachusetts, are diligently glued to *Masterpiece Theatre*. And many of us cannot fathom why the students of Santiago de Cuba, the most musically vibrant city in the hemisphere, are listening to the New Kids on the Block, or why Emperor Hirohito, having seen his country laid waste by American bombs, sported a Mickey Mouse wristwatch. But we are no different, in our hunger for Le Cars, and tiramisù, and Ayurvedic medicine. And American culture always becomes something else, and something more, as it takes on a native coloring: the McDonald's outlets in Bangkok feature floor-to-ceiling windows so that diners can, quite literally, engage in conspicuous consumption, watched by all their envious friends as they pay five times more for their burgers than they would elsewhere. What draws people to the Pizza Hut in Moscow is not, one suspects, its special sauce, but rather what it stands for: a way of aligning oneself, however fleetingly, with a world that is—in imagination at least—quick and flashy and rich. The Kentucky Fried Chicken store in Tiananmen Square has place mats telling the whole of Colonel Sanders's history, and framed posters of San Francisco and L.A. on the walls; its customers, paying a week's wages to dine there, troop around the place, taking photos, as if it were a rival to Mao's mausoleum nearby. The lure of the foreign is quickened by the lure of the forbidden.

I got my own best sense of this in a friend's apartment in Havana some years ago. My friend was an intellectual dissident, fluent in several languages, eager to talk about Spinoza and Saroyan, and able to make a living by reading people's futures from their photographs and translating the latest Top 40 hits—recorded from radio stations in Miami—into Spanish. One night, trying to convey his desperation to escape, he pulled out what was clearly his most precious possession: a copy of Michael Jackson's "Bad," on which he had scrawled some heartfelt appeals to Jackson to rescue him. He did not, I suspect, know that Jackson was reclusive, eccentric, and about as likely to respond to political appeals as Donald Duck. What he did know was that Jackson was sexually ambiguous, black, and rich—all things it was not good to be in Castro's Cuba. What he also knew was that Jackson had succeeded on his own terms, an individual who had proved himself stronger than the system.

The less my friend knew about Jackson the man, the closer he could feel to Jackson the symbol. And so it is with America.

And since the America that he was coveting does not quite exist, it is, I think, immutable: a talisman that will fail him only if he comes here. Besides, America, of all countries, is still best able to identify itself with abstractions, and to present itself as an image for the world's consumption. There is a sense, in fact, in which America is perceived to be the home of the "image" and of all the forms associated with it: the theme park, the sound bite, the video, and the thirty-second commercial. That is why politicians from Managua to Manila seek out Madison Avenue techniques, and Roger Ailes–like TelePrompTers. America seems so much the leader in packaging and promotion that it has become the leader in packaging and promotion. Fast food—not good food, but cheap, convenient, smartly packaged food, democratic food—is one example. Another is "American football," which is fast gaining ground on what the rest of the world calls football, not least, I think, because it is American (even as the real football World Cup is about to be held in America). These days, Redskins stickers and 49ers caps are *de rigueur* in Europe. More than 300 million Chinese watch the Super Bowl. Even Fidel Castro has been seen doing the Wave. This is not, I think, because American football is so exciting; it is, rather, because it embodies so much of what the world loves about America: it is flashy, it is full of show-biz frills (cheerleaders and electronic scoreboards and high tech and high fives)—and most of all, it is telegenic.

The single most extraordinary example of this phenomenon today is Madonna. It would be easy to write her off by simply calling her the first Virgin Queen of the Video Age, the prima ballerina of MTV, the maiden megastar of the graven-image world. Certainly, she is in part a product of her place and time—America, 1960–90—perfectly positioned to be in tune with all the latest fads and to be the first to cash in on a global village small enough for one figure to girdle. Not, by her own admission, an exceptional dancer, or actress, or singer, she is, rather, something else, a full-time professional icon. Her job is to be a star, to play the part of a celluloid hero. And Madonna, the classic vid kid and baby boomer, growing up at the same time as TV, sharpening her moves in the discos of Motown and New York, anthologizing the devices of Hollywood's glamour queens and attuning herself to the ten-second attention span of video, has turned herself into a kind of synthetic phenomenon, as compulsively watchable as the tube itself.

In some ways, indeed, she has shown us just how cable knit, and media made, the world around us is. When Madonna first appeared on the cover of *Time*, six years ago—in a story that described her as a "trash-flash star" and "1985's rock supernova"—it seemed a safe bet that she would remain in the limelight about as long as all the other flavors of the moment (Cyndi Lauper, Molly Ringwald, Tama Janowitz). Yet here we are, three hundred issues later, and she's bigger than ever, wreathed in Homeric images in *Time*, dilating on public morality on *Nightline*, delivering reasoned arguments against censorship outside the Vatican, and being lionized and anatomized by professors (even in 1985, the interview with her that *Time* printed was, by its own admission, one of the longest in its history, given more space than had been allotted to Churchill or Nixon or Mao). The astonishing achievement of Madonna is not just to reinvent herself constantly but to have the whole world hanging on her every reinvention: she has succeeded in doing what many more interesting and intelligent artists—Bob Dylan, say, or Norman Mailer—have tried, and failed, to do. And what people seem to enjoy in following her is watching her pull our invisible strings: as her movie *Truth or Dare* shows very clearly, she is a figure more of power than of sex (which is one reason why she appeals to women as much as to men and, among men, especially to those other seditious ironists, the gays). Nowadays, everyone wants to be Madonna because everyone wants to be Madonna.

I do not believe that Madonna is enormous simply because she is American; yet it is hard to imagine her dominating the world were she not American. Can one picture a Madonna from Stockholm, or Tokyo, or even London? The Beatles, of course, had some of the same appeal, but their marketing was based in large part on their air of shaggy innocence (here were pop stars you could take home to introduce to Grandma), and they began to fade as soon as they began to get far-out; Madonna somehow has all the world following an ideology that could not be more disruptive to established codes. And much of her success seems to have something to do with growing up in America in the era of the small screen and developing an almost intuitive sense of how to play the media and how to deal in images (as those other infant prodigies of the star-making machinery Michael Jackson and Brooke Shields have, in their more passive way, also done). These days, the canny superstar knows that even absence and aberration are good PR (as brilliantly explored by perhaps the most clairvoyant and contemporary of chroniclers of America, Don DeLillo, whose latest hero is a novelist who advances his literary career simply by sitting for a photo session). It is not just that Madonna cannot live off-camera; it is that she knows how to perform in real life as if on-camera (as Reagan did too, in a sense), till there is no gap between public and private self. She is the first celebrity willing to play the part around the clock—the cultural world's first answer to the actor politician. Madonna is as American as ambition.

The other factor in all this, and a more fundamental one, perhaps, is you, and me, and the man next door. As borders crumble, and cultures mingle, and more and more of the world acquires a lateral mobility, more and more of us are becoming hyphenated. In that sense, all the world's a melting pot these days, and culture increasingly seems bound to carry two passports, or three. Tourism alone will be the most important economic activity in the world by the year 2000, according to the United Nations. And as the power brokers of a departing Hong Kong scatter around the world, to Vancouver, and London, and Bermuda, more and more of the world is coming to seem like Hong Kong, a collection of hybrids and exiles and mongrels living in an entrepôt of convenience to do business, in dollars (and in English), in a community tied together by links less political than commercial. Culturally speaking, few people now have a fixed address. Just take, as an almost random example, some of the "Indian writers" flourishing today in English. V. S. Naipaul is an Indian born and raised in Trinidad, who carries himself like an Englishman from an England that no longer exists; Bharati Mukherjee is a Calcuttan married to a Canadian, partially educated in the United States, and writing in the voices of the latest immigrants from Central America and the Caribbean; Anita Desai, half German, spends a third of the year in England, a third in the United States, and a third in India (as, famously, did Ruth Prawer Jhabvala); and Vikram Seth went to school near Delhi, went to college at Oxford, and wrote the "Great California Novel" while a student at Stanford doing research in China. Nowadays, one suspects, it is R. K. Narayan, living for nearly all his life in the same tiny area, and writing mostly about it, who is the rare exception, with a sense of belonging that seems to place him in a never-never land.

This feverish international crosscutting can only have happy effects on the cultural plane. Perhaps the best example of the new globoculturalism is music, the least tongue-tied of forms and the one most able to cross borders and travel without a visa: World Music has already lasted longer than any mere fashion in ethnic chic and has already succeeded in putting countries like Yemen and Bulgaria on the cultural map. One German group, called Cusco, and playing haunting Andean melodies on authentic panpipes, is all the rage in Japan (challenged only by the Gipsy Kings); another German band has produced a best-selling, all but definitive, recording of original Javanese gamelan music. Influences are flashing between cultures at the speed of light, forming a laser latticework of images: one could almost say that William Faulkner begat Gabriel García Márquez begat Salman Rushdie. And the most fashionable authors of today—Kundera, say, or Rushdie, or Allende—are all in some sense spokesmen for a kind of floating culture, international citizens who are never local in the way that Thomas Hardy, or Tolstoy, or even Balzac, were. Meanwhile, Malinese movies are appearing on screens in Los Angeles, and the Chinese film *Ju Dou* was the top hit in Oslo last summer; some of the glossiest art-house successes of recent years—*The Last Emperor*, say—are coproductions quite as multilingual as many of their stars. Arnold Schwarzenegger, Rubén Blades, Ryuichi Sakamoto— who can say where any of them is from?

The danger in all this, as Peter Brook has said, is that if cultures are mixed too self-consciously or dilettantishly, one ends up with a kind of artistic Esperanto, a simple smorgasbord of styles whose whole is always less than the sum of its promiscuous parts; yet the promise of it all, as Peter Brook exemplifies, is the creation of a work in which many tongues are blended into a single chorus that cuts deeper than language or geography. It is not the differences between cultures, but the convergences, that Brook celebrates, and in so doing, he exalts and explodes the whole notion of cultural mix. And though Paris and Tokyo and Sydney and Toronto are all becoming natural meeting points for this multipolar culture, America is still the spiritual home of the very notion of integration: everyone feels at home in only two places, Miloš Forman has said—at home, and in America. That is one reason why I suspect that America's domination of pop culture will continue, even if the reality of American power increasingly seems a thing of the past. The notion of America itself attracts more and more people to come and revive or refresh the notion of America. And the more international a culture is, the more, very often, it draws from the center of internationalism, the United States. The French may rail against cultural imperialism, and try to enforce a kind of aesthetic protectionism by striving to keep out *le burger* and *le video*. But as soon as Madonna shows up in Cannes—so efficient is her command of all the media and so self-perpetuating her appeal—she sets off the biggest stir in thirty years. Professors at the Sorbonne continue to remind us that Charles Bukowski is the greatest American of our times and Mickey Rourke the finest actor since—well, since Jerry Lewis at least. And the English routinely complain that their whole country is being turned into a theme park for American consumption—then take their holidays in Disney World (and promise the children that next year they can go to Euro-Disney—not far from central Paris!).

The likely dominance of American culture is best borne out, I think, by the Japanese example. As more and more of the world is, quite literally, being bought and taken over by the Japanese, the first outlines of a Japanese Empire are increasingly in evidence: not just in the new Japanese colonies, such as Hawaii, the Champs Elysées, and Australia's

Gold Coast (where shopgirls speak entirely in Japanese, prices are routinely quoted in yen, and locals pull along Osaka couples in rickshas), but even in more far-reaching fashions. "Sushi" and "karaoke" are as universally understood now as "disco" and "bar." Japanese comic books, fashions, and inventions are defining trends in every *Blade Runner* future. Some Australian schools have made classes in Japanese compulsory; Berlitz in Paris is offering 2,200 classes in the language this year; and even in the wilds of Java, the hustlers who formerly prided themselves on mastering such slogans as "No money, no honey" are now adding Japanese catchphrases to their repertoire. Tokyo-style traffic lights, Comme des Garçons fashions, and Mitsukoshi department stores are more and more the model all over the Far East. Even the wooden footpath signs in the Yorkshire Moors around the Brontë cottage are written now in katakana.

Yet of all the peoples in the world, none is more heavily influenced by American culture, at some level, than the Japanese, with their baseball games, their McDonald's outlets (featuring Teriyaki McBurgers and Corn Potage Soups), and their whole areas done up to simulate New World optimism (as in Osaka's "America-mura"). The Japanese, more than anyone, feed and live off brand names, and America has, in the world of entertainment, the biggest brand name of all (Kurosawa is honored by many young Japanese only because he is regarded as a protégé of George Lucas and Steven Spielberg). Such fashions are, to be sure, no more than that, and surface deep; yet there is still a strong sense among the Japanese that, however much American businesses are taking their cues from them, America is still the ultimate pleasure zone, the place they look to for their honeymoons and holidays. And the Japanese belief that they are different from the world—or even superior to it—tends to distance them from even the outposts of their empire in a way that could never happen with the Pax Americana (for America *is* the world, a heterogeneous collection of all its scattered parts). The common viewer will always, I suspect, have a hunger for innocence, for storytelling, and for special effects, and somehow—perhaps because they were immigrants themselves, with half a heart still on the streets they left—the moguls of Hollywood and Broadway and Nashville seem never to have lost their common touch: *E.T.* and *Back to the Future* strike universal chords as surely as *Gone With the Wind* and *Casablanca* did half a century ago. Besides, the reigning stars of pop culture have a kind of durability—the immunity of myth—that many politicians would die for (and try to acquire, increasingly, by turning themselves into pop or video stars). Even figures as dominant as Gorbachev and Thatcher can disappear overnight, mired as they are in the demeaning and slippery world of decision making; yet there is almost nothing that Michael Jackson or

Madonna can do to lose their fascination. They have, in a sense, a sort of provisional immortality. And people will almost never renounce them, if only because to do so is, in a way, to renounce their past, and to repudiate what appeals to the most innocent part of them, and the most private.

So it is that many of us, I think, feel a little wistful as we see that whatever happens in the world of geopolitics, America will continue ruling the airwaves. Midway through *The Quiet American*, when Fowler is summoned back to England, his Vietnamese lover, Phuong, promises to come with him. "Are there skyscrapers in London?" she asks eagerly. "No," he tells her patiently. "You have to go to America for them." "And the Statue of Liberty?" "No, Phuong," he replies, "that's American too."

(1991)

# A Midsummer
# Night's Dream:
## *The Sequel*

There has been so much talk of late of the cold war ending and the arms race receding, the whole geopolitical world shifting on its very foundations, that we have had little time, perhaps, to notice how quickly the battle of the sexes has been heating up. These, in fact, are hard times for lovers: in the age of AIDS and the palimony suit, an affair of the heart seems less a matter of chemistry than of law and medicine and politics. The pattern now, it seems, is boy meets girl (or sometimes boy), quizzes significant other on her sexual history, comes clean with an update on his own antisocial diseases, and puts it all down in writing for the lawyers. Precoital tristesse, in short. Shall I compare thee to a summer's day? Okay. But remember that in 1989, summer days are apt to be murky with smog, uncomfortably hot thanks to the greenhouse effect, and filled with lo-cal sequels.

What, then, one wonders on an idle summer evening, would the Shakespeare of *A Midsummer Night's Dream* make of us, and what can we make of him? The first thing we notice when we see his play today is how little love has changed, with all its harsh geometry of triangles and unrequited passions; nor do we have any difficulty recognizing its ageless cast of characters—the impatient suitor trying to persuade his girl to let him share her bed, the fair-weather swain shifting in an instant from rhapsody to rancor, the lovers plotting to escape a tyrannical father (only to find that they cannot so easily escape themselves). Puck, we realize, would make a dream host on *Love Connection*, and the rude mechanicals, rehearsing "most obscenely and courageously," would surely be an instant hit on prime time. We can recognize, too, that the malaprop artists' confusion of "paragon" and "paramour" is not an idle joke; the idealizing of love is as old as broken hearts. "Reason and love keep little company now-a-days."

In some respects, indeed, the comedy of musical beds and drugs and knockabout buffoonery seems almost made for MTV. The scene of two young men playing mixed doubles with their interchangeable girlfriends, Hermia and Helena ("like to a double cherry"), would not seem strange to the kids in Bret Easton Ellis novels, who fall into bed with anyone at all, scarcely stopping to ascertain identity, or even sex. Titania's sudden passion for ass-headed Bottom seems almost natural in the Age of

Ecstasy, when someone who takes a tab of MDMA is liable to open her heart to the first person she sees. And Pyramus and Thisbe, wooing each other through a chink in a wall, might almost be model paramours—paragons, in fact—for the "safe sex" generation.

Besides, "the course of true love never did run smooth," as Lysander observes, and in seeing the muddle of our own times we are apt to overlook the fact that it was ever so. Faithlessness was hardly patented by Cressida, and even in Shakespeare's day the theaters were full of Roman numerals. Sequels follow sequels. Romeo, let us not forget, was a heartstrong adolescent rhyming "sighs" with "eyes" and unable to imagine any girl save Rosaline—until he set eyes on Juliet; and Juliet was a thirteen-year-old upstart who roundly abused both her murdering Romeo and her devoted nurse. Shakespeare himself addresses some of his most heartfelt statements of love to a beautiful young man, and to some mysterious "Dark Lady" who was not his wife.

Yet even though the heart may not have changed, the pressures and restrictions brought to bear on it have surely done so. The whole thrust of Shakespeare's play, after all, is that "lovers and madmen have such seething brains," that lovers, in short, are too full of folly, too much aflame, too rich in their imaginations. Nowadays, often, our problem seems just the opposite. Prudence makes us measure out our hearts with coffee spoons, and discretion is the better part of Valium. Love has always been a messy affair, and that is precisely why it cannot be easily legislated. Make romance a thing for lawyers, and callousness and shame turn into crime and punishment. Yet today we have girls suing their dates for standing them up, and star-crossed ex-lovers—the former partners of William Hurt, Mike Tyson, and Rock Hudson, to name but three—counting the emotional cost in millions. Litigation means never having to say you're sorry.

All this is not to suggest that caution is a bad thing: Romeo and Juliet died prematurely, after all. Romance has always included some degree of calculation. Indeed, the very notion of true love, according to many scholars, is a relatively recent invention: in most places, in most times, marriage has been a practical arrangement. Those who scoff at matrimonial ads in Indian papers may have few qualms about placing SWM notices in their local tabloids; a blind date is only an arranged marriage *in potentia*. If disease and collision liability have put a crimp in promiscuity, that may be all to the good. But just because love cannot be free, does it have to be so costly?

Perhaps in the end, then, the thing that separates us most from Shakespeare is simply his belief in fairies who can solve all our confusions by going above the heads of lawmakers. The classic premise of comedy, and the ritual revelry from which it springs, is a story that concludes with a vision of unity, of natural harmony. So after all the lunacies and bumps of Shakespeare's starlit night are over, the spirits come down to put everything to right, and the lovers awaken with the morning lark, only to suspect that it was all a dream. Love is blind, and its victims are mad, the poet suggests, but only for a night, a brief, forgetful spell. Perhaps even in 1600 that might have seemed an escapist thought; in 1989, however, a midsummer night's dream may be our best hope of a happy ending.

(1989)

# The Ultimate
## Near-Life Experience

One of the liveliest topics of the moment—even as life expectancies increase and it is the proliferation of births that worries many of the world's thinkers—seems, improbably, to be death. The best-seller lists are crowded with titles such as *How We Die* and *The Tibetan Book of Living and Dying*, and even *The New Yorker*, that beady-eyed spotter of new trends, has run a last-page interview with the Reaper. Perhaps it is because AIDS and cancer have implicated us all in the abruptness of extinction; or merely that publishers see a killing in the most universal experience of them all. But that, in either case, may be a blessing: when we spend months, even years, learning to fix a car, or speak Portuguese, why should we not try to learn how to die?

One reason, of course, is that death is the one great adventure of which there are no surviving accounts; death, by definition, is what happens to somebody else. Empiricism falters before death. Yet it is more certain than love and more inevitable than health.

And its very inevitability prompts us to find ways to domesticate it. Some of us try to take the sting out of mortality by talking of "passing away" or going to "the Great Dugout in the Sky" (while doctors, who have to deal with it daily, refer, even more coolly, to "coding" or "circling the drain"). Others try to romanticize it as the great escape, the best anesthetic this side of Prozac. Those who cannot countenance any hope in the world find it the ultimate—indeed—confirmation of their grimmest fears. Death, after all, is the only reality that never lets you down. Yet that, too, can be an escape, a projection of our fantasies upon the dark unknown. Keats, who admitted to being "half in love with easeful Death," died at twenty-five, penniless and spitting blood.

Others would try to outlast it, or at least outwit it, through cryonics, say (though it may be no coincidence that their most famous example is said to be Walt Disney). And others talk blithely of Dr. Kevorkian or 200,000 dead in Rwanda, as if to avoid its more immediate implications for us. But the fact remains: this article will soon be posthumous. That face I touch will, in the not too distant future, be out of reach. Tibetan Buddhists meditate upon images of dancing skulls, and ancient Egyptians, during feasts, had skeletons brought to their tables, all to remind them of a single fact: that smile we love will soon be food for worms.

Perhaps the most common way of making peace with death—getting over it, in a sense—is by thinking of it as a way to "meet one's Maker." Religions, of every kind, might almost be said to exist to help us deal with our extinction. They tell us that something is waiting for us on the other side; that death may be a pilgrimage and not a destination; that the after-life is a warm awakening after the fretful dream of life. The huge best-seller *Embraced by the Light* returns from the hereafter with the news that "*All* experiences can be positive." In my local bookstore, the Death and Dying section is right next to Recovery and Affirmations, and the titles themselves sound like holiday brochures: *The Trip of a Lifetime, Heading Toward Omega, Companion Through Darkness.*

Not coincidentally, in William Osler's classic medical textbook of 1892, he recommended opium as the one great help for some diseases (words for Karl Marx to chew on), and that may be especially true now that our sense of the transcendent is diminished. The man who gave us "the death of God" also wrote *The Birth of Tragedy*; a sense of eternity is much less cold and abstract if linked to a sense of divinity.

Yet none of this helps us in the here and now. And thinking about death is useful only if it makes us concentrate on life. All of us, after all, are dying every moment, and, as Montaigne wryly remarked, "the goal of our career is death." The other world is relevant only in the shadow it casts on this one; or, as Thoreau implied upon leaving the woods, he didn't want to die feeling he hadn't lived.

Many of us—this writer included—have been lucky enough never to have had to face death close-up, even in a loved one; it remains as remote to us as the other great challenges of Hunger and Poverty and War. Of course we have our dress rehearsals, all the time: for as much as every death is a separation, every separation is a little death, and one that may be even harder, because protracted and reversible. Yet still we would do well to recall that at least a fifth of all Americans die without warning (and the onset of fatal disease is equally unexpected): suddenly there is a knock on the door, a telephone ringing, a messenger in black.

There is nothing any of us can do about death, and there is no virtue in dwelling on it, or trying to penetrate its mystery. In any case, phi-losophy is famously helpless before a toothache. But there may be some good in coming to death as least as well prepared as we go to our vaca-tions, our driving tests, or our weddings. If I were to die tomorrow, as the old saw has it, what would I wish to have done today? Or, as the Tibetan Sogyal Rinpoche says, "If you're having problems with a friend, pretend he's dying—you may even love him." Especially good advice if that friend happens to be yourself.

(1994)

Charles Waterton was just another typical eccentric. In his eighties, the eminent country squire was to be seen clambering around the upper branches of an oak tree with what was aptly described as the agility of an "adolescent gorilla." The beloved twenty-seventh lord of Walton Hall also devoted his distinguished old age to scratching the back part of his head with his right big toe and ministering to a young, but ailing, lady chimpanzee, whom he visited daily and left each day with a kiss on the cheek. Not that such displays of animal high spirits were confined to the gentleman's old age: when young, Waterton made four separate trips to South America, where he sought the wourali poison (a cure, he was convinced, for hydrophobia), and once spent months on end with one foot dangling from his hammock in the quixotic hope of having his toe sucked by a vampire bat.

James Warren Jones, by contrast, was something of a weirdo. As a boy in the casket-making town of Lynn, Indiana, he used to conduct elaborate funeral services for dead pets. Later, as a struggling preacher, he went from door to door, in bow tie and tweed jacket, selling imported monkeys. After briefly fleeing to South America (a shelter, he believed, from an imminent nuclear holocaust), the man who regarded himself as a reincarnation of Lenin settled in northern California and opened a pet shelter, three convalescent homes, and some kitchens for the poor. Then, one humid day in the jungles of Guyana, the former human rights commissioner of Indianapolis ordered his followers to drink a Kool-Aid–like punch soured with cyanide. By the time the world arrived at Jonestown, 911 people were dead.

The difference between the eccentric and the weirdo is, in its way, the difference between a man with a teddy bear in his hand and a man with a gun. We are also, of course, besieged by other kinds of deviants—crackpots, oddballs, fanatics, quacks, and cranks. But the weirdo and the eccentric define between them that invisible line at which strangeness acquires an edge and oddness becomes menace.

The difference between the two starts with the words themselves: "eccentric," after all, carries a distinguished Latin pedigree that refers, quite reasonably, to anything that departs from the center; "weird," by comparison, has its mongrel origins in the Old English *wyrd*, meaning fate or destiny; and the larger, darker forces conjured by the term—Macbeth's Weird Sisters and the like—are given an extra twist with the slangy bastard suffix *-o*.

Beneath the linguistic roots, however, we feel the difference on our pulses. The eccentric we generally regard as something of a donny, dotty, harmless type, like the British peer who threw over his Cambridge fellowship in order to live in a bath, and became so ardent a champion of water that he would press silver coins on anyone who drank his favorite beverage; the weirdo is an altogether more shadowy figure—Charles Manson acting out his messianic visions. The eccentric is a creature of fancy, the weirdo one of fantasy. The eccentric is a distinctive presence; the weirdo something of an absence, who casts no reflection in society's mirror. The eccentric raises a smile; the weirdo leaves a chill.

All too often, though, the two terms are not so easily distinguished. Many a criminal trial, after all, revolves around precisely that gray area where the two begin to blur. Was Bernhard Goetz just a volatile Everyman, ourselves pushed to the limit, and then beyond? Or was he in fact an aberration? What do we make of Jerry Lee Lewis, the maniacal rock 'n' roller who boasts of how he earned his nickname, "the Killer"? Or, conversely, of Gary Gilmore, the convicted killer with a scrupulous, if erratic, sense of moral justice?

Often, moreover, eccentrics may simply be weirdos in possession of a VIP pass, people rich enough or powerful enough to live by their own laws. Who knows what Howard Hughes might have done had he not enjoyed the resources to create his own private world in which uncleanliness was next to godliness? Elvis Presley could afford to pump bullets into silhouettes of humans and never count the cost; lesser mortals, however, after shooting their dummies, must find another kind of victim. Eccentricity can thus become almost a sign of aristocracy, the calling card of those who do not have to defer to convention, but live above it, amoral as Greek gods. It is no coincidence, perhaps, that Charles Waterton was a nobleman descended from Sir Thomas More, Saint Matilda Queen of Germany, Saint Margaret Queen of Scotland, and Saint Vladimir of Russia. Or that the man who lived in a tub, a beard stretching down to his knees, was a peer of the realm, Lord Rokeby. These days, it is our modern ruling class—the Superstars—whose idiosyncrasies we devour in the tabloids.

To some extent, too, we tend to think of eccentricity as the prerogative, even the hallmark, of genius. And genius is its own vindication. Who cared that Glenn Gould sang along with the piano while playing

Bach, so long as he played so beautifully? Or if Sir Ralph Richardson, the very patron saint of oddness, bursts into *The Tempest* in the middle of *Volpone*, so long as he can carry it off convincingly? Even the Herculean debauches of Babe Ruth did not undermine so much as confirm his status as a legend.

Indeed, the unorthodox inflections of the exceptional can lead to all kinds of dangerous assumptions. If geniuses are out of the ordinary and psychopaths are out of the ordinary, then geniuses are psychopaths and vice versa, or so at least runs the reasoning of many dramatists who set their plays in loony bins. If the successful are often strange, then being strange is a way of becoming successful, or so believe all those would-be artists who work on eccentric poses. And if celebrity is its own defense, then many a demagogue or criminal assures himself that he will ultimately be redeemed by the celebrity he covets.

All these distortions, however, ignore the most fundamental distinction of all: the eccentric is strange because he cares too little about society, the weirdo because he cares too much. The eccentric generally wants nothing more than his own attic-like space in which he can live by his own peculiar lights. The weirdo, however, resents his outcast status and constantly seeks to get back into society, or at least get back at it. His is the rage not of the bachelor but of the divorcé.

Thus the eccentric hardly cares if he is seen to be strange; that in a sense is what makes him strange. The weirdo, by contrast, wants desperately to be taken as normal and struggles to keep his strangeness to himself. "He was always such a nice man," the neighbors ritually tell reporters after a sniper's rampage. "He always seemed so normal."

And because the two mark such different tangents to the norm, their incidence can, in its way, be an index of a society's health. In her very English and very eccentric book, *English Eccentrics*, Edith Sitwell asserts that "Eccentricity exists particularly in the English, and partly, I think, because of that peculiar and satisfactory knowledge of infallibility that is the hallmark and birthright of the British nation." She might have added that the height of British eccentricity coincided with the height of British power, if only, perhaps, because Britain in its imperial heyday presented so strong a center from which to depart. Nowadays, however, with the empire gone and the center vanishing, Britain is more often associated with the maladjusted weirdo—the orange-haired misfit or the soccer hooligan.

At the other extreme, the relentless and ritualized normalcy of a society like Japan's—there are only four psychiatrists in all of Tokyo—can, to Western eyes, itself seem almost abnormal. Too few eccentrics can be as dangerous as too many weirdos. For in the end, eccentricity is a mark of confidence, accommodated best by a confident society; whereas weird-ness inspires fear because it is a symptom of fear, and uncertainty and rage. A society needs the eccentric as much as it needs a decorated frame for the portrait it fashions of itself; it needs the weirdo as much as it needs a hole punched through the middle of the canvas.

(1987)

Ꭵt passes through our minds, it tumbles off our fingers every day. Regardless almost of our race or tongue, it is as close to us as the date of our birth, the number of our telephone, the house in which we live. Yet how often do we ever think of 9? In numbers, Pythagoras and Plotinus and other worthies have believed, lie the secrets of the universe; God and Nature move in 40-day rotations, 28-day cycles, passages of 9 months. And in 9 alone is a universe—maybe even a paradise—if only we would stop and look.

Every number has its character, its own distinctive coloring: 5, for instance, is the gray accountant, the user-friendly solid citizen, the John Major, if you like, of integers; 6 has the springtime bounce of a perky cheerleader, though taken too far it leads straight to hell (666 is the number of the Beast). And 7 is everybody's lucky number—we base our lives around 7 seas, 7 heavens, and 7 graces (as well, inevitably, as their shadow side, the 7 Deadlies). But what of 9? It is, we all know, an odd number (very odd) and one of the earliest squares. It is a 6 on its head, a circle and a line, the highest digit, and the last, with something of the darkness that attaches to last things. Yet it has strange magic in it. Multiply any number by 9, and the sum of the digits will also come to 9 (7 times 9 equals 63; 6 plus 3 equals 9). Reverse the digits, and the number you get (36) will also be a multiple of 9. Take any number you choose (4321), and divide it by 9. The remainder you get (1) will be the same as the remainder you get when you add the digits and divide by 9. That is why mathematicians check their calculations by "casting out nines."

Thus 9 is the source of magic squares, pool-table pyramids, and various patterns that reproduce themselves indefinitely. Most of us, however, know it on less formal terms: as a friend to decision making (9 judges on the Supreme Court) and the key to the heavens (9 planets and 9 Muses). Statisticians covet it—since if all 9 members of a baseball team have 9 at bats (in any number of 9-inning games), their batting averages will be instantaneous to compute (2 for 9 is .222, 3 for 9 is .333, 4 for 9 is .444, and so on to infinity). And 9 is a priceless aid to shopkeepers, who will keep on charging $9.99 or $49.95 till the end of time. In binary terms, 9 is 1001—the number of adventure and romance; in England, you dial 999 for emergencies (to reverse, perhaps, the diabolic effect of 666). Yet 9 also has an edge to it, the menace that comes from lying along a fault line: it is the number just before the boxer is counted out, the cat runs out of lives, the lover slams the door.

Every number, of course, is only what we make of it, and one man's anguished 10 minus 1 is another's rosy 2 plus 3 plus 4. Indeed, 4 was the divine *tetraktys* for Pythagoras, and we comfort ourselves still with 4 seasons, 4 directions, and 4 elements. Yet in China there are 5 of each—not least, perhaps, because the character for "4" is a homonym of the character for "death" (even now, in many Far Eastern hotels, a 4th floor is as rare as a 13th).

Nine is equally 2-faced. Christ died at the ninth hour, and Macbeth's Weird Sisters chant eerily, "Thrice to thine, and thrice to mine, / And thrice again, to make up nine." Yet the Egyptians were devoted to the Enneads (a triple triad). The legends of northern Europe revolve around 9 bards, 9 dragons, 9 stones in a circle. We all know of Dante's 9 Circles of Hell, but few, perhaps, remember that they were merely the inversion of the 9 he associated with Heaven. In the Middle Ages, indeed, 9 was "first and foremost the angelic number." Milton divided his Nativity ode into 3 sections of 9 stanzas each; one sixteenth-century church in Venice has, quite consciously, a nave 9 paces wide and 27 paces long.

All this, you may say, is mere antique superstition. Yet many lives, even today, still hang in the balance of numbers. The bustling contemporary city of Kyoto, in Japan, is divided into 9 auspicious sections. In Beijing, within an old man's memory, the Emperor would ascend the Altar of Heaven—a perfect circle inside a perfect square—and, his 9 grades of mandarins performing a ninefold bowing before him, survey a world of 9s. "From the center of the topmost tier nine rings of paving-stones radiated out in concentric multiples of nine," explains Colin Thubron, "and fanned down into the lower terraces, nine rows to each, in everexpanding manifolds of nine." To this day, the 37 million citizens of Burma are ruled not only by the shadow dictator Ne Win but by his favorite number, 9 (a near anagram of his name). A devotee of golf (no coincidence), Win governs his life by 9s—he took 45 people with him on a trip to America; he overthrew an upstart civilian government on the 18th day of the 9th month; he gave his party the 9th, 18th, and 27th slots on electoral ballots. Yet he finally exhausted his people's patience (throwing the country into turmoil) when, four years ago, he decided on a whim to replace all 25-, 35-, and 75-kyat banknotes with 45- and 90-kyat notes—thus, at a stroke, rendering half the currency in Burma worthless and many Burmese citizens, who kept their savings at home, penniless.

"The number nine is not just lucky," a Western diplomat told *The New Yorker*. "It is a powerful number, which has to be conquered. Otherwise, it's a danger to you."

Does any of this have any bearing on us? Even Goethe might not too readily say, *"Nein."* For this, let us remember, is a palindromic year, the first since 1881; and those still alive 11 years from now will be the first for a millennium—since 1001, in fact—to experience two palindromic years. Anyone who doubts the power of the number 9 need only talk to someone who was 39, or 49, last night, and is 40, or 50, today. Nine, in short, is no 9-day wonder; it is, for many, "the number of heaven itself." So this week, as we prepare to note the date 9/9, let us spare a thought for the number that will be keeping us close company for 9 more years at least. And ponder the reverberations of Emerson's pregnant epigraph to Nature: "The rounded world is fair to see / Nine times folded in mystery."

(1991)

One of the most revealing moments in Norman Sherry's massive, ongoing biography of Graham Greene (with the second volume just published, he has now devoted 1,352 pages to Greene's first fifty-one years) comes at the very beginning, when Greene charges Sherry with compiling a list of his, the novelist's, enemies. Every man has enemies, Sherry replies. By the time the night is over, Greene has composed, with the help of his brother Hugh, his own extensive list of his lifetime's opponents and handed it to his biographer.

That might be said to be the paradoxical trademark of Graham Greene: that he rarely gave himself the benefit of his unending doubt, and that he invariably gave the men he was supposed to hate his best lines. He saw the folly, and the frailty, of everyone around him. Thus adulterers come to feel compassion for the husbands they're cuckolding; victims see the human side of their criminal tormentors; Fowler in *The Quiet American* comes to mourn the death of his rival in love and opponent in politics (*Schadenfreude* in reverse, you could say). Even when he was writing wartime propaganda for the British government, Greene described an Englishman shooting a German lieutenant—and then finding in the dead man's pocket a picture of his baby.

That issue is one of the hardest dilemmas in every serious life, and one that faces us daily in the office, the bedroom, even the income tax form we sign: what to do with the person who opposes us? We know, more or less, how to deal with our friends, but what to do with those who tempt us to awaken the devil in ourselves (a far more pernicious temptation than any external devil affords)? Many religions counsel us to forgive those who trespass against us and to extend charity even to the Jeffrey Dahmers of the world; Buddhists actually argue that our enemies are our best friends because they challenge us to transcend ourselves. Yet still the debate between mercy and justice is as unending as the one between duty and love.

If all Greene's novels are essays on fallenness (and self-accusations), they are also, by the same token, arguments against the whole notion of enmity, or reminders, at least, that our enemies are no less vulnerable, and right in their own minds, than ourselves. With his famous taste for

ambiguity and refusal to see things in black and white (except in his con-
demnation of any institution that would treat humans as tokens, statistics, or pawns), Greene made it his life's work to understand every
position. In Vietnam, in the 1950s, he sympathized with the Vietnamese
guerrillas, and with the French colonialists they opposed; if he couldn't
say no very easily, he couldn't say yes. And as a headmaster's son, he was
a lifelong connoisseur of divided loyalties, knowing that for every commitment you honor, you betray another. As he put it in *The Power and
the Glory*, "When you visualized a man or a woman carefully, you could
always begin to feel pity. . . . When you saw the corners of the eyes, the
shape of the mouth, how the hair grew, it was impossible to hate. Hate
was just a failure of imagination."

To many, that kind of sympathy with the enemy could seem the worst
kind of two-facedness or moral relativism: not so much turning the other
cheek as sheer turncoatism. And by trying to see both sides of every argument, Greene contrived to make enemies on both sides of every fence:
Catholics and agnostics, McCarthyites and Communists, all found his
conviction wanting. A would-be Christian who admits to putting people
before principles gets accused of sentimentality by skeptics and of
hypocrisy by believers. Those issues found their focus in Greene's
unshakable loyalty to his old boss in British intelligence, the Soviet
double agent Kim Philby: which of us, he wrote, in introducing Philby's
memoirs, has not betrayed something even more important to us than
country?

Yet it could be said that Greene was never a truer Christian than
when forgiving even his un-Christian enemies. This is not to whitewash a
self-styled scapegrace who had so many treacheries and transgressions
to confess (though it is to give him credit for confessing so openly to
them). If he could be unusually tender toward his enemies, he could be
unnaturally negligent of his loves. In his championing of the voiceless,
the forgotten, the oppressed, he could conceive irrational and implacable
prejudices against those he regarded as Established (Noël Coward, say).
And sometimes, by his own admission, he could do the right thing for
the wrong reasons, refusing to be straight with someone because he
lacked the nerve.

It is, in fact, the ultimate strength of Greene's books that he shows us
the hazards of compassion. We all know, from works like *Hamlet*, how
analysis is paralysis, and the ability to see every side of every issue prevents
us from taking any side at all. The tragic import of Greene's work is that
understanding can do the same: he could so easily see the pain of the
people he was supposed to punish that he could not bear to come down

hard on them. He became hostage to his own sympathies, and railed at pity with the fury of one who was its captive. The most sobering lesson of Greene's fiction is that sleeping with the enemy is most with us when we're sleeping alone; and that even God, faced with a wounded murderer, might sometimes feel Himself agnostic.

(1994)

When autumn comes to the cities of Japan, supermarkets hang paper leaves from their cash registers, and cigarette makers issue packages featuring autumn colors. In spring each year, salarymen dutifully assemble under cherry blossoms and drunkenly bawl songs in what is really only a quainter version of Saint Patrick's Day. To a jaded foreigner, the observation of seasons in a traditional culture such as Japan's can seem as formulaic and debased as the Muzaked versions of "Jingle Bells" that torment every department store from Bangor to Bangkok.

And yet the very qualities we admire in Japan—its safety and solidarity and sense of long-term planning—are in some ways the result of such promptings as the leaves. For seasons release us from time and space: a Japanese stockbroker is marveling at the same cherry tree that his grandfather, and his grandfather's boss, gaped at once upon a time; and if he is a good Japanese, he will enjoy the *sakura* even in Washington, D.C. Seasons take us into an order higher than ourselves, or nation, or ideology; not so much a collective religion, perhaps, as a religion of collectivism. And seasons rescue us from our private winters and admit us to a larger rhythm, as unanswerable as the dawn. Autumn leaves are early harbingers of spring, they say, and however dark our present mood, change is on the way.

The seasons, in fact, teach us two lessons that both steady and chastise: all things must pass, and all things shall return. They tell us that every new beginning brings us closer to an end, and every elegy has within it the echo (and the promise) of a future celebration. They say that love that seems eternal now may soon be a distant memory; and that a new love may come along to revive our sense of eternity. They teach us that suffering is inevitable, and in that inevitability is a constancy that helps to take the edge off suffering. We cherish flowers more than evergreens, precisely because they do not last.

Seasons instruct us, then, in a subtler way of being; they initiate us into a process more universal than New Year (which is, after all, celebrated at one time in Chinatown and another time in midtown) and more flexible than moons. All of us have our own calendars (April 15 means taxes, and next Thursday is Cindy's birthday), and all of us think in terms of spring cleaning or fall fashions. But seasons induct us into a world of divisions that are never hard and fast (soft and slow, rather); they offer lessons about constancy and flux (*The Winter's Tale* is an affirmation of spring) and show us that there are some things—for all our fears of global warming and a nuclear winter—we cannot much affect. Seasons teach us about transitions, for winter elides into spring as gently as remorse into regret, or adolescence into youth. And just when we assume that winter's gone, an "unseasonable" blizzard will come down to remind us we were wrong.

Seasons are important, of course, because they take place in all of us, and all our days and loves (even if Paris in the spring is Perth in the fall). They are as close to us as the spring in our step or the dying fall in a lover's lament; and the high incidence of alcoholism and suicide in far northern countries is routinely ascribed to their extreme rhythms of three months of white nights giving way to three months of absolute dark. That seasons affect our sense of order is reflected in the fact that doctors speak of "seasonal affective disorder." And though the pattern of the skies is still felt on the pulse and in the bones of every farmer and nomad, those of us immured in fourteen-story office blocks, under fluorescent lighting, need artificial reminders of the weather: if we can't "go back" to nature, we have to let nature come back to us.

In America, we hymn a gospel of progress, and the great premise, and promise, of the country is its continual forward motion. One reason so many people migrate to the New World is to escape the hidebound traditions and confining circles of the Old, to flee changeless cycles for a world of never-ending blue. America revels in a child's sense that the future is illimitable, and tomorrow need not bring with it any taint of yesterday.

Yet a land that is entirely linear is itself limited, and the sorrow of a place like California, it often seems, is that no one there knows who he will be (or who he will be with) a year from now. The absence of external rhythms forces everyone to try to make his own. And a world without seasons is as unnatural as a person without moods: even tropical islands speak of wet seasons and dry, or hot seasons and tourist seasons; and even places with climatic changes often add divisions of their own (thus the English ruling class follows the "season" from Henley to Ascot to Wimbledon). Everyone needs some stability in his life, whether it be from a partner, a routine, or a home; and that is what the seasons are to us—our loves, our habits, and our living rooms.

So even as we jeer at the paper cherry blossoms fluttering off Kyoto lampposts, we may also envy the sense of continuity, and history, and community, they enforce; and marvel at how a society can function like an orchestra, each person playing his part while attending to a common score. A country with a sense of seasons has greater respect for the old, and a clearer sense of tomorrow. That is why newspapers in Japan that meticulously chart the dates on which the leaves will fall may be precious in not just the derogatory sense. And why a Japanese would understand why this most autumnal of meditations is being published at the very time when most of us—in the north at least—are exulting in the resurgences of spring.

(1994)

# SQUIBS

For many years now, I have had a secret addiction. It is an increasingly common problem, though unknown until about a decade ago, and one for which doctors and psychologists have no cure. If religion is the opium of the masses, this might be said to be the lithium.

It all began innocently enough when a travel agent said to me, as if guilelessly, "Since you're taking all these flights, why don't you sign up for a frequent flier program? It's easy, it's free, and you can earn free tickets. Since you're traveling anyway, you've got nothing to lose." That is how it always begins: "Bill, have you heard about this new kind of glue? They say it has the most incredible effect." "All this I will give to you if only . . ." "I guess it can't hurt. They say everyone is doing it."

Because my miles weren't accumulating fast enough, I began taking trips I didn't need, or routing myself from L.A. to New York by way of Anchorage. If I went all around the world, I figured, I could earn a free ticket to Alpena. Then I acquired a credit card that would allow me to get one mile for every dollar spent. The credit line was tiny—lower than the price of most international plane fares—but the sense of possibility was enormous; why, if I just spent $20,000—if I just bought a car, a VCR, a computer, a fax machine, and a washer-dryer set—I could go to State College, and back, for free (depending on availability, blackout dates, and routings)!

But was I satisfied? No. Is any addict ever satisfied? I needed to know that if I bankrupted my entire family, we could all fly free—or get upgrades at least—to debtor's prison. So I hooked my telephone up to another carrier's frequent flier program. That didn't help my principal account at all, but it did mean that I got five miles for every phone dollar spent; thus, if I called Zaire every day for a week—for 177 straight weeks—I could get a free ticket to Detroit. Indeed, if I called a friend in Japan for forty minutes a day every day for 84 weeks—or made a three-minute call once a week for 101 years—I could earn enough miles to go and visit the friend in person (though then we'd have no incentive to talk, since we wouldn't be earning miles).

For a while that seemed enough: I spent as much money as possible, charged everything to my credit card, and made all my reservations by international phone call. Then the airlines got wise to me. If I stayed in an Exorbitant Suites Hotel (on their new Executive Floor), they said, or rented an Expense-o-Car, I could earn one-fortieth of a ticket to Kalamazoo. And if I hopped in and out of forty airports and rented a car from the same agency in every one, regardless of price, model, and need, I might be able to go to the next two airports free!

Then, just as I was getting giddy, they introduced segments. This meant that if I flew from Seattle to Vancouver via Chico, Oshkosh, Bullhead City, and Purgatory (Colorado), I might clock up enough miles to make the same trip for free! Alternatively, if I flew to Casper instead, stayed in the most expensive hotel around, made some calls to Zaire at prime rates, and rented a car to drive back to the airport, I might be able to return home without paying. The shortest distance between two points was the slowest way to get ahead.

If only it had ended there. But now, every day, new permutations come flying in the door. If I go first class to Paris, I can bring a companion along free—so long as she has the same itinerary. Having the same itinerary will likely mean the end of our friendship, but the offer does ensure that if I spend $6,846 on a ticket that would otherwise cost $768, I can get another ticket (for which I would have had to pay $768) for nothing. If I make five round trips to Taipei, a city I have always tried to avoid, I can go again—to Taipei—free of charge. If I play my miles right, in fact, I need never leave the plane. As soon as I embark, I can buy things—key chains, duty-free perfumes, souvenirs, and razors—and put them on my credit card. Then I can acquire more goods on the Airfone, charged to my special phone carrier. By the time I land, I might have earned enough miles to get the next leg free. I can even earn tickets while six miles high! (Vertical miles don't count, however, and horizontal ones are not what they seem: the frequent flier is the only bird of prey that flies even more directly than a crow—thus for a standard 3,000-mile cross-country flight, I'm lucky to get 2,470 miles.)

By now, however, I anyway spend all my free hours—and cash—hunting down old boarding passes, ticket receipts, and hotel vouchers. If ever I do get a free ticket through the mail, I have no time to use it (since I am always flying)—and, in any case, don't want to use a ticket that will give me no miles. More and more companies, besides, have got in on the act, so that soon, I suspect, I'll be earning miles from using the same brand of diaper, from walking or talking, or from *not* going by air (but charging long-distance bus rides to my credit card). Even the woman who runs the largest mail-order-bride service on the mainland accepts credit cards: now I can earn miles by choosing a wife!

And then came the killer blow! If only I could persuade my friends to develop the same habit, I could earn one-tenth of a free trip to Menominee. If only, in short, I could turn my friends into addicts as demented as myself, I could empirically prove that there *is* such a thing as a free lunch. Nowadays, I hardly ever think about the credit I could get by attending frequent flier support groups around the globe—or the five miles I could earn by transmitting this article to the office on my modem. Mostly, I'm to be found saying, "Come on. Why don't you sign up? It's easy, it's free, and you can earn free tickets. They say this guy Faust never had to pay for a ticket in his life."

(1993)

T he ink is dry. The revisions are over. He has produced what he regards as a pitiless dissection of something demonic in the human heart, an archetypal tale of how the nay-saying spirit, simply because it has no beliefs, can play havoc with vulnerability; a play, in fact, about how innocence has no recourse against the dark.

"Oh, Bill. Just a minute. There's someone here who wants to talk to you. Seems they're planning some kind of conference on Afro-European relations. They've heard about the new thing and want you to be on the panel."

"Wait. Before you get back to them, this just came in on the fax. Some women's group wants you to go to Venice, California. They're putting together some lecture series on Women Who Love the Men Who Kill Them. Webster's going to be there; Jonson too. You'd be perfect, Bill: you use women characters, you've been in love."

"Hold it. What about that exclusive contract we signed with the guys who did *Two Gentlepeople of Verona*?"

"Sure. But this is different. Plus, there's a guy here from some cable station in Naples. Says you've worked up a lot of excitement over there by using an Italian as the heavy. No, of course they haven't seen the script yet. But they're wild about it. They want you on their morning show. Tomorrow. In Naples. Could be great exposure for the Euromarkets."

"Bill, you've got to understand something. You're sitting on a gold mine here. This thing is dynamite. If you play your cards right, this thing could touch all the bases. A black guy; a high-society blonde whose old man's a senator. This Cassio guy, fooling around with a streetwalker. That stuff about Cyprus, Rhodes, the Middle East. Even the gays are claiming it as their own—'From Bonding to Bondage,' or something. There isn't a guy in the country who can't relate to this. Daughter's off on some interracial kick. Colleague's got the hots for her husband. And the immigrant war hero's out to lunch."

"Yeah. This just arrived. West Point wants you to teach a course this fall on the new spirit in the military: how to be a man without losing the woman inside."

"No way. That's when we're shooting this TV thing Bill's going to present. Remember? 'Venice: Love and Death.' "

·   ·   ·

When Cyril Connolly wrote *Enemies of Promise* half a century ago, he didn't know the half of it. In 1938, there were only a handful of radio stations in all England. Today there are more than that in Stratford alone. And TV stations, pay-for-view stations, home video shoots. Not just in London, but in Shibuya, Jo'burg, the Bastille. All the enemies that Connolly listed—"journalism, reviews, advertising, broadcasting and the cinema"—are a hundred times stronger than before, and now they've been joined by a thousand other media around the globe. Audiotapes. Satellite hookups. Internet chats. Panels, conferences, conference calls. In Rio, Rome, Bangkok. There are spinoffs, options, prequels; courses on workshops, workshops on courses, conferences on conference calls. There are made-for-TV specials, made-for-cable-TV spectaculars, made-for-MTV extravaganzas.

"Bill? Some guy from the Stratford *Sun*, wants to cover the local angle?"

"No way. We're giving an exclusive to the Mauritanians—this is the first plug these guys have got in years."

"Yeah, but I have a request here from the Stratford, Ontario, *Gazette*. Seems you're a local story there too. And in Othello, Washington."

"Sure. But you've got to go easy with those guys. That bit about the cannibals, the Anthropophagi? The macrobiotic crowd's going crazy."

"Maybe you could just hold a press conference or two. Put out some comments about interracial murder. Maybe a few lines about mixed marriages. A couple of bites on the buddy theme. How the boozing songs aren't meant to be a number on AA. Seems like you're the only guy in Warwickshire who can talk for white men."

"And for white nay-saying spirits."

"And for white murderers."

"Sure. But what about the tour? We've already committed to the breakfast shows, the major bookstores, that playwriting gig at Bard."

"That reminds me, Bill. What do you think of an Esalen seminar with Bly? Then we could follow by getting Tannen, Steinem, a few others, for some kind of Town Hall meeting? Great documentary potential."

"Right. Maybe work in a plug for that bar that wants to call itself The Turbaned Turk."

"Easy there. Remember we've already optioned some of the lines to those characters from Hong Kong who are making *Beast with Two Backs*."

"Hey, Bill! Some girl on the phone. Says she sent you her autobiography, in six volumes. The only copy she had. Wants it back. Right now."

"You interested in a kind of hair promotion tie-in? Male pattern baldness thing?"

"Jim, he just did a . . ."


Just blurb this book, support this cause. Take a look at this project, review this manuscript. Just one more benefit, guest appearance, survey for *The New York Times*. Just 250 words on girls you'd hate to love, just thirty seconds for PBS on the new Islamic paradigm. Just give a word, lend your name, sign on the dotted line. Maybe a few minutes with a Handycam? An honorary seat on the board? Some off-the-record comments on the Marlowe thing that's breaking?

It's not PC, it's not PR, it's acronym consciousness that's seizing us. Make it short, make it simple, make it snappy: turn yourself into a jingle.


"The thing is, Bill, you may know about pentameters, but you know nothing about marketing. You want people to see your play or not? If not, fine, just tell me, and we'll call the whole thing off. Pull the plug. Kaput. Nada. Sayonara."

"I mean, it's not like we're asking you to sell your soul to the devil. All we're saying is, 'Be yourself.' Take your show on the road. Let them get a taste of who you are. The play's the thing, sure. But the play's going to be around for two months, three months tops. Maybe get a second life when *Moor's the Pity* hits the stage. But you—you're here for the duration. You've got to get your name out there, your face."

"Just think of it this way: you're trading in one kind of communication for another."

"Face it. Writing's just a way of laying the table. Now you've got to eat."

"What is this thing with purity you've got? Burroughs does the Laurie Anderson movie—even appears in *Heavy Petting*—and you can't go out and talk to Regis and Kathie Lee?"

"It's the first law of motion. If you can't move the product, move the audience. Raising funds is the first step toward raising consciousness. Remember what that Connolly guy said: it's not the creation of art that's important, it's the 'diffusion.'"

"Look, Bill, we've got the whole strategy mapped out. We're playing it close, real close to the chest. Just a few advance copies targeted at the right players: *Ebony, Soldier of Fortune, Cosmo*. Get the Willow Song into an Avon commercial or two. Then get the teasers out: 'The First Frank Look at the Love Between Three People!' Blond hair, black limbs, Venice vistas: you know the scene. Then you go out there and just play up the deep stuff. 'Base Indian / Base Judean,' 'Barefoot to Palestine for a taste of his nether lip'—there's something here for everyone. But we can't hang around. We've got to get moving. If they start digging up that old Earl of Oxford thing, our bacon's cooked."

"Remember, Bill, just work out a few lines in advance—'Merchant of Menace,' 'Jennets for Germans,' 'Cassio's Clay,' that kind of thing—and you'll be on every talk show in the country."

"Oh, Bill, before you go. There's a guy on the line, Sellinger, I think he said. Says he's got a message for you. From a guy called Pynchon."

"Never heard of him. Where's he at?"

"I don't know. Some no-name agency. Never seen him on Letterman."

"Hey, listen up! The handkerchief manufacturers are going ballistic. Say you're accusing them of murder."

"Great. All news is good news."

"What was that name you wanted, Bill? Beckett with two *t*'s? And this is about a one-word play? Okay. But don't forget: one-word plays are hot right now with all the textual scholars. More bang for the buck."


Nobody begrudges an author his moment in the sun; after the creation of a thirteen-hundred-page novel—or even a ninety-page book of poems—he deserves a break: some readings to make contact with his audience, a few five-by-seven glossies to get the book at the front of the store, three months of touring to sell six years of hard work. No one would recommend failure: as Gore Vidal once said, "Absence of money is a bad thing because you end up writing 'The Telltale Clue' on television—which I did."

But as Connolly knew, much more dangerous than failure is success. It begins with an offer to write a column; a column becomes a TV spot; a TV spot becomes a regular slot. Before long, a writer is being paid to play himself, and not to express himself; to lend his name to something, and not his talents; to speak in short words, and not in long ones. And before much longer, he's getting paid—and paid handsomely—to do everything but write. By then, in any case, he has nothing to write about but TV studios, tours, and hotel rooms.

"Sales? No sweat, Bill. Sure they're not what we figured they'd be, even after the Italian-American boycott. But there's a lot of interest—big interest, global interest—in your next thing. You're bringing back the Italian guy, right? Just make sure he's in the opening scene—for the credit sequence. And maybe give him some kind of Eurasian feel—the Saigon market's almost as big as the Italian one. And go easy on that bed scene—we don't want to lose a PG-13. Just think Gap ad, *Vanity Fair*, Jenny Holzer kind of thing. Maybe ask Kathie Lee for a couple of tips.

"And this time he's going to be with an old guy, right? And three daughters? Perfect! That whole child-abuse, sibling-rivalry thing. Family values through the kazoo! I can almost see the prime-time billing. Bill, I have a feeling this could be the big one. Forget about sales; we're talking residuals!"

(1992)

$S$ee, the thing is, I come from this really dysfunctional family. The old man is just the usual raving white patriarch who's never taken the time to get in touch with his feminine side—it's like he doesn't even know how to interact with women! My sisters have no time for bonding at all—Cordelia, in fact, likes to go around saying nothing, with this crazy smile on her face. Talk about denial! And all the time I was growing up, I never had any positive female role models, anyone who could teach me about mothering, or mentoring. Who ever heard of Mrs. Lear?

So all of us are a long way from wellness. But the way to look at it, according to my stress consultant, is that the root of the problem is my father. Just because he's a king, he thinks he owns the world. And the only counselor around is this really repressed kind of guy called Kent, who's got some kind of thing for him and is heavily into astrology.

Anyway, one day my father gets into this whole inheritance trip—you know how death duties can be murder around here! So suddenly all of us have to come together like we're in some kind of EST seminar, and tell him how much we love him. Talk about low self-esteem!

So Regan and I more or less reinforce him, tell him what he wants to hear, get into the whole "nuclear family" bit. But Cordelia—out to lunch, as usual—must have been told by her shrink to go with her feelings. Next thing you know, she's laying a whole number on him, and he's power-tripping like crazy.

I know you'll say this is a classic case of blame-the-victim. But I can tell you, my father's real uptight: like a control freak with all this negative energy he hasn't worked through. So he decides to move in with about a hundred other reinforcers—really into partying—and he gets into this real abusive relationship with the help, and I begin to feel like he's in need of a twelve-step recovery program. Finally I tell him, "Codependency no more!" Well, he totally freaks and takes this guilt trip thing over to my sister's house. Pretty soon we both feel like we're ready for a Children of Recovering Tyrants workshop. It's like he's only just learning how to reclaim his inner child.

Anyway, before you know it, he's off on some empowerment kick, deciding to get in touch with his wild man. You know the scene: racing around the heath in the middle of the night, shouting at the skies and beating his chest and hanging out with some Fool who probably did a shamanism seminar at Esalen once. Telling us he's tired of being gentle and nurturing, he wants to take the warrior path! Deciding all of a sudden that he's got to do some grieving, learn to access his rage. Soon he's talking to the other guys in his men's group—real flakes—as if they were philosophers.

So now we've got a father who's into this back-to-nature trip and a sister who's on her way to jail. My husband, as usual, is totally judgmental, tells me that the problem is we never spend any quality time together. Every time I talk about my father, he says I'm just projecting. Our marriage counselor says we've got to learn to be friends with ourselves before we can be friends with each other. And my lawyer tells me that divorce is not a growth experience. So what can I do? I find this really cute guy—high-energy, take-charge, real centered. But as soon as my back is turned, I find my sister's coming on to him. Talk about sibling rivalry! Meanwhile, there's all this stuff coming down—someone's knocked off my secretary, the old guy next door's gone south, Cordelia's husband's acting out. Just then my girlfriend tells me about this holistic new book by Derek Humphry. So I think, what the hell? It's always darkest before the dawn.

(1992)

Every sport, the cliché tells us, is a game of inches. But at the Olympics one is reminded how much each one is also a game of instants: not just in the milliseconds ticking away at every scoreboard in the Savoie this fortnight, but in the larger way in which fifteen years of determination can turn on a single moment. Look away from the slope for an instant, touch the side of the run for a second, and ten thousand hours of practice are gone. The athletes carry alarm clocks—or time bombs—in their heads, and measure their lives in heartbeats (193 a minute for a biathlete). "Luge is all feeling," explained Duncan Kennedy, an American luger who won by placing tenth (higher, at the time, than any U.S. luger in history). "You can have a 'great run,' but if you're not feeling the track, you end up a second behind, and you don't know where the time went."

Time, in that sense, is the referee at every Olympic event, the ghost in the machine, as fickle a third party as in the Shakespeare sonnets. Biathletes begin their runs, like every amateur at home, the minute the second hand hits .00, and pay for their shooting misses with penitential thirty-second loops; hockey players serve sentences for penalties that can doubtless seem like sixty years. Of course, this is true in every sport, or every life that knows a slip, a birth, a marriage; but in the Olympics, an athlete comes into the spotlight for a second, and then, in most cases, disappears into oblivion for four years. Even these Olympians, the first in almost a century lucky enough to have to wait only two years for a rematch, are waiting twice as long as Wimbledon losers or narrow misses in the Masters. The first question asked of the first male gold medalist, Austrian downhiller Patrick Ortlieb, was whether he had thought, during his run, of his teammate Gernot Reinstadler, who died in a race last year. He couldn't, the affable big man said simply; he couldn't afford to think of accidents, or of anything but the course. One moment of sentiment could mean a lifetime of regret.

Time plays strange tricks in the Winter Games. Ortlieb was the first one down, whooshing through the course in 1:50:37; then, like the rest of us, he could do nothing but watch the scoreboard as fifty-five others, one by one, tried to eclipse his time. He had been competing only against himself; they were up against the clock. Athletes, at their greatest, can attain almost meditative states—the so-called zone—in which time slows down, or seems suspended. We, however, bring them back to earth with our deadlines. Hardly had the majestic figure-skating pair, Natalia Mishkutienok and Artur Dimitriev, claimed their gold when they were being asked about the World Championships in March, the next Olympics, the future of the Soviet Union. "Only thirty minutes, one hour, has passed, and already you are thinking about our great plans," admonished their commanding coach, Tamara Moskvina. "As you understand, such great decisions cannot be made in such a short time." Then, speaking as one who knows about glacial change even in the midst of the accelerated history of her homeland, she added, "Nowhere in the world, and in our country especially, nothing happens quick."

For the winners in these Games, the tyranny of time was partially reversed, and the payoff was a moment that seemed to last forever. "It's wonderful that such an investment has a return all in one day," said Georg Hackl, a silver medalist in 1988, now claiming his gold in the luge. But even for champions, there are a hundred clocks working simultaneously, not all of them benign. Bonnie Blair, after winning a gold, coolly outlined her four-year plan, taking her from the Calgary Games to Albertville, and how "I took each year a little differently." But not in the plan was the death of her father two years ago, and when his name came up, the smilingly efficient woman suddenly choked over her words.

Time takes its toll on everyone in the Games, especially the ones in the stands: on the ubiquitous mothers recalling 5 a.m. drives to the rink, on the spectators who stop breathing while they wait for a figure skater to land. The fans of Franz Heinzer, the great favorite in the downhill, stomped, rang bells, and waved heraldic banners when their hero hit the slopes; less than two minutes later, their hopes were dead. When AJ Kitt came down the course, eight Americans huddled round walkie-talkies and urged him on through clenched teeth: "Go, go, be aggressive, be aggressive. That's it, come on. Be aggressive!" He finished ninth. And when longtime local favorite Fabrice Guy finally crossed the finish line for gold, in Nordic Combined, and another Frenchman, Sylvain Guillaume, even more miraculously, snatched the silver, grown women wept and kissed everyone in sight.

The Winter Games are very much the blue-eyed Games, more informal and convivial than the summer ones: at Les Saisies, a picturesque winterscape of red bridges in the snow, where the first women's biathlon in Olympic history was being held, snowballing was actually the favorite event, and children's bobsledding without benefit of sleds. Scores of jolly Norwegians sang folk songs around an accordion and swayed in place, beating time with the poles of enormous Norwegian flags. But even here, clocks were ticking everywhere, and as the athletes set off on their lonely twenty-five-minute journeys, instants were getting ready to be replayed in the pause and rewind sections of the mind.

The watcher on television cannot see so clearly the effect of the internal wake-up calls, the biological clocks, the steady tick-tock-tick. Ye Qiaobo, just after becoming the first Chinese athlete in history to win a Winter medal, in the Women's 500 meter Speed Skating event, got up on a podium, a composed twenty-seven-year-old in a purple track suit who had been done out of her gold, she felt, by a competitor's error. Would she protest? "Maybe I will try"—and the whole room held its breath— "to set my sights for the next Olympic Games, if possible." Then, gallantry exhausted, suddenly she thought of all the years going by. Her first three years of training had been wiped out, she explained, when she was disqualified for doping just before Calgary (the result of a doctor's trick, she said). The next fifteen months were lost in a suspension. "What can I say?" she said, voice cracking. "What can I answer to my parents, my sisters, my best of friends?" Now she had seen another three years leave her 18/100ths of a second short (and four days later she would lose another gold to Blair by 2/100ths of a second). "I spend so many times for skating," she went on, tears streaming down her cheeks, "also I gave up so many hobbies for this." Why should the first Asian woman medalist in Winter history cry? "Because the Olympics are four years in time. And I am old."

That same day, thirty-eight miles away, in La Plagne, the Canadian luger Harington Telford was saying the same thing. "The last four years have been a struggle to get here," he said, noting how his nineteenth-place finish in Calgary had become an eighteenth-place finish here. "I am twenty-five years old now, and I've really managed to make zero progress in the past four years. There's no way to express the disgust I have with myself." Someday he would look back on this with pride, said a bystander. "I hope so," he said without much conviction. A few feet away, Robert Pipkin, a nineteen-year-old American in the first flush of Olympic enthusiasm, his beaming parents waving a "Go Rob. Slide in Pride" banner around him, looked over at the snowcaps, the blue skies, and the pines, and, finishing twenty-first, told reporters that he hoped to compete in the next two—or even three—Olympics.

(1992)

E<small>very</small> one of us knows the sensation of going up, on retreat, to a high place, and feeling ourselves so lifted up that we can hardly imagine the circumstances of our usual lives, or all the things that make us fret. In such a place, in such a state, we start to recite the standard litany: that silence is sunshine, where company is clouds; that silence is rapture, where company is doubt; that silence is golden, where company is brass.

But silence is not so easily won. And before we race off to go prospecting in those hills, we might usefully recall that fool's gold is much more common, and that gold has to be panned for, dug out from other substances. "All profound things and emotions of things are preceded and attended by Silence," wrote Herman Melville, one of the loftiest and most eloquent of souls. Working himself up to an ever more thunderous cry of affirmation, he went on: "Silence is the general consecration of the universe. Silence is the invisible laying on of the Divine Pontiff's hands upon the world. Silence is the only Voice of our God." For Melville, though, silence finally meant darkness and hopelessness and self-annihilation. Devastated by the silence that greeted his heartfelt novels, he retired into a public silence from which he did not emerge for more than thirty years. Then, just before his death, he came forth with his final utterance—the luminous tale of Billy Budd—and showed that silence is only as worthy as what we can bring back from it.

We have to earn silence, then, to work for it: to make it not an absence but a presence; not emptiness but repletion. Silence is something more than just a pause; it is that enchanted place where space is cleared and time is stayed and the horizon itself expands. In silence, we often say, we can hear ourselves think; but what is truer to say is that in silence we can hear ourselves not think, and so sink below our selves into a place far deeper than mere thought allows. In silence, we might better say, we can hear someone else think.

Or simply breathe. For silence is responsiveness, and in silence we can listen to something behind the clamor of the world. "As soon as you are alone, you are with God," wrote Thomas Merton, who was, as a Trappist, a connoisseur, a caretaker of silences. It is no coincidence that places of worship are places of silence: if idleness is the devil's playground, silence may be the angels'. It is no surprise that "silence" is an anagram of "license." And it is only right that Quakers all but worship silence, for it is the place where everyone finds his God, however he may express it. Silence is an ecumenical state, beyond the doctrines and divisions created by the mind. If everyone has a spiritual story to tell of his life, everyone has a spiritual silence to preserve.

So it is that we might almost say that silence is the tribute that we pay to holiness; we slip off words when we enter a sacred space, just as we slip off shoes. A "moment of silence" is the highest honor we can pay someone; it is the point at which the mind stops, and something else takes over (words run out when feelings rush in). A "vow of silence" is for holy men the highest devotional act. We hold our breath, we hold our words; we suspend our chattering selves and let ourselves "fall silent," and fall into the highest place of all.

It often seems that the world is getting noisier these days: in Japan, which may be a model of our future, cars and buses have voices, doors and elevators speak. The answering machine talks to us, and for us, some-where above the din of the TV; the Walkman preserves a public silence but ensures that we need never—in the bathtub, on a mountaintop, even at our desks—be without the clangor of the world. White noise becomes the aural equivalent of the clash of images, the nonstop blast of fragments that increasingly agitates our minds. As Ben Okri, the young Nigerian novelist, puts it, "Where chaos is the god of an era, clamorous music is the deity's chief instrument."

There is—of course—a place for noise, as there is for daily lives. There is a place for roaring, for the shouting exultation of a baseball game, for hymns and cries of pleasure. The great charm of noise, however, is when it ceases. In silence, suddenly, it seems as if all the windows of the world are thrown open, and everything is as clear as on a morning after rain. Silence, ideally, hums. It charges the air. In Tibet, where the silence has a tragic cause, it is still quickened by the fluttering of prayer flags, the tolling of temple bells, the roar of wind across the plains, the memory of chant.

Silence, then, could be said to be the ultimate province of trust: it is the place where we trust ourselves to be alone; where we trust others to understand the things we do not say; where we trust a higher harmony to assert itself. We all know how treacherous are words, and how often we use them to paper over embarrassment, or emptiness, or fear of the larger spaces that silence brings. "Words, words, words" commit us to positions we do not really hold, the imperatives of chatter; words are what we use

for lies, false promises, and gossip. We babble with strangers; with inti-
mates we can be silent. We "make conversation" when we are at a loss; we
unmake it when we are alone, or with those so close to us that we can
afford to be alone with them.

In love, we are speechless; in awe, we say, words fail us.

(1992)

# Permissions Acknowledgments

Some of these essays were originally published, in somewhat different form, in the following publications: *Civilization, Condé Nast Traveler, Islands, Los Angeles Times Book Review, Los Angeles Times Magazine, The Nation, New Perspectives Quarterly, The New Republic, The New York Review of Books, The New York Times Book Review, Partisan Review, The Smithsonian, The Times* (London), *The Times Literary Supplement* (London), *Tricycle,* and *The Village Voice.*

The following essays were originally published in *Time* magazine: "The New World's New World: Making Itself Up and Over" (Nov. 18, 1991); "Tenzin Gyatso: Tibet's Guiding Star" (April 11, 1988); "Peter Matthiessen: In Search of the Crane" (Jan. 11, 1993); "Prosaic Justice All Around: Salman Rushdie vs. the Ayatollah" (March 6, 1989); "Private Eye, Public Conscience: The Works of Raymond Chandler" (Dec. 12, 1988); "An American Song of Enthusiasm: Henry Miller at 100" (July 22, 1991); "In Praise of the Humble Comma" (June 13, 1988); "Excusez-moi! Speakez-vous Franglais?" (July 2, 1990); "For Japan, See Oscar Wilde" (May 25, 1992); "The Rise of Minority Terrorism" (Sept. 3, 1990); "History? Education? Zap! Pow! Cut!" (May 14, 1990); "*A Midsummer Night's Dream:* The Sequel" (Aug. 7, 1989); "The Ultimate Near-Life Experience" (Aug. 3, 1994); "Of Weirdos and Eccentrics" (Jan. 18, 1988); "9/9/1991" (Sept. 16, 1991); "Sleeping with the Enemy" (Feb. 20, 1995); "The Competitive Advantage of Seasons" (April 1, 1996); "Confessions of a Frequent Flyer" (Feb. 14, 1994); "A Game of Instants" (Feb. 24, 1992); "Silence" (Jan. 25, 1993). Copyright © 1988, 1989, 1990, 1991, 1992, 1993, 1994, 1995, 1996 by T, Inc. Reprinted by permission.

Grateful acknowledgment is made to Farrar, Straus & Giroux, Inc., for permission to reprint an excerpt from "Sea Canes" and an excerpt from "The Divided Child" from *The Collected Poems 1948–1984* by Derek Walcott, copyright © 1986 by Derek Walcott.

"Tibet: The Life and Times of the Potala Palace" by Pico Iyer from *Great Residences: Living in a Dream,* published by Mitchell Beazley, London. Reprinted by permission of Reed Books.

## A Note About the Author

Pico Iyer has been a writer for *Time*, principally of essays, since 1982, and his pieces appear often in *Harper's*, *The New York Review of Books*, *The New York Times*, *Sports Illustrated*, and many other publications on both sides of the Atlantic and Pacific. He lives as much as possible in Japan.

## A Note About the Type

This book was set in Adobe Garamond. Designed for the Adobe Corporation by Robert Slimbach, the fonts are based on types first cut by Claude Garamond (c. 1480–1561). Garamond was a pupil of Geoffroy Tory and is believed to have followed the Venetian models, although he introduced a number of important differences, and it is to him that we owe the letter we now know as "old style." He gave to his letters a certain elegance and feeling of movement that won their creator an immediate reputation and the patronage of Francis I of France.

Composed by Creative Graphics Inc., Allentown, Pennsylvania
Printed and bound by Berryville Graphics,
Berryville, Virginia
Designed by Anthea Lingeman